CRITICAL THEORY

———

SÖDERTÖRN
PHILOSOPHICAL STUDIES 28
2021

SÖDERTÖRN PHILOSOPHICAL STUDIES

The series is attached to Philosophy at Södertörn University. Published in the series are essays as well as anthologies, with a particular emphasis on the continental tradition, understood in its broadest sense, from German idealism to phenomenology, hermeneutics, critical theory and contemporary French philosophy. The commission of the series is to provide a platform for the promotion of timely and innovative philosophical research. Contributions to the series are published in English or Swedish.

Critical Theory

Past, Present, Future

Edited by
Anders Bartonek & Sven-Olov Wallenstein

Södertörns högskola

Södertörns University
Library
SE-141 89 Huddinge
www.sh.se/publications

Cover layout: Jonathan Robson

Cover image: Kristoffer Nilson, *System (Portrait of a Swedish Tax Form)*, 2020, Lead pencil drawing on chalk paint, on mdf 59.2 x 42 cm. Photo: Jesper Petersen.

The Swedish tax form is one of many systems designed to handle and present information. Mapped onto the surface of an artwork, it opens a free space; an untouched surface where everything can exist at the same time – Kristoffer Nilson

Graphic form: Per Lindblom & Jonathan Robson

Södertörn Philosophical Studies 28
ISSN 1651-6834

Södertörn Academic Studies 83
ISSN 1650-433X

ISBN 978-91-89109-35-3 (print)
ISBN 978-91-89109-36-0 (digital)

Contents

Introduction

ANDERS BARTONEK & SVEN-OLOV WALLENSTEIN

From its inception in the 1920s, Critical Theory as it developed under the auspices of the *Institut für Sozialforschung* in Frankfurt, was a project that by drawing on a series of disciplines and traditions not only intended to study modern bourgeois society as a factual reality, but also, in line with Marx's eleventh Thesis on Feuerbach, sought to transform it. Today, almost a century after the founding of the Institute, more than three generations of theorists have reworked the initial critical program in different ways. Whether, though, this development can be unified into one single trajectory is doubtful. Beginning with the forced relocation of the Institute to US in the 1930s, its influence spread to the Anglophone world; various responses have developed, and what from the outset appeared like a substantially German debate today extends across the world, absorbing influences from many other intellectual traditions. Today, the existence of something like the "Frankfurt School" is tenuous, and even more so, the existence of a "Critical Theory" that could be circumscribed by a set of problems or methods; the term has acquired a life of its own and is used across the intellectual field, institutionally as well geographically. If, then, there is unity, it is one cribbed together through a set of family resemblances rather than augmented through conceptual coherence.

Thus, to ask about the past, present, and future of Critical Theory does not imply that an answer is forthcoming that would demarcate an inside from an outside, or determine what the legitimate descendants of the initial program would be. Rather, it opens up towards many new influences. This malleability is in fact a direct consequence of the claim that theory is not outside history, but must always respond to a changing present, which in turn requires that the perspective from which the past is apprehended and assessed cannot be fixed. Similarly, the idea of critique implies that the point of departure must be the present instead of some fixed eternal standard, that is, a present grasped in its contradictions and opened up to other possibilities. To inquire into the past, present, and future of critical theory is thus not to ask three separate questions, but rather involves a process of constant reappraisal.

Marx and Freud, system and subject

If one were to delineate the development of Critical Theory by trusting the reference to stages, generational shifts, and proper names, the most important figures of the first generation would be Max Horkheimer, Theodor W. Adorno, Herbert Marcuse, and Walter Benjamin; in the second Jürgen Habermas, Alfred Schmidt and Albrecht Wellmer; and in the third, Axel Honneth, Rahel Jaeggi, Christoph Menke, and Martin Saar, to name but a few. While obviously simplified, and also more debatable as we approach the present—as well as downplaying the fact that the past is always open to revision on the basis of current concerns—this chronology nonetheless still retains pedagogical merit; it allows us to understand this development as a series of problems, imposed both from within and without.

In fact, the very distinction between internal theoretical problems and external pressures emanating from society is precisely what is rejected from the outset. This comes across in the program proposed by Max Horkheimer in his "Traditional and Critical Theory" (1937), a key idea of which is that society must be understood as a totality constituted by contradictions that need to be theorised at the systemic level as well as mapped onto individual configurations that cannot be simply reduced to passive reflections. In bridging the gap between totality and subjectivity in terms of a dialectical whole, Critical Theory obviously followed Hegel, on the one hand, but on the other, in stressing contradictions as necessarily unresolved, it also drew on Freud and Marx, and engaged in turning each into a mutual support for the other. The question of how political economy and the economy of the drives intersect in the formation of the subject—how its preferences, fantasies, and desires, ranging from everyday life to the spheres of politics and aesthetics—thus resonates through the first phase of the Frankfurt School.

The emphasis on subjectivity and experience also implied that economic factors always had to be understood in their implications for consciousness, the latter of which gained a new quasi-autonomy. If Marx in *The German Ideology* once could claim that historical materialism dispelled the vacuous idealist "phrases" about consciousness, since the latter is finally never anything other than "conscious being" (*Das Bewusstsein kann nie etwas Andres sein als das bewusste Sein*), i.e. a reflection that arises directly out of the actual life process according to the model of the camera obscura, to the effect that forms of ideology will lose all semblance of autonomy and no longer have a history and development of their own—then Critical Theory, notwithstanding its many reverent references to Marx and to the theory of ideology, stakes out a different route. Determinism is no longer the key problem, but rather how the base is taken up—to be sure in ways that are distorted and reflected. Here, Critical Theory draws upon themes in Hegel, which Marx, in his eagerness to reject idealism, at least in this context, appears to have repressed. If consciousness is nothing but conscious being, Hegel might have retorted how being amounts to very little but *being having become conscious*, in a process of mediation for which the mechanical model of the camera obscura is wholly inadequate, and any theory that wants to account for the correlation of system and subject simply by explaining away the latter will be just as inadequate.

The term "Western Marxism" probably locates these discussions in a far too unequivocal geographical scheme that only later would congeal into the East-West divide, and we should rather see the conflicts over base and super-structure, determination "in the last instance", consciousness, ideology etc., as a series of shifting positions responding to both internal theoretical factors and external socio-political events. A central question that obviously deter-mined most discussions of the implications of this divide was why the pro-mised socialist revolution never happened—or, when it did take place in Russia, soon failed to make good on its promises—and whether this needed to be accounted for precisely in terms of consciousness, and how seemingly mere superstructural phenomena could take the lead over the basic con-tradictions of capital. This first question then came to resonate with a second one, which soon became even more urgent: how to explain the rise of National Socialism. In the analysis proposed by Adorno and Horkheimer in *Dialectic of Enlightenment*, this violent irruption of brutality cannot be accounted for only in terms of the pathologies of capitalism—although it is obviously that too—but must be located as the catastrophic end point of a historical dialectic that emerges already in the archaic phase of history. Thus, for Adorno and Horkheimer, "Enlightenment" does not refer to a particular historical period, but spans the whole of history, from the first step out of myth to modern scientific rationality. Enlightenment reason, they propose, is always double-edged: as instrumental rationality it seizes control over both outer and inner nature, and rationality is gradually severed from all sub-stantial aims until it becomes its own myth and relapses into irrationality. National Socialism cannot then be understood as merely an aberration from the progressive trajectory of reason, but is deeply rooted in the ambivalences of the Enlightenment itself; it is a catastrophe of reason that is prefigured in its own trajectory, and thus calls for a critique of reason that must draw on the legacies of "critique" from Kant and Hegel to Marx and Freud, while also remaining attentive to the blind spots of its predecessors.

Nature and art

Crucial here is the transformation of nature, and in *Dialectic of Enlightenment* Horkheimer and Adorno propose Odysseus as an exemplary case where the first fateful implications already can be discerned. Faced with the alluring song of the sirens, Odysseus keeps the distance required for attaining subjectivity by fettering himself to the mast while propping the oarsmen's ears with wax; he is able to enjoy the sirens without being led into their trap, just as the oarsmen can go performing their task, although cut off from enjoying the song. In this he installs a complex figure of domination, based in a division of intellectual and manual labour, which also allows for aesthetic pleasure to emerge as memory of nature and myth; the deadly song is henceforth heard as music, which will always retain a trace of a first nature now lost. As the process of Enlightenment unfolds, this mastering of inner as well as outer nature becomes a defining feature of Western philosophy and science (the extent to which it also applies to other cultures is never addressed), and a certain theory of the subject fuses with the socio-historical development, so that a critique of social domination must always involve a critique of epistemology and subjectivity.

While many of the sombre and pessimistic features of this analysis can undoubtedly be accounted for by the immediate context of writing during the war, they also point to one of its main dilemmas, later addressed by the second generation of Critical Theory, notably Habermas, and then echoed by many others: how can the inherited tools of rationality be turned against themselves without simply engaging in a form of self-destruction? If instrumental rationality and identity thinking are the ineluctable result of a tradition whose emergence even antedates the first philosophers, in what way could a different rationality at all begin to articulate itself? In short: even if a wholesale rejection of Enlightenment reason is by no means what the analysis proposes, is it not yet an outcome that is difficult to avoid?

Hinted at in the interpretation of Odysseus in the *Dialectic of Enlightenment*, and increasingly present in Adorno's subsequent writings, there is an appeal to art and aesthetic experience as an antidote to instrumental rationality and the domination of nature. In the excursus on the sirens we find the paradigm for art as a particular way of approaching nature and the world of non-human life (features of which are discussed by Camilla Flodin and Rolf Wiggershaus below)—art as a stylised song of what is lost, which is either exiled in aesthetic autonomy of the concert hall, severed from physical response and action, or allows for a remembrance of nature that holds regression at bay. Art, in Adorno's case specifically music, to which he devoted a long series of analyses that both make vast philosophical claims and immerse themselves in minute details (the latter aspect is treated by Anne Boissière below), thus holds out a promise of happiness necessarily broken because of art's position in a broken world. Art cannot deliver what it promises, not least since it just as much as everything else partakes in reification (a theme dealt with in different ways in Gérard Raulet's and Josefine Wikström's respective contributions), and yet, in its very manner of delivering the promise, in its refusal, simply by being art, to accept the given state of things, it opens a different perspective of what an object—and consequently a subject—could be outside of conceptual subsumption. The culture industry, the discussion of which forms a kind of counterpoint to the analysis of the siren song, instead affirms commodification, standardisation, and reification, and it solidifies both object and subject by appealing to a regressive promise of immediate identification and pleasure. While the analysis of the culture industry has been challenged on many points, notably in a long tradition of "cultural studies", which stresses that reception always implies transformation and cannot be reduced to passive consumption, it retains a relevance, specifically in relation to the spectacularisation of politics (discussed in Douglas Kellner's contribution).

Theory and praxis

The claim that there must exist a unity of theory and praxis has been interpreted differently in the Marxist tradition, from the stress on authoritarian party leadership as the only means for radical change, to a distrust in top-down organisation and the belief that the revolution can only come from the spontaneous actions of the masses. But while a stress on the autonomy of theory and the emphasis on subjective mediation, which we find in Critical Theory does not as such entail any break with practice, the rejection of Soviet-style Marxism as a viable option, together with the far-reaching claims that National Socialism were rooted in the history of philosophy, nevertheless resulated in a distancing from political practice that was chastised by opponents such as Bertolt Brecht, György Lukács, and many others who cannot be unequivocally aligned with Soviet Marxism. That, in the face of the imminent disasters of world history, the Frankfurt School would have comfortably checked in at the "Grand Hotel Abgrund" and lamented the spectacle of destruction from the ivory tower of philosophy and aesthetics, as was later claimed by Lukács, is as such an unjust allegation; and yet the problem remains: what, if any, political practice is consonant with the dark picture painted by the dialectic of enlightenment?

The first generation never wholly abandoned the idea of a revolutionary transformation, but in the post-war political landscape their paths would diverge. Whereas Marcuse in his American exile became a prominent figure in the student movement, and his project for concrete and radical philosophy advocated direct revolutionary transformation, Adorno, after returning to Germany, was far more cautious. He suspected that what the student revolts in Germany would accomplish was only a "pseudo-praxis", compensating for the fact that current society made any genuine action impossible (a theme discussed in various ways by both Sven Anders Johansson and Anders Bartonek). This caused severe conflicts between the Frankfurt school and the student movement; even though to a large extent they shared the same goals, their respective ways to get there were significantly different (see here Stefan Müller-Doohm's contribution). In Adorno's own writings from the period, the claim recurs constantly that theory cannot forever remain external to praxis if it is not to dwindle, at the same time as their fusion at present must be postponed: from the initial paradox in *Negative Dialectics* onwards, namely that philosophy lives on because the moment where it could have been realised was missed, the link between interpretation and transformation proposed in the last of Marx's theses on Feuerbach become increasingly tenuous, or itself increasingly a matter of interpretation rather than action.

Communicative action, intersubjectivity, the good life

If the first generation never wholly abandoned the prospect of a revolutionary transformation of society, then the second and third, for whom the reconstruction and re-founding of the post-war state and civil society was the central task, gradually shifted the terrain to a reformist politics. The task was no longer to formulate an idea of utopia, no matter how hesitant and aporetic, in which communal life, philosophy, and art would be radically different, but rather to pose the question of the foundations for rational discourse and a rational society in a way that does not require a radical break with the present, but sets itself goals reachable through gradual improvements (see Andreas-Arpad Sölter's contribution). This was largely the achievement of Jürgen Habermas, and already in his first major work, on the transformations of the public sphere (*Strukturwandel der Öffentlickeit*, 1962) while the structural matrix of cultural decline was still operative, the stress on the enlightenment, and particularly Kant, as a project that has remained unfulfilled, pointed beyond the darker aspects of the dialectic of enlightenment. This stress on the public nature of reason (aspects of which are discussed by Cecilia Sjöholm by way of Hannah

Arendt) was later developed into a grand theory of communicative action and intersubjective reason, in which rational dialogue and deliberative democracy was to counterbalance the harmful effects of the supremacy of market economy and the way in which technology tends to colonise the life-world. If there is a promise of utopia in the second generation of Critical Theory, it is not one that aspires to go beyond bourgeois society, but to achieve a better balance between different forms of rationality inside society as it exists.

For this project, the earlier critique of reason now appeared as too encompassing in its rejection of all the normative standards and rational procedures that modern societies have developed, and in subsuming rationality under "instrumental rationality" it sometimes became indistinguishable from the irrationality it wanted to denounce. This went hand in hand with a more specific claim that the first generation of Critical Theory, and specifically Adorno, would have remained oblivious to the turn from a philosophy of consciousness to a philosophy of language, and thus caught up in "metaphysical thinking" and in a series of unresolvable paradoxes that arise from taking the subject-object relation as the ground of reason, whereas a shift to language and intersubjectivity simply would take us into a "postmetaphysical thought" that exorcises the spectre of foundationalism.

Another aspect of this is the rejection of the idea of mimesis, a relation to things that precedes conceptual subsumption and survives inside it, and which is crucial for both Adorno's epistemology and his aesthetics. In Habermas' reading mimesis is proposed as an alternative to discursive rationality, although without being able to supply any normative criteria for its application. In aesthetics, which was largely pushed to the side in this type of theory, there was a similar shift to what Albrecht Wellmer termed a "post-metaphysical aesthetics of modernity" that emphasises the communicative role of art, and suggests that Adorno, precisely because of his dependence on the subject-object paradigm, remained entrenched in late modern strategies of refusal and negation (different aspects of which are treated in Lydia Goehr's and Sven-Olov Wallenstein's texts below).

This internal polemic and self-criticism was also fuelled by another debate, the quarrel over modernism and postmodernism in the mid-1980s, which created new links as well as divisions between German and French philosophy. In his lectures at the Collège de France, which became the basis for *Der philosophische Diskurs der Moderne* (1985), Habermas aligned earlier Critical Theory not only with what he saw as an irrationalist tendency in French thought, but also with Heidegger, and inserted his own defence of the Enlightenment in a vast historical panorama from Hegel onwards. The tenor of these lectures had the effect of making philosophical dialogue across the Rhine more difficult, but also made the question whether there was any real continuity in the tradition of Critical Theory more acute, as well as, perhaps unwittingly, opening up a new avenue for Adorno in France (the historical irony here being that if Adorno's lectures at the Collège de France some twenty years earlier, in which he outlined *Negative Dialectics*, dismayed some of his listeners because of his treatment of Heidegger, then Habermas, in chastising French philosophers for their dependence on Nietzsche and Heidegger, pushed Adorno into their camp). Internal to Critical Theory however, the question had to be raised whether the rejection of the earlier program in favour of communicative rationality was a logical progression that provided the critique of current society with a more sound foundation, or whether something essential had been lost, i.e. the very sense of the "critical". If contemporary political institutions are integral moments in the logic of global capitalism (which now seemed to take on the role earlier ascribed by Adorno to the "administered world"), to what extent is an appeal to these very institutions not simply acquiescent to society as it is?

In the wake of these debates, we find the work of Axel Honneth, who grappled with the work of both the first and second generations, but in the end sides with Habermas' constructive approach. Original however is Honneth's affirmative retrieval of Hegel, specifically the *Philosophy of Right*, which is taken to demonstrate the need for public recognition between members of a democratic society. Taking issue with the earlier interpretation we find in Adorno that mostly gives a picture of Hegel as the philosopher of the closed system (even though Adorno's reading is in fact far from univocal), Honneth wants to resuscitate the idea of an "ethical order (*Sittlichkeit*) as the element of intersubjectivity that gives orientation to the lives of individuals. This also includes a new take on the socialist tradition, although now without reference to Marx, which seems to effectively exclude the dimension of antagonism and conflict and is now replaced by the idea of the individual as "suffering from indeterminacy". Freedom, Honneth argues, can only be achieved to the extent that the individual becomes a recognised part of an ethically normative society.

If the ethical order derived from Hegel is supposed to give direction to individuality, what remains of individual experience precisely as individual? If normative ethical orders provide the bedrock for freedom, does this not once more imply that the "system" (to be sure in a more benevolent and supple version based on "recognition") swallows the subject, installing something like a "malignant normality" (Shierry Weber Nicholsen) that evacuates the possibility of resistance and critical intellectual work? On the other hand, one might argue that the attempt to develop a moral reflection in a work like Adorno's *Minima Moralia* is caught up in a romantic idea (Anke Thyen), and that the claim to have access to true, authentic individuality, even if expressed obliquely and aporetically, as in Adorno's writings, is just as repressive and presupposes insights without normative guidelines. Or, might it not be the case that the insistence on the singular and opaque, that which is irreducible to universal standards, itself already contains an ethical intuition that releases the present from its false immediacy, and that necessitates a philosophy expressing itself in a particular form of writing (Helena Grass)?

In this sense, what we take to be the present—and even more so the future—of Critical Theory depends to a large extent on how we assess its past, i.e. which of the earlier ideas are adjudged to be pertinent and which need to be discarded. Should it avoid the stance of radical theory and engage in constructive contributions to feasible and already existing programs of liberal democracy, or should it rather insist on incommensurable experiences and residues that rational communication must overlook? The claim that Critical Theory requires a set of normative commitments can be understood in different ways, for instance in the form of a "procedural rationality" that safeguards minimal basic rules for rational debate, or more substantially, as a set of philosophical commitments that themselves must always remain open to debate, and cannot be decided by any reference to pre-existing rules. If at present no solution to this problem seems available, this is perhaps not so much a weakness as a strength, and it is what makes Critical Theory open to a not yet determined future.

*

In his "Thinking against and through the Protest Movement: Adorno, Habermas, and the New Left", Stefan Müller-Doohm offers a historical scrutiny of Adorno's and Habermas's respective skirmishes with the student protest movements in Germany in the 1960s. Re-opening the historical archives, Müller-Doohm sheds light on important aspects of the history of Critical Theory and its connections to the political praxis of the students, providing us with a more nuanced version than the simplified accounts often given. While both Adorno and Habermas were sympathetic to some of the claims of the protest movement, neither of them saw themselves as active parts, and they reacted against what they perceived as a threatening ir-rationality and a cult of immediate action. Their arguments, however, were in fact very different: whereas Adorno assumed the role of a "general intellectual" and criticised the student movement for undermining academic freedom, the autonomy of theory, and the independence of the subject, Habermas assumed the role of a "specific intellectual", and his objections were motivated by an idea of radical reform-driven politics. In the end, Müller-Doohm suggests that the dynamics of these debates were one of escalating incomprehension, and no constructive dialogue between the representatives of Critical Theory and the new left took place.

In his contribution, "The Lava of Thought: The Future of Critical Theory beyond Cultural Criticism", Arpad-Andreas Sölter examines the potential of Critical Theory and its methods to produce cultural criticism and radical social questioning. The main issue is whether the intimate connection to a particular German tradition of cultural criticism in fact is an obstacle to fulfilling this task. The text deals mainly with Adorno's and Habermas' respective conceptions: while they share the critique against conservative bourgeois cultural criticism, and hold on to the unfulfilled ideals of enlightenment, which they perceive as having become perverted, the outcome of their respective analyses are quite different. According to Sölter, what is needed in order for Critical Theory to make a difference is the development of a normative theory of rationality that, to some extent following the claims of Habermas, incorporates a democratic fallibilism, and that by proceeding step by step aims to initiate gradual improvements. Only by prioritising feasibility over wishful thinking, as well as advocating an ethics of responsibility that incorporates the self-reflexivity of Enlightenment, will Critical Theory be relevant to the future tasks of social philosophy.

Douglas Kellner's "Donald Trump, the Culture Industry, and Authoritarian Populism" also addresses the theme of cultural criticism, and attempts to explain the Trump phenomenon by drawing specifically on some of the key concepts derived from the encounter between first generation Critical Theory and American mass culture. Kellner discusses two main issues: on the one hand, how the concept of the cultural industry, which we find in *Dialectic of Enlightenment*, might be useful in accounting for the rise of the "master of media spectacle", and on the other hand, how the concept of the authoritarian personality, which plays a decisive role in the theories of several scholars tied to the Frankfurt school—here particularly Erich Fromm—can provide an understanding for the specific "mind-set" that makes authoritarian populist politics attractive. While there are parallels to other political leaders (notably Mussolini, Kellner suggests), historically as well as in the present, Trump is also rooted in a long history of American populism and its anti-establishment sentiments.

Rolf Wiggershaus' "Elements of a Critical Environmental Philosophy" connects political issues to the analysis of the domination over nature, a key element in Adorno and Horkheimer's analysis of the enlightenment. What is at stake, he suggests, is a "remembrance of nature" in the subject; not distance and autonomy, but rather the acknowledgement that we are inevitably part of a natural order while still avoiding a regression to myth. Drawing on examples from recently discovered biotopes with extreme life conditions, and citing controversies over whether such environments should be protected as common heritages of humanity and be studied scientifically, instead of being exploited as objects of deep sea mining, Wiggershaus widens the perspective and questions the implications of the very idea of a seamless monitoring of nature and its connection to social monitoring. From quantified self-practices, smart devices in homes and cars, to mass surveillance of urban space, "smart cities" or "honest cities", where norms are upheld through constant monitoring on an individual level, he identifies a process in which humans have become increasingly estranged from one another and from themselves, precisely through the demand for security and protection. A critical analysis of this, Wiggershaus proposes, must treat the alternative between conquering and saving as merely a starting point for a thinking of "remembrance" as sketched in *Dialectic of Enlightenment*, and of the possibility of "freedom in the midst of the natural", as Adorno writes in a later discussion of Kant in *Negative Dialectics*.

Camilla Flodin too, in her "Adorno's Utopian Animals", pursues the question of nature in Adorno's writings, although with a particular focus on the place of the animal, which until recently has been largely neglected. In the face of an exorbitant loss of species, Flodin argues that a renewed interpretation of Adorno's ideas on natural history and human domination over nature, especially as they emerge in his writings on art and aesthetics, can open a different avenue for thought. Here a way out of the dialectic of enlightenment is sketched, which gives a voice to subjugated nature, particularly in the form of natural beauty. This concept was suppressed in the tradition from Hegel onwards, but was still present as a trace in the Kantian analysis of the sublime, even though it was obscured by being tied to the human being's moral superiority precisely as separated from nature. Transposed to art, however, the sublime can bear witness to the subjugation of nature and reveal human beings as natural. Citing Adorno's interpretation of Mahler's Third Symphony, Flodin suggests that the idea of a "likeness to animals" (*Tierähnlichket*) has a critical and utopian potential, in showing us both difference and affinity, which is a source of joy as well as an imperative: to try to be "a good animal", as Adorno writes in *Negative Dialectics*.

In his "On Reification: Some Thoughts on Adorno, Benjamin and Honneth", Gérard Raulet first establishes a link between Adorno's early work on phenomenology and the later reflections of reification and the primacy of the object. This primacy is, on the one hand, a consequence of reification, and, on the other hand, a possibility of overcoming it through a "second reflection" that shows how the non-constitutive role of the subject can lead to a fuller experience of the subject. These ideas, Raulet suggests, which we find fully worked out in Adorno's two final works, *Negative Dialectics* and *Aesthetic Theory*, draw substantially on Walter Benjamin, and the idea of a divine language beyond subject and object—that is, a memory of the "name" that gestures towards nominalism and yet remains different from it. Art is one way of giving voice to this "unreconciled reconciliation" or "transcendental affinity", and Benjamin and Adorno provide two different answers to the question of what this means: while Benjamin tends towards the psychophysical order of the body, for Adorno, affinity must be approached through history. Contemporary representatives of Critical theory have however taken a different path; such is the case with Axel Honneth, who, in his influential theory of recognition, evacuates mimesis as well as giving an impoverished version of reification, all of which, Raulet argues, has considerable consequences for our relation to nature as well as social theory.

Josefine Wikström also brings up a problem connected to reification and the body, in her "Interest in the Body': Art, Autonomy, and Natural Beauty in Adorno". Starting out from *Dialectic of Enlightenment*, where Adorno and Horkheimer, on the one hand, trace a repression of the body and its passions throughout the tradition, and, on the other, the desire for the pure and perfect body in Fascism, she proposes a reading of our contemporary focus on the body, both in various forms of philosophical materialisms and in performance and dance. While Adorno's ideas on performance are largely contained in his writings on musical reproduction, an alternative point of access can be found in his theory of natural beauty. The dialectical relationship between art and natural beauty in Adorno first hinges, Wikström argues, on separation and abstraction understood as a social form: art's autonomy is a social fact conditioned by the production and circulation of other commodities. In natural beauty, a separation from nature takes place, which then, as the residue of nonidentity in things, returns as both a promise and a threat. Art, Wikström argues, imitates not nature, but the act of separation, intensifying it, first in the ambiguous form of the commodity, and then as a historical construction. In contemporary dance and performance Wikström then discerns both a tendency towards extreme control and a trust in the body as somehow real and true, and a locus of inner feelings, none of which succeed in showing the contradictory aspect of natural beauty crucial for Adorno's critique of human domantion over nature.

Lydia Goehr's contribution, "Painting in Waiting: Prelude to a Critical Philosophy of History and Art", explores the dimensions of waiting: temporal suspension, hesitation, anticipation, but above all artworks that are imageless, unwritten pages, blanks, and silences. Drawing on a wide variety of examples from literature, visual art, music, and philosophy, she traces the multiple connotations of the figure of the blank, from the claim to artistic freedom, to a politics of the not-yet that oscillates between prophesy and the demand that the future must be left open. The underlying question is whether the structure of "waiting for" always implies an object, or if we can think of it in an intentionless fashion, as an existential mood. In Adorno she finds an imageless waiting that refuses the mimetic verisimilitude to *what is*, thereby retaining an utopian, even messianic mode, mimesis in waiting for *what of the not yet*. Citing a passage from Habermas, Goehr places Adorno's idea alongside the claim that we must find the ground for communicative action among subjects, which, Habermas suggests, must not be pictured as the totality of a reconciled form of life and cast into the future as utopia: what is at stake are necessary, not sufficient conditions, so that the situation is never fully determined, and philosophy, as a particular form of waiting, can remain critical.

Sven-Olov Wallenstein, in his "Adorno's Aesthetics Today", discusses the present relevance of Adorno's aesthetics in light of changes that have become greatly intensified since the 1960s: the nominalism of the arts; the fusion of high and low, and Adorno's own distance from those emerging forms of artistic practice in his own time that were to become decisive for later developments. But if we follow Adorno's own claim that theory needs to be written from the vantage point of the present, then, being faithful to him must mean that we answer his questions anew, instead of repeating answers given more than half a century ago. Wallenstein particularly stresses four points in which a rethinking might be needed (a process that, to be sure, is already underway in Adorno's own texts). *Interpretation*, first, should be seen as a second work, an invention of a particular kind, rather than something merely grafted onto the first object, so that they cease to appear as a subjective power exerted on a passive object. Second, the concept of *autonomy* must be articulated differently than the one available to Adorno, since the idea of a substantial closure that guided him now appears as a framing condition that the works themselves assume as a problem. Third, *contradiction* must be rendered more fluid so as to incorporate a more expansive sense of difference. Fourth and finally, the *utopian* dimension of the work must be pluralised, which does not mean to simply abandon the idea of reconciliation, but to think it as necessarily multiple.

Anne Boissière's "Orientation towards the Concrete" focuses on Adorno's writings on music, and the kind of philosophical gesture they contain. In opposition to a prevailing tendency to theorise art in general, Adorno's reflections on music bear on the concrete, in which the presence of the non-identical in details is at stake. This also implies a different manner of philosophising. This immersion in details, she argues, requires a form of passivity or relaxation, an abandonment of oneself to the experience of the object rather than an attempt at dominating it through concepts. In the radio talk "Beautiful Passages", built on citations and fragments of music, as well as in the unfinished magnum opus on Beethoven, Adorno connects this to his own childhood and memories outside of the socio-historical sphere: these are glimpses of a metaphysical experience, Boissière proposes, which require an "exact imagination" to break up the movement of dialectics. Similarly, in the monographs on Mahler and Berg, we encounter a different take on subjectivity: the element of lingering in Mahler, technically expressed in the "extensive type" that breaks with quantitative and measured time, in Berg, a subjectivity that is transformed into a mortal disappearance. Reading Adorno against the grain (just as he himself wanted to do with Hegel), means focusing on these singular moments; it is to think in "models" instead of falling back into the trap of a general theory.

Cecilia Sjöholm, in her "Arendt on Aesthetic and Political Judgement: Thought as the Pre-Political", addresses the legacy of Critical Theory through the work of Hannah Arendt and the idea of the public sphere. From Kant to Habermas the public sphere has served as an element of rationality, which today finds itself challenged in many respects. The question, then, is whether Arendt's idea of an "inner voice" might allow us to approach this idea differently. If the thinking individual in dialogue with itself—which Arendt develops in her reading of Shakespeare—is in fact already marked by a constitutive plurality that replaces the transcendental subject as the agent of experience, this might provide a new model for critical thought at a time when the idealised notion of a public sphere seems problematic. For Arendt, in always implying a plurality that also goes beyond the collective, the inner voice presents this plurality already in thought itself, and in this way it orients us towards a horizon that supports a common grasp of the world. To Arendt, then, we can only really think when others are encroaching upon us; only in a world of plurality can we truly reflect on our actions and ourselves.

In his contribution "The Future of Saying No: The Non-Identity and Incompatibility of (Critical) Theory", Anders Bartonek examines the relation of theory to praxis in the thought of Adorno, with a focus on the tension that the question of the non-identical entails with respect to society as it is. On the one hand, it is necessary for theory to preserve a moment of the non-identical, in order to remain critical and to hold on to a minimal utopian hope; on the other hand, since the path to a genuinely liberating praxis in Adorno's view is blocked, the alternative option for critical theory seems to be to make itself incompatible with social praxis, cutting off the possibility of having an impact as well as protecting itself from being swallowed up by the cunning of society. This might leave no other perspective for Critical Theory than a future of saying No; the question that remains is whether there is a way around this steadfast negative approach, since every "constructive" attempt must overcome this, otherwise it risks remaining an unsuccessful endeavour.

Sven Anders Johansson too, in his "What is a Revolutionary Subject? Activism, Theory, and Adorno's Conception of the Subject", addresses the issue of the possibilities of resistance and revolutionary praxis, but sees the question of the subject of activism as the crucial hinge on which the future of Critical Theory hangs. Discussing Adorno's critique of the student movement in Germany in the late 1960s, as well as addressing a contemporary event of activist subjectivity, Johansson highlights the crucial role that historical context plays in deciding which political possibilities are available at any given moment. Johansson furthermore stresses the importance of passivity, corporeality, and frailty for a fruitful understanding of the critical and theoretical subject as a point of departure for a revolutionary praxis. The question is: how to establish a critical subject—one which no longer remains within the confines of the personal established by liberal and capitalist logics, but rather gestures towards the pre- or non-personal. Adorno's stress on thinking as a connection to the "happiness of humanity" points to another sense of the subject, Johansson proposes, a subject that necessarily implies a somatic dimension and an openness to its surroundings, without the desire for control; it is one that acknowledges the relative powerlessness of the individual and the illusory quality of its freedom and self-determination.

In "Adorno's *Minima Moralia*: Malignant Normality and the Dilemmas of Resistance", Shierry Weber Nicholsen discusses Adorno's claims about the "workings of malignant normality", both in the context of its origin in the immediate aftermath of the second world war, as well as its further development in the larger trajectory of advanced capitalism. Nicholsen sees Adorno's *Minima Moralia* as a reflection on the "slight possibilities of resistance" that could be developed within this totalising form of negative normality or normalized suffering. She thus situates her own contribution within the twilight of negativity and resistance. In order to locate the possibility of resistance in such a situation of seemingly normal inhumanity, the critical intellectual, Nicholsen suggests, faces a difficult dilemma since any use of normalised language risks maintaining precisely such a semblance of normality. But in this situation, it seems just as essential to resist the image of an absolute negative totality; only then can resistance retain a minimal hope. For Adorno, the individual plays a significant role in carrying out such an engagement, and Nicholsen argues that individual experience must be the starting point in a situation of overwhelming malignancy.

Anke Thyen's "'In many people it is already an impertinence to say I': Some critical observations" undertakes a critical examination of Adorno's *Minima Moralia*, questioning its moral merits due to what she perceives as an aggressive and mocking tone in relation to the oppressed individuals that Adorno claims to defend. Thyen sees in Adorno's thinking a vagueness concerning the qualities of individuals, and whether they are at all able to transcend false consciousness and develop a critical perspective on society. Who can have this ability and why, and how did Adorno reach this level of reflection and insight? Is it legitimate for him to take this position of representing individuals that have lost their genuine individuality? Thyen addresses a series of problems concerning individuality and the idea of the "I" from various conceptual perspectives, and in the end questions the status of Adorno's moral philosophy and its ability to offer a description of normative foundations in society. Therefore, she concludes, it is questionable whether it is more than just a romantic idea—an idea that also robs the individuals of their capacity for reasoning and for genuine moral judgement.

Helena Grass' "Critical Theory and the Good Life: Do All Good Things Go Together?" poses a similar question as Thyen: can Critical Theory point towards what a good life would be in contemporary society? First, she suggests that there today exists no such thing as a single, uniform Critical Theory, and furthermore that such a corpus in fact never existed; simply, there are only multiple forms of critical theorising. Unlike Thyen, however, Grass proposes that the writings of Adorno, and particularly his *Minima Moralia*, are able to bring together critique and ethics. Instead of reducing the question of the good life to a matter of personal opinion or taste, while without appealing to a universal standard, Adorno's focus on the singular, the "tiny pieces of morality", cuts across these distinctions. The good life can only be lived in a good society, which is only realised in the particular; at present, damaged life can only find expression in damaged forms, in the fragmented reflections of a text that yet gestures towards a horizon of an as yet non-existing common, be it in the form of "Rien faire comme une bête". However, for Grass, Adorno's own insistence on negativity, which seems to block all positive precepts, does not do him justice; so for instance, the idea of negative dialectics must always be guided by an idea of what lies beyond identity thinking—utopia, as it sometimes appears in Adorno's writings—if it is not to relapse into sheer nothingness. We must ask, Grass suggests, what kind of possibilities and potentialities are hidden in the here and now? She proposes that subjectivity would then be recognised as something singular, unrepeatable, as having dignity, just as objects would too be respected as unique and valuable entities, and tenderness would be a guiding category for social life.

*

The editors would like to thank the Goethe-Institut in Stockholm for co-organising the conference that formed the basis for this volume, and David Payne, whose assistance with proofreading and comments on style as well as content have been essential throughout the editorial process.

Thinking against and through the Protest Movement: Adorno, Habermas, and the New Left

STEFAN MÜLLER-DOOHM

As is commonly known, a complex series of causes account for the contemporary historical turbulence of the late sixties and the genesis of transnational revolt. In part, these causes include:

1. The escalation of the Vietnam war, which the government of the federal republic of Germany, as an alliance partner to the US, diplomatically supported;
2. The activities of the CIA, the US-secret service, in South America, as well as the increasingly radicalised civil rights movement in the US;
3. The world-wide eruption of Anti-colonial struggles, e.g. the six-day war in the Middle East as well as the military putsch in Greece.
4. The debates surrounding domestic policy regarding the planned Emergency Acts in the federal republic, as well as the formation of a power cartel between Christian and Social democrats under the leadership of the former NSDAP-member and staunch anti-communist Kurt Georg Kiesinger, who helped form the government of 1966, and finally the entry of a far-right party in many of the federal parliaments, e.g. Hessen and Bavaria.

As a result of both this global and domestic situation, youth cultural and student protest movements steadily grew and developed, something that was partly caused by state sanctions, itself a dynamic for radicalisation. At the same time protests gained greater public visibility, in part because extra-parliamentary opposition employed forms of expression that were more effective medially: direct actions, happenings, sit-ins and the like were gratefully received by the press and television coverage, thus helping to broaden the movement's effects.

In what follows, I intend not to further discuss the broad response to the protests provided by the media. Rather, my focus will be on the special role that Theodor W. Adorno and Jürgen Habermas played in this particular moment. As left-wing intellectuals they, both in their own way, set the tone by providing analyses and publicised commentaries on ongoing events. In offering this particular focus, I begin with the premise—contrary to the stereotypes typical of the time, according to which having seeded the wind, critical theory now harvested a storm—that the implied reciprocity between the critics of society, on the one hand, and the politics of the new left, on the other, does not conform to any simple causal schema.

I will proceed in the following way: first, I shall describe a few of the activities that hypothetically contributed to create an intellectual climate in which the core of the undogmatic new left crystallised around the *Sozialistische Deutsche Studentenbund* (SDS), with respect to it serving as a political driver for particular impulses and catchwords by which the protest movement positioned itself. Subsequently, I will, with some necessary simplifications, further discuss the history of that present through the interpretative figures of Adorno and Habermas. It seems plausible to me that both thinkers have been positioned within a quite heterogeneous line of thinking, not only within the West German but also the international New Left. In the centre of this thinking stood a humanistic motivated Marxism that tried to overcome orthodox economism and the determinism of the philosophy of history.

From the beginning one must bear in mind that, in contrast to Herbert Marcuse, at no point did Adorno and Habermas see themselves as part of the protest movement. Rather, they enquired into its thinking and acting without—despite growing reservations—completely demarcating themselves from the movement *coram publico*. Conversely, though, the case is somewhat different with the students themselves, at least regarding the short phase of the protest movement from the late sixties: students' criticisms of Critical Theory became open agitation against its key representatives, Adorno and Habermas. Towards the end of this essay, I shall accentuate several aspects of Adorno's and Habermas' critique of the procedural changes that the protest movement underwent (impressively documented in the film *Ruhestörung* (*Disturbance of the Peace*) by Hans Dieter Müller and Günter Hörmann). The movement transmogrified from a pluralistic culture of debate, exercising (basic-) democratic decision-making, to provocative and divisive action-taking. Here, I am particularly interested in how Adorno and Habermas acted as public intellectuals alongside the specific character of the intellectual dispute that ensued between Critical Theory and the New Left.

II

Besides Berlin, in Germany many of the major protest events took place in Frankfurt. On point of this fact, it is only natural that the two prominent representatives of Critical Theory, Adorno and Habermas, would find themselves in the middle of political events. This applies more to the younger representative, for whom everything political has always been of the utmost urgency. As regards Adorno, well, he may have followed the politics of the day attentively, but in no way did he relinquish his repeatedly pronounced distance to the sphere of politics and was indeed sceptical about a socially transformative praxis.

Nevertheless, ongoing anti-Semitism, the existence of old Nazis in positions of government in Adenauer and in the judiciary, nuclear armament, the Social Democratic Godesberger programme from 1959, the Emergency Acts and the grand coalition, were reasons enough to reflect on the stability of both democracy and the constitutional state. And all the more so after the results of a study published in 1967 by the Institute for Social Research gave further reasons to doubt the future of German parliamentary democracy.

It is striking that a group of researchers from the institute, under the direction of Adorno, found an alarmingly high degree of political disinterest in the population. Especially in situations of crises, e.g. strikes resulting from wage disputes, the danger is that an already widespread tendency of political apathy turns into an affirmative attitude towards state authorities. This authoritarian personality exhibited by people was associated with a real feeling of powerlessness in society, thereby resulting in a strong tendency towards political resignation.[1] In the collected data, people reacted negatively towards Adolf Eichmann's conviction by an Israeli court—findings interpreted as a form of resistance against the events surrounding the Nazi past. This confirmed the results of a prior "group experiment" study from 1955, namely that the general population's attitude towards past crimes was characterised by defence reactions, leading to a secondary antisemitism, which expressed itself in the refusal to remember.[2]

In summary, the results of the study showed that in a majority of the population there was a general aversion towards the political sphere, something that could have fatal consequences for democracy. From this, the principal researchers, Egon Becker and Regina Schmidt, drew pessimistic conclusions; and, as explored in his essay, "The Meaning of Working through the Past" from 1959, these were thoughts shared by Adorno also.

---

[1] See Regine Schmidt and Egon Becker, *Reaktionen auf Politische Vorgänge: Drei Meinungsstudien aus der Bundesrepublik* (Frankfurt am Main: Europäische Verlagsanstalt, 1967), 81.

[2] See Lars Rensmann, *Kritische Theorie über den Antisemitismus: Studien zu Struktur, Erklärungspotential und Aktualität* (Berlin: Argument, 1998), 231ff.

Like Adorno, Becker and Schmidt claimed that identification with West German democracy remained superficial. This identification is "not considered under the aspect of political self-determination, but primarily from the perspective of the consumer and the de-politicised private individual, who wants to see the status quo guaranteed".[3]

As a public intellectual, Adorno's criticism was at the time mainly directed at two things. Firstly, in many of his publicly aired statements, he accused society for not struggling hard enough against anti-Semitic tendencies. Secondly, he criticised the plans for the Emergency Acts, proposed by the grand coalition of the Christian Democrats and Social Democrats in 1966.

The event "Democracy in the state of emergency", which took place in May 1968 in the large broadcasting room of the Hessischer Rundfunk (Hessen's public broadcast corporation) was in part arranged by Adorno, who also chose to speak. He pointedly remarked that one does not have to be full "of political hysteria to be afraid of what is on the horizon". On this occasion, he spoke of the false accusation of treason levelled at the head editor of the weekly magazine *Der Spiegel* as well as the cynical attitude adopted by leading politicians against the constitution. In light of what remained an unstable democratic order in Germany, it was imperative to protest vociferously against the emergency laws, which represented the legal exhumation of democracy.[4]

While Adorno left no doubt about his solidarity with the protest movement surrounding the Emergency Acts, at the same time (and just like Max Horkheimer) he was also a critic of a prevalent Anti-Americanism, which had already began to show itself after the murder of John F. Kennedy, as well as during the violent suppression of the black civil rights movement and the assassination of Martin Luther King. This tendency began to spread further with increasing opposition in Germany against the Vietnam war. Despite his sympathies for the democratic tradition in the US, in the lecture he gave on metaphysics in the summer of 1965, Adorno described the war in Vietnam as a sign for the further existence of the "world of torture" that began in Auschwitz.[5]

A test-case for examining the actual condition of West German democracy was finally provided when in the summer of 1967 the Shah of Persia visited. Due to secret service activities against Iranian students and the use of torture against members of the opposition, the regime overseen by the Shah exhibited certain totalitarian characteristics. This visit was carried out with unusually

[3] Schmidt and Becker, *Reaktionen auf Politische Vorgänge*, 137f
[4] Adorno, *Gesammelte Schriften* (Frankfurt am Main: Suhrkamp, 2003) (= GS), 20.1: 396 f.
[5] Adorno, *Nachgelassene Schriften* (Frankfurt am Main: Suhrkamp, 1998), 14: 160.

high security measures. Calls for demonstrations followed, with thousands of students taking to the streets in several big cities, such as on June 2 in Berlin in front of the Schöneberger town hall and the German opera house. Here a student, Benno Ohnesorg, was shot from behind by a police superintendent during skirmishes with police, resulting in chaotic scenes of students fleeing from violence. The Berlin Senate immediately issued a ban on demonstrations in response to the "unannounced emergency" by the extra-parliamentary opposition. This emergency order became the main topic for many student meetings taking place within universities at the time.[6]

This specific event, as well as the media campaign organised by the Springer publishing group against the demonstrating students, led to Adorno making the following comment in a sociology seminar: "The students have in some sense taken over the role of the Jews".[7] Shortly afterwards, on the June 6, he would speak directly about the death of the student, as well as the so-called six day-war between Egypt and Israel, opening one of his lectures on aesthetics with the following statement:

> It is not possible for me to begin the lecture without saying a word about the events in Berlin, as much as they are overshadowed by the awful events threatening Israel, home to many Jews who fled from the horror. I am aware how hard it is after this to come to a just and responsible view about what is nonetheless factually so simple, since all news reaching us is already controlled. But that cannot stop me from expressing my sympathy for the student whose destiny – no matter what is reported – has no relation to his participation in a political demonstration. Not only the urge to do justice to the victims, but also the worry that the democratic spirit in Germany— which is, truly, only starting to emerge— makes it even more necessary that those ongoing investigations in Berlin are led by authorities who are wholly unconnected to the individuals who shot and swung the batons, and remain impartial with respect to the direction that these inquiries may lead. It is not my private wish. It rather springs from the objective situation that investigations are conducted swiftly, with fullest freedom, unbridled from authoritarian interests, and carried out in accordance with the spirit of democracy. I suppose you share this wish. I ask you to stand up in memory of our dead fellow student from Berlin.[8]

---

[6] See Wolfganf Kraushaar, Wolfgang (ed.), *Frankfurter Schule und Studentenbewegung: Von der Flaschenpost zum Molotowcocktail* (Hamburg: Rogener & Bernhard, 1998), vol. 1, 254
[7] Ibid.
[8] *Frankfurter Adorno Blätter* III (1994): 145.

The disturbing news that the policeman was acquitted from the charge of manslaughter by the largest criminal court in Moabit was an opportunity once more for Adorno to offer further comment, this time at the beginning of his lecture on aesthetics on November 23, 1967:

> If the officer cannot be convicted since it cannot be proven if he is guilty in the eyes of the law, then the guilt of his employer is all the more great. That the police were armed at a student demonstration, carries in itself the temptation to carry out what the police chief wanted to justify when he appealed to the word "mission" (*Auftrag*). In Frankfurt it was shown repeatedly that the police do not need to deploy such measures. As a result, it is all the more urgent to receive information why such measures were used in Berlin: who gave the directives and what the status is of the so-called order. But the impression that I had from Mr Kurras when he appeared on TV goes beyond all of that. I heard a sentence like this: 'I'm sorry that a student died'. The tone was unmistakably reluctant, as if he had laboriously wrestled with those meagre words, not seriously aware of what he was doing.[9]

While Adorno is open to discussing with the students—expressing his understanding for their motives on many occasions—at the same time he clearly expressed his own doubts surrounding the strategies adopted by the students, especially their purposeful violation of the law, which gave rise to a violence towards things and the provocation of persons. Adorno's scepticism towards the political consequences of this form of activism was even more openly expressed in his letters.[10] As early as the summer of 1967 he wrote to Marcuse, the theorist and "sacred animal" of the student movement, that some of its representatives tended to "synthesise their kind of practice with a nonexistent theory, out of which emerged a decisionism reminiscent of the horror".[11] Moreover, Adorno spoke out against the conduct of members of the protest movement towards Israel.

Even though the Left supported pro-Israeli policies during the immediate decades after the war, by the end of the six day-war there was an active distancing from the government of the Israeli state, and the preventative war that it waged; the Left connected this conflict to an anti-colonial struggle, and for this reason showed solidarity with the Arab states. When in the turbulent June of 1969, a speech by the Israeli ambassador Asher Ben-Nathan in

---

[9] Ibid, 146.
[10] See *Frankfurter Adorno Blätter* VI (2000): 42ff.
[11] Ibid, 59.

Frankfurt was disrupted, Adorno was greatly irritated. The extent of this irritation was clearly conveyed in a letter to Marcuse:

> The danger that the student protest turns into fascism is a risk I take a lot more seriously than you. After the Israeli diplomat was denounced, the guarantee that it didn't happen because of Anti-Semitism […] doesn't help in the slightest […]. You should once see the manic frozen eyes of those who— possibly with reference to ourselves— direct their anger against us.[12]

Habermas was in contrast less ambivalent than Adorno. He refused to shy away from offering a clear critique of US foreign policy on the grounds of the Vietnam war. For this reason, it was his name that headed a public statement, which was handed over in November 1965 to to the Federal Chancellor Ludwig Erhard. The statement requested an immediate halting of the air strikes in Vietnam, along with a peaceful solution to the conflict and a guaranteeing of the political neutrality of Vietnam as a whole. At a conference organised by Rudi Dutschke and the SDS on the May 22 1966 at the Goethe University, entitled "Vietnam— analysis of an example", the plenary speaker was Herbert Marcuse. Among others, Wolfgang Abendroth, Norman Birnbaum and Oscar Negt also addressed the conference. On this occasion, Habermas did not mince his words, describing the Vietnam war as illegitimate and an expression of anti-Communist aggression.[13]

Before the big coalition was formed, Habermas—alongside Iring Fetscher, Ludwig von Friedeburg and Alexander Mitscherlich—was one of the co-signatories of an open letter addressed to the SPD-chairman, Willy-Brandt. The letter warned of the emergence and consolidation of a power cartel between the major parties. Under the influence of Herbert Wehner and Helmut Schmidt, the Social Democratic Party (SPD) were strategically prepared "to enter the ruined government of CDU/CSU", and according to Habermas, in an intervention made during a podium discussion organised by the SPD student union in Frankfurt, in December 1966, the risk was that the party would provide "the alibi for concealing bankruptcy […]. We have reason to fear the new government more than the old".[14] Habermas feared that parliamentary democracy itself was in peril; "when nine tenths of the members of the Bundestag belong to the governing parties, conflicts are closed to public scrutiny".[15]

---

[12] *Frankfurter Adorno Blätter* VI (1992): 112.
[13] See Kraushaar, *Frankfurter Schule und Studentenbewegung*, vol. 1, 226 and 228.
[14] Ibid, 231.
[15] Ibid, 216.

On the June 9, Benno Ohnesorg, the student who was shot by the police at the Berlin protest, was buried with a large outpouring of public sympathy. Immediately after, a conference took place entitled "University in democracy – conditions and organisation of resistance", and was dedicated to the dead student. Only four professors were invited to speak: Wolfgang Abendroth, Margherita von Brentano, Hartmut von Hentig and Jürgen Habermas. In a speech about the political role of the student body in the Federal Republic, Habermas described the state sanctioned police actions against the demonstrators in Berlin as an act of terror, an example of systematic intimidation. For him the student protests were legitimate, a much needed expression of democratic consciousness and political engagement.

Furthermore, Habermas declared that "the task of the student opposition in the Federal Republic was and remains a means for compensating for society's failures, namely the lack of any theoretical perspective, for the lack of sensitivity towards obfuscations and denunciations, for a lack of radicality in interpreting and practicing our welfare state and democratic constitution, and a lack of both anticipatory consciousness and an alert imagination".[16] Habermas called on others to resist the emerging "authoritarian meritocratic society" by means of public protest. At the same time, he warned of an activism at all costs that sought "to challenge the sublime violence of state institutions by means of open violence". Such a strategy was "masochistic, and offered no satisfaction therefore, other than one's further submission under this very violence".[17]

When Rudi Dutschke, the then head of the student movement, declared that violent actions should not be ruled out, Habermas was startled and criticised Dutschke for his voluntarism: "it was called Utopian Socialism in 1848, but under today's conditions it has to be called—or, at least, I think there are reasons to suggest this terminology—"left fascism".[18] In the lecture hall, this pronouncement of Habermas was met both with hostile heckles as well as applause.

A decade later Habermas confessed that, even though intended as "an internal criticism of the methods of the protest movement", the accusation of left fascism was "somewhat misplaced"; he had himself "acted a shade too much like a typical bourgeois intellectual".[19] At this time Habermas' relationship to the protest movement began to change. Up to this point the students had lined up with him, but soon significant parts of the movement began to

---

[16] Jürgen Habermas, *Protestbewegung und Hochschulreform* (Frankfurt am Main: Suhrkamp, 1969), 141.
[17] Ibid, 145.
[18] Ibid, 148.
[19] Jürgen Habermas, *Kleine Politische Schriften I–IV* (Frankfurt am Main: Suhrkamp, 1981), 519f

distance themselves from his work, in some cases they were directly confrontational. This did nothing to dissuade Habermas from engaging all the more intensely with the political self-understanding of the New Left and the protest movement.

In a lecture delivered in November 1967 at the New York Goethe-Institute, Habermas interpreted the recent processes of politicisation in West Germany as generally positive, describing them as a reaction to the authoritarian sedimented structures of post-war society. A new generation, which grew up under conditions of affluence, were now critical towards the existing system, taking seriously the principle of democratic participation in the constitution. This generation refused to accept that "despite the high level of technological development, the life of the individual is still determined by the ethic of competition, the pressure of status-seeking, and the values of possessive individualism and socially dispensed substitute-gratifications."[20]

Shortly afterwards, Habermas further presented his thoughts in Frankfurt in February 1968, as part of a series of events, entitled "critical universities" on "the role of students in the extra-parliamentary political opposition", initiated by the SDS. In open dispute with Hans-Jürgen Krahl, a prominent spokesperson for SDS, Habermas was on the offensive, referring explicitly to the mistakes the protest movement had made. He recommended to the SDS that they search for alliance partners with progressive parts of the unions and the media. Habermas was also present at an event on June 2 1968, this time in the context of a nationwide student congress at the University of Frankfurt, which the students had re-named the Karl Marx University. Here, he explored two questions. First, what risks were the extra-parliamentary opposition taking with their militant actions, which were in direct response to the passing of the Emergency Acts in the Bundestag just three days before? Secondly, how does one foster the conditions under which the old structures of authority in the education system might be replaced with institutionalised spaces for processes of self-clarification within and between academic cultures?

Here, Habermas' starting point was that there is no alternative to the constitution underpinning parliamentary democracy, even if the gap between the norms of the constitution and its reality remains stark. To investigate this very discrepancy is the task of societal critique. According to Habermas, in order to counteract depoliticisation, the tactics of the demonstrators, i.e. the calculated violation of rules by students, are not only an effective means, but are legitimate forms of non-violent resistance. However, since the societal situation in

---

[20] Habermas, *Protestbewegung und Hochschulreform*, 170.

Western Europe can in no way be interpreted as revolutionary, violent actions against reactionary counter-forces would not only be dangerous but entirely ineffective.[21] Habermas thus concluded: "Under these circumstances, whosoever tactically considers the fomenting of revolutionary practices to overthrow the system simply falls into illusion".[22] For this reason, the protest movement has to relinquish any kind of direct use of violence and thereby restrict itself to provocations with symbolic means.[23]

III

In different ways Adorno and Habermas have played a central role for the New Left. To begin with, both had an enormous influence as university teachers; they addressed philosophical and socio-theoretical themes that fell within the New Left's horizon, themes that members of the New Left would otherwise have not encountered at such an elevated intellectual level. Secondly, Adorno and Habermas functioned in their own way as non-conformist public intellectuals. Both took risks to repeatedly intervene politically, not least in order to support the demands of the protest movement for the expansion of democracy, so that it would encompass pre-political spheres of living, e.g. the family, the market, school and the university. Thirdly, Adorno and Habermas provided, in different ways and with particular accents, contemporary interpretations and analytical categories that broadly became part of a neo-Marxist vocabulary,

[21] Ibid, 248.

[22] Ibid, 196

[23] The Criticism that Habermas raised surrounding the actionism of the students, tending towards "left fascism" is not without consequences. A volume, published in 1968, entitled *Die Linke antwortet Habermas* contains strong counter-criticisms. Fifteen authors who were close to the SDS engaged with Habermas' six theses on the tactics, aims and situation analyses of youth protests. In the introductory contribution Oskar Negt writes: "What connects all these articles is […] neither an unconditional solidarity with the protest movement nor the confirmation and explanation of a closed theory, of which one could claim that the tactics of indirect action are founded in the long-term strategies of politicisation of the public sphere and the socialist transformation of society". From a political point of view Habermas represents a "residual liberalism", which he has overcome socio-theoretically. It was the "fear that the violent potential of outdated forms of authority, still institutionally bound, with little reason, that could be actualised at any time" which accounts for why Habermas appealed to the students not to provoke sublime violence and not to touch liberal institutions, even if their emancipatory function has for a long time proved to be questionable. For the publisher, the volume was to be understood as "a publicly led controversy within the new left, that in the first instance serves its political self-understanding". It was meant to be "no anti-Habermas" tract. Habermas however refused to take part in this controversy, and so rejected the invitation to contribute and respond directly to his critics. See Wolfgang Abendroth and Oskar Negt (eds.), *Die Linke antwortet Jürgen Habermas* (Frankfurt am Main: Europäische Verlagsanstalt, 1968).

and to which the New Left, with its fundamental criticisms of late capitalist societies and its crisis phenomena, referred.

Primarily, four key thematic areas had an increasingly important role to play in critical thinking for the New Left, and were common topics addressed by important academic journals such as *Neue Kritik, Diskurs* and *Das Argument*.[24] On the one hand, there were treatments of discourses on the past and guilt, and, on the other, there was an attempt to renew traditional concepts from the critique of capitalism as well as broadening this account in order to provide a critique of the culture industry. There were also investigations into the structural and functional change of the public sphere and finally a critique of the education system. So as to make it evident in what way these criticisms spread into the thinking of the New Left, I shall illustrate by way of an example. After returning to Germany, it was Adorno who warned of the afterlife of National Socialism in democracy. Indeed, already in 1951 he had provocatively written how it would be barbaric to write poetry after Auschwitz. When due to the Auschwitz trial in Frankfurt and the Eichmann trial in Israel, discourses about the past began to stir, Adorno awoke public consciousness with lectures such as "The Meaning of Working through the Past" as well as "The Struggle against anti-Semitism today" and "Education after Auschwitz". Adorno thus positioned himself as the prototypical taboo breaker. This was also the case with Habermas. In 1953, in the *Frankfurter Allgemeine Zeitung* Habermas accused the much admired Martin Heidegger who, in his republished lectures on the *Introduction to Metaphysics* "spoke without further comment on the greatness and inner truth of national socialism and the planned murder of millions of people [...] as the destinal error that is made intelligible within the historicality of being."[25]

When Horkheimer in his essay "The Jews and Europe" (written with Adorno's significant involvement at the end of 1939) formulated "whoever does not want to speak about capitalism, should keep silent about fascism",[26] with the two keywords of capitalism and fascism he set the (albeit temporary) course for how critical theory would approach the analysis of capitalism.

---

[24] The political convictions of the New Left were originally "with some socialist elements, e.g. radical-democratic-reformist, not Marxist-revolutionary or even Marxist-eschatological". See Albrecht et al, *Die intellektuelle Gründung der Bundesrepublik: Eine Wirkungsgeschichte der Frankfurter Schule* (Frankfurt am Main and New York: Camp, 1999), 316.

[25] Habermas, *Philosophisch-politische Profile* (Frankfurt am Main: Suhrkamp, 1998), 72.

[26] GS 4: 308f.

This view of interpreting the totalitarian system as a contemporary manifestation and result of a monopolistically organised, state regulated capitalism, was rediscovered in the middle of the 60s by parts of the New Left.

In Habermas' essay, "Technology and Science as 'Ideology'", the concept of the system already had a prominent place—it would later become all the more significant in his study about the *Legitimation Crisis in Late Capitalism.* In the politically controlled system, increases in productivity and in the accumulation of capital had priority over all other criteria. Habermas diagnosed three tendencies in the development of late capitalism: first, "a growth of interventionistic state action, which has to secure the stability of the system" and on the other hand "a growing interdependence of research and technology that turns science into the first productive resource".[27] Finally, he concludes that the stability of state regulated capitalism is dependent on conflicts remaining invisible. Whence the problem of the depoliticisation of the public sphere.

With this assumption Habermas returned to his influential study on *The Structural Change of the Public Sphere* from 1962, which was adopted by the New Left. He feared that a manipulated public could potentially arise in which "a mood that is ready for acclamation", that is, "a climate of opinion" could be established.[28] Since the fact that the public is directed by hegemonic mass media, a new influence is born, according to Habermas, namely media power, as practiced by privately organised press companies, in fact amounting to the refeudalisation of the public.[29]

In this study Habermas took up some critico-ideological motifs Adorno had previously developed in his theory of the culture industry. The term culture industry directs attention to the fact that the products of music, visual arts, and literature are produced as commodities in capitalist organised societies. Their use value is no more than a diversion: to distract and to entertain culture consumers. The overall effect of the culture industry thus runs counter to the enlightenment: Adorno writes that the culture industry prevents the formation of "independent and judicious individuals. But those would be a precondition of a democratic society".[30] The emphasis placed on the enlightenment as a condition for self-determination and democracy was a leitmotif in many of the statements and analyses that Adorno and Habermas published on the reform

---

[27] Habermas, *Legitimationsprobleme im Spätkapitalismus* (Frankfurt am Main: Suhrkamp, 1973), 74.

[28] Habermas, *Strukturwandel der Öffentlichkeit: Untersuchungen zu einer Kategorie der bürgerlichen Gesellschaft* (Frankfurt am Main, Suhrkamp, new ed. 1990), 321.

[29] Ibid, 292

[30] Adorno GS 10.1: 345.

of the education system, already before Georg Picht's and Ralf Dahrendorf's warning of an education catastrophe, and before the maxim that 'education is a civil right'.[31] During the mid-1950s, Adorno would write about the crisis in school and university education, alongside the general collapse in education. He was to further sharpen his critique in his *Theory of Half Education*.

After the collapse of the emancipatory ideal, education ends up functioning as a means for social selection. What remains is the notion of "half education", which limits citizens' knowledge to things for which only the standards of utility apply, thus feeding "the very reification of consciousness from which education should be protected".[32]

In his theses "On the Democratisation of German Universities", Adorno welcomed the reduction of authoritarian structures and hierarchies within universities, claiming that their amelioration is a precondition for the cultivation of a "type of free human being" who can develop through self-determination. At the same time, Adorno demanded that the academic must face the public sphere and should not privately dedicate himself/herself merely to his or her subject, to the occupation of knowledge and to the pursuit of one's own career. Because "the withdrawal from politics itself negates the democratic principle when one lets oneself be valid only contemplatively. That is the Achilles heel of the democratisation of German universities".[33]

Habermas deepens this thought with his article "On the Social Change of Academic Education" from 1963. There he argues that the aim of university education should question the social system of authority and interests, by which the direction of techno-scientific development is determined. As a deepening of this insight, in 1967 Habermas demanded the democratisation of universities as a "political necessity of the highest importance", thereby constituting the precondition of critique of science, which must be able to develop unimpeded within the academic sphere "since no longer can we afford an unreflected implementation of scientific information in the context of social (life) practice".[34] Habermas connects this extensive understanding of democracy with earlier analyses about the norms and reality of the constitution, i.e. the deficits of parliamentarianism as a mere formal democracy that under the

---

[31] Georg Picht, *Die deutsche Bildungskatastrophe: Analyse und Dokumentation* (Freiburg: Walter, 1964); Ralf Dahrendorf, *Bildung ist Bürgerrecht: Plädoyer für eine aktive Bildungspolitik* (Hamburg: Nannen, 1965).
[32] Adorno GS 8: 112.
[33] Adorno GS 20.1: 335f.
[34] Habermas *Protestbewegung und Hochschulreform*, 121, 104

exorbitant power of administrative machineries, parties and interest groups tend to take an "authoritarian form".[35]

IV

How did Adorno and Habermas understand their respective role as public intellectuals in the debates surrounding the protest movement? A comparative perspective shows that the particular differences separating them is akin to the difference between the figure of the *general* and the *specific* intellectual.[36] Adorno criticised as delusional the extremism expressed in the actionist practices of the protest movement. He placed his focus on those principles that were under attack. This put him on a defensive footing, since he saw the validity of certain principles at risk—e.g. the principles of academic freedom, scientific truth, the autonomy of theory, the self-determination and maturity of the subject. Political views were only of secondary importance to Adorno, who pointed out the fatal consequences to be feared if the imperfect and always endangered constitutional laws of a democratic order or the freedom of the individual are ignored. His public engagement was ultimately directed paternalistically towards the project of a critical theory as a radical project of enlightenment, whose defence (or rescue) motivated and drove him.

In his intellectual interventions Habermas acted more offensively, and in his prescriptive articles he clearly opposed those evaluations made by the protest movement on their own historical present. His criticism of "actionism" was principally politically motivated, i.e. from the perspective of a politics of radical reformism. Habermas sought to overcome the risk of polarisation; despite all polemical traits, he tried performatively to take over perspectives, trying to argumentatively empower his own interpretations and categories in the mode of "pros and cons" surrounding interpretations of the situation.

An obvious sign of the public debate between representatives of the New Left, on the one hand, and Adorno and Habermas, on the other hand, is that the intellectual formation of fronts follows its own dynamic. This dynamic takes the form of an escalation that typically goes from a first step of cooperation on a factual level to a second step of controversially carrying out different interpretations, through a third step of dispute and finally to a fourth and final

---

[35] Habermas et al, *Student und Politik* (Neuwied: Luchterhand 1961), 15f, 43ff.
[36] Ingrid Gilcher-Holtey, *Eingreifendes Denken: Die Wirkungschancen von Intellektuellen* (Weilerswist: Velbrück, 2007), 390f.

phase of open discord.[37] Retrospectively, the controversies of 1967 and '68 show clearly that in the formation of intellectual camps it happens that opponents block one another, making consensus an impossible task—a consensus, that is, predicated on being convinced by the arguments of the other.

—Translated by Dana Schmidt.

[37] Hartwig Germer, Stefan Müller-Doohm, Franziska Thiele, "Intellektuelle Deutungskämpfe im Raum publizistischer Öffentlichkeit", *Berliner Journal für Soziologie* (Wiesbaden: Springer, 2013): 513–520

"The Lava of Thought":
The Future of Critical Theory beyond Cultural Criticism[1]

ARPAD-ANDREAS SÖLTER

The critique of reason is realised already in early Critical Theory "by reflecting on the disease of the world".[1] To this end its proponents even reverted to medical-organicist metaphors. Evidently, the use of the notion of disease is not restricted merely to cultural-conservative and pre-fascist journalism.[2] With reference to Fromm's *The Sane Society*, Marcuse assessed the state of health of present industrial societies and proclaimed them to be "sick."[3] Marcuse's normatively laden analysis of crisis, which is conceived in cultural-critical terms, declares *qua* medical analogy the "pathological state" of "society as a whole."[4] In other words, Marcuse assigns society a medical certificate.[5] Habermas states his concerns and worries with regard to metaphors that refer to the body and disease: he rejects the "transferring of the doctor-patient model to political praxis of large groups."[6] The use of these metaphors would be problematic, as it "would encourage the uncontrolled exercise of force on the part of self-appointed elites, who close themselves off against potential opponents with dogmatic claims of privileged access to true insight."[7] He regards the concept of alienation in "bourgeois cultural criticism" as too vague, "too blurred", since it announces "a kind of anthropological, even metaphysical damnation."[8] Therefore it must be detached from the analysis of the commodity form and

---

[1] "die Lava des Gedankens im Fluß". Jürgen Habermas, "Die Zeit hatte einen doppelten Boden: Theodor W. Adorno in den fünfziger Jahren: Eine persönliche Notiz", in Stefan Müller-Doohm (ed.), *Adorno-Portraits: Erinnerungen von Zeitgenossen* (Frankfurt am Main: Suhrkamp, 2007), 15–23, 18. I am grateful for critical comments from Richard Wolin, Volker Heins, and Alix Landgrebe. Any shortcomings in this article, however, are my responsibility entirely. Antonia Hofstätter has translated an earlier version of this chapter.

[1] Max Horkheimer, *Eclipse of Reason* (London: Continuum, 2004), 120.

[2] On this metaphor see Jürgen Habermas, *The Theory of Communicative Action* (Vol. 1): *Reason and the Rationalization of Society*, trans. Thomas McCarthy (Boston: Beacon Press, 1984), 101; Habermas, *The Theory of Communicative Action* (Vol. 2), 303–331.

[3] Herbert Marcuse, "Aggressiveness in advanced industrial societies", in *Negations: Essays in Critical Theory*, trans. Jeremy Shapiro (London: Mayfly Books, 2009), 187–202, 189ff.

[4] Jürgen Habermas, *Knowledge and Human Interests*, trans. Jeremy J. Shapiro (Boston: Beacon Press, 1972), 274.

[5] Herbert Marcuse, "Aggressiveness in advanced industrial societies", 189 (translation modified).

[6] Jürgen Habermas, *Theory and Practice* (Boston: Beacon Press, 1974), 16.

[7] Ibid.

[8] Jürgen Habermas, *Kleine politische Schriften I–IV* (Frankfurt am Main: Suhrkamp, 1981), 479.

abstractly reformulated in terms of a critique of instrumental and functional reason to capture modernity's ills and pathologies.[9] Obviously, Habermas also regards his own theory as a continuation of the experiences and problems with which cultural criticism has been dealing. However, it would be absolutely misguided to equate Adorno, Horkheimer, Marcuse, Benjamin, Leo Löwenthal or Habermas's thought with anti-modernist cultural criticism.[10] From their point of view, this oxymoronic 'conservative revolutionary' cultural criticism aimed at preserving bourgeois culture as a form of authority in the Mandarin tradition of German aristocratic elitism. In diametrical opposition, far from encouraging political quiescence and passivity Adorno and Benjamin were guided by fundamentally different intentions. Unquestionably, as Marxists they strove to refunction cultural criticism during the 1920s and 1930s to the political left, and unlike their political opponents without neglecting a critique of the very material conditions of society. The ambivalences about this entire project to repurpose conservative versions and tropes of cultural criticism for progressive ends surfaced multiple times. The melancholic reference to "the sacrifices and outstanding utopian contents of bourgeois emancipation [...] is not yet cultural pessimism. [...] And opposition against scientism, which denies the nexus between the theory of science and the basic questions of practical philosophy is not yet obscurantism."[11] It is by no means necessary to 'harmonise' the fundamental differences between the individual representatives of the 'cultural-critical paradigm' to notice their apparent convergences and affinities.[12] Hence, the affinities between Critical Theory and this German specialty, a diagnosis of the times and the ills of modern society, need to be researched and emphasised. In this respect, the important distinctions and differences between the Frankfurt School and their political opponents on the Right deserve to be carefully considered. They lie in the detail and as a result, are often quite subtle.[13]

The notion of our modern world gone wrong and human beings suffering from severe deformations and pathologies has in conjunction with key con-

---

[9] Ibid. 479–80.

[10] Jürgen Habermas, *Philosophisch-Politische Profile* (Frankfurt am Main: Suhrkamp, 1981), 467.

[11] Ibid. 467.

[12] Richard Wolin, *The Terms of Cultural Criticism: The Frankfurt School, Existentialism, Poststructuralism* (New York: Columbia University Press, 1992); Herbert Schnädelbach, "Kultur und Kulturkritik", in *Vorträge und Abhandlungen*, vol. 2 (Frankfurt am Main: Suhrkamp, 1992), 169.

[13] Marcuse's early "idea of fusing Heidegger with Marx" is just as astonishing as the fact that Walter Benjamin was deeply attracted to the "doctrines of C. G. Jung and Ludwig Klages" who became reactionary "supporters of Germany's Brown Revolution"; see Richard Wolin, *The Frankfurt School Revisited: and Other Essays on Politics and Society*. (London: Rutledge, 2006), 80, 36.

cepts and reformulated ideas, such as alienation and reification, formed a unity in Critical Theory's many versions and traditions.[14] As *basso continuo* combined with a critical Post-Kantian theory of reason it unfolds a diagnosis of modernity. In this respect, it is consistent with Kant's project of self-determination maturity, and responsibility. Critical Theory's focuses on the crucial link between reason and emancipation, insight and autonomy. It is set in motion by reflexion and radical critique. According to Adorno and Horkheimer, alienation is a fatal result of instrumental reason.[15] In a context of total delusion under the spell of commodity fetishism human beings are reduced to mere objects in the machinery of capitalism. What is supposed to be a subject ultimately becomes just an object, an exchangeable commodity in the marketplace of a "one-dimensional society" (Marcuse).[16] In this view, the present age is a manifestation of degeneration and decline with increasing enhanced technological oppression.

Critical theorists argue that a fundamental critique of Western modernity can be formulated on the basis of a radical critique of reason, reification and alienation. This claim implicitly coincides with the core thesis of cultural criticism.[17] "Modernity *is* the crisis"—and the cultural-critical paradigm understands itself as an intellectual answer to this crisis of Western culture.[18] Hence, cultural criticism is presented as a theory of the crisis of modernity, that is, as a comprehensive, mostly negative assessment of the present age, which aims to decipher the "pathologies of modernity" and subject these alleged pathologies to fundamental critique.

In this contribution, I will explore the key coordinates and the productive research potential of Critical Theory's approach to cultural criticism and social critique. And I will analyse the *instrumentarium* of cultural criticism itself—that is, its modus and its perception of the modern world. Adorno and

---

[14] Axel Honneth, *Reification: A New Look at an Old Idea.* (Oxford: Oxford University Press, 2008); Axel Honneth, *Pathologien der Vernunft: Geschichte und Gegenwart der Kritischen Theorie.* (Frankfurt am Main: Suhrkamp Verlag, 2007); Rahel Jaeggi, *Alienation (New Directions in Critical Theory),* trans. Frederick Neuhouser (ed.) and Alan E. Smith (New York: Columbia University Press, 2016).

[15] Sonja Lavaert and Winfried Schröder (eds.), *Aufklärungs-Kritik und Aufklärungs-Mythen: Horkheimer und Adorno in philosophiehistorischer Perspektive,* (Berlin: de Gruyter, 2018).

[16] Volker M. Heins, "Herbert Marcuse, One-Dimensional Man", *The Oxford Handbook of Classics in Contemporary Political Theory,* ed. Jacob T. Levy (Oxford: Oxford University Press, 2015), 1–14.

[17] Arpad-Andreas Sölter, *Moderne und Kulturkritik: Jürgen Habermas und das Erbe der Kritischen Theorie* (Bonn: Bouvier, 1996), 250ff. and 274ff; Arpad-Andreas Sölter and Alix Landgrebe, "Kulturkritik today: Adorno's Sting", Moskau 2011 (in Russian). Kritika kultury segodnja. Zhalo Adorno. In *Filosofia. Kultura. Istorija: Materialy mezhvukovskoj konferenzii* (Moscow 12–13. dekabrja 2011 g. Moscow 2011), 88–97.

[18] In his most recent assessment of scenarios of crises and narratives of decline Habermas summarizes: "Die Moderne *ist* die Krise". Jürgen Habermas, *Auch eine Geschichte der Philosophie, Band 1. Die okzidentale Konstellation von Glauben und Wissen* (Berlin: Suhrkamp 2019), 41.

Habermas have explicitly emphasised many shortcomings of classical, so-called bourgeois conservative cultural criticism. I will demonstrate, however, why their respective critiques do not go far enough. They do not abandon all patterns, *topoi* and arguments as ingredients of cultural criticism in their analyses of modern society. To the contrary, Critical Theory's understanding of the modern age as a time of crisis and social ills is shaped by conventional cultural critical tropes: it is presented in form of a primarily negative judgement on the *conditio moderna* based on a critical diagnosis of the contemporary age. This means that also some of the serious problems, effects and burdens of older versions of cultural criticism are implicitly adopted even by its more recent variants. In the final part of this article, I will explore the question, if, and if so, how, Critical Theory, which is deeply embedded in, and until today connected to, the heritage of cultural criticism, can still make innovative contributions to the rational critique of society and the analyses of the present.

I argue, first, that there is an internal coherence and motivic cohesion of the cultural-critical paradigm in a comprehensive Kuhnian sense.[19] Adorno's and Habermas's different approaches seamlessly fit the wide-ranging paradigm of cultural criticism. Analytical diagnoses of the present are thus not merely accidental to Critical Theory. Rather, as cultural-critical force, these diagnoses determine the substance of Critical Theory in its essential core. They illustrate it in a symptomatic manner. Their own explicit critique of older forms of cultural criticism thus only applies to a specific type and to particular representatives of cultural criticism, however, not to the whole paradigm as such. Adorno's and Habermas's fundamental cultural-critical convictions play a crucial role in disclosing and making intelligible to them the key elements of a modern worldview. This factor has also decisively contributed to the international success of their oeuvres and of the entire paradigm of cultural criticism.[20]

Second, I argue that radical patterns of perception in cultural criticism lead to deeply deficient, even catastrophic misjudgements in the sphere of the political. Critical theorists themselves provide striking proof of this point. They convey the fatal nexus between philosophy inspired by cultural criticism and

---

[19] Thomas S. Kuhn, *The Structure of Scientific Revolutions* (Chicago: University of Chicago Press, 1970).

[20] Luca Corchia, Stefan Müller-Doohm, and William Outhwaite (eds.), *Habermas global: Wirkungsgeschichte seines Werks* (Berlin: Suhrkamp Verlag, 2019); Karsten Fischer/Raimund Ottow, "Sammelrezension Das 'Godesberg' der Kritischen Theorie: Theorie und Politik im Generationenwechsel von Horkheimer/Adorno zu Habermas Teil II", *Politische Vierteljahresschrift*, Volume 43, Issue 4 (December 2002): 653–669. Their review systematically denies significantly crucial motifs shared by "left wing", democratic cultural critics like Habermas or his predecessors, and "right wing" critics of civilisation, 659–660.

(misguided) political perception. Habermas's critique of the Federal Republic of Germany and his most recent vision for a future European Union will serve as an example to illustrate this crucial relationship.

Third, I argue, *pars pro toto*, that questions concerning the future of Critical Theory open up the possibility to disclose and address deeper layers of mentality. In this context, Habermas and Adorno will serve as examples with the help of which I will analyse the paradigmatic coordinates of cultural criticism to unfold its most important layers and dimensions. The discussion about the validity and dignity of these respective philosophical positions and their methodology also touches on future options and political perspectives. This is why the discussion on the motifs, argumentative structure and evaluation of cultural criticism as a holistic paradigm, to which both philosophers belong, coincides with a debate on the actual and future determinations of political thinking today.

Fourth, I argue that the future of Critical Theory crucially depends on whether it can move beyond philological 'musealisation' and whether it can rid itself of the old burden of cultural criticism. To accomplish this shift, Critical Theory must transform itself into a rational critique of society. This is to be characterised in a threefold manner: (a) by a capacity to reflect conflicts between certain normative ideals, aims and objectives; (b) by an ability to reflect on problems of realisation with reference to ideal social situations, and thereby to expose the illusiory nature of political wishful thinking by juxtaposing it with empirical evidence offered by social research, and (c) by an aptitude to articulate innovative impulses of analysis and for society's organisation and social distribution, in order to initiate gradual improvements increasing the problem-solving capacity of democratic fallibilism.

Cultural criticism, its proponents and multiple variations

Philosophy offers a mode of communication and understanding for the pressing questions of the modern age, an age that has attained reflexivity and come to problematise itself through cultural criticism. Furthermore, philosophy helps to overcome the deficits of modernity in a constructive manner.[21] This,

---

[21] Jürgen Habermas, "The Undermining of Western Rationalism Through the Critique of Metaphysics: Martin Heidegger", in *The Philosophical Discourse of Modernity: Twelve Lectures*, trans. Frederick Lawrence (Cambridge: Polity Press, 1990); Jürgen Habermas, "Work and Weltanschauung: The Heidegger Controversy from a German Perspective", trans. John McCumber, *Critical Inquiry*, Vol. 15, No. 2 (Winter, 1989), 431–456; Jürgen Habermas, "Mit Heidegger gegen Heidegger denken", *Frankfurter Allgemeine Zeitung*, 25.07.1953. Arpad-Andreas Sölter, "Mirrors of Evil: Cultural criticism, critique of modernity, and

however, poses a problem: philosophy "is credited with and thought capable of omni-competence, as it were, and this also concerns the political."[22] This specific assignation of tasks to philosophy relates to decisive weaknesses in the spheres of political understanding and praxis, as manifested by the eccentric German cultural consciousness.[23]

The cultural-critical response to the *conditio moderna* is an international phenomenon. The German cultural consciousness and self-consciousness, however, is not only decisively shaped by cultural criticism. In Germany, almost without exception, the Western theory of the present age is presented in the terms of cultural criticism.[24] The dominant system of coordinates in this perception functions as a selective filter of interpretation for all the alleged impertinences of the process of modernisation. The paradigm of cultural criticism is characterised by three dimensions, which lend space to the different variations of cultural criticism. These different versions share a common denominator. A critical view or even a fundamental opposition to the modern age is articulated in terms of a rejection of or, even, a contempt for modernity.

1. The *first axis* of this system of coordinates indicates the radical nature of the cultural-critical analysis of crisis. Cultural pessimism and cultural criticism must be regarded as different degrees on the spectrum of radicalness within the same discourse of alienation. The ascending line, which signifies a fundamental aversion against modernity, rises on a scale from A to C up to

---

Anti-Semitism in Heidegger's Thought", in *Cosmopolitism, Heidegger, Wagner – Jewish Reflections*, ed. Daniel Pedersen (Stockholm: Judisk kultur i Sverige, 2019, 2nd expanded edition), 199–222. Arpad-Andreas Sölter, "Und das jetzige Menschentum verschwindet'; Heideggers kulturkritische Diagnose des gegenwärtigen Zeitalters in den Schwarzen Heften" *Heidegger-Jahrbuch* 12 (2019).

[22] Ernst Vollrath, *Was ist das Politische? Eine Theorie des Politischen und seiner Wahrnehmung* (Würzburg: Königshausen und Neumann, 2003), 171.

[23] For very recent attempts to rehabilitate cultural criticism, see: Alexander Grau, *Kulturpessimismus: Ein Plädoyer* (Lüneburg: Zu Klampen Verlag, 2018), special issue "Kulturkritik", *Kultursoziologie*, No. 1/ 2017, and *Formen der Kulturkritik*, ed. Sebastian Baden et. al. (Munich: Wilhelm Fink, 2018), Erik Lehnert, Kulturkritik, *Sezession* 62, Oktober 2014, 8–11. https://sezession.de/uploads/Sez_62-Lehnert.pdf Accessed Feb. 16, 2020. Heiko Christians noted that "[a]part from presentations that paraphrase or collect the programmes of cultural criticism, there exist no fundamental accounts of cultural criticism" (Heiko Christians, "Kulturkritik", in *Metzler Lexikon Literatur und Kulturtheorie*, 2nd rev. edition, ed. Ansgar Nünning [Stuttgart: Metzler, 2001], 347–348). Only partly was this gap filled by Georg Bollenbeck, *Eine Geschichte der Kulturkritik: Von J.J. Rousseau bis Günther Anders* (München: Beck, 2007). For a critical review see Clemens Albrecht, "Sammelrezension Kulturkritik", *Clio Online: Fachportal für die Geisteswissenschaften*, accessed August 26, 2018, https://www.hsozkult.de/publicationreview/id/rezbuecher-11106.

[24] Dieter Henrich, "Die Grundstruktur der modernen Philosophie. Mit einer Nachschrift: Über Selbstbewußtsein und Selbsterhaltung", in *Subjektivität und Selbsterhaltung: Beiträge zur Diagnose der Moderne*, ed. H. Ebeling (Frankfurt am Main: Suhrkamp, 1976), 124. Ernst Vollrath, *Was ist das Politische?*, 173.

the point of apocalyptic consciousness. This trajectory expresses the conviction that

a) material elements of civilisation—such as technology or the commodity form—damage the true essence of culture. Indeed, it indicates that there are losses to be mourned and even pathologies to be attested in the processes of modernisation.
b) culture is in decline—even though this decline is not specified in temporal terms—and that symptoms of decay are perceptible.
c) culture moves irrevocably towards its imminent downfall.

2. The *second axis* defines the cultural quality and tone of the arguments advanced. According to these coordinates, the intellectual altitude of the different varieties of cultural criticism move in a continuum of extremes. The paradigm of cultural criticism appears in form of a vulgar version and in a version that defines the top performances of intellectual history, i.e. in a decisively ambitious and highly cultured form. However, both versions share basic deficits regarding their political perception, no matter whether they are located on the left or on the right of the political spectrum.[25]

2.1 The tradition of high culture and the widely ramified landscape of cultural criticism with its critique of modernity can be detected within a continuum of tradition: inspired by Rousseau's critique of civilisation it stretches via 'The Oldest Systematic Program of German Idealism' to Schiller, Marx, Nietzsche, Freud, Max Weber, Spengler's *The Decline of the West*, Thomas Mann's *Reflections of a Nonpolitical Man*, Karl Jaspers' *Man in the Modern Age*, Heidegger, Carl Schmitt, Gehlen,[26] on the one side, and from the Neo-Marxism of Critical Theory up to French poststructuralism, on the other. Interestingly, in order to juxtapose an authentic (cultural) sphere to an allegedly lower sphere of civilisation, there developed a widespread dichotomy

---

[25] See Ernst Vollrath, *Was ist das Politische?* The inner core of Critical Theory has never developed a coherent theory of politics or the political. See Ulf Bohmann an Paul Sörensen (eds.), *Kritische Theorie der Politik* (Berlin: Suhrkamp, 2019).

[26] Arnold Gehlen, "Die Seele im technischen Zeitalter", in Gehlen, Gesamtausgabe ed. Karl-Siegbert Rehberg. Bd. 6: *Die Seele im technischen Zeitalter und andere sozialpsychologische, soziologische und kulturanalytische Schriften* (Frankfurt am Main: Vittorio Klostermann, 2004), 1–137. Daniel Morat, "Der lange Schatten der Kulturkritik: Arnold Gehlen über "Die Seele im technischen Zeitalter", *Zeithistorische Forschungen/Studies in Contemporary History* 6, vol. 2 (2009): 320–325. https://zeithistorischeforschungen.de/2-2009/4606 Accessed Feb. 16, 2020.

between culture and civilisation in Germany. Since the beginning of the twentieth century, the German *Zeitgeist* has been shaped by these kind of polarisations and degradations of core areas of civilisation, such as state, economy and technology.[27] The cultural-critical repertoire goes hand in hand with the capitalist mode of production, which creates, by means of universal rationalisation, an "iron cage" (Weber), which forces the individual into the straightjacket of instrumental rationality, disenchantment, bureaucratisation, specialisation and secularisation. Horkheimer and Adorno's notion of "instrumental rationality" serves to criticise a lack of holistic, critical thinking. After World War II cultural criticism underwent a renaissance.[28]

2.2. The vulgar-cultural variant which can be contrasted to this high-cultural version is described by Fritz Stern in *The Politics of Cultural Despair*. The German translation of *Kulturpessimismus als politische Gefahr* (lit. cultural pessimism as political danger) signifies already with its title the immediate connection between cultural-critical positions and political perception and effect. Repeatedly, the affinity between certain tendencies of vulgar cultural criticism and National Socialism has been pointed out.[29] It included, furthermore, the rejection of emancipatory movements and change, which the advocates of cultural criticism did not regard as typical for the "German intellect [*Geist*]."[30]

Surprisingly, Cultural criticism can appear in both forms mentioned above and even oscillate between them. At any time, its concepts, motifs and justifications can be interchanged. This makes it particularly problematic. The line of demarcation between the two variants remains muddy.[31] Its odious variant can profit from the prestige of the esteemed one, not just because the border between the two versions is blurred, but also because no criteria of demarcation

---

[27] Wolf Lepenies, *The Seduction of Culture in German History* (Princeton: Princeton University Press, 2006).

[28] See Bollenbeck, *Eine Geschichte der Kulturkritik*.

[29] This study discusses critics of Germany's cultural crisis, such as Lagarde, Langbehn, and Moeller van den Bruck serving as examples for a particular type of cultural despair; see Fritz Stern, *Kulturpessimismus als politische Gefahr: Eine Analyse nationaler Ideologie in Deutschland* (Stuttgart: Klett-Cotta, 1963); Georg Bollenbeck, *Bildung und Kultur: Glanz und Elend eines deutschen Deutungsmusters* (Frankfurt am Main and Leipzig: Insel, 1994).

[30] Barbara Besslich, *Wege in den "Kulturkrieg": Zivilisationskritik in Deutschland 1890–1914* (Darmstadt: Wissenschaftliche Buchgesellschaft, 2000).

[31] Andrei S. Markovits, *Uncouth Nation: Why Europe Dislikes America* (Princeton: Princeton University Press, 2007).

apply to the realm of alienation and decay. Does this overlap devalue cultural criticism itself? Not necessarily. For inasmuch as the paradigm of cultural criticism is comprised of different qualitative dimensions and a far-ranging spectrum, it can include either regressive or emancipatory aspects. It contains liberating forces as long as it is directed at emancipation, enlightenment and progress (understood as the abolition of injustice, suffering, and superfluous domination). However, it can also contain conservative, restitutive and even regressive versions, which bitterly oppose any move towards emancipation, social change, and human progress.[32]

The classical *topoi* of cultural criticism articulate the discontent regarding modernity. Universal decay, alienation, the emergence of the masses and the 'death of the individual', the domination of money, technology, media, the decline of culture and education—these issues are still the topics of cultural criticism today. Cultural criticism circles around negative findings, such as the process of economisation (understood as the invasion of profit-maximising imperatives into spheres outside of the economy), quantification, uniformity, homogenisation *qua* mass culture through the narcotic 'culture industry' (Adorno and Horkheimer),[33] and the "colonisation of the lifeworld" by systemic imperatives, such as power and money (Habermas).[34]

3. On the third axis, democratic as well as anti-democratic versions of cultural criticism exist. The political camps are divided into conservative, regressive or even restitutive tendencies (Jünger, Benn, Schmitt, Heidegger, Gehlen),

---

[32] Ralf Konersmann, *Kulturkritik* (Frankfurt am Main: Suhrkamp, 2008).

[33] Negative assessments of the culture industry and its social function can also be found in Heidegger. His description "corresponded to the metaphysical diagnoses of the times which were undertaken by Lukács, Bloch, Kracauer and Benjamin" (Rolf Wiggershaus, *The Frankfurt School: Its History, Theories, and Political Significance*, trans. Michael Robertson [Cambridge: MIT Press, 1998], 99). However, if the present time appeared "as inauthentic, alienated, dominated by the 'they'", there remained only "a muted protest against existing conditions, which did not describe the causes of those conditions, and whose chief characteristic was an emotional sense of heroic fatalism" (Ibid., 100–1). Adorno and Horkheimer's critique of rationality and science in *Dialectic of Enlightenment* and other works is highly compatible with Heidegger's criticism of instrumental reason and the "instrumental character of modern science" (Martin Heidegger, "Anmerkungen I–V", in *Gesamtausgabe*, IV. Abteilung: Hinweise und Aufzeichnungen, Vol. 97, ed. Peter Trawny (Frankfurt am Main: Vittorio Klostermann, 2015), 252). Rolf Wiggershaus, "Max Horkheimer/ Theodor W. Adorno, Dialektik der Aufklärung (1947)", in *Geschichte des politischen Denkens: Ein Handbuch*, 4th edition, ed. Manfred Brocker (Frankfurt am Main: Suhrkamp, 2012), 540–553.

[34] Jürgen Habermas, *The Theory of Communicative Action* (Vol. 2): *Lifeworld and System: A Critique of Functionalist Reason*, trans. Thomas McCarthy (Boston: Beacon Press, 1987). Peter Niesen, "Jürgen Habermas, Theorie des kommunikativen Handels (1981)", in *Geschichte des politischen Denkens: Das 20. Jahrhundert*, ed. Manfred Brocker (Berlin: Suhrkamp, 2018), 639–653.

on the one hand, and progressive left positions, which are derived from or inspired by Marxism, on the other (Marx, Lukács, Bloch, Fromm, Marcuse, Horkheimer, Adorno, Habermas). Critical Theory regards the ideas of enlightenment—freedom and equality, emancipation, autonomy, and the subject—as unfulfilled promises of bourgeois society. In diametrical opposition and in their anti-liberal resentment other cultural critics consider these very ideas and ideals already as grave mistakes and aberrations.

Despite these substantial differences, there are also shared *topoi* and overlaps with respect to content and argumentation, which ultimately weld the paradigm of cultural criticism into a mental unity. This framework constitutes a dominant filter of interpretation through which reality is perceived. Across the entire political spectrum in Germany during the twentieth century—from the political left to the political right—cultural criticism and the radical critique of reason appear as two sides of the same coin. Often, strategies of immunisation are employed as soon as the cultural-critical disposition clashes with experience and counterevidence. All varieties of cultural criticism share a completely inadequate relationship to the civil-political concept of the political in the West. This is characterised *inter alia* by an inability to act pragmatically, a contempt for reality, an intellectual radicalness that tends towards extreme views and favours apocalyptic tendencies and catastrophic scenarios, a dualistic approach to thinking that reduces complexities and moves in binaries, a degradation of democratic institutions and liberal orders, and a contempt for politics or a call for its aestheticisation. Due to this misdirected impetus, wide sections of the German population in particular are enticed by mythological and aesthetic spheres of displacement. Consequently, political thinking is dominated by genuinely unpolitical images and categories and by a desire for 'unpolitical politics' or 'meta-politics'.[35] This moment conferred on German culture a particular intellectual radicalness, which crucially contributed to the international profile, standing and attractiveness of German culture. This eccentricity is extremely attractive to members of other cultures and not only to them. If greatness of intellect and political weakness are immediately linked in Germany, the taming of precisely this intellectual radicalness—which bestows finesse, admiration, and greatness on the German spirit—will lead to a loss of substance and to the levelling of cultural depth. Nevertheless, Germany's understanding of politics must become less radical. If the German political perception is to be re-integrated

---

[35] Ernst Vollrath, *Was ist das Politische?*, 176.

into the overall Western cultural understanding, it will have to change substantially. Only if it does so, can German culture fully become a part of the Western political culture. Politics must neither be dismissed as trivial, nor must it be burdened by unrealistic expectations. Politics can neither save mankind and the world, nor is it simply just a dirty business. Max Weber, despite his cultural-critical sympathies, describes politics as "a strong and slow boring of hard boards [that] takes both passion and perspective."[36] This process of reflexive civilising which will have to go hand in hand with Germany's integration into the West, demands the probing of its intellectual, institutional, and economic history.[37] However, relics of cultural criticism hamper the required disposition and make the cultural and political assimilation to the West difficult. Germany's cultural-critical paradigm constitutes a moment of demarcation with Western civil-political culture, precisely because of the extreme recklessness of its anti-civilisational impulses. This contributes to the erosion of trust in the democratic state and its constitutional mechanisms. This is reflected even in current debates.

Adorno's and Habermas' Critique of Bourgeois Cultural Criticism

The central concern of and interest in the dissolution of universal alienation reveals an affinity not only of representatives of Critical Theory to the overarching cultural-critical paradigm. The overcoming of alienation, as Critical Theory itself aspired to reach, must be understood as a process of healing and reconciliation—even if, by virtue of the so-called ban on images in Judaism,[38] the state of ultimate redemption remains foreclosed. The affinity between Critical Theory and cultural criticism remains valid despite the explicit claim of critical theorists to occupy a standpoint *above and beyond* earlier forms of cultural criticism. First, however, I want to disclose Adorno's and Habermas's arguments against conservative, bourgeois cultural criticism and its approach to culture. Both theorists uphold the ideals of enlightenment as unfulfilled

---

[36] Max Weber, "Politics as Vocation", in *Max Weber: Essays in Sociology*, ed. H. H. Gerth and C. Wright Mills (New York: Oxford University Press, 1946), 128 (translation modified).

[37] Arpad-Andreas Sölter, "Der europäische Sonderweg zur offenen Gesellschaft", in *Mensch und Gesellschaft aus der Sicht des kritischen Rationalismus*, ed. Hans Albert and Kurt Salamun (Amsterdam/Atlanta: Rodopi, 1993), 143–179.

[38] Micha Brumlik, "Das Bilderverbot im Judentum", *Blickpunkt.e* 06, 2011, in Dan Diner (ed.), *Enzyklopädie jüdischer Geschichte und Kultur* (Stuttgart: Metzler Verlag 2011) http://www.imdialog.org/bp2011/06/10.html, Accessed Feb 16, 2020.

promises, while claiming that these ideals have been perverted.[39] Both share, second, a defiance to regard as absolute the value of cultural ideals and to treat them as higher ends-in-themselves. This goes hand in hand with their refusal to ignore material interests and conditions, which bourgeois cultural criticism had dismissed as belonging to a lower sphere. In contrast to the conservative versions of cultural criticism, Critical Theory intends to reveal the social nexus between mass culture and the perpetuation of domination, social injustice, and extreme social inequality.[40] Adorno and Horkheimer assume that the culture industry—with its pre-formed, organised, all-round all-inclusive-amusement-operations—fulfils some kind of narcotic social function. By the same token, for Adorno, in fetishising the concept of culture, cultural criticism shares the "blindness"[41] of its subject matter.[42] Inspired by cultural criticism, Adorno's judgements about jazz, sport events or popular music are crushing. All he saw were recipients, who had degenerated into passive "amphibians."[43] Since his time in exile in the US, however, Adorno increasingly viewed the German concept of *Kultur* as dubious and the antithesis between *Kultur* and culture even as "fatal."[44] He fiercely criticises in particular the tendency of German intellectual culture to be detached from "real humanity" and thereby to become an end in itself. In *Negative Dialectics*, Adorno even establishes a connection between cultural criticism and fascist barbarism: "Cultural criticism and barbarism are not without affinity".[45] For Adorno, after fascism, immortal cultural values and norms, even theological ones, are discredited.[46]

"The end of the individual" as advocated by the older variant of Critical Theory, is a *topos* Habermas deals with critically.[47] His conclusive assessment is

---

[39] Martin Jay, *The Dialectical Imagination*, 295.

[40] Theodor W. Adorno, *Prisms*, trans. Shierry and Samuel Weber (Cambridge: MIT, 1981), 125. Martin Jay, *The Dialectical Imagination: A History of the Frankfurt School and the Institute of Social Research 1923–1950* (London: Heinemann Educational Books, 1973), 215.

[41] Adorno, *Prisms*, 23.

[42] For Adorno's relationship to US culture and to US cultural criticism, see Adorno, *Prisms*, 95ff.

[43] See Hans Joas "Die unterschätzte Alternative: Amerika und die Grenzen der 'Kritischen Theorie'", in Hans Joas, *Pragmatismus und Gesellschaftstheorie* (Frankfurt am Main: Suhrkamp, 1992), 109.

[44] T.W. Adorno, *Critical Models: Interventions and Catchwords*, trans. Henry Pickford (New York: Columbia University Press, 1998), 210.

[45] Ibid, 368. T.W. Adorno, *Negative Dialectics*, trans. E.B. Ashton (London and New York: Routledge, 1973), 366–7 (trans. mod.)

[46] See Herbert Schädelbach, "Kultur und Kulturkritik", in Herbert Schnädelbach, *Vorträge und Abhandlungen*, vol. 2 (Frankfurt am Main: Suhrkamp, 1992), 158ff. See also Horkheimer's essay "Philosophie und Kulturkritik". Max Horkheimer, *Sozialphilosophische Studien: Aufsätze, Reden und Vorträge 1930–1972*, ed. Werner Brede (Frankfurt am Main: Suhrkamp, 1981), 90ff.

[47] Habermas, *Legitimation Crisis*, trans. Thomas McCarthy (Cambridge: Polity Press, 1988), 117 ff.

negative: "Until now no one has succeeded in extracting the thesis of the end of the individual from the domain of the malaise and self-experience of intellectuals and made it accessible to empirical tests."[48] Habermas, too, deals repeatedly with the "unreflected prejudices of bourgeois cultural critique."[49] He traces back the phenomena of anomie, alienation, and the deprivation of meaning (i.e. the pathologies of post-traditional societies) either to the rationalisation of the lifeworld—as in bourgeois cultural criticism—or to deformations, which are caused by relations of production—as in Marxism.[50] A theory of modernity aiming at the radical critique of society, as presented by older Critical Theory, does not just repudiate its foundations. Rather, for Habermas, it cannot synchronically draw a distinction between manipulation and enlightenment or the deprivation of freedom and the protection of freedom.[51] The ominous context of total delusion and blindness (*Verblendung*) and reification of "a totally administered, calculated, and power-laden world' erases any substantial differences."[52] Even if looked at diachronically, when modern life-forms are compared with pre-modern life-forms, the fatal effects of a critique of modernity that levels off all distinctions come to the fore in the conjuring up of nostalgic, romanticising, and retrogressive ideals of life: "The high price earlier extracted from the mass of the population (in the dimension of bodily labour, material conditions, possibilities of individual choice, security of law and punishment, political participation, and schooling) is barely even noticed."[53] As a result, Habermas rejects the conservative variant of cultural criticism. In doing so, he follows the earlier generation of Critical Theory.[54] He repudiates in particular the latent "desire for de-differentiated forms of life" expressed by conservative cultural criticism.[55] Akin to Adorno, who castigates the "fetishism of culture" of conservative cultural criticism,[56] Habermas turns against *bourgeois cultural apologetics*, who understand the 'pathologies of modernity' only as inevitable effects of the process of disenchantment and

---

[48] Ibid, 128.

[49] Jürgen Habermas, *The Philosophical Discourse of Modernity.* 140. See also Jürgen Habermas, *The Theory of Communicative Action* (Vol. 2), 329 ff.; Jürgen Habermas, *Legitimation Crisis*, trans. Thomas McCarthy (Cambridge: Polity Press, 1988); Jürgen Habermas, *Die neue Unübersichtlichkeit: Kleine politische Schriften*, vol. V (Frankfurt am Main: Suhrkamp, 1985), 30 ff.

[50] See Habermas, *The Theory of Communicative Action* (Vol. 2), 329.

[51] See Habermas, *The Philosophical Discourse of Modernity*, 338.

[52] Ibid.

[53] Ibid; See also Habermas, *The Theory of Communicative Action* (Vol. 2), 341.

[54] See Habermas, *Die neue Unübersichtlichkeit*, 53.

[55] Ibid, 27.

[56] See Adorno, *Prisms*, 22ff.

social differentiation.[57] According to Habermas, however, bourgeois cultural apologetics advocate the misguided assumption that "disenchantment and alienation are structurally necessary conditions of freedom."[58] He distinguishes himself from so-called bourgeois cultural criticism by refusing to accept the two causes that are apologetically invoked by cultural criticism to explain deformations. According to him, neither the "increasing system complexity as such" nor the "rationalization of the lifeworld as such", sweepingly invoked, are responsible for social pathologies.[59] For him, it is the destructive process of social colonisation alone.

The suspicion that the fatal binary between culture and civilisation, revitalised by communications theory, might have crept into Habermas's dichotomous distinction between system and lifeworld is well founded. It is not just based on the flagrantly dualistic conception of Habermas's theoretical framework and his deeply ambivalent analyses of modern societies. Traditionally, the success-driven spheres of politics and economy are resigned to the inferior sphere of civilisation. Discursive self-assurance in authentic communicative situations, however, is construed as coinciding with participation in a cultural community. Habermas recognises the problems and dangers inscribed in "the anti-civilizational undercurrent of the German tradition"[60] and identifies them for instance in Heidegger's anti-western cultural criticism.[61] Habermas regards "the rather conventional dichotomy between culture and civilisation, style and technique, genius and talent, [...] the critique of social progress, [...] the lament over permissive pedagogics, [...] the distancing from the public or from philosophical journalism," as *indicators* of a specifically German tradition of cultural criticism: the 'ideology of the German mandarins' embraces *inter alia* 'a fetishizing of intellect [*Geistfetischismus*],' which goes hand in hand with the 'elitist self-perception of the academic,' 'an idolising of the mother tongue,' a polarising juxtaposition of the humanities and the natural sciences, 'contempt for all things social,' and a lack of a sociological framework for analysis, as it exists in the US or in France.[62] This phalanx of *topoi* from the realm of cultural criticism can be complemented with other concepts, such as: an anti-modern attitude; theories of decay or the pessimism of history; a radical scepticism of technology; an emphatic plea for non-alienated life-forms; a critique of the

---

[57] Habermas, *The Theory of Communicative Action* (Vol. 2), 330.

[58] Ibid.

[59] Ibid.

[60] Habermas, *Texte und Kontexte* (Frankfurt am Main: Suhrkamp, 1991), 59.

[61] Ibid, 49ff.

[62] Ibid. 57; see also Hauke Brunkhorst, "Ansichten des Intellektuellen: Vom deutschen Mandarin zur Ästhetik der Existenz", in *Raum und Verfahren: Interventionen 2* (Basel: Stroemfeld and Roter Stern, 1993).

emergence of the masses and of de-individualisation; a rise of conformity and mediocrity; a loss of authority; a critique of mechanisation; bureaucratisation; commercialisation and of consumerism in general; the domination of the media; the decline of education, ultimate values and morals; the critique of materialism and hedonism, anti-Americanism and anti-Semitism. Usually, this kind of a critique of life in industrialised civilisations is supplemented and contrasted with a 'vision of "true" culture.'[63] However, the *constellation* of different motifs and their respective argumentative nexus, which anchors the specific variant within the system of coordinates of cultural criticism, is decisive, of course.[64] The modernist wing of cultural criticism (Tönnies, Simmel, Weber) neither desires the retrogressive escape from modernity nor does it condemn modernity as such.[65] Rather, it pleads for the acceptance of its inevitable aspects. Considering the apparent 'at least partial alignment' of their analyses of modernity with cultural criticism, the legitimate question emerges as to whether 'ultimately, traditional "left" and "right" yardsticks (…) converge in the conjuration of the present as a time of catastrophe.'[66]

In Habermas' critical engagement with German cultural criticism he argues that a 'diagnosis of the contemporary age', appropriate to occidental modernity, must no longer 'follow in the footsteps of the cultural criticism of the German mandarins.'[67] He vehemently has distanced himself from 'the notorious clichés of cultural criticism.'[68] Habermas advocates 'the westernisation of our cultural order of values;' he challenges the 'fading dream of a triumph of depth' and the explosive traits of German cultural production with a plea for 'self-confident normality,' which does not descend into 'mediocracy.'[69] He rejects both a German *Sonderbewusstsein* (a consciousness of exception)—'that this land in the heart of Europe is destined to proceed into modernity on a privileged path'—and a German self-understanding that focusses on language and

---

[63] Schnädelbach, "Kultur und Kulturkritik", 161.

[64] Martin Jay has associated Fritz Ringer's famous study "The Decline of the German Mandarins" with the Frankfurt School but concludes that substantial differences between the two frameworks prohibit them from being equated. Jay, *The Dialectical Imagination*, 292ff.

[65] Fritz Ringer, *Die Gelehrten: Der Niedergang der deutschen Mandarine 1890–1933* (Munich: DTV, 1987), 152ff and 120ff.

[66] Michael Th. Greven, "Konservative Kultur- und Zivilisationskritik in der 'Dialektik der Aufklärung' und 'Schwelle der Zeiten'", in, *Konservatismus*, ed. Iring Fetscher et. al (München: Piper, 1983), 145 and 156; for Habermas' relationship to the leftwing spectrum of cultural criticism, see also Micha Brumlik, "Jürgen Habermas und die kulturkritische Linke", in *Vernunft der Moderne? Zu Habermas"Theorie des kommunikativen Handelns"*, ed. Rainer Danielzyk and Fritz Volz (Münster: Edition Liberacion, 1986), 15–23.

[67] Jürgen Habermas, *Justification and Application* (Cambridge, Mass.: MIT, 1994), 97.

[68] Jürgen Habermas, *Stichworte zur geistigen Situation der Zeit* (Frankfurt am Main: Suhrkamp, 1979), 28.

[69] Habermas, *Texte und Kontexte*, 208–9.

culture and which is associated with the idea of a 'cultural nation,' which, in turn, is shaped by the cultural bourgeoisie [*Bildungsbürgertum*].[70] However, Habermas distances himself exclusively from the conservative and regressive or vulgar-cultural variant of cultural criticism, but not from wider cultural criticism *per se*. Thus, he turns against a version thereof, which either blocks the process of westernisation by upholding an obsolete canon of values or which aims at reversing this process by means of romanticising transfiguration or with the help of an antirationalistic critique of modernity. While conservative cultural criticism cultivates a hostile-melancholic attitude towards modernisation, according to Habermas, its progressive variant, despite its 'insights into the dialectic of progress,' trusts 'the productive forces of the modern world.'[71] This is why Habermas always emphasises that the contemporary critique of reification cannot take its impetus from 'the nostalgically loaded, frequently romanticized past or premodern forms of life.'[72] However, his critical engagement with the specific forms of cultural criticism inadmissibly reduces the discussion of the problematic nature and the dangers of cultural criticism. Apparently, Habermas presumes that he can refrain from re-examining the *whole* system of coordinates of cultural criticism. He brackets Marxism and its development within the tradition of Critical Theory, because the Marxist framework of modernity does not criticise the original intentions of the enlightenment, but only its failed realisation. Yet, this selective understanding of the problem ignores that the German tradition of cultural criticism also includes an emancipatory variant, which is indebted to high culture. Without doubt, elements of this specific variant have influenced Habermas' theory of society and critique of modernity's distortions and social pathologies and thus, creating a distant echo of Horkheimer's notion of Critical Theory as critique of reason being realised 'by reflecting on the disease of the world.'[73]

Positioning Critical Theory within the Paradigm of German Cultural Criticism

The entirety of Critical Theory—not just its individual moments or critical motifs and phases—is part of the cultural-critical paradigm. This includes even its recent modifications and corrections. Critical Theory must be understood as a Western theory of the contemporary age, which is based on a cultural-

---

[70] Ibid, 215
[71] Habermas, *Die neue Unübersichtlichkeit*, 40.
[72] Habermas, *The Theory of Communicative Action* (Vol. 2), 342.
[73] Max Horkheimer, *Eclipse of Reason* (London: Continuum, 2004), 120.

critical analysis of the present and opposes the alienation and deformation of human beings. As such, it entails all of the above-mentioned key elements and characteristics in different variations.

1. *Consciousness of crisis and the critique of pathologies in the present age*: Key ideas of the Frankfurt School, such as Horkheimer's notion of a "totally administered world"—using a Spenglerian idiom[74]—were formulated during times of Nazi dictatorship and totalitarianism in the 1940s. Similarly, the narrative of Western civilisation was shaped. This is an understanding of modernity as a story of decline signifying a total triumph of "instrumental reason" and the reduction of humans to the stuff of domination. Critical Theory, as indicated earlier, justifies its self-understanding by an analysis of the sad pathological state of the world. According to Critical Theory, structurally pathological conditions within modern society correlate inevitably with cognitive deformations, which affect the *consciousness* of human beings. Habermas, for whom a "permanent consciousness of crisis" [*Krisensbewusstsein*] is the symptom of modernity,[75] criticises a phenomenon that Horkheimer already mourned as an indicator for a substantial loss in the age of modernity: the "fragmentation" of "the consciousness of the common man," which is an image of the pathological conditions of modern societies.[76] "In place of false consciousness we today have a fragmented consciousness that blocks enlightenment by the mechanism of reification."[77] In short, this 'fragmentation' forestalls enlightenment by reification.[78] According to Habermas, it is the task of an 'analysis of modernity' to explain the "fragmentation of everyday consciousness."[79] Due to the differentiation of science, morality, and art in the process of Western rationalisation, comprehensive relationships (of meaning) are lost. For him, this is reflected by individual consciousness: "*Everyday consciousness*

---

[74] Richard Wolin, *The Frankfurt School Revisited: And other essays on politics and society.* (New York/London: Rutledge, 2006), 58.

[75] Jürgen Habermas, *Auch eine Geschichte der Philosophie*, vol 2: *Vernünftige Freiheit: Spuren des Diskurses über Glauben und Wissen* (Berlin: Suhrkamp 2019), 801.

[76] Max Horkheimer, "Der Planet– unsere Heimat", in *Gesammelte Schriften*, vol. 8, ed. Gunzelin Schmid Noerr (Frankfurt am Main: Fischer), 320.

[77] Jürgen Habermas, *The Theory of Communicative Action* (Vol. 2), 355.

[78] Jürgen Habermas, *Die neue Unübersichtlichkeit: Kleine politische Schriften* (Frankfurt am Main: Suhrkamp, 1985), 252.

[79] Jürgen Habermas, *The Theory of Communicative Action (Vol. 2)*, 355; Jürgen Habermas, *Die neue Unübersichtlichkeit*, 252.

is robbed of its power to synthesize; it becomes *fragmented*."[80] In his view, this fragmentation of everyday consciousness is a condition of the colonialisation of the lifeworld.[81] The cultural-critical perception regards modernity as a nexus of alienation. It follows that a substantial analysis of crisis and a diagnosis of the present time must be based on a foundation that is *critical* of alienation. The different variants of the cultural-critical perception meet in the assumption that the alienation-critical approach is the only conception suitable to understanding modernity through a universal theory of crisis. This is why there exist analogous views and patterns of justification, which connect conservative cultural criticism with the cultural criticism of Critical Theory, despite their different aims. The assumption that modernity is in 'a state of all-embracing alienation' creates a unifying bond between the different varieties of cultural criticism.[82] Any analysis of modernity that proceeds along cultural-critical lines, however, is marred by considerable conceptual and empirical deficits. As a result, this paradigm can by no means do justice to the 'European miracle' (Eric L. Jones).[83] The cultural-critical theory of civilisation presented in *Dialectic of Enlightenment* reduces the process of modernisation to a history of mounting repression: enlightenment's ideal of rationality providing the key to social progress begins with the domination of outer nature and culminates in the comprehensive oppression of human beings. Besides these reductionist tendencies, diffuse causal connections (characterised as completely inevitable by Adorno and Horkheimer) reveal that this kind of critique is part of the paradigm of cultural criticism: "industrialism makes souls into things."[84] In conjunction with the fatalist theory of history their cultural-critical argumentation results in a total blockade of practice. In his *Philosophical Discourse of Modernity* Habermas is extremely critical of Adorno and Horkheimer's diagnosis—just as he is justly critical of their poststructuralist, neo-Nietzschean heirs, such as Bataille, Foucault, and Derrida.

---

[80] Jürgen Habermas, *The Theory of Communicative Action* (*Vol. 2*), 355.

[81] See Ibid. 356.

[82] Wiggershaus, *The Frankfurt School*, 541.

[83] For a discussion see Arpad-Andreas Sölter, "Der europäische Sonderweg zur offenen Gesellschaft", in *Mensch und Gesellschaft aus der Sicht des kritischen Rationalismus*, ed. Hans Albert/Kurt Salamun (Amsterdam/Atlanta: Rodopi, 1993), 143–179. Arpad-Andreas Sölter, *Moderne und Kulturkritik: Jürgen Habermas und das Erbe der Kritischen Theorie* (Bonn: Bouvier, 1996), 151–182.

[84] Theodor W. Adorno and Max Horkheimer, *Dialectic of Enlightenment*, trans. Edmund Jephcott (Stanford: Stanford University Press, 2002), 21.

2. *The irreconcilability of antagonisms:* The imposition of structural dicho-
tomies and binary oppositions—such as culture and civilisation, *Geist* and
power, individual and society—on social reality is symptomatic for the
cultural-critical paradigm. This discourse is shaped by a tendency to "pit
one section of culture as a whole against *other* sections."[85] Striking in this
context is the proneness of this paradigm to produce abstract polarisations
and reductionist perspectives. The basic categories of cultural criticism are
grouped around an antagonistic constellation of the core concepts of
alienation and reconciliation. The 'desire of the unreconciled world' for
reconciliation is a desire for overcoming the state of alienation.[86] Hence, the
paradigm is dominated by an 'exodus-impulse,' by a desire to return home
or to 'move out of the disenchanted world' and into a realm in which the
fragmentation of the present age will have been overcome.[87]

3. *The invasion by the civilisational sector:* Critical Theory's many representatives have offered variations of the thesis that capitalism is responsible for
the fundamental pathologies of human existence. This conviction is one of
its common denominators. *Dialectic of Enlightenment* shares with *The
Theory of Communicative Action* the basic cultural-critical assumption that
the formalisation and *reification of life forms*[88]—which is set in motion by
the political and economic 'system'—hampers the possibility of 'unscathed
inter-subjectivity' within an authentic communicative society. It also causes
deformed interpersonal relationships and individual psychological pathologies. Because of all this, it matters little whether the cultural-critical argumentation of Critical Theory focuses on the intentions and ideals of the
enlightenment. For ultimately "almost all *topoi* of argumentation are shared
by 'left wing' cultural critics and "right wing" cultural critics."[89] Habermas
stresses the fact that Critical Theory sees itself as a continuation of the
philosophy of the enlightenment and its ideals. This self-understanding,
however, cannot hide the formative influence of the distinction crucial to
German cultural-critical thinking as such, that is, the dichotomy between
culture and civilisation. Its echo from afar can be heard even in in
Habermas' critique of "the colonization of the lifeworld" by impersonal

---

[85] Herbert Schnädelbach, "Kultur und Kulturkritik", 176.
[86] Gert Hummel, *Sehnsucht der unversöhnten Welt: Zu einer Theologie der universalen Versöhnung* (Darmstadt: Wissenschaftliche Buchgesellschaft, 1993).
[87] Norbert Bolz, *Auszug aus der entzauberten Welt: Philosophischer Extremismus zwischen den Weltkriegen* (München: Fink, 1991).
[88] Habermas, *The Philosophical Discourse of Modernity*, 352.
[89] Herbert Schnädelbach, "Kultur und Kulturkritik", 169.

forces, such as economic and administrative rationality. The colonisation thesis criticises the civilisational-systemic mechanisms of organisation, which encroach upon the refuge of culture and lifeworld, in which the solidary efforts of social reproduction take place. The endangered sphere is parasitically hollowed out by the civilisational imperatives, such as power and money. For Habermas, this illegitimate encroachment constitutes the heart of a crisis, which he frames in terms of a critique of society. Critical Theory is part of the paradigm of cultural criticism, because its analyses show that social ills—understood as boosts of alienation—result from the threats that are posed by the civilisational sector.

According to Habermas, modernity as such has "derailed",[90] because economic and administrative imperatives increasingly continue to monetarise and bureaucratise ever larger areas of life in the form of practical necessities. During this process in which the life-world is colonised and exploited an increasing number of human relations are turned into objects of administration and commodities.[91] For Habermas, then, the whole discourse of modernity has only one theme: the deformations within the life-world create "the need for something equivalent to the unifying power of religion."[92] From this perspective, the civilisational structures of liberal democratic orders based on market capitalism evoke serious pathological side-effects.[93] Because in Western liberal societies, Habermas claims, "the necessary conditions for a "good life" are carelessly and arbitrarily violated."[94]

4. *The extra-territorialising of the political and the degradation of liberal-democratic institutions*: Related to the specific German understanding of culture is a tendency to bracket the political. This inclination, however, leads to an implicit or even explicit misjudgement and degradation of the civilisational sector of society. For the cultural-critical perspective must regard the lawful institutions of liberal-democratic constitutional democracies exclusively as contaminated by alienation and domination. This

---

[90] Jürgen Habermas, *Auch eine Geschichte der Philosophie, Band 2. Vernünftige Freiheit. Spuren des Diskurses über Glauben und Wissen.* Berlin: Suhrkamp 2019, 807.

[91] Jürgen Habermas, *Die neue Unübersichtlichkeit: Kleine politische Schriften*, vol. V (Frankfurt am Main: Suhrkamp, 1985).

[92] Jürgen Habermas, *The Philosophical Discourse of Modernity*, 139.

[93] Jürgen Habermas, *Kleine politische Schriften*, vol. I–IV (Frankfurt am Main: Suhrkamp, 1981), 517.

[94] Jürgen Habermas,"Questions and Counterquestions", in *Habermas and Modernity*, ed. Richard J. Bernstein (Cambridge: Polity Press, 1985), 216.

reveals the specific problem of cultural criticism: once the entire civilisational complex is theorised as having fallen prey to alienation, it is impossible to distinguish between perverted and successful forms of the political. Hence, all forms of the political are interpreted as forms of alienation.[95] Thus, the institutional apparatus of liberal societies is seen in a negative and distorted light. Habermas' narrow interpretation of German cultural criticism implicitly upholds the regressive component of conservative cultural criticism as the *conditio sine qua non* of the modern cultural-critical perception. He thus misjudges both the scope of political trends that are shaped by the paradigm of cultural criticism and the variety of expressions it can take. These varieties, however, entwine with each other in structural commonalities, such as the critique of alienation and civilisation. Yet, the disastrous consequences of cultural criticism—the degradation of political and economic institutions—become apparent even where this regressive moment—the nostalgic desire for the lost age of mankind—is not present. Rather, the crucial point is that "from the perspective of the German cultural consciousness," the entire "complex of civilisation," which forms the heart of the "Western European world of ideas," appears as a threat to the cultural sphere and its presumed authenticity.[96] "Systemically induced social pathologies": the systemic sphere of civilisation increasingly colonises the authentic sphere of the lifeworld. It undermines the internal functional sequences of the lifeworld and therefore threatens the latter's entire capacity for reproduction. In Habermas's critique of mediatization,[97] instrumentalization,[98] technisation, formalisation, pathologisation, monetarisation, bureaucratisation, legalisation, and "the colonialization of the lifeworld,"[99] which focuses on the category of domination, Adorno and Horkheimer's echo of the accusation of "alienation"[100] and the turning of human beings "into things",[101] identified as distorting the psycho-social sphere, can be perceived.

---

[95] See Ernst Vollrath, "Was ist das Politische?"

[96] Ernst Vollrath, "Historische und naturrechtliche Apperzeption des Politischen: das deutsche und anglo-amerikanische Paradigma", in *Naturrecht und Politik*, ed. K.G. Ballestrem (Berlin: Duncker und Humblot, 1993), 88.

[97] Habermas, *Theory of Communicative Action* (Vol.2), 186.

[98] Ibid, 325.

[99] Ibid, 332ff.

[100] Adorno/Horkheimer, *Dialectic of Enlightenment*, 49.

[101] Ibid, 204.

According to Marcuse, too, the capitalist economy produces symptoms of reification, which correlate with deformations in both the psychological and interpersonal sphere. For him, this structurally endangers the possibility of authentic interaction within "any authentic form of human community."[102] Inspired by Heidegger, Marcuse argues in 1929 "that the crisis of capitalism is a crisis of existence, which has truly been shaken to its foundation."[103] In this view, capitalist commodity management—the central economic form of the present age—spurs a loss in solidarity and meaning, the destruction of all "personal values"[104] or subjugates these values to "technological and rational objectivity".[105] During the course of this reification, human beings are reduced to economic objects to the extent that "a true mode of existence" becomes impossible.[106]

All varieties of cultural criticism within Critical Theory are marked by the assumption that psycho-social deformations must be understood as indicators of the fundamental crisis of modernity. This crisis can only be understood and rectified by a comprehensive critique of rationality: "The crisis of reason is manifested in the crisis of the individual, as whose agency it has developed."[107] Of course, pointing out the consequences and incidental consequences of modernisation in the psycho-social sphere is not the same as committing to dogmatic anti-modernism.[108] Furthermore, it is not necessary to deny the costs of modernity, such as the breaking down of traditional forms of life and stable social structures, which is connected to rapid urbanisation and to processes of anonymisation under industrial conditions of life. In order to understand and criticise the destructive consequences of rationalisation or even the self-endangering tendencies of industrialised societies, however, cultural-critical patterns are not needed as an intellectual framework.

Ultimately, we can conclude that Habermas' revision of Critical Theory did not eliminate *all* components of cultural criticism. His endeavour to

---

[102] Herbert Marcuse, "On Concrete Philosophy", in *Heideggerian Marxism*, ed. Richard Wolin and John Abromeit (Lincoln and London: University of Nebraska Press, 2005), 42. For a most recent, political assessment of Heidegger's "Being and Time" (1927) see Arpad-Andreas Sölter: "Review of Marion Heinz, Tobias Bender (ed.): Sein und Zeit neu verhandelt. Untersuchungen zu Heideggers Hauptwerk", *Philosophischer Literaturanzeiger* 73, Heft 1 (2020): 22–38.

[103] Ibid.

[104] Ibid, 44.

[105] Ibid.

[106] Ibid.

[107] Horkheimer, *The Eclipse of Reason*, 87.

[108] See Habermas, *Philosophisch-Politische Profile* (Frankfurt am Main: Suhrkamp, 1981).

distance himself from cultural criticism and to protect Critical Theory from attempts to bend it along "the ordinary tracks of cultural criticism" does not go far enough.[109] In contrast to conservative cultural criticism, Critical Theory, whilst upholding the intentions of enlightenment, denies that the latter was realised in society. However, this fact ought not to blind us to the thematic overlaps of conservative and progressive forms of cultural criticism. Already Adorno remained rooted within the dualisms and "the dilemma of all cultural criticism,"[110] despite recognising and criticising the central problems of traditional cultural criticism.

Between Philosophy and Politics: The Degradation of Democracy and Liberalism

For Habermas, it was only after its total defeat in World War II that Germany accomplished its greatest intellectual achievement in the twentieth century: "The unreserved opening of the Federal Republic to the political culture of the West."[111] During this period, Habermas emerged as a cultural critic committed to democratic values defending a pro-European Union and pro-Western stance.[112] In the following, I will show how his theory of crisis shaped by cultural criticism nevertheless results in distorted political misconceptions which are connected precisely to his indebtedness to a dubious intellectual heritage of cultural criticism. Habermas has declared that existing democracies, such as the Federal Republic of Germany, suffer from "legitimation problems in late capitalism."[113] 'Late' in the temporal use of the prefix [*Spät-*] suggests that the beginning of a system different from capitalism is imminent. This alternative new order on the horizon, however, is never outlined. He has recently renewed his critique of capitalism with respect "to the putatively coercive systemic imperatives of a global economic order embodied by remote international organizations" and decries "the social destruction caused by untamed capitalism."[114] He refers to the high unemployment of young people in Southern

---

[109] Ibid, 429.

[110] Schnädelbach, "Kultur und Kulturkritik", 158.

[111] Jürgen Habermas, "A Kind of Settlement of Damages", *New German Critique*, No. 44, Special Issue on the Historikerstreit (Spring/Summer, 1988): 25–36, 39.

[112] See Rolf Wiggershaus, *The Frankfurt School*.

[113] Jürgen Habermas, *Legitimation Crisis*, trans. Thomas McCarthy (Cambridge: Polity Press, 1988).

[114] Jürgen Habermas, "What Macron Means for Europe: 'How Much Will the Germans Have to Pay?'", *Spiegel Online International*, accessed 7 March, 2019, http://www.spiegel.de/international/europe/

Europe as an example. Habermas, for whom the progress of rationalisation helped to spark 'societal pathologies', deformation and destruction criticises the "undemocratic constitutional state—something we experienced long enough in Germany."[115] In the 1990s, he demanded a *Western* (sic!) *"Perestroika."*[116] Habermas' postulate, however, does not specify the particular direction the demanded 'conversion' of constitutional liberal democracies should take. In connection with the fall of the Berlin Wall and German Reunification, Habermas even criticises an alleged "consolidation [*Gleichschaltung*] of media" (sic) in the new states of Eastern Germany.[117] By using the term 'consolidation', which is historically associated with the Nazi regime and its euphemism for the elimination of political opposition, Habermas indicates as if indeed the media in the bankrupted GDR was not consolidated by the SED dictatorship and as if a reunified Germany did not deliver freedom of the press! Thus, he propagates an absurd understanding of social and political reality in Western Germany after 1989: the total control, steering, and manipulation of all media with the aim to distribute false information via TV, radio and the internet. Both statements—Habermas' call for a second *'perestroika'* and his critique of 'the consolidation of media'—suggest quasi-totalitarian conditions. The underlying assumption is that allegedly non-democratic domination in Germany testifies to a political condition that must be overcome. To be sure, Habermas does not employ these terms in a naïve way; they are simplified and truncated perspectives, which do not adequately characterise democracies as only "halfway liberal".[118] They reveal his disapproval of an economic imperialism with market mechanisms penetrating every corner of society. And they mischaracterise the democratic and capitalist reality in constitutional states, for instance, in the Federal Republic of Germany and its welfare state based on a regulated market economy. Again, this misperception is induced by cultural criticism. The idea of a 'civil society', for instance, is pitted against the concept of liberal democracy. Similar to Habermas' notion of true, 'radical democracy' it signifies the exercise of democracy 'from below' as opposed to the dominance of elites,

---

juergen-habermas-on-the-european-vision-of-emmanuel-macron-a-1174721.html. Jürgen Habermas, *Auch eine Geschichte der Philosophie*, vol. 2, 799.

[115] Jürgen Habermas/Joseph Ratzinger, *Dialectics of Secularization: On Reason and Religion*, ed. Florian Schuller, trans. Brian McNeil (San Francisco: Ignatius Press, 2006), 31.

[116] Jürgen Habermas, *Vergangenheit als Zukunft*, ed. Michael Haller (Zurich: Pendo Verlag, 1990), 109.

[117] Jürgen Habermas, "Die zweite Lebenslüge der Bundesrepublik: Wir sind wieder "normal" geworden", *Die Zeit*, December 11, 1992, accessed August 20, 2018, https://www.zeit.de/1992/51/die-zweite-leben sluege-der-bundesrepublik-wir-sind-wieder-normal-geworden/komplettansicht.

[118] Jürgen Habermas, *Zur Verfassung Europas: Ein Essay.* (Frankfurt am Main: Suhrkamp, 2011), 38.

the political system, the administrative apparatus, and economic centres of power.[119] However, it is obvious that corrective democratic mechanisms become necessary, once allegedly salutary movements of the civil society aim at the abolition of the democratic and civilisational achievements of Western societies. In other words, civil societies potentially also harbour malicious trends and phenomena, which do not deserve our support and agreement.[120] Rather, vigorous democratic resistance is required against these elements of 'bad civil society.' Thirty years on, Habermas reflects on the state and future of Europe.[121] Again, he assesses "democratic deficits"; for him, European politics suffers from being "elitist and bureaucratic."[122] Again, links to earlier forms of cultural criticism are here recognisable.

Future Perspectives for Critical Theory

Critical Theory's future needs to focus on the fault lines of democracy and its neuralgic points in the current contestations of the liberal Western script with new and old authoritarian regimes gaining strength and nationalism on the rise. Today, when the freedom and the system of liberal democracy is put into question, critical-rational thought must advocate the credo 'in dubio pro libertate' and defend it against its opponents.[123] Innumerable motives, scenarios, and points of reference, which currently emerge as lines of argumentation and discourses of the new right, are a distant echo of the cultural-critical perception. Issues crucial to this intellectual portfolio are back on the agenda: a consciousness of fundamental crisis, understood as the turn of an era. Against this backdrop, future research to cover this trend might cover the following areas: an updated analysis of the authoritarian personality and authoritarian societies and the roots and causes of Fascism. All mechanisms of and instruments for mass manipulation, counter-enlightenment, incapacitation, control and repression, as well as all indications of political danger, such as a return to pre-democratic conditions remain the goal of any political and intellectual critique.

---

[119] Arpad-Andreas Sölter, "Zivilgesellschaft als demokratietheoretisches Konzept", *Jahrbuch für Politik*, vol.3, no.1 (1993): 145–180. Arpad-Andreas Sölter, *Moderne und Kulturkritik: Jürgen Habermas und das Erbe der Kritischen Theorie* (Bonn: Bouvier, 1996), 283, 378–399.

[120] Simone Chambers and Jeffrey Kopstein, "Bad Civil Society", *Political Theory*, vol. 29, no. 6 (2001): 837–865.

[121] Jürgen Habermas, Die Stimme Europas in der Vielstimmigkeit seiner Nationen", in Jürgen Habermas, *Der gespaltene Westen* (Frankfurt am Main: Suhrkamp 2004), 43–82; Jürgen Habermas, *Ach, Europa: Kleine politische Schriften XI* (Frankfurt am Main: Suhrkamp 2008); Jürgen Habermas, *Zur Verfassung Europas.*

[122] Jürgen Habermas, *Ach, Europa*, 98–99.

[123] Steven Levitsky and Daniel Ziblatt, *How Democracies Die* (New York: Crown, 2018).

A growing economic inequality has over recent years gradually started to erode the lower and the middle-class in Western societies, for which even affordable housing has become increasingly scarce, among other multiple causes of increased status anxiety in OECD-countries. Therefore, the taming of excessive, 'wild capitalism' and 're-feudalization' (Habermas) is back on the agenda.[124] Refugees, asylum seekers, and immigrants in great numbers arrive on the shores of Western societies stretching their capacities as welfare states. This trend has been perceived by many as a 'wave' initiating increased cultural conflicts and debates on inclusion and exclusion, integration and separation. The demand for (impossible) cultural homogeneity along binary and xenophobic lines has resurfaced on the agenda.[125] The *classa politica,* in collaboration with elites in the media is perceived by large circles of the population as inadequate. The (mal)functioning of public institutions is ascribed to the failure of the state and understood as being caused by detached political elites and the media. The political centre is denounced as 'pseudo-liberal mainstream' and accused of submitting to political correctness. Fake news, trolls and bots are blurring fact and fiction in an unparalleled transformation of the digital public sphere. Facebook, Google and Twitter call for a new comprehensive analysis of internet-based hyper-capitalism. Consequently, Habermas' earlier assessment requires an update.[126] Public discourse in social media has by and large not followed his notion of an unconstrained reflective discourse. Instead, it has created so-called influencers, echo chambers reinforcing preconceived attitudes and opinions, and digital platforms for unfiltered resentment, fake news, propaganda, and even hate speech. Equally, the relationship between art, culture, TV, entertainment and market capitalism is in need of a re-assessment.[127] Adorno's diagnosis of mass culture will in the future only serve as an inspiration if new trends and phenomena, such as Amazon, Google and Netflix, are

---

[124] Jürgen Habermas, *Zur Verfassung Europas,* 117.

[125] Arpad-Andreas Sölter, "Die Einbeziehung des Fremden: Reflexionen zur kulturellen Fremdheit bei Simmel, Habermas und Huntington", in *Der fremde Blick: Perspektiven interkultureller Kommunikation und Hermeneutik,* eds. Ingo Breuer and Arpad-Andreas Sölter (Bozen, Innsbruck and Vienna: Studien Verlag 1997), 25–51. Samuel P. Huntington, *Who are we? The Challenges to America"s National Identity* (New York: Simon & Schuster, 2004).

[126] Jürgen Habermas, *The Structural Transformation of the Public Sphere: An Inquiry into a Category of Bourgeois Society,* trans. Fredrick Lawrence (Cambridge, Mass.: MIT, 1989).

[127] Don Thompson, *The $12 Million Stuffed Shark: The Curious Economics of Contemporary Art* (New York: Palgrave Macmillan 2008); Sarah Thornton, *Sieben Tage in der Kunstwelt* (Frankfurt am Main: Fischer, 2009); Julia Voss, *Hinter weißen Wänden / Behind the White Cube* (Berlin, Merve-Verlag, 2015); Wolfgang Ullrich, *Siegerkunst: Neuer Adel, teure Lust.* (Berlin: Klaus Wagenbach Verlag, 2016).

taken into consideration by further empirical research.[128] For example, the so-called 'culture industry' with its 'mass deception', implemented by deeply invasive manipulative regimes, has transformed into today's festivalisation of culture as spectacle. The fun-driven event machinery, people-oriented entertainment and a growing festival landscape shape a competitive context manufactured by market conditions and sales-driven programming. Festivals have become marketing and branding tools for corporate entities. As a result, public festivals need to provide solid return on investment (ROI) in terms of their marketing value.

Despite everything that can be justly said and has already been written against cultural criticism: are its concerns not justified? Is cultural criticism not often right? Is cultural diagnostics beyond *Kulturkritik* even possible? And what could it look like? Who would deny the fact that we live in the age of 'information-dementia' as the cultural critic Botho Strauss puts it harshly in his 1993 essay in Der Spiegel, "Anschwellender Bockgesang" ("Swelling He-Goat Song") and in his stream-of-consciousness novella *Die Unbeholfenen*?[129] Yet, this critique of society and civilisation proves to be essentially abstract and indeterminate. It remains unsatisfactory, not least because it hardly shows any concrete connections with a politics focused on a piecemeal engineering approach—that is, a politics that proceeds in evolutionary steps and implements small and secure improvements of society. Critics of cultural criticism argue unanimously that democracy does not need a sweeping and generalising form of critique. Rather, it demands a differentiating rational analysis of society, which forms the basis for the implementation of social improvements

---

[128] For an assessment of recent trends in the "culture industry" such as festivals, see Arpad-Andreas Sölter, "Festival circus, golden gnomes and cultural diplomacy: The Audi festival of German films in the context of multicultural films in Australia", in *Studies in Australasian Cinema*, Vol. 9, No. 2, (2015): 190–204; Arpad-Andreas Sölter, "Strategically Shaping International Cultural Relations in a Changing Competitive Environment: Reflections on Recent German-Australian Encounters", in Benjamin Nickl/Irina Herrschner and Elsbieta M. Gozdziak (eds.), *German-Australian Encounters and Cultural Transfers: Global Dynamics in Transnational Lands* (Singapore: Springer VS, 2018), 3–28. For a discussion of culture"s international scope in its use as "soft power" (Joseph Nye), see Arpad-Andreas Sölter, "Auswärtige Kulturpolitik und die Erfolgsbedingungen interkultureller Verständigung", in: Peter Wapnewski and Christoph Mücher (eds.), *Realitäten und Visionen: Hilmar Hoffmann zu ehren* (Cologne: DuMont 2000), 226–245; Arpad-Andreas Sölter, "Cats statt Kafka? Kultur und auswärtige Kulturpolitik im Zeitalter der Globalisierung", *lendemains: Französisch-deutsche Kulturbeziehungen, Entente cordiale* 26. Jahrgang (103/104) (2001): 147–166. Arpad-Andreas Sölter, "Massiver Wandel und neue Ziele: Strategisches Veränderungsmanagement in Kulturbetrieben am Beispiel der Reform im Goethe-Institut", in *Handbuch für Kulturmanagement und Kulturpolitik. Eds.* Friedrich Loock and Oliver Scheytt (Berlin: Raabe 2010), 1–29: Arpad-Andreas Sölter, "Hochkultur ist subversive: Kultur, Bildung und Gleichheit in Schweden", I *Politik und Kultur* 3 (2019): 10. https://www.goethe.de/ins/se/de/kul/mag/21526796.html (In Swedish: https://www.goethe.de/ins/se/sv/kul/mag/21526796.html), Accessed Feb 16, 2020.

[129] Botho Strauß, *Die Unbeholfenen: Bewußtseinsnovelle* (Muniche: Hanser, 2007).

by means of piecemeal social engineering. While Habermas adopts Popper's idea of piecemeal engineering, his remarks on practice are extremely imprecise. It leaves us in the dark with respect to what a concrete practical politics, which takes seriously the colonialisation thesis and aims at the 'decolonialisation' of social lifeworlds, would look like, both in general and in particular.

The deficits of blanket cultural criticism, as outlined above, oppose the search for realisable political alternatives, which are informed by an ethics of responsibility. These alternatives must take the form of a democratic fallibilism, which moves step-by-step—via trial and error—towards better solutions. It must be based on an awareness of all the privileges of an open society. In these societies human dignity is valued, and its form of governance guarantees freedom. Human and civil rights are upheld by the constitution. A separation of powers is implemented and independent courts, pluralism and competition are established alongside the levelling of interests, freedom of press, media and the arts, and a public civil society is active, which forms a necessary corrective to truth claims—in short, a political form has been created in which responsibility and creative forces are periodically transferred to newly elected representatives without bloodshed, in which old governments are superseded peacefully in order for other and perhaps better solutions to be tested.

Any rational critique of society describes the collateral damages of progress. Usually, they occur as unintended effects or side effects. Ideally, with the help of a cultural critical frame of reference, experiences and problems can be identified and reformulated.[130] A modernised, appropriate variant of a rational critique of society does not represent an anti-modern ideology or any of its former components. Rather, it offers a legitimate and consistent continuation of the enlightenment by pointing out deficits, losses, aberrations, and ambivalences in modernity and by correcting them step-by-step as far as possible. Within the limits of feasibility, critical-rational methodology can help to develop solutions for problems. Cultural criticism, then, applies enlightenment reason reflexively to itself.[131] If understood in this way, cultural criticism is not formed by resentment and restitutive transfiguration, but by truth claims, analyses of deficits, and epistemological achievements. This kind of criticism continues to unfold its effects, which are critical of society and intellectually stimulating. Hence, this approach identifies concrete deficits beyond conventional and generalising cultural-critical judgements. This approach is characterised by its search for politically realisable alternatives. In line with social

---

[130] See Habermas, *Philosophisch-Politische Profile*, 466.
[131] See Georg Bollenbeck, *Eine Geschichte der Kulturkritik* and Ralf Konersmann, *Kulturkritik.*

critique, it takes seriously the problem of viability with respect to continued comparison of possible social alternatives.[132] Questions of implementation and feasibility will enjoy priority over wishful thinking, chasing rainbows, and total blockade. It reflects and incorporates the research of the empirical sciences and their results as well as the conflicting aims and objectives of different socio-political ideal conceptions. A Critical Theory of society must confront these ambitious demands. The idea of redeeming and fulfilling modernity's emancipatory potential with its egalitarian promise invites more contemporary perspectives. Humanitarian interventions and international law, human rights and the values of citizenship, point in this direction.

[132] Arpad-Andreas Sölter, "Philosophie ohne archimedischen Punkt: Imperative kritisch-rationalen Denkens für die offene Gesellschaft", in *Begegnungen mit Hans Albert: Eine Hommage*, ed. Franco Giuseppe (Wiesbaden: Springer, 2019), 309–318.

Donald Trump, the Culture Industry, and Authoritarian Populism

DOUGLAS KELLNER

Explaining the Donald Trump phenomenon is a challenge that will occupy critical theorists of contemporary society and politics for years to come. In this article, I will argue that the Frankfurt School provides a set of categories and theories that help illuminate the Trump phenomenon. First, I suggest that the Frankfurt School's conception of the culture industry helps explain Trump's success in business and politics. Next, I argue that the Frankfurt school's notion of the authoritarian personality illuminates Trump's mind-set and helps explain the connection between Trump and his followers who provide the base of his support. The article purports to show the contemporary relevance of key categories and theories of the Frankfurt School in explaining the rise of Donald Trump and authoritarian populism. I argue that the global rise of authoritarian politics in the US, Europe, and throughout the world demonstrates the continuing relevance of the Frankfurt School in presenting analysis and critique of the contemporary moment.

Donald Trump and the Culture Industry

To a large extent, the Frankfurt school inaugurated critical studies of mass communication and culture, and produced the first critical theory of the cultural industries. Moving from Nazi Germany to the United States, the Frankfurt School experienced at first hand the rise of a media culture involving film, popular music, radio, television, and other forms of mass culture. In the United States, where they found themselves in exile, media production was by and large a form of commercial entertainment controlled by big corporations. Two of its key theorists Max Horkheimer and Theodor W. Adorno developed an account of the "culture industry" to call attention to the industrialisation and commercialisation of culture under capitalist relations of production. This situation was most marked in the United States that had little state support of film or television industries, and where a highly commercial mass culture emerged that came to be a distinctive feature of capitalist societies and a focus of critical media/cultural studies.

During the 1930s, the Frankfurt school developed a critical and transdisciplinary approach to cultural and communications studies, combining political economy, textual analysis, and analysis of social and ideological effects of the media. They coined the term "culture industry" to signify the process of the industrialisation of mass-produced culture and the commercial imperatives driving the system. The critical theorists analysed all mass-mediated cultural artefacts within the context of industrial production, in which the artefacts of the culture industries exhibited the same features as other products of mass production: commodification, standardisation, and massification. The culture industries had the specific function, however, of providing ideological legitimation of the existing capitalist societies and of integrating individuals into its way of life.

Furthermore, the critical theorists investigated the cultural industries in a political context as a form of the integration of the working class into capitalist societies. The Frankfurt school theorists were among the first neo-Marxian groups to examine the effects of mass culture and the rise of the consumer society on the working classes, which were to be the instrument of revolution in the classical Marxian scenario. They also analysed the ways that the culture industries and consumer society were stabilising contemporary capitalism and accordingly sought new strategies for political change, agencies of political transformation, and models for political emancipation that could serve as norms of social critique and goals for political struggle. This project required rethinking Marxian theory and produced many important contributions—as well as some problematical positions.

Updating the classic theory of the culture industry, I would argue that Donald Trump won the Republican primary contest and then the U.S. Presidential Election because he is the *master of media spectacle*, a concept I have been developing and applying to U.S. politics and media since the mid-1990s.[1] In the following pages, I will discuss Trump's use of the media spectacle and the culture industry in his business career, in his effort to become a celebrity and reality-TV superstar, and his political campaign.

In the 2016 U.S. presidential election, obviously Donald Trump emerged out of the culture industry as a major form of media spectacle; he has long been a celebrity and master of the spectacle with promotion of his buildings and casinos from the 1980s to the present, his reality-TV shows, self-promoting events, and now his presidential campaign. Hence, Trump was able to run for the presidency in part because the media spectacle has become a major force in US politics, helping to determine elections, government, and more broadly the

---

[1] On my concept of media spectacle, see Kellner, *Grand Theft 2000: Media Spectacle and a Stolen Election* (Lanham: Rowman and Littlefield, 2001); *From September 11 to Terror War: The Dangers of the Bush Legacy* (Lanhan: Rowman and Littlefield, 2003); *Media Spectacle* (London and New York: Routledge, 2003); *Media Spectacle and the Crisis of Democracy* (Boulder, Col.: Paradigm Press, 2005).

ethos and nature of our culture and political sphere. Trump is a successful creator and manipulator of the spectacle.

Hence, it is no surprise that political campaigns are run as media spectacles and that masters of the spectacle like Donald Trump are playing the spectacle to win and then perform the presidency, even if it is quite possible that the Donald himself will fall victim to the spectacle: after two years of relentless criticism by the mainstream media, a resistance movement that began the day after his 2016 election, and the Mueller probe, which has led to the prosecution of many of Trump's major associates as well as minor players in the Trump Reality TV Show.

The Apprentice, Twitter and the Trump Presidential Campaign

Since Trump's national celebrity derived in part from his role in the reality-TV series *The Apprentice*,[2] we need to interrogate this popular TV phenomenon to help us explain the Trump phenomenon. The opening theme music "For the Love of Money", a 1973 R&B song by The O'Jays, establishes the capitalist ethos running throughout the competition. For the winning contestant, a job with the Trump organisation. Obviously, money is the key to Trump's business and celebrity success, although there is much controversy over how rich Trump is and so far he has not released his tax returns to quell rumors that he isn't as rich as he claims, that he does not contribute as much to charity as he has stated, and that for many years he has been paying little or no taxes.

The Apprentice's TV Producer Mark Burnett broke into national conscious-ness with his reality-TV show *The Survivor*, a neo-Darwinian epic of alliances, backstabbing, and nastiness, which provides an allegory of how one succeeds in the dog-eat-dog world in which Donald Trump has thrived, and spectacu-larly failed as many of the books about him document. Both Burnett and Trump share the neo-Darwinian (a)social ethos of 19th century ultracompeti-tive capitalism with some of Donald Trump's famous witticisms proclaiming:

> When somebody challenges you unfairly, fight back—be brutal, be tough—don't take it. It is always important to WIN!

> I think everyone's a threat to me.

> Everyone that's hit me so far has gone down. They've gone down big league.

---

[2] Trump's book *The Art of the Deal*, co-written with Tony Schwartz (New York: Ballantine Books [1987, 2005), helped introduce him to a national audience and is a key source of the Trump mythology; see Gwenda Blair, *The Trumps* (New York: Simon and Schuster, 2000), 380ff.

I want my generals kicking ass.

I would bomb the shit out of them.

You bomb the hell out of the oil. Don't worry about the cities. The cities are terrible.[3]

In any case, *The Apprentice* made Trump a national celebrity, and he became well known enough to plausibly run for president. Indeed, throughout the campaign Trump used his celebrity to gain media time. In addition to his campaign's ability to manipulate broadcast media, Trump is also a heavy user of Twitter, tweeting his messages day and night. Trump has thus emerged as a master of digital culture as well as media culture, the latter of which is itself undergoing transformations in the digital era. Donald Trump was arguably the first major U.S. presidential candidate to use Twitter, and as President he continued to use Twitter aggressively and frequently with arguably contradictory results.

Twitter is a perfect vehicle for Trump as you can use what was first a 140 character framework—and which, by November 2014, was expanded, to a 280 character platform—for attack, bragging, and getting out simple messages or posts that engage receivers who when they get pinged and receive his tweets, feel they are in the know and involved in Trump World. When asked at an August 26, 2015, Iowa event as to why he uses Twitter so much, he replied that it was easy, it only took a couple of seconds, and that he could attack his media critics when he "wasn't treated fairly". Trump has also used Instagram—an online mobile photo-sharing, video-sharing and social networking service that enables its users to take pictures and videos, and share them on a variety of digital social networking platforms, such as Facebook, Twitter, Tumblr and Flickr.

Twitter is perfect for General Trump who can blast out his opinions and order his followers what to think and in some cases what to do. It enables businessman and politician Trump to define his brand and mobilise those who wish to consume or support it. Trump Twitter gratifies the need of narcissist Trump to be noticed and recognized as a master of communication who can bind his warriors into an on-line community. Twitter enables the Pundit-in-Chief to opine, rant, attack, and proclaim on all and sundry subjects, and to subject Trump World to the indoctrination of their fearless leader.

---

[3] *Quotations From Chairman Trump*, ed. Carol Pogash (New York: Rosetta Books, 2016), 30, 152, 153.

Hence, Trump is mastering new digital media as well as dominating television and old media through his orchestration of media events as spectacles and his daily Twitter feed. In Trump's first presidential campaign speech on June 16, 2015, when he announced he was running for president, Trump and his wife Melania dramatically descended the stairway at Trump Towers, and the Donald strode up to a gaggle of microphones and dominated media attention for days with his drama. The opening speech of his campaign made a typically inflammatory remark that held in thrall news cycles for days when he stated: "The U.S. has become a dumping ground for everybody else's problems. [Applause] Thank you. It's true, and these are the best and the finest. When Mexico sends its people, they're not sending their best. They're not sending you. They're not sending you. They're sending people that have lots of problems, and they're bringing those problems to us. They're bringing drugs. They're bringing crime. They're rapists. And some, I assume, are good people".

This comment ignited a firestorm of controversy and a preview of the things to come concerning vile racism, xenophobia, Islamophobia, and the other hallmarks of Trump's cacophony of hate. Debate over Trump's assault on undocumented immigrants would come to dominate the daily news cycles of the Republican primaries and would continue to play out in the general election in Fall 2016 and throughout Trump's presidency. In the lead up to the first Republican primary debate in Fall 2015, Donald Trump received the majority of media time, and his daily campaign appearances and the Republican primary debates became a media spectacle dominated by Trump. Every day that Trump had a campaign event, the cable news networks would hype the event with crawlers on the bottom of the TV screen proclaiming "Waiting for Trump", with air-time on cable TV dominated by speculation on what he would talk about. Trump's speeches were usually broadcast live, often in their entirety, a boon of free TV time that no candidate of either party was awarded. After the Trump event, the pundits would for the rest of the day dissect what he had said and evaluate his standing vis-à-vis the other Republican candidates. If Trump had no campaign event planned, he would fire off a round of Tweets against his opponents on his highly active Twitter account—which then would be featured on network cable news discussions as well as social media.

Hence, Trump's orchestration of the media spectacle and a compliant mainstream media was a crucial factor in thrusting Trump ever further in front of the other Republican candidates during the primaries, gaining him an overwhelming amount of media attention and eventually the Republican nomination. The first major quantitative study shows that from mid-June 2015, after Trump announced he was running, through to mid-July, Trump was in 46%

of the news media coverage surrounding the Republican primaries, based on Google news hits, and 60% of Google news searches were about him. I think we can expect that future academic studies will also show how during the Republican primaries and then during the general election he dominated all media, from newspapers to television to Twitter and new media to social networking.[4]

In his 1989 book, *Fast Capitalism*, and *Speeding Up Fast Capitalism*, Ben Agger presented a Frankfurt School-inspired framework for analysing mutations in society, culture, and politics that have made possible a Donald Trump.[5] Without a media-saturated cybercapitalism, new technologies like Twitter and social networking, and a celebrity culture that has morphed into politics, there could never be a Donald Trump who used the culture industry and communications technology as a candidate and president to sell himself and his agenda to the U.S. public.

Trump rose to prominence in New York during the Reaganite '80s as an embodiment of wild, entrepreneurial cowboy capitalism in an era of deregulation, the celebration of wealth, and the "greed is good" ethos of Wall Street, enabled by the Reagan administration. Trump's success was tied to an unrestrained finance capital that loaned him immense sums of money, often with minimal and problematic collateral, to carry through his construction projects.

The delineation of consumer capitalism as a new stage of capitalism was one of the Frankfurt School's major contributions during their US exile from Hitler's fascism, and Trump embodies the consumer ethos that the Frankfurt School denounced. Trump was an extravagant consumer with a three-storey penthouse at the top of Trump Towers, a 118-room mansion in Palm Beach, Florida Mar-A-Lago that he immediately opened for TV interview segments, and an obscene array of properties. He flaunted a yacht bought from Saudi arms dealer Adnan Khashoggi, and a personal airplane to jet-set him around the world to luxury resorts. Trump was featured on TV shows like *Life Styles of the Rich and Famous,* and his life-style was the subject of multi-page spreads in fashion and other popular magazines, making Trump the poster-boy for excessive "conspicuous consumption", to a degree that I doubt Veblen could have imagined.

---

[4] Ravi Somaiya, "Trump's Wealth and Early Poll Numbers Complicate News Media's Coverage Decisions", *The New York Times*, July 24, 2015 at http://www.nytimes.com/2015/07/25/business/media/donald-trumps-wealth-and-poll-numbers-complicate-news-medias-coverage.html (accessed July 22, 2016).
[5] See Ben Agger, *Fast Capitalism* (Champaign-Urbana: University of Illinois Press, 1989), and *Speeding Up Fast Capitalism* (New York and London: Routledge, 2015.

Trump's financial fortunes hit the economic slowdown that followed the Reagan orgy of unrestrained capitalism in the late 1980s,[6] and in the 1990s Trump almost became bankrupt. Fittingly, Trump had overinvested in the very epitome of consumer capitalism by buying a string of luxury gambling casinos in Atlantic City. The financial slump hit Trump's overextended casinos, driving him to put them on the market. The banks called in loans on his over-extended real estate investments, and he was forced to sell off properties, his yacht, and other luxury items. Having temporarily lost his ability to borrow from finance capital to expand his real estate business, Trump was forced to go into partnerships in business ventures, and then sold the Trump name that was attached to an array of consumer items ranging from water to vodka, and men's clothes to fragrances.

Most significantly, Trump has been particularly assiduous in branding the Trump name and selling himself as a businessman, a celebrity, and a presidential candidate. Indeed, Trump's presidential campaign represents an obscene branding of a conman from the culture industry into an alleged super capitalist and then into a political candidate whose campaign was run on bombast, hype, and crude expressions of obscene forms of racist, sexist, anti-immigrant, and capitalist ideology which on a daily basis dominated the mediascape of the culture industry, thus gaining the attention of voters/consumers. Trump is also the first authoritarian populist to have been a party nominee and then the President in recent times in the United States.

Donald Trump and Authoritarian Populism

Much has been made of Donald Trump's character and whether he is fit to be president of the United States. In the following analysis, I want to suggest that the theories of Erich Fromm and his fellow German-Jewish refugees known as the "Frankfurt School" provide an analysis of authoritarian populism that helps explicate Trump's character, his appeal to his followers, and in general the Trump phenomenon.

Erich Fromm was a strong critic of Hitler and German fascism and I believe that his major books and some key ideas help explain the character, presidential

---

[6] For the story of Trump's financial down-fall and near collapse in the 1980s and 1990s, see the detailed and well-documented narratives in Wayne Barrett, *Trump: The Greatest Show on Earth: The Deals, the Downfall, the Reinvention* (New York: Regan Books, 2016); John O'Donnell and James Rutherford, *Trumped!: The Inside Story of the Real Donald Trump-His Cunning Rise and Spectacular Fall* (New York: Simon and Schuster, 1991); Michael D'Antonio, *Never Enough: Donald Trump and the Pursuit of Success* (New York: Thomas Dunne Books, 2015); and Michael Kranish and Mark Fisher, *Trump Revealed: An American Journey of Ambition, Ego, Money and Power* (New York: Scribner, 2016).

campaign, and supporters of Donald Trump. Hence, in this discussion, I develop a Frommian analysis of Trump and his followers and take on the issue of what American authoritarian populism looks like. This project begins with Fromm's *Escape from Freedom*, which explains how in modernity individuals submitted to oppressive and irrational regimes and in particular how Germans submitted to Hitler and fascism. *Escape* combines historical, economic, political, ideological and socio-psychological analysis, as is typical of the best multi-dimensional work of Fromm and the Frankfurt School, and provides a model that we can apply to analysing Trump and our current political situation.

Other members of the Frankfurt School developed analyses of the authoritarian personality while in exile from German fascism in the United States. The book *The Authoritarian Personality* (edited by Adorno, Frenkel-Brunswik, Levinson, and Sanford and published in 1950) found authoritarian tendencies, like those found in earlier Frankfurt School analyses of the middle and working class submission to German fascism during the 1920s and 1930s. Certainly, Trump is not Hitler and his followers are not technically fascists,[7] although I believe that we can use the terms authoritarian populism or neo-fascism to explain Trump and his supporters.[8]

Authoritarian movements ranging from German and Italian fascism to Franco's Spain to Latin American and other dictatorships throughout the world centre on an authoritarian leader and followers who submit to their leadership and demands. I argue that Donald Trump is an authoritarian leader

---

[7] Parenthetically, there were enough media comparisons between Trump and Hitler and fascism for Trump to say with some perhaps genuine perplexity "I'm not Hitler! I don't like the guy!" See Sam Sanders, "Trump Champions The 'Silent Majority', But What Does That Mean In 2016?" *NPR,* January 22, 2016 at http://www.npr.org/2016/01/22/463884201/trump-champions-the-silent-majority-but-what-does-that-mean-in-2016 (accessed on July 20, 2016). At this time, Trump was asking his followers to raise their hands if they would vote for him as President, and the simultaneous raised hands going up looked like a mob of Hitler salutes! And there is a story out there that Trump keeps a book of Hitler's writings by his bedside; see Timothy O'Brien, *TrumpNation: The Art of Being the Donald* (New York: Grand Central Publishing, 2016 [2005]), 200; the story originates from a *UPI* report, August 9, 1990, cited in O'Brien, 260.

[8] Carl Bernstein started calling Trump a neo-fascist and an American-brand fascist on CNN on June 19, 2016. See Tom Boggioni, "Carl Bernstein: Donald Trump is a 'pathological liar' and America's first 'neo-fascist' nominee", *Rawstory,* June 19, 2016 at http://www.rawstory.com/2016/06/carl-bernstein-donald-trump-is-a-pathological-liar-and-americas-first-neofascist-nominee/ (accessed on July 20, 2016). In an article by Adam Gopnik, "Being Honest About Trump", *The New Yorker,* July 14, 2016 at http://www.newyorker.com/news/daily-comment/being-honest-about-trump (accessed on July 20, 2016), Gopnik comments: "It is the essence of fascism to have no single fixed form – an attenuated form of nationalism in its basic nature, it naturally takes on the colors and practices of each nation it infects. In Italy, it is bombastic and neoclassical in form; in Spain, Catholic and religious; in Germany, violent and romantic. It took forms still crazier and more feverishly sinister, if one can imagine, in Romania, whereas under Oswald Mosley, in England, its manner was predictably paternalistic and aristocratic. It is no surprise that the American face of fascism would take on the forms of celebrity television and the casino greeter's come-on, since that is as much our symbolic scene as nostalgic re-creations of Roman splendors once were Italy's".

who has mobilised a populist movement that follows his leadership. Arguably, Trump is an authoritarian populist in the traditions of Ronald Reagan and Margaret Thatcher. Like Reagan, Trump comes out of the culture industry and was a popular celebrity when he announced his candidacy in summer 2015; it was thanks in part to his television celebrity status that every mainstream media outlet touted the announcing of his candidacy. Trump does not share the conservative ideology of Reagan and Thatcher, although he shares their electoral strategy of taking a populist pose claiming to represent the people against the political establishment. Yet Trump lacks Reagan's disciplined skills as a performer and Thatcher's "Iron Lady" self-discipline and political rationality. Instead, Trump shoots from the hip and cannot resist insults, attacks, impolitic language and rants against those who dare to criticise him, and thus resembles Mussolini and Latin American dictators like Juan Peron. While Trump does not have a party apparatus or ideology like the Nazis, parallels to Nazism appeared clear to me last summer at Trump's August 21, 2015, Alabama mega-rally in Mobile, Alabama. I watched all afternoon as the cable news networks broadcast nothing but Trump, hyping up his visit to a stadium where he was expecting 30–40,000 spectators, the biggest rally of the season. Although only 20-some thousand showed up, which was still a "huge" event in the heat of summer before the primaries had even begun in earnest, Trump's flight into Alabama on his own Trump Jet and his rapturous reception by his admirers became the main story of the news cycle, as did many such daily events in what the media called "the summer of Trump".

What I focused on when watching the TV footage of the event was how the networks began showing repeated images of Trump flying his airplane over and around the stadium before landing and then cut away to big images of the Trump Jet every few minutes. This media spectacle reminded me of one of the most powerful propaganda films of all time—Leni Riefenstahl's *Triumph of the Will*—a German Nazi propaganda film of 1935. *Triumph* focuses on Hitler flying in an airplane through the clouds, looking out the window at the crowds below, landing, and driving through mass crowds applauding him as he proceeded through the streets of Nuremburg for a mass rally. The crowds along the way and in the stadium greeted Hitler with rapture as he entered the spectacle of a highly touted and orchestrated Nuremburg mass Nazi rally that Riefenstahl captured on film.

I do not know if the Trump operatives planned this parallel, or if it was just a coincidence, but it is clear that Trump, like Hitler, has organised a fervent mass movement outside of the conventional political party apparatuses. The anger and rage that Fromm attributed to Nazi masses in *Escape from Freedom* is also exhibited in Trump's followers as is the idolatry towards their Führer, who arguably see Trump as the magic helper who will solve their problems by building a giant wall to keep out the threatening Other, a Fairy Tale scenario that Fromm would have loved to deconstruct.[9]

Like followers of European fascism in the 1930s, Trump's supporters over the years have suffered economic deprivation, political alienation, humiliation, and a variety of hard times, and they appear to be looking for a political saviour to help them out with their problems and to address their grievances. Trump proposes magical solutions like a wall along the Mexican border that will keep out swarms of immigrants he claims are taking away jobs in the US, as well as committing waves of crime. Trump claims he will create millions of "great" jobs without giving specific plans—a claim refuted by his problematic business record that includes many bankruptcies, hiring of foreign workers to toil on his projects, some of whom he does not pay, and his failures to pay many sub-contractors who worked on his projects.[10]

While Trump plays the role of the *Übermensch*, celebrated by the Nazis and embodies their *Führerprinzip* Trump is a very American form of the Super-hero, and lacks the party apparatus, advanced military forces, and disciplined cadres that the Nazis used to seize and hold power. Like other rightwing American populists, Trump bashes the Federal Reserve, the U.S. monetary system, Wall Street hedge fund billionaires, and neoliberal globalisation, in the same fashion as Hitler attacked German monopoly capitalism.[11] While Hitler ranted against monopoly capitalists, at the same time he accepted big donations from German industrialists, as brilliantly illustrated in John Heartfield's famous graphic, "the meaning of the Hitler salute", which showed Hitler with his hand up in the Nazi salute, getting bags of money from German capitalists. Just as Hitler denounced allegedly corrupt and weak party politicians in the

---

[9] The notion of "the magic helper" to whom the follower submits in the hopes their problems will be solved is found in Erich Fromm's *Escape from Freedom* (New York: Holt. 1941), 174–178; on "authoritarian idolatry", see Fromm's *The Sane Society* (New York: Holt, 1955), 237f. *Escape from Freedom* not only critiqued Nazi ideology, the party apparatus, the concept of the Fuhrer, and the psychology of Nazi mass followers of Hitler, but also illuminated the role of fairy tales and magical thinking in National Socialism, a theme Fromm expanded in later writings like *The Forgotten Language: An Introduction to the Under-standing of Dreams, Fairy Tales and Myths* (New York: Random House, 1988).

[10] On Trump's business failures, see references in note 6, and "The Art of the Bad Deal: Donald Trump's Business Flops, Explained", *Newsweek*, August 8, 2018: 24–33.

[11] One should note, however, that Trump's attacks on finance and corporate capitalism during the campaign was fraudulent as he loaded his cabinet with billionaires and his few policies that were actually passed by Congress were all in the interests of deregulation and serving the interests of the rich (see Douglas Kellner, *The American Horror Show: Election 2016 and the Ascendency of Donald J. Trump* [Rotterdam, The Nether-lands: Sense Publishers., 2017]; Trump's serving of Russian interests will be a story for another time).

Weimar Republic, Trump decries all politicians as "idiots", "stupid", or "weak" —some of the would-be strongman's favourite words. In fact, Trump even attacks lobbyists, and claims he alone is above being corrupted by money, since he is self-financing his own campaign (which is not really true but seems to impress his followers).[12]

Trump has his roots in an American form of populism that harkens back to figures like Andrew Jackson, Huey Long, George Wallace, Pat Buchanan and, of course, the American carnival barker and snake oil salesman. Like these classical American demagogues, Trump plays on the fears, grievances, and anger of people who feel that they have been left behind by the elites. Like his authoritarian populist predecessors, Trump also scapegoats targets from Wall Street to a feared mass of immigrants allegedly crossing the Mexican border and pouring into the States, overwhelming and outnumbering a declining White population.[13]

Trump's followers share antecedents in the Know Nothing movement of the 1850s, the Ku Klux Klan movement which achieved popularity and media in the 1920s, with Donald's father, Fred Trump, arrested at one of its rallies,[14] and the movement that made George Wallace a popular candidate in the 1960s. Like the alienated and angry followers of authoritarian populist movements throughout the world, Trump's admirers had suffered under the vicissitudes of capitalism, globalisation, and technological revolution. For decades, they have watched their jobs being moved overseas, displaced by technological innovation, or lost through unequal economic development amid increasing divisions between rich and poor. With the global economic crisis of 2007–8, many people lost jobs, housings, savings, and suffered through a slow recovery under the Obama administration. The fact that Obama was the first black president further outraged many who had their racism and prejudices inflamed by eight

---

[12] After bragging how his campaign was self-funded during the Republican primaries, Trump released a statement showing that much of the money he spent was paid into his own companies; see Nicholas Confessore and Sarah Cohen, "Donald Trump's Campaign, Billed as Self-Funded, Risks Little of His Fortune", *The New York Times*, February, 5, 2016 at http://www.nytimes.com/2016/02/06/us/politics/donald-trumps-campaign-billed-as-self-funded-risks-little-of-his-fortune.html?_r=0 (accessed July 29, 2016). During the Fall 2016 Presidential election, Trump was forced to court donors and raise funds, thus undercutting his claims to be the only self-financing candidate.

[13] Trump's vision of Latin American immigrants pouring over the border into the U.S. is a fantasy, as studies have shown that more Mexicans are returning to Mexico after working in the U.S. than coming into the country, illegal or not; see Ana Gonzalez-Barrera, "More Mexicans Leaving Than Coming to the U.S. Net Loss of 140,000 from 2009 to 2014; Family Reunification Top Reason for Return", November 19, 2015 at http://www.pewhispanic.org/2015/11/19/more-mexicans-leaving-than-coming-to-the-u-s/ (accessed September 3, 2016).

[14] Kranish and Fisher, *Trump Revealed* 27–28.

years of attacks on Obama and the Obama administration by the rightwing media and the Republican Party.

Indeed, Donald Trump was one of the most assiduous promoters of the "birther" myth, erroneously claiming that Barack Obama was born in Africa and was thus not eligible to serve as President of the United States.[15] In the 2008 presidential election, Trump made a big show of insisting that Obama make public his birth certificate to prove he was born in the U.S., and although the Obama campaign provided photocopies of the original birth certificate in Hawaii and notices of his birth in Honolulu newspapers at the time, Trump kept insisting they were frauds and many of his followers continue to this day to believe the myth that Obama was not born in the USA.[16]

Yet unlike classic dictators who are highly disciplined with a fixed ideology and party apparatus, Trump is chaotic and undisciplined, viciously attacking whoever dares criticise him in his daily Twitter feed or speeches, thus dominating the daily news cycles with his outrageous attacks on Mexicans, Muslims, and immigrants, or politicians of both parties who dare to criticise him. Trump effectively used the broadcast media and social media to play the powerful demagogue who preys on his followers' rage, alienation, and fears. Indeed, by March 2016, media companies estimated that Trump received far more media coverage than his Republican Party contenders, and by June *MarketWatch* estimated that he had received $3 billion worth of free media coverage.[17] Yet, at his whim, Trump bans news media from his rallies, including *The Washington Post*, if they publish criticisms he does not like.

Like followers of European fascism, Trump's authoritarian populist supporters are driven by rage: they are really angry at the political establishment and system, the media, and economic and other elites. They are eager to

---

[15] On the birther myth, see D'Antonio, *Never Enough*, 283ff.

[16] Public Policy Polling reported that a "new poll finds that Trump is benefiting from a GOP electorate that thinks Barack Obama is a Muslim and was born in another country, and that immigrant children should be deported. 66% of Trump's supporters believe that Obama is a Muslim to just 12% that grant he's a Christian. 61% think Obama was not born in the United States to only 21% who accept that he was. And 63% want to amend the Constitution to eliminate birthright citizenship, to only 20% who want to keep things the way they are". *Public Policy Polling*. "Trump Supporters Think Obama is A Muslim Born in Another Country", September 01, 2015 at http://www.publicpolicypolling.com/main/2015/08/trump-supporters-think-obama-is-a-muslim-born-in-another-country.html (accessed August 3, 2016).

[17] Nicholas Confessore and Karen Yourish, "$2 Billion Worth of Free Media for Donald Trump", *The New York Times*, March 15, 2016 at http://www.nytimes.com/2016/03/16/upshot/measuring-donald-trumps-mammoth-advantage-in-free-media.html?_r=0 (accessed August 6, 2016) and Robert Schroeder, "Trump has gotten nearly $3 billion in 'free' advertising". *Marketwatch*, May 6, 2016 at http://www.market watch.com/story/trump-has-gotten-nearly-3-billion-in-free-advertising-2016-05-06 (accessed August 6, 2016).

support an anti-establishment candidate who claims to be an outsider (which is only partly true since Trump has, following his father, been a member of the capitalist real estate industry for decades, and has other businesses as well, many of which have failed).[18] Trump provokes their rage with classic authoritarian propaganda techniques like the Big Lie; for example, when he continuously repeats that immigrants are pouring across the border and committing crime, or when he accuses all his primary opponents, the media, and Hillary Clinton of being "big liars", or—clearly the biggest lie of all—when he claims that he is the only one telling the truth .[19]

Trump's anti-immigrant and racist rhetoric, his Islamophobia, and his xenophobic nationalism plays into a violent racist tradition in the U.S. and activates atavistic fears of other races and anger among his white followers. Like European fascism, Trump draws on restorative nostalgia and promises to "Make America Great Again". Thus, to mobilise his followers, Trump arguably manipulates racism and nationalism and plays to the vile side of the American psyche and the long tradition of nationalism, America First-ism, and xenophobia, wanting to keep minorities and people of color outside of the country and "in their place".

Like fascists and authoritarian populists, Trump thus presents himself as the Superhero leader who, appearing from the from outside, believe they can solve the problems that Washington and politicians have created. In the form of authoritarian idolatry described by Fromm,[20] his followers appear to believe that Trump alone can stop the decline of the United States and make it "great" again. Over and over, Trump supporters claim that he is the only one who talks about issues like immigration, problems with Washington and politics, and the role of money in politics. Trump promotes himself as the tough guy who can stand up to the Russians and Chinese, and to "America's enemies". In the Republican primaries, he presented himself as "the most militarist" guy in the field and promised to build up the US military, and to utterly destroy ISIS and America's enemies, restoring to the U.S. its status as a superpower, which he says was relinquished by the Obama administration. Trump embodies the figure to excess of strong masculinity that Jackson Katz describes as a key motif in recent U.S. presidential elections. With his bragging, chest-pounding, and

---

[18] On Trump's business failures, see 6 and 10 above.

[19] At the Republican convention, Trump insisted that "you won't hear any lies here". For documentation of Trump's Big and little lies, see Hank Berrien, "Lyin' Donald: 101 Of Trump's Greatest Lies", *Dailywire*, April 11, 2016 at http://www.dailywire.com/news/4834/trumps-101-lies-hank-berrien (accessed August 8, 2016).

[20] On Fromm and "authoritarian idolatry", see *Sane Society*, 237f.

hypermacho posturing, Trump provides a promise of restoration of White Male Power and authority that will restore America to its greatness.

Trump repeatedly uses the discourse of national crisis also deployed by classic fascist and authoritarian regimes to describe the situation in the U.S. and the need for a saviour to solve all problems. In contrast to the Nazis, however, Trump tells his followers that it's his deal-making skills as a supercapitalist billionaire which credentials him to be the President, and he induces his followers to believe he will make a "great deal" for them and "Make America Great Again".

The slogan "Make America Great Again" refers for some of Trump's supporters to a time where White Males ruled and women, people of color, and others knew their place. It was a time of militarism where U.S. military power was believed to position America as the ruler of the world—although as the ambiguous Cold War and U.S. military defeats in Vietnam and the uncontrollable spaces of Iraq and Afghanistan suggest, this era of American greatness was largely a myth. Yet the slogan is vague enough that Trump's followers can create a fantasy of a "great" past and dream that Trump will resurrect it—a fantasy conceit nourished by many authoritarian leaders in the twentieth century.

Trump is thus an authoritarian populist and his campaign replicates in some ways the submission to both the leader and the cause found in classic authoritarian movements. In some ways, however, it is Mussolini, rather than Hitler, who Trump most resembles. Hitler was deadly serious, restrained, and repressed, while Trump is comical, completely unrestrained, and arguably unhinged. Curiously, on February 28, 2016, Trump used his Twitter feed to post a quote attributed to Mussolini, which compared the Italian dictator to Trump, and in an interview on NBC's "Meet the Press" that morning he said: "It's a very good quote", apparently not bothered by being associated with Mussolini.[21] There were also news clips that showed Trump speaking, chin jutting out in Mussolini-like fashion, and making faces and performing gestures that seemed to mimic characteristics associated with Mussolini. Like Mussolini, Trump has a buffoonish side which his mobocracy finds entertaining, but which turns off more serious people. Trump is the embodiment of the trend towards celebrity politics and the implosion of politics and entertainment that is becoming an increasingly important feature of U.S. politics. Yet, his presidency also embodies a growing global trend towards authoritarianism, thus

---

[21] Maggie Haberman, "Donald Trump Retweets Post With Quote From Mussolini", *The New York Times*, February 28, 2106 at http://www.nytimes.com/politics/first-draft/2016/02/28/donald-trump-retweets-post-likening-him-to-mussolini/ (accessed August 8, 2016).

showing the contemporary global relevance of the Frankfurt School theories of the authoritarian personality and critiques of authoritarian regimes.

Elements of a Critical Environmental Philosophy

ROLF WIGGERSHAUS

In 1930, the philosopher Max Horkheimer became the director of the Institut für Sozialforschung, which had been founded only a couple of years before in Frankfurt am Main. His goal was to establish an interdisciplinary social theory with the purpose of providing a critical diagnosis of the present. Since then, this enterprise and its meaning for Frankfurt and the Frankfurt University has undergone significant transformations. Today, both main protagonists of the classical phase, Theodor W. Adorno and Max Horkheimer, in many ways belong to the foundation of the Westend-Campus of the Goethe-University, connecting Humanities and Social and Economic Sciences as well as Jurisprudence. The central square is named after Adorno, and a little bit further away, in a street named after Max Horkheimer, a building can be found in which the cluster of excellence "The Formation of Normative Orders" is located. Its founders and spokespersons—the philosopher Rainer Forst and the jurist Klaus Günther—understand themselves as standing in the tradition of the Frankfurt School and continuing the project of Critical Theory. The theme of one of its projects is "Sustainable Development, Global Governance, and Justice". It addresses highly significant problems, such as how to limit global warming, which can be traced back to the beginning of industrialisation. This goal cannot be achieved unless the industrialised countries shoulder the greatest responsibility for emission reduction, as well as to help expand the possibilities for action of the developing countries. Ultimately, the wealth and leading position of the industrial countries depended on a long phase of unrestrained anthropogenic greenhouse emissions. A connection can be made between this project to the theme repressed by the social-philosophical paradigms of communication and recognition, and whose relevance and significance the authors of *Dialectic of Enlightenment* realised so early: we are a part of nature—and we have been unable to establish a normative order that provides us with the ability to create a sustainable handling of it.

To begin with, I want to recall the central motif of classical Critical Theory. Hereafter, I will provide some examples in order to point to the characteristics of the current treatment of the external nature and the creation of artificial environments, and finally, I will formulate the theoretical motives of Adorno and Horkheimer with renewed urgency and actual concreteness.

On the Fundamental Preconditions for the Emancipation of Society from Antisemitism

The Frankfurt School and Critical Theory represent a wide theoretical field. But there is one central motif that Horkheimer and Adorno followed in their work *Dialectic of Enlightenment*, and that had a particularly inspiring effect on different parts of Adorno's work, traces of which can be found in the work of Habermas, particularly his essays on the future of human nature.

The pithiest formulation of this motif can be found in the last essay of *Dialectic of Enlightenment*: "Elements of Anti-Semitism: Limits of Enlightenment". Here a diagnosis of the present and a theory of civilisation are brought together in an attempt to answer the following question: on what, ultimately, does "the emancipation of society from anti-Semitism" depend? In many ways, the answer given by the authors connects to Freud. In his late book, *Moses and Monotheism*, Freud's position concerning those who hate Jews was that they had become Christians late and often only through bloody coercion—they were "mis-baptised",[1] and had, under a thin layer of Christianity, remained true to their ancestry, which paid homage to barbaric polytheism. Horkheimer and Adorno transform this into the diagnosis that anti-Semitism is a symptom of a society of "superficially civilised people" that only dominates nature through force. What served as a reminder about how immediacy was repressed within civilisation, or what testified to a suffering from the failures of civilisation and thus created images of a preexisting time free from coercion or of an untroubled life, caused rage in those who only dominated nature through force. The "anti-Semitic reaction-formation" served as substitute satisfaction for this rage. The authors formulated the meaning of this with help from the example of the most animal-like sensation.

> When we see we remain what we are; but when we smell we are taken over by otherness. Hence the sense of smell is considered a disgrace in civilization, the sign of lower social strata, lesser races and base animals. The civilized individual may only indulge in such pleasure if the prohibition is suspended by rationalization in the service of real or apparent practical ends. The prohibited impulse may be tolerated if there is no doubt that the final aim is its elimination.[2]

---

[1] Sigmund Freud, *The Origins of Religion: Totem and Taboo, Moses and Monotheism and other works* (London: Penguin, 1990), 336.

[2] Max Horkheimer and Theodor W. Adorno, *Dialectic of Enlightenment*, trans. John Cumming (London: Verso, 1992), 184.

Another vivid example of the forceful domination over nature can be found in the last part of *Dialectic of Enlightenment*. The topic of the text called "The importance of the body" is the "love-hate relationship to the body". To be caught within one's body without appreciating that it is part of nature, in unity with what is non-human, is, instead of being a medium for a being at home in the world, turned into the means of abstract self-preservation. The body then becomes "a moving mechanism", according to which the flesh is seen "as cushioning the skeleton" and "a walk [is transformed] into motion and a meal into calories".[3] The exoneration of labor from physical effort and the liberation of the body from restrictive conventions regarding clothing, self-presentation, and forms of social interaction have not—according to Horkheimer and Adorno—led to a more "tender" and "rich" connection of human and external nature, but rather to an increase in their mutual distance and alienation.

The aphorism entitled "Paysage" from Adorno's *Minima Moralia*, a book written during a pause in the work with Horkheimer on *Dialectic of Enlightenment*, highlights such distance and alienation by way of another example:

> The shortcoming of the American landscape is not so much, as romantic illusions would have it, the absence of historical memories, as that it bears no traces of the human hand. This applies not only to the lack of arable land, the uncultivated woods often no higher than scrub, but above all to the roads. These are always inserted directly in the landscape, and the more impressively smooth and broad they are, the more unrelated and violent their gleaming track appears against its wild, overgrown surroundings. [...] Just as they know no marks of foot or wheel, no soft paths along their edges as a transition to the vegetation, no trails leading off into the valley, so they are without the mild, soothing, unangular quality of things that have felt the touch of hands or their immediate implements. [...] And it is perceived in a corresponding way. For what the hurrying eye has seen merely from the car it cannot retain, and the vanishing landscape leaves no more traces behind than it bears upon itself.[4]

The achievement of *Dialectic of Enlightenment*, often misunderstood as a pessimistic and even dark philosophy of history, is its early emphasis on the close connection between the human treatment of its own nature, its external nature, alongside its treatment with one another. In *Dialectic of Enlightenment* Horkheimer's and Adorno's formula for the desirable relation between civilised

---

[3] Ibid. 235
[4] Theodor W. Adorno, *Minima Moralia*, trans. E. F. N. Jephcott (London: Verso, 2005), 52–53

people and nature amounts to a "remembrance of nature in the subject".[5] But how should one conceive of this in practical terms?

Furthermore in later works, variations of this conceptual motif of a "self-reflection of nature in the subject" remain present, for example in Adorno's lectures on *Problems of Moral Philosophy*, delivered during the summer semester of 1963.

> The truth is that we are no longer simply a piece of nature from the moment we recognize that we are a piece of nature. [...] Moreover, any being that stands outside nature and might be described as a human subject in a very emphatic sense can be said to possess the capacity for self-reflection in which the self observes: I myself am a part of nature. By virtue of that fact the human subject is liberated from the blind pursuit of natural ends and becomes capable of alternative actions.[6]

The question remains: turning to what? Turning to nature? If so, from what position? From within or from outside nature? And ultimately, what possibilities of action does such a turning afford?

One thing is clear: the enterprise of disputing and disavowing an understanding of humanity that is part of nature, and that advances how humanity is emancipated from nature, is countered with the notion that humanity appears as itself simultaneously intertwined with nature. In this regard, a formulation from Adorno's *Negative Dialectics*, which at first sounds very speculative, is worth quoting: "The reconciled condition would not be the philosophical imperialism of annexing the alien. Instead, its happiness would lie in the fact that the alien, in the proximity it is granted, remains what is distant and different, beyond that which is one's own."[7]

"Black Smokers" – or Approximations on Nature that remove Nature

"Black Smokers", these deep-water geysers, arise from weak spots at the bottom of the ocean. With high pressure, water advances through cracks down into deeper layers of the earth, where it encounters glowing basaltic magma and then, enriched with volcanic gases and minerals as well as having a temperature of up to 400 degrees Celsius, bursts out from the bottom of the deep sea. This mixture, which for most living species is fatal, arises in the form of black smoke

---

[5] Max Horkheimer and Theodor W. Adorno, *Dialectic of Enlightenment,* 40

[6] Theodor W. Adorno, *Problems of Moral Philosophy,* trans. Rodney Livingstone (Cambridge: Polity, 2000), 103–104.

[7] Theodor W. Adorno, *Negative Dialectics,* trans. E. B. Ashton, (New York: Continuum, 1990). 191.

from out of meter-long chimneys, which derive from sedimentations of minerals. Where such chimneys are frequent, kilometre-wide hydrothermal fields are developed.

Black smokers are extraordinary biotopes. In these dark depths, life energy is not produced through photosynthesis, as is the case with plants. Primary energy is rather produced by bacteria through chemosynthesis. They are the foundations for life spaces in the deep sea and are the most densely settled ones. It is said that the diversity of species in the areas of black smokers is higher than those in the tropic rainforest. But black smokers, with their metal enriched layers of massive sulphate, are also places for a high degree of valuable ore. Research tests have shown that 30 grams of gold are contained per 1 ton of rock. This is more than in deposits found on land that are considered lucrative when comprised of 1 gram per 1 ton of rock.

In the darkness of the deep sea, where there is additionally extreme water pressure and ice-cold water temperatures, dark smokers had remained un-discovered for a long time. In 1977 the first were identified near the Galápagos Islands. Since then they have become the object of multiple forms of human interest and action. This opens up a variety of research fields for the life sciences. Evolutionary biologists are fascinated by a biotope whose extreme life conditions seem close to those conditions often connected to the notion of the origin of life on earth. Biotechnologists have already used special albumens in recently discovered species for genetico-technological purposes within com-mercial enterprises. The Canadian mining company Nautilus Minerals is striv-ing to become the first company to initiate the mining of the deep-sea area in the waters of Papua New Guinea with the permission of their government.

Other organisations are making efforts for the sake of protecting the "treasures of the deep sea." In 2002, the Worldwide Fund for Nature praised the regional government of the Azores because of their preparedness to mark two hydrothermal fields in the deep sea of the Atlantic as marine protected areas. The Worldwide Fund for Nature is also adviser for the International Seabed Authority that administrates international seabed areas as "common heritage of humanity" and has within its powers the allocation of mining rights. In a text by WWF Germany on deep sea mining, it states, under the title "To reduce the results of exploitation", that:

> To begin with, a network of marine protected areas must be established worldwide, which identifies important representative areas and protects them from destruction by prohibiting every form of mining resources in these areas.

Not even knowledge presented by an international research team, and published by the scientific journal *Geology*, could either interfere with those big interests in the resources of the deep sea—interests relying on technological development and raw material prices—or change the fact that opportunities in deep sea mining often are overestimated and that mining could destroy entire biospheres of animals and plants about which we know only little. The WWF in the US formulated what is to expected: "The life of the deep sea is very complex and we don't know much about it. There is a risk that we destroy something that we not yet have understood entirely".

But what perspective is required in order to reach complete "understanding" about life communities of animals and plants that until now remain unknown or are barely known? Wild animal telemetry and bio-blogging are two examples of this. Modern electronic behavioural biology makes it possible to measure the movement and position of animals in geographic spaces through the use of advanced nanotechnology, in which breathing and heart frequencies can be monitored, as well as dietary intake can be documented, through stomach probes. Researchers now also want to equip small birds, bats, and even insects with transmitters that weigh less than one gram, which would lead to entirely new knowledge about their life so it would be possible for the archived data, which flows from the "Movebank", to be searched on the basis of posing a variety of different questions. In addition to developments in basic research, new technologies are meant to optimise conceptions we have about the protection of threatened species, that is, about a better understanding of how animals react to environmental changes caused by climate change, as well as about the possible utility of monitored animals, for instance as warning systems in the case of natural catastrophes.[8]

But the idea that nothing should be external to research and that research should be predicated on (as far as it is possible) a seamless process of monitoring—even if this only relies on apparatuses and databanks—does not seem solid. In reports on diverse projects, the terms "protection" and "monitoring" are used seemingly interchangeably. "We want to understand how 'green' and 'brown' parts of an ecological system interact with each other, and for this purpose we need to gather as much data as possible"—this is the motivation of the German centre for integrated research of biodiversity in Leipzig for "Ecotron", an establishment with 24 mini greenhouses at the cost of approximately 3,7 million Euros. This means: "total monitoring" with help from every-

---

[8] Georg Rüschemeyer, "Tierisch viele Daten", *Frankfurter Allgemeine Sonntagszeitung*, October 1, 2017.

thing that technology offers—from cameras in the ceiling with a range of 360 degrees, which document the growth and behaviour of plants and animals, to suction probes, which collect the leachate for chemical analyses.[9]

Smart Worlds— or, No one Should Feel Alone or Unacknowledged

In his essay "Die Welt als Phantom und Matrize" (in the book *Die Antiquiertheit des Menschen*, first published 1956), the philosopher and publicist Günther Anders offered a passage from his "Kindergeschichten" as a motto:

> But since the king did not like the fact that his son left the controlled streets and instead wandered all over the land with the purpose to obtain his own opinions of the world, he gave his son a carriage and a horse as a gift. "Now you do not need to walk", were his words. What they meant was: "You are no longer allowed to walk". And their impact was: "You can no longer walk".[10]

Today's kings act no differently; they simply practice it as a business model. To become irreplaceable in the customers' everyday life—this is the explicit goal of Amazon's echo devices, which are linked to the speech assistant Alexa. We should get used to having such devices everywhere in the apartment, waiting for their orders. Without using any hands, the user can switch household appliances on and off, monitor sleeping kids or wake them up with music, generating shopping lists, or making orders from Amazon. Explaining why Amazon's appliances are so cheap, the boss for the department of appliance says, "other hardware firms make money when the customers buy their products. What happens later is of no importance. We make money afterwards—through all the services that the customers use. For us it is a failure when people buy an Echo and then put in the drawer".[11]

An example of the services that Amazon wants you to add is the network camera "Echo Look", which provides the network loudspeaker Echo with eyes. As the journalist, Adrian Lobe, remarks: "the customer can through a spoken order ("Alexa, take a picture of me") take photos of two different outfits, which are then assessed by a computer through the so-called Style Check Function. The whole thing is marketed as an artificial intelligence style counsellor".[12] The "Alexa camera for those that are into fashion" is an example what the sociologist Gary T. Marx has called the "soft surveillance" of consumption.

---

[9] Hubertus Breuer, "Die Kammern der Erkenntnis", *Frankfurter Allgemeine Zeitung*, July 16, 2017.
[10] Anders Günther, *Die Antiquiertheit des Menschen* (Munich: Beck, 1961), 97.
[11] Katrin Werner, "Alexa, warum bist du so billig?", *Süddeutsche Zeitung*, September 29, 2017
[12] Adrian Lobe, "Trautes Heim", *SüddeutscheZeitung*, May, 30, 2017.

Firms like Walmart and Amazon compete for control over a 600 billion-dollar US market, testing how far one can penetrate into the last recesses of private life. The solution is seen to lie in surveillance systems that enable a fail-safe execution from a distance of one's choosing. This is why Walmart has begun collaborating with the security firm August Home. By using a one-time security code, delivery personnel can open a lock placed at the customer's door, who then can monitor the delivery person's activities through a security camera, and in the end receive confirmation that the door has been closed.

Here too, protection is made dependent on surveillance, according to which surveillance appears as self-evidently the best form of protection. Further examples underscore this point. For instance, in Germany, there has been much reaction to the fact that the most common cause of traffic deaths is no longer alcohol, but distraction. In the future, anyone using tools of "communication, information, or organization"—including tools of navigation or tablets—while driving will incur a 100 instead of 60 Euro fine. As long as cars do not drive on their own, they should at least protect the driver from himself. "Already today there exists technologies that can detect, for instance, that the driver is tired, and provide him with a warning. In order to do this, these systems observe how he uses the gas pedal and the steering wheel. Newer versions also gauge eye activity with the use of special cameras. To take one example, the car supplier Boschis has developed a package that identifies the driver by means of a camera that adjusts the car accordingly. The camera is so precise that it can also detect possibilities." It measures the extent to which the eye is open or how often the driver blinks. If the car decides that the driver is too tired, it will recommend that he take a pause. Inducements encouraging surveillance include, for instance, financial advantages relating to insurance. In the case of self-driving cars too, attention surveillance is recommended, so that control is not handed over to a driver who is incapable of driving. "The car of the future will not just have to know exactly what happens in the street, but also what happens in the human being's inner space".[13]

In order for the communication of such things to function, smart homes and smart cars require smart cities. In Songdo, South Korea, which calls itself "the smartest of the smart cities of the world," the residents are to be spared the noise of garbage trucks and the sight of overfilled rubbish containers. After having requested personal identification, permanent video surveillance of collection points monitor with the use of sensors, whether garbage has been correctly sorted and placed into the appropriate areas of the waste disposal unit.

---

[13] Piotr Heller, "Mensch, leg das Handyweg!", *Frankfurter Allgemeine Sonntagszeitung*, October 1, 2017.

In Rongcheng and other cites among China's pilot projects for "honest cities", the task is through surveillance to form better and more disciplined citizens who live up to its norms. So, for instance, in May 2017, the bike rental firm Ofo proudly presented its newest bike model, equipped with a computerized transmitter, which, in real time transmits not only the profile of the cyclist's movement, but also the biker's body postures, to the Cloud.[14] This is wholly in line with a government that as of 2020 will introduce a social credit system that rewards norm conforming behaviour while punishing non-conformism. As a preparation for this, and in order to ensure that people become more accustomed to it, there is now in operation a Chinese counterpart to the Western selfies or putting-yourself-on display. In the West, internet pages like "insecam" or "opentopia", have long since gathered transmissions from webcams, making them available online, without the user's knowledge. In China something bigger is taking place. Here, there are hundreds of surveillance camera streams, ordered into categories, often with more than ten thousand viewers. "Apart from the sheer size of these pages, it is above all the types of places being filmed that appear crasser than examples from the Internet in the West. The images come not only from public places, but also from sports facilities, restaurants, supermarkets, and even schools."[15] The behaviour of those filmed is then commented upon and evaluated by viewers, and in this way they participate in the normalisation of camera and sensor surveillance, and behaviour evaluation through "social scoring".

Smart are obviously also quantified self-practitioners who use devices and measurements as means to control and discipline their own existence as a functioning organism. Taken together, as a piece of nature equipped with capacities for sensing, reflecting and communicating, in living contact with their equals and capable of caring for themselves and for others, this smartness results in a distancing or an alienation of humans from themselves. In this victory of smart worlds, the theme of protection also plays a role. At stake is the protection of privacy, of public spaces, and of human rights. But this seems just as modest as the claim that the conquering of nature should be accompanied with the establishment of protected zones. What, then, would a critique of smart worlds look like if it were focused on the connection between the relation to external nature and the human being as a part of nature? Could smart worlds pave the way for the human's apparent emancipation from nature? They cannot really make themselves independent from it, even if they make the remainder of

---

[14] Kai Strittmatter, "Schuld und Sühne", *Süddeutsche Zeitung*, May 20, 2017.
[15] Michael Moorstedt, "Edle Menschen vor der Kamera", *Süddeutsche Zeitung*, August 14, 2017.

autonomous and informed interaction with nature appear as superfluous and unnecessarily tiresome, in the face of the promise that we, as consumers of technologisation, are able to enhance the utility of our urban environment and, in so doing, approximate the ideal of an unmoved mover.

Value or Dignity of Nature, or what?

For Horkheimer in the mid-1930s, the ideal of a future society was characterised by the "mastery of classless humanity over nature".[16] Similarly, in the 1939 essay "Die Juden und Europa" he writes that a society based on reason can only be determined by coming to terms with nature,[17] and in "The Authoritarian State" in 1941,[18] he characterises social transformation as based on the socialisation and planning of the economy, which would increase domination over nature beyond measure, and simultaneously on an active resistance that would spell the end of exploitation. It is only towards the end of the essay "The End of Reason",[19] eventually appearing in the last issue of the Institute's journal, that an idea of emancipation from nature emerges that does not aim for domination, but for an understanding of nature. The demand for liberating the forces of production in a society predicated on reason and justice is replaced with a critique of humanity's domination over nature that serves to uphold social relations of domination. This diagnosis amounts to an image of society as a "mass racketeering in nature", which, with its technological visions and technological developments, represses any thought of social progress.[20]

A quite different understanding of the relation between technological and social utopias was developed by Walter Benjamin in his last text, the theses on the concept of history. In thesis eleven Benjamin identified a fateful connection between "progress in the domination over nature" and the "regressions of society". In contrast he imagines a state in which the "beneficent division of social labour" of those that no longer are a mere work force enslaved to the owners of the means of production, will no longer exploit nature, but instead will be "capable of delivering creations whose possibility slumbers in her womb". In order to paint this picture, Benjamin draws on the utopian socialist Charles Fourier—utopias of the sort in which "four moons would illuminate the night sky; ice would be removed from the polar cap; saltwater from the sea

---

[16] Max Horkheimer, *Gesammelte Schriften* (Frankfurt am Main: Fischer, 1985), vol. 12, 246.
[17] Max Horkheimer, "Die Juden und Europa", in *Zeitschrift für Sozialforschung* VIII (1939).
[18] Max Horkheimer, "The Authoritarian State", *Telos*, Vol 15: 1973.
[19] Max Horkheimer, "The End of Reason", *Studies in Philosophy and Social Science*, 9 (1941).
[20] Ibid.

would no longer taste salty; and wild beasts would enter into the service of human beings".[21] This came very close to an idea of nature as the cradle of a paradisiac high-tech environment.

Regarding the abolition of night, the receding of ice, the transformed taste of the oceans, and service to humans by predators for touristic and scientific aims, Benjamin's technological utopia seems to have become reality, courtesy of highly developed productive forces, or, at least, is in the process of realising itself, even without "social labour" as the principal beneficiary. For many this is not a problem, rather a normal challenge for the future of human civilisation. If environmental problems occur, one seeks to compensate for the loss of nature's functioning with technical means that not infrequently even surpass nature. As a logical consequence of this attitude and strategy there lies, as the historian Rolf Peter Sieferle writes in *Die Krise der Menschlichen Natur*, from 1989:

> that in the end it largely will renounce from drawing on the preceding workings of natural systems, even strive to wholly eliminate them since, to the extent that they are not under human control, they can produce disturbances. In the end a way must be found for humanity to master the integral biosphere, or at least the part that functions as the space for human production and consumption; this must be controlled on a planetary level. In such a system of total technologico-ecological planning the integral apparatus of production and consumption must operate as a space station in stationary orbit, independent of natural spatial conditions, for these cannot be trusted.[22]

Just as earlier, there is in many projects unconditional trust in the boundless possibilities of human science and technology. Examples of this can be found, for instance, in the emerging field of synthetic biology, whose motto reads: "What I have understood, I can build". One of the largest research projects in this field bears on artificial endosymbiosis. The principle of photosynthesis in plants should be transferred to animals. What took "evolution" hundreds of millions of years to accomplish—the transformation of cyanobacteria into chloroplast leading to endosymbiosis—should be applied to animals. "The whole effort of ingestion" would then be abolished, so researchers argue. Such animals could themselves carry out photosynthesis, and thus live off light. Even biologists, who were once sceptical of the idea, today hold that the vision of

---

[21] Walter Benjamin, *Selected Writings*, 4: 1938–1940 (Cambridge: Harvard University Press, 2003), 394.
[22] Rolf Peter Sieferle, *Die Krise der menschlichen Natur* (Frankfurt am Main: Suhrkamp, 1989), 201.

artificial endosymbiosis is a realistic project. To be sure, this is a project "on the same scale as the mission to the moon", which "surely requires a billion dollars and a whole generation of scientists", says the chloroplast researcher Andreas Weber, from Heinrich-Heine-Universität in Düsseldorf.[23] That millions of years of evolution have involved complex co-evolutionary processes is obviously no reason to doubt the possibility of both technologically controlled and accelerated development without well-considered and acknowledged goals. The traditional world, determined by birth and death, health and sickness, nature and cultivation, is seen as a laboratory, in which the task is to displace, transgress and abolish borders previously taken to be natural.

In addition to the pressure to grasp and objectivise everything in a scientific manner is the further pressure to subject everything to economic evaluation and categorisation. A few years ago, an investigation, originally based on a German initiative that then continued under the auspices of the United Nations Environmental Program (UNEP), presented the interim conclusion that the economic value of how the ecosystem was performing was much higher than economists and natural scientists had hitherto assumed. In a statement issued by Federal Ministry for the Environment, Nature Conservation and Nuclear Safety, we read:

> So the approx. 100 000 protected areas each provide human beings with ecosystem performances evaluate to 4,4 to 5,2 billion USD. This value surpasses the turnover of the global car industry, steel industry, and IT service sector. The investments required to sustain the performances of a nature with 'ideal' worldwide protection net (15 percent of the terrestrial surface and 30 percent of the marine surface) at the level of a value of 5,000 billion USD would, according to expert judgment, amount to app. 45 billion USD. This corresponds to a very good cost-benefit relation of 1:100.[24]

But what happens when something is evaluated as worthless or replaceable with technical means that even may surpass it? Then the insecurities involved in protecting, if this very protecting is made dependent on an evaluation of nature as "ecosystemic performance", become evident.

---

[23] Sascha Karberg, "Tiere, zur Sonne, zur Mahlzeit", *Frankfurter Allgemeine Sonntagszeitung*, May 15, 2011.
[24] Federal Ministry for the Environment, Nature Conservation and Nuclear Safety, "Die Ökonomie von Ökossystemen und der Biodiversität", August 2010.

Protection as a Business Model: "Freedom within the natural" vs. Comfortable Journeys to Nature

On the basis of what has been said, the question that imposes itself is the following: do the prevailing metaphors of conquering and saving, and the link between grasping and evaluating, get in the way of an adequate perception and understanding?

For Horkheimer and Adorno, *Dialectic of Enlightenment* was to be only a beginning. For them, in the end it was a question of "true reason". And yet a collaborative follow-up to the study never materialised. Instead what remains are partly formulaic analyses and constructions, for instance that the "remembrance of nature in the subject" would open a path towards an emancipation from a socially organised, ruthless domination over nature.

How might we understand the miraculous process of a "remembrance of nature in the subject", as well as the even more miraculous transcending of nature and reconciliation with it? Adorno tries to explicate it in the chapter on freedom in *Negative Dialectics*. If humans are subject to the laws of nature like all other natural entities, does the moral law put an impossible burden on them? In making Kant's problem his own, but rejecting Kant's dualist construction of a determined nature and intelligible world, Adorno presents his own considerations.

In the *Critique of Pure Reason* Kant had shown how a human being, when confronted with the problem of relating human freedom to natural causality, must end up in a ceaseless vacillation.

> Today it would strike him as convincing that the human will is free; tomorrow, when he considered the indissoluble chain of nature, he would side with the view that freedom is nothing but self-deception, and that everything is mere nature. But now if it came to be a matter of doing or acting, then this play of merely speculative reason would disappear like the phantom images of a dream, and he would choose his principles merely according to practical interest.[25]

Referring to this vacillation, Adorno suggests:

> Freedom and intelligible character are akin to identity and nonidentity, but we cannot clearly and distinctly enter them on one side or the other. The subjects are free, after the Kantian model, in so far as they are aware of and identical with themselves; and then again, they are unfree in such identity in

---

[25] Kant, *Critique of Pure Reason*, trans. Norman Kemp-Smith, (London: Macmillan, 1929), A 475.

> so far as they are subjected to, and will perpetuate, its compulsion. They are
> unfree as diffuse, nonidentical nature; and yet, as that nature they are free
> because their overpowering impulse – the subject's nonidentity with itself is
> nothing else – will also rid them of identity's coercive character.[26]

Only when the "becoming-conscious-of-oneself" takes place in a subject that is not identical with itself does what would be "freedom in the midst of the natural" come into being. A society on the other hand, which only thinks and acts in categories of conquest and protection, and does not flinch from genetic self-manipulation, such a society cannot grasp and master what can only be attained differently, i.e. as that which becomes perceptible and present for a subject that reflects on itself. The formula "freedom in the midst of the natural", which only occurs fleetingly in Adorno's debate with Kant, makes it particularly clear what is at stake in the idea of a reason interwoven with nature. At stake is a freedom born out of nature, but at the same time can only be lived in the midst of nature.

But what shape could this take in a time where the contacts between humans and extra human nature intensifies, accelerating through the mediations of science, technology and business models? It seems fruitful to take examples from nature tourism as a starting point for such reflections. In these cases, persons seek contact with extra human nature, free from the existential pressure and needs as well as from the drudgery of work assignments and everyday burdens. Corporations working within maritime-tourism promise "direct and intense" nature experiences of a special kind. This is especially the case when it comes to journeys to the Arctic or the Antarctic. They are marketed as "discovery", even as "individual discoveries" to "largely unknown" or "untouched" natural environments. At present, the most intensive form of maritime nature-experience is, according to the French shipping company Ponant, offered by their newest expedition ships: the "Ponant Explorers Serie", named after French discoverers. Their guests are put on the same exploratory tracks as the scientists, who work in "remote and untouched areas, which are not reachable for larger ships". The main attraction of these boats is the "multisensory underwater lounge called 'Blue Eye Underwater Lounge'", equipped with "Body Listening Sofas" and integrated panoramic windows. Underwater microphones receive sounds from the oceans, combined with music produced by an in-house electro composer, a specialist in transforming ambient sounds

---

[26] Theodor W. Adorno, *Negative Dialectics*, 299.

into music. In addition, underwater cameras transmit images from the ocean to plasma screens installed on the ship.

According to Ponant's head of marketing and sales, the aim is to communicate the beauty of the oceans to passengers, but also its vulnerability and its need for protection. "Through the windows you will not only see picturesque reefs and colorful fishes, but also rubbish on the bottom the ocean or drifting plastic bags". This break with the illusion will hopefully lead to greater awareness among the passengers".[27]

An experienced expedition leader, who has been on dozens of journeys to the Arctic and the North pole, also points to this kind of change of attitude through expedition tourism. She was interviewed in connection to a tourist expedition organised by Hapag-Lloyd to the Spitsbergen, where a polar bear was shot dead. The bear had attacked a guide, who had disembarked with the so-called "polar bear guardians" in order to secure the area. These guardians are not supposed to protect the polar bears and their life space; rather, their role as guardians is meant to protect the tourists from the polar bears, whose life spaces are designed to become a trafficable zoo. "If no one would go there, it would be ice deserts", claims the expedition leader. Accordingly, it is reasoned that the pictures and reports from these regions are good for the world. "In this way it is possible to create awareness for the sake of its protection". But this also means: protection, not of the ice deserts and the animals living there, but of the business model of polar trips in grandiose landscapes. The sensibility of the expedition leader addresses the "eternal contradiction", with which the companies and the guests have to live: "that the love for this region also in some sense damages the region".[28]

The companies formulate their marketing of expeditions to untouched areas of nature with the promise that the guests will be taken "to interesting places in a secure and comfortable manner". But the information they give also includes references to the fact that the underwater cameras, which deliver the images to the plasma screens on Ponant's ships, work with photo luminescence, in order not to disturb underwater life; so that not one tourist footprints is left behind. Only "impressions, emotions and pictures" are meant to be brought home. And so that Co2-emissions can be compensated, a donation to "Trees for the Arctic" is included in journey price.

But little appears—to use an image from Adorno's aphorism "Paysage"—so "immediately blasted out of the landscape" than cruise ships in the Arctic or

---

[27] Ingrid Brunner, "Wale spüren", *Süddeutsche Zeitung*, August 23, 2018.
[28] Max Sprick, "Der wahr gewordene Albtraum" (interview with Birgit Lutz), *Süddeutsche Zeitung*, 31.7.2018.

Antarctic. If someone, who experiences such "untouched" nature from his or her box seat, thinks of the need for protection, it probably would be about these kind of thoughts and feelings, expressed by a tourist who uploaded a photo on the internet with a polar bear on the ice: "One of my most impressive moments of all my travels was to look into a polar bear eyes! Knowing that they are an endangered species is so sad to see!" Hereby she distances herself from the powerless inhabitants of a world in which they are no longer at home, and she avoids becoming aware of her own existential bond with them beyond the arranged comfortable and isolated world of a cruise journey. If the tourist really had met the eyes of the polar bear, her pleasure for photographs would have disappeared; she would have experienced the bear's rejection of her. The emphasis on vulnerability and the need to protect nature that is visited and photographed distracts our attention away from the aggression of human life, thereby hindering the possibility of fostering an ethos of "civilised" care for extra human nature, whether this is on ice deserts, on journeys or at home.

Adorno's Utopian Animals

CAMILLA FLODIN

Scientists warn us that we are living in an era of human-induced mass extinction of species caused by our social practice of "co-opting resources, fragmenting habitats, introducing non-native species, spreading pathogens, killing species directly, and changing global climate".[1] Mass extinction is characterised by a dramatic reduction in species during a geologically short interval. This kind of species extinction has happened five times over the last half billion years—referred to as the Big Five. And now we are entering into a sixth, expected to be the most detrimental since the asteroid impact eradicated the dinosaurs 66 million years ago.[2] Today, over 26,500 species are threatened with extinction, according to the IUCN Red list.[3] Even without the impact of humans, species would die out, but, as an example, the extinction of anthropogenic vertebrae is estimated to be up to 100 times higher than what scientists refer to as "the background rate".[4]

The future of many of the species existing today is thus uncertain, thanks to the triumph of the self-proclaimed cleverest one, *homo sapiens*. That this triumph threatens to become a pyrrhic victory was clear already to Adorno and Horkheimer in the 1940s:

> The human capacity for destruction promises to become so great that – once this species has exhausted itself – a *tabula rasa* will have been created. Either the human species will tear itself to pieces or it will take all the earth's fauna and flora down with it, and if the earth is still young enough, the whole procedure – to vary a famous dictum – will have to start again on a much lower level.[5]

---

[1] Anthony D. Barnosky et al., "Has the Earth's Sixth Mass Extinction Already Arrived?", *Nature* vol. 471 (2011): 51.

[2] For an illuminating account, see Elizabeth Kolbert, *The Sixth Extinction: An Unnatural History* (New York: Henry Holt and Company, 2014).

[3] The International Union for Conservation of Nature, "The IUCN Red List of Threatened Species", Version 2018–2, http://iucnredlist.org. Accessed 5 February 2019.

[4] Gerardo Ceballos et al., "Accelerated Modern Human-Induced Species Losses: Entering the Sixth Mass Extinction", *Science Advances* vol. 1, no. 5 (2015), e1400253. DOI: 10.1126/sciadv.1400253

[5] Max Horkheimer and Theodor W. Adorno, *Dialectic of Enlightenment: Philosophical Fragments*, ed. Gunzelin Schmid Noerr, trans. Edmund Jephcott (Stanford: Stanford University Press, 2002), 186; *Dialektik*

The above quote is from the sketch "On the Critique of the Philosophy of History" in *Dialectic of Enlightenment*. But already from the early essay (originally a lecture) on natural history from 1932, Adorno is concerned with the relationship between human beings and the rest of nature, including non-human animals. He is relentless in his critique of a domination of nature that has entrapped human beings despite its promise to deliver freedom from external constraints. Furthermore, according to him, this domination finds its most obvious expression "in the exploitation and maltreatment of animals".[6] Adorno is, however, not generally regarded as a prominent contributor to the field of Critical Animal Studies.[7] The role of animals in Adorno's philosophy is a theme that until quite recently has been neglected in Adorno scholarship too.[8] In the following, I shall argue that Adorno's writings contain some fundamental insights that can contribute to a critique of our current relationship towards external nature, especially our relationship to non-human animals, and where the most suitable way to grasp Adorno's contribution to this field is through his aesthetics. A first clue as to why art and aesthetics are fundamental for understanding Adorno's take on nature and non-human animals is to be found in another sketch in *Dialectic of Enlightenment*, namely the one entitled "Man and Beast" (a sketch I will return to below): "In this society there is no longer any sphere in which domination can profess its contradictions, as it does in art; there is no longer any means of duplication by which the distortion

---

der Aufklärung: Philosophische Fragmente, in Theodor W. Adorno, *Gesammelte Schriften* vol. 3, ed. Rolf Tiedemann (Frankfurt am Main: Suhrkamp, 2003), 255.

[6] Theodor W. Adorno, *Problems of Moral Philosophy*, ed. Thomas Schröder, trans. Rodney Livingstone (Stanford: Stanford University Press, 2000), 145; *Probleme der Moralphilosophie*, in *Nachgelassene Schriften* section IV, vol. 10 (Frankfurt am Main: Suhrkamp, 1996), 215.

[7] A notable exception is Marco Maurizi, "The Dialectical Animal: Nature and Philosophy of History in Adorno, Horkheimer and Marcuse", *Journal for Critical Animal Studies* vol. 10, no. 1 (2012): 67–103.

[8] Fredric Jameson briefly considers Adorno and Horkheimer's sketch "Man and Beast" from *Dialectic of Enlightenment*, see Jameson, *Late Marxism: Adorno, or, the Persistence of the Dialectic* (London: Verso, 1990), 96. In the anthology *Das steinerne Herz der Unendlichkeit erweichen: Beiträge zu einer kritischen Theorie für die Befreiung der Tiere*, ed. Susann Witt-Stahl (Aschaffenburg: Alibri, 2007), all contributions analyse the human–animal relation in critical theory, and some explicitly consider Adorno's ideas on this topic. The role of art in the liberation of animals is nevertheless only briefly touched upon in a few of the essays in the anthology, see Arnd Hoffmann, ""Ein Königstiger als Vegetarianer": Zur Kritik an der Utopielosigkeit von Antispeziesismus und Veganismus", 191; Esther Leslie and Ben Watson, "Tiere, Geschichte und Kunsttriebe", 217–218. Christina Gerhardt discusses Adorno's ideas on the human–animal relation in "The Ethics of Animals in Adorno and Kafka", *New German Critique* vol. 33, no 1 (2006): 159–178, and in "Thinking With: Animals in Schopenhauer, Horkheimer, and Adorno", in *Critical Theory and Animal Liberation*, ed. John Sanbonmatsu (Lanham MD: Rowman & Littlefield, 2011): 137–146. The latter anthology contains another essay on Adorno and animals, which briefly discusses his ideas on the relationship between art and animals, Eduardo Mendieta, "Animal Is to Kantianism as Jew Is to Fascism: Adorno's Bestiary", see 153–154.

might be expressed".[9] Art may offer a glimpse of the way out of the fatal dialectic of enlightenment; at the same time as it is part of the process of enlightenment, in becoming precisely *art*, and thus regarded as an autonomous sphere separated from scientific knowledge and social praxis, it is able to preserve the memory of what has been deformed in this development. Art is thus, according to Adorno, able to give voice to subjugated nature and animals.[10]

For Adorno, art is never merely a human affair. This is one of the chief criticisms he levels at Hegel's aesthetics: the philosophical aesthetics of Hegel may well be the most adequate comprehension of art in its own time, nevertheless, from Adorno's standpoint, Hegel's outright dismissal of natural beauty from aesthetics also testifies to the increasing subjugation of nature characteristic of the dialectic of enlightenment.[11] What is objective in art for Hegel is something *Geistliches*, and while this is in accord with art's own movement away from the merely sensuously pleasing (i.e. subjective) to becoming "the expression of an idea",[12] it also contains the "arrogance of the spirit towards that which is not spirit".[13] By understanding natural beauty as deficient, in other words, not objective enough, and falsely equating this proclaimed non-objectivity with the "feebly subjective"[14]—regarding it thereby as abstract, as lacking in substance—in Hegel's aesthetics "the essence of natural beauty, the anamnesis of precisely what does not exist for-an-other, is let slip".[15]

This remembrance of what does not exist for-an-other, in other words, what would be allowed to exist for itself, is essential in natural beauty, according to Adorno. And the artistic beauty that counts can convey this memory:

[9] Horkheimer and Adorno, *Dialectic of Enlightenment*, 209; *Dialektik der Aufklärung*, 289.

[10] See also Camilla Flodin, "Of Mice and Men: Adorno on Art and the Suffering of Animals", *Estetika: The Central European Journal of Aesthetics*, no. 2 (2011): 139–156 and "The Wor(l)d of the Animal: Adorno on Art's Expression of Suffering", *Journal of Aesthetics & Culture* vol. 3, no. 1 (2011), https://doi.org/10.3402/jac.v3i0.7987.

[11] For this dismissal, see G. W. F. Hegel, *Aesthetics: Lectures on Fine Art*, trans. T. M. Knox, vol. 1 (Oxford: Clarendon Press, 1975), 1–2; *Vorlesungen über die Ästhetik I*, in *Werke* vol. 13, ed. Eva Moldenhauer and Karl Markus Michel (Frankfurt am Main: Suhrkamp, 1979), 13.

[12] Theodor W. Adorno, *Aesthetics 1958/59*, ed. Eberhard Ortland, trans. Wieland Hoban (Cambridge: Polity Press, 2018), 20; *Ästhetik 1958/59*, in *Nachgelassene Schriften* section IV, vol. 3 (Frankfurt am Main: Suhrkamp, 2009), 37.

[13] Adorno, *Aesthetics*, 21; *Ästhetik*, 39.

[14] Theodor W. Adorno, *Aesthetic Theory*, ed. Gretel Adorno and Rolf Tiedemann, trans. Robert Hullot-Kentor (London and New York: Continuum, 1997), 75; *Ästhetische Theorie*, in *Gesammelte Schriften* vol. 7 (Frankfurt am Main: Suhrkamp, 2003), 116.

[15] Adorno, *Aesthetic Theory*, 74; *Ästhetische Theorie*, 116.

> The artwork, through and through θέσει, something human, is the plenipotentiary of φύσει, of what is not merely for the subject, of what, in Kantian terms, would be the thing itself. The identity of the artwork with the subject is as complete as the identity of nature with itself should some day be.[16]

What is seemingly most determined by human spirit, the artwork, is the proxy of nature's determination of itself, that is to say, nature liberated from dominating subjective rationality's attempt to determine nature. This becomes increasingly problematic, since the development in society at large is precisely in the other direction: everything is exchangeable, nothing exists for itself. Consequently, what does not exist for-an-other remains a possibility, and in order not to betray this possibility, art cannot depict it as something already achieved. That is why Adorno appeals to Plato's theory of *anamnesis*: "Ever since Plato's doctrine of anamnesis the not-yet-existing has been dreamed of in remembrance, which alone concretizes utopia without betraying it to existence."[17] Kant's *thing in itself* is evoked for the same reason: it indicates that which is beyond human immanence. And in Kant's aesthetics, there is also an attempt to move beyond the merely subjective and formal characteristics of beauty, which is why Adorno appeals to him as a dialectical counterpart to Hegel's objective aesthetics. In Adorno's lectures on aesthetics from 1958–59, he claims that Kant's description of the dynamic sublime and the conflict between humanity and nature that appears therein is a more suitable account of aesthetic experience than the notion of pleasure associated with formal properties. Well aware of the Kantian division between the beautiful and the sublime, Adorno nevertheless insists that "this fundamentally dissonating character of all comprehensively modern art is in fact an expression of the dialectic which Kant encountered in natural beauty".[18] What Adorno finds problematic, however, is that for Kant the experience of the sublime in nature becomes a sign of human being's moral superiority. According to Kant, nature is not sublime in itself. What causes the subject's sublime feeling is the experience of his own determination over nature.[19]

---

[16] Adorno, *Aesthetic Theory*, 63; *Ästhetische Theorie*, 99.

[17] Adorno, *Aesthetic Theory*, 132; *Ästhetische Theorie*, 200.

[18] Adorno, *Aesthetics*, 31; *Ästhetik*, 54.

[19] Immanuel Kant, *Critique of the Power of Judgment*, trans. Paul Guyer and Eric Matthews (Cambridge and New York: Cambridge University Press, 2000), 145; *Kants Gesammelte Schriften*, ed. by the Preußischen Akademie der Wissenschaft, Berlin: Walter de Gruyter, 1902– [henceforth: AA], vol. 5, *Kritik der Urteilskraft*, 261–262. I am deliberately using "his", because there is a gendered aspect of this dominance, which I unfortunately do not have space to analyse further here. For discussion of the gendered aspect of

Despite correctly recognising the tension involved in aesthetic experience, Kant's theory of the sublime and the description of the human being's rational superiority is regarded by Adorno as a stage in the intensified domination of nature which characterises the process of enlightenment at large. In the theory of the sublime Kant defines the human being *qua* rational creature as separated from nature, and Adorno also perceives the same trait in Kant's moral philosophy. In *Critique of Practical Reason* Kant argues that humans cannot have respect for animals, merely inclination (*Neigung*); respect is reserved for persons, Kant argues, and can never be felt for "things".[20] In his unfinished book on Beethoven, published posthumously, Adorno criticises Kant's ethics for its denigration of nature and animals:

> What I find so suspect in Kantian ethics is the "dignity" which it attributes to man in the name of autonomy. A capacity for moral self-determination is ascribed to human beings as an absolute advantage—as a moral profit—while being covertly used to legitimize *supremacy* [*Herrschaft*]—supremacy over nature. This is the real aspect of the transcendental claim [in *Critique of Pure Reason*] that man can dictate the laws of nature. Ethical dignity in Kant is a demarcation of differences. It is directed against animals. Implicitly it excludes man from the rest of creation [*Schöpfung*], so that its humanity threatens incessantly to revert to the inhuman. It leaves no room for compassion [*Mitleid*]. Nothing is more abhorrent to the Kantian than a reminder of man's likeness to animals [*Tierähnlichkeit*]. This taboo is always at work when the idealist berates the materialist. Animals play for the idealist system virtually the same role as the Jews for fascism. To revile man as an animal—that is genuine idealism. To deny the possibility of salvation for animals absolutely and at any price is the inviolable boundary of its metaphysics.[21]

the mastery of nature, see e.g. Val Plumwood, *Feminism and the Mastery of Nature* (London and New York: Routledge, 1993). Plumwood explicitly refers to the *Dialectic of Enlightenment* as a forerunner to the ecofeminist critique of nature-dominating rationality, see *Feminism and the Mastery of Nature*, 24. For a reading that emphasises the possibility of Adorno's thinking contributing to ecofeminist theory, see D. Bruce Martin, "Mimetic Moments: Adorno and Ecofeminism", in *Feminist Interpretations of Theodor Adorno*, ed. Renée Heberle (University Park, PA: The Pennsylvania State University Press, 2006), 141–171. Martin does not, however, discuss Plumwood. Deborah Cook briefly notes the similarities between Plumwood and Adorno in Cook, *Adorno and Nature* (Durham UK: Acumen, 2011), 125.

[20] Immanuel Kant, *Critique of Practical Reason*, in Kant, *Practical Philosophy*, trans. and ed. Mary J. Gregor (Cambridge: Cambridge University Press, 1996), 202; *Kritik der praktischen Vernunft*, AA vol. 5, 76–77.

[21] Theodor W. Adorno, *Beethoven: The Philosophy of Music*, ed. Rolf Tiedemann, trans. Edmund Jephcott (Cambridge: Polity Press, 1998), 80 (translation modified); *Beethoven: Philosophie der Musik*, in *Nachgelassene Schriften* section I, vol. 1 (Frankfurt am Main: Suhrkamp, 1993), 123–124. This passage is quoted by Derrida in his acceptance speech for the Theodor W. Adorno Award in 2001, see Jacques Derrida,

Admittedly, the truth content of the structural comparison between the Jew and the animal, both of which function as "the other" upon which fears are projected, has arguably at least been tarnished (if not altogether lost)—through, for example, PETA's (People for the Ethical Treatment of Animals) macabre campaign "Holocaust on Your Plate" in 2003 in which photographs of Nazi concentration camps were juxtaposed against images from today's industrialised animal husbandry—a campaign which also included a quote falsely attributed to Adorno. As a consequence, we need to pay careful attention to what Adorno is *actually* saying in the above passage.[22] He points to the *affinity* between an idealistic metaphysics, which grounds the dignity of human beings in their *separation and elevation* from other animals, and a fascist ideology that establishes the idea of a superior race by denigrating Jews.

As Christina Gerhardt has noted, what Adorno aims at is to reveal "the ideals of idealism that were not realised and to pinpoint precisely what prevented them from being realised or, worse, allowed them to turn into their opposite".[23] Adorno is of course very aware of the myth of the Nazis as animal lovers—this was a myth they themselves created in order to mask their hatred towards certain humans,[24] and still is today maintained in order, through *guilt by association,* to smear those who, like Adorno himself, advocate "the possibility of salvation for animals". In the fragment "Man and Beast" from *Dialectic of Enlightenment*, Horkheimer and Adorno write:

> In this world liberated from appearance—in which human beings, having forfeited reflection, have become once more the cleverest animals, which subjugate the rest of the universe when they happen not to be tearing themselves apart—to show concern for animals is considered no longer merely sentimental but a betrayal of progress. In the best reactionary tradition Göring linked animal protection to racial hatred, the Lutheran-Germanic joys of the happy murderer with the genteel fair play of the aristocratic hunter. The

---

Fichus: Discours de Francfort (Paris: Galilée, 2002), 54–55. See also Gerhardt, "The Ethics of Animals in Adorno and Kafka", 162–163.

[22] PETA, founded in the US in 1980, is the world's largest animal rights organization and has by several animal rights theorists been criticized for its problematic, and many times sexist, campaigns. For an anti-speciesist critique of the comparison between the situation of non-human animals and Jews, see Susann Witt-Stahl, "Das Tier als 'der ewige Jude'? Ein Vergleich und seine Kritik als Ideologie", in *Das steinerne Herz der Unendlichkeit erweichen: Beiträge zu einer kritischen Theorie für die Befreiung der Tiere*, ed. Susann Witt-Stahl (Aschaffenburg: Alibri, 2007), 278–309. See also Maurizi, "The Dialectical Animal", 68.

[23] Gerhardt, "The Ethics of Animals in Adorno and Kafka", 163.

[24] See Horkheimer and Adorno, *Dialectic of Enlightenment*, 210; *Dialektik der Aufklärung*, 291. This is still an established *modus operandi* for racist ideologists of today, for instance in their criticism of halal and/or kosher slaughtering because of alleged concern for animal welfare.

fronts are clearly drawn; anyone who opposes Hearst and Göring is on the side of Pavlov and vivisection; anyone who hesitates between the two is fair game for both.[25]

Adorno attempts to overcome this "either/or" option, in order to preserve the idea of a possible future free from *both* Nazism *and* vivisection. A condition for the actualisation of such a possible future is if human beings stop ascribing themselves dignity by separating themselves from, and denigrating other, animals. As long as the "animal" is perceived as an abuse it can also be used to denigrate human beings. Denying the human being's likeness to animals is to deny the existence of nature in the subject. According to Adorno, such a denial entails a backlash against humanity.

Grounding the dignity and exceptional position of the human being on its separation from and denigration of both other animals and nature is a trait Kant shares with his successors, Schiller and Hegel. Indeed, Adorno connects Hegel's dismissal of natural beauty from the realm of aesthetics with this idealistic anthropocentrism.[26] True freedom cannot be achieved by elevating the human being above nature and understanding dignity as a sign of the human's exemption from the natural and animal world, thereby sanctioning human being's dominion over the rest of nature. This is why Adorno claims: "If the case of natural beauty were pending, dignity would be found culpable for having raised the human animal above the animal."[27]

In his lectures on moral philosophy from 1963, Adorno instead draws attention to Schopenhauer's view of other animals, and the need to show compassion towards them—an idea which at the time was regarded as eccentric, but from which Adorno says we can learn a great deal. What Schopenhauer reacts to is the fact that Kant does not regard animals as worthy of sympathy for their own sake. Kant claims that we practice compassion towards human beings by showing compassion towards animals.[28] Adorno argues that Schopenhauer is on to something important, namely

---

[25] Horkheimer and Adorno, *Dialectic of Enlightenment*, 211; *Dialektik der Aufklärung*, 291–292.

[26] See also Flodin, "Of Mice and Men", 144–145.

[27] Adorno, *Aesthetic Theory*, 62; *Ästhetische Theorie*, 99.

[28] See Arthur Schopenhauer, "Über die Grundlage der Moral", in *Kleinere Schriften, Sämtliche Werke* vol. 3, ed. Wolfgang Frhr. von Löhneysen (Frankfurt am Main: Suhrkamp, 1993), 690–691 (§ 8). For Kant's argument that compassion towards animals is merely to be practiced because it promotes compassion towards human beings, see Immanuel Kant, *The Metaphysics of Morals*, in Kant, *Practical Philosophy*, 564 (§17); *Die Metaphysik der Sitten*, AA vol. 6, 443. For a discussion of Schopenhauer's influence on especially Horkheimer and Adorno regarding the human–animal-relation, see Gunzelin Schmid Noerr, "Mitleid mit der gequälten Kreatur: Zur Anwesenheit Schopenhauers in der Kritischen Theorie", in *Das steinerne Herz der Unendlichkeit erweichen*, 50–69.

that the establishment of total rationality as the supreme objective principle of mankind might well spell the continuation of *that blind domination of nature whose most obvious and tangible expression was to be found in the exploitation and maltreatment of animals.* He [Schopenhauer] thereby pointed to the weak point in the transition from subjective reason concerned with self-preservation to the supreme moral principle, which has no room for animals and our treatment of animals. If this is true, we can see Schopenhauer's eccentricity as the sign of great insight. If we picture to ourselves what an institutionalized reason as the supreme principle of mankind might actually look like, we should surely think of it as something from which this dominant principle has been eradicated. [...] Certainly, it would be better to eliminate it than to install it in perpetuity, in order, finally, in the name of morality to establish society itself as a vast joint-stock company for the exploitation of nature.[29]

From Adorno's perspective, the notion of humankind's elevation of itself over nature and over other animals, which Kant also expresses in his theory of the sublime, is part of the destructiveness characteristic of the domination of nature. But Adorno argues that the sublime changes once it has been transferred onto art.[30] This is because spiritualisation—itself an aspect of the process of enlightenment, as we have seen in Hegel's aesthetics—takes a different course in art than outside it. For Adorno, art's spiritualisation simultaneously bears witness to the subjugation of nature, which has occurred through the process of enlightenment and the domination of nature. In *Aesthetic Theory*, Adorno argues that "the telos of aesthetic spiritualisation" is "to give the historical figures of the natural and subordination [*Unterordnung*] of the natural their due".[31] Art is, as we saw earlier in a quote from *Dialectic of Enlightenment*, a reflection on the process of enlightenment, and is able to express the distortions accompanying this process. Unlike the rest of society and its established practices, art is also able to reflect on and acknowledge its own dependence on nature: "Art's spirit is the self-recognition [*Selbstbesinnung*] of spirit itself as natural [*sein eigenes Naturhaftes*]."[32] In mediating the moment (*Moment*) of the sublime—that is to say, the moment in which natural beauty shakes the human subject's feeling of superiority—art reveals the human being as natural, as a mortal creature among other mortal creatures. Spirit is thus

---

[29] Adorno, *Problems of Moral Philosophy*, 145 (my emphasis); *Probleme der Moralphilosophie*, 215–216.
[30] See Adorno, *Aesthetic Theory*, 197; *Ästhetische Theorie*, 293.
[31] Adorno, *Aesthetic Theory*, 93 (translation modified); *Ästhetische Theorie*, 144.
[32] Adorno, *Aesthetic Theory*, 196; *Ästhetische Theorie*, 292.

"brought down to its natural dimension [*auf sein naturhaftes Maß gebracht*]".[33] In other words, through art's mediation, the sublime becomes a genuine experience, something which has the capacity to transform the subject:[34]

> Rather than that, as Kant thought, spirit in the face of nature becomes aware of its own superiority, it becomes aware of its own natural essence [*Naturhaftigkeit*]. This is the moment when the subject, vis-à-vis the sublime, is moved to tears. Recollection of nature breaks the arrogance of his self-positing: "My tears well up; earth, I am returning to you." [quote from Goethe's *Faust*[35]] With that, the self exits, spiritually, from its imprisonment in itself. Something of freedom flashes up that philosophy, culpably mistaken, reserves for its opposite, the glorification of the subject. The spell that the subject casts over nature imprisons the subject as well: Freedom awakens in the consciousness of its affinity with nature [*Naturähnlichkeit*].[36]

For Adorno, the idea of human supremacy over both nature and non-human animals is something that limits Kant's philosophy and aesthetics. The devaluation of animals is at the same time what makes possible the devaluation of (certain) humans as "mere" animals, even if all humans are in fact animals. And as Adorno argues in *Minima Moralia*, something haunts us in the claim "it is 'only an animal'": we know it is not true, not "even of animals".[37]

Adorno scholars often have a hard time accounting for his dialectical view of animals. Even commentators writing on nature, like Deborah Cook, fail to engage fully with this aspect of his thinking. In *Adorno on Nature*, Cook correctly observes that Adorno believes that damaged nature is given voice through the ideas of "justice, equality and freedom",[38] which develop as an answer to oppression. Here she emphasises that oppressors often compare the people they want to oppress with animals, thus identifying them with nature in order to subjugate them, just as nature has been subjugated. Cook also correctly

---

[33] Adorno, *Aesthetic Theory*, 198 (translation modified); *Ästhetische Theorie*, 295.

[34] See Brian O'Connor, *Adorno's Negative Dialectic: Philosophy and the Possibility of Critical Rationality* (Cambridge, Mass. & London: MIT Press, 2004), 2: "For Adorno, experience is the process in which ideally, that is, in its fullest possibility, one (a subject) is affected and somehow changed by confrontation with some aspect of objective reality (an object)".

[35] See Adorno, *Aesthetic Theory*, 375 note 7. The quote is from J. W. von Goethe, *Faust*, part 1, conclusion of scene "Night".

[36] Adorno, *Aesthetic Theory*, 276; *Ästhetische Theorie*, 410.

[37] Theodor W. Adorno, *Minima Moralia: Reflections from Damaged Life*, trans. E. F. N. Jephcott (London and New York: Verso, 2005), 113; *Minima Moralia: Reflexionen aus dem beschädigten Leben*, in *Gesammelte Schriften* vol. 4 (Frankfurt am Main: Suhrkamp: 2003), 118.

[38] Cook, *Adorno on Nature*, 89.

accredits Adorno with a reconfigured idea of humanity that "supersede[s] the antagonism between the animal and the human, instinct and reason, body and mind".[39] But in the conclusion of her book she nevertheless ascribes to Adorno the notion that "we [humans] will continue to behave like other animals as long as survival instincts shape our behaviour".[40] This fails to do justice to Adorno's dialectical understanding of non-human animals. In denial that they are themselves part of nature, human beings do not act like other animals, according to Adorno, but they act in accord with *a defective conception* of other animals, a conception indicative of our petrified society and of identity thinking. He does not regard other animals as mere slaves to their own instincts. Here, Cook would have profited from engaging more with Adorno's writings on aesthetics and art in which the concept of *Tierähnlichkeit,* i.e, a resemblance to animals, is deployed. Adorno regards this concept as having both critical and utopian potential: when we humans deny our likeness to animals, defining ourselves as radically distinct from other animals, we become increasingly like the false (but socially real) conception of animals subtending this denial—*instinctual creatures trapped in existing conditions.* This is precisely what Mahler is able to reveal to us in the third movement of his Third Symphony:

> Its light-beam falls on that perverted human condition that, under the spell of the self-preservation of the species, erodes its essential self and makes ready to annihilate the species by fatefully substituting the means for the end it has conjured away. Through animals humanity becomes aware of itself as impeded nature and of its activity as deluded natural history; for this reason Mahler meditates on them. For him, as in Kafka's fables, the animal realm is the human world as it would appear from the standpoint of redemption, which natural history itself precludes. The fairy-tale tone in Mahler is awakened by the resemblance of animal and man [*Ähnlichkeit von Tier und Mensch*]. Desolate and comforting at once, nature grown aware of itself casts off the superstition of the absolute difference between them.[41]

If we reflect on our resemblance to animals, and acknowledge both our affinity (identity) with them and our difference (non-identity) from them—which is concurrently also an acknowledgement of their identity with themselves and

---

[39] Cook, *Adorno on Nature,* 89.

[40] Cook, *Adorno on Nature,* 160.

[41] Theodor W. Adorno, *Mahler: A Musical Physiognomy,* trans. Edmund Jephcott (Chicago and London: The University of Chicago Press, 1996), 9; *Mahler: Eine musikalische Physiognomik* in *Gesammelte Schriften* vol. 13 (Frankfurt am Main: Suhrkamp, 2003), 157. I discuss Adorno's interpretation of Mahler's Third Symphony further in Flodin, "The Wor(l)d of the Animal".

their non-identity with our attempts to exhaustively define them—we would allow for a reconciliation that at the same time permits us and other animals to realise our (inherently different) potentials. Adorno argues that through engaging with authentic artworks, like Mahler's Third Symphony, humankind can catch a glimpse of its own repressed animal likeness and thus achieve an insight into why this repression is challenging.

Adorno is often accused of having an elitist conception of art. However, if one is attentive to his considerations of the art–animal relationship then it is possible to identify a much broader conception of art. Ridiculousness and clownishness are important aspects of art for Adorno, and there exists a close affinity between art, animals, and the standpoint of the child:

> In its clownishness, art consolingly recollects prehistory in the primordial world of animals. Apes in the zoo together perform what resembles clown routines. The collusion of children with clowns is a collusion with art, which adults drive out of them just as they drive out their collusion with animals. Human beings have not succeeded in so thoroughly repressing their likeness to animals that they are unable in an instant to recapture it and be flooded with joy; the language of little children and animals seems to be the same. In the similarity of clowns to animals the likeness of humans to apes flashes up; the constellation animal/fool/clown is a fundamental layer of art.[42]

In the encounter with art, not only do adult human beings remember instantly their own repressed likeness to animals, but art also indicates the possibility of a reconciliation of human being and animal. This indication is a source of joy, for it reveals the possibility of a transformed relationship between human beings and other animals. Moreover, in the aphorism "Bequest" from *Minima Moralia*, Adorno speaks about the truth content of certain children's books. Here I would like to suggest that Adorno's reasoning turns precisely on the way in which the human–animal relation is presented in those books. Adorno picks up on Walter Benjamin's thesis "that history had hitherto been written from the standpoint of the victor, and needed to be written from that of the vanquished", adding to this that knowledge "should also address itself to those things which were not embraced by this dynamic, which fell by the wayside— what might be called the waste products and blind spots that escaped the dialectic [between victory and defeat]".[43] He argues that this lack of fit

---

[42] Adorno, *Aesthetic Theory*, 119; *Ästhetische Theorie*, 181–182.
[43] Adorno, *Minima Moralia*, trans. Jephcott, 161; *Minimal Moralia*, 172.

can most readily be seen in art. Children's books like *Alice in Wonderland* or *Struwwelpeter*, of which it would be absurd to ask whether they are progressive or reactionary, contain incomparably more eloquent ciphers even of history than the high drama of Hebbel, concerned though it is with the official themes of tragic guilt, turning points of history, the course of the world and the individual [...].[44]

Implicitly containing a critique of his own perspective in *Philosophy of New Music*, which pits Schönberg against Stravinsky as composers of progressive and reactionary music, respectively, Adorno here contrasts the nineteenth century dramas by Christian Friedrich Hebbel with Lewis Carroll's *Alice in Wonderland* and Heinrich Hoffmann's *Struwwelpeter*.[45] What is it, then, that makes these children's books a better place for the interpretation of history than Hebbel's high drama, influenced by, among other things, Hegelian philosophy?[46] One of the reasons, I would like to suggest, is precisely the relationship between human and non-human animals as it appears in these books. For example, after Alice falls down a rabbit hole and in diminutive form swims around in the tears she has cried in her previous giant form, she meets a mouse and calls out to it. In the conversation that ensues, Alice cannot help but talk about cats, and begins to tell the mouse about the family cat Dinah:

> ["]I think you'd take a fancy to cats, if you could only see her. She is such a dear quiet thing", Alice went on, half to herself, as she swam lazily about in the pool, "and she sits purring so nicely by the fire, licking her paws and washing her face – and she is such a nice soft thing to nurse – and she's such a capital one for catching mice – oh, I beg your pardon!" cried Alice again, for this time the Mouse was really bristling all over, and she felt certain it must be really offended. "We won't [sic] talk about her any more, if you'd rather not".[47]

Both in the nineteenth century poet Eduard Mörike's "Mousetrap Rhyme" ("Mausfallen-Sprüchlein"), which Adorno considers in *Aesthetic Theory*,[48] and

---

[44] Adorno, *Minima Moralia*, trans. Jephcott, 161; *Minimal Moralia*, 172–173.

[45] *Struwwelpeter* appears in two other aphorisms, it is the title of #20 (see *Minima Moralia*, trans. Jephcott, 44; *Minima Moralia*, 44) and #56, called "Genealogical research", argues for the "deep affinity" between *Struwwelpeter* and Ibsen's plays (see *Minima Moralia*, trans. Jephcott, 98; *Minima Moralia*, 102–103).

[46] Adorno also refers to Hebbel's dramatic works in a similar manner in the section on natural beauty in *Aesthetic Theory*, 75; *Ästhetische Theorie*, 118.

[47] Lewis Carroll, *Alice in Wonderland*, in *The Annotated Alice: The Definitive Edition*, introduction and notes by Martin Gardner (New York and London: W. W. Norton & Company, 2000), 26.

[48] Adorno, *Aesthetic Theory*, 123–124; *Ästhetische Theorie*, 187–188. For a discussion, see Flodin, "Of Mice and Men", 149–154.

in *Alice in Wonderland*, it is the children who uphold the common view of mice—i.e., that they are vermin either to be tortured by mousetraps or killed by animals we have domesticated (there is a cat in "Mousetrap Rhyme" as well). At the same time, these artistic renderings implicitly point towards the possibility of relating to mice differently, through offering a change of perspective, which unsettles our habitual gaze on these animals.

Alice in Wonderland also unsettles the habitual way of regarding non-human animals as food. Such is the case when Alice meets the Mock Turtle:

> At last the Mock Turtle recovered his voice, and, with tears running down his cheeks, he went on again: –

> "You may not have lived much under the sea –" ("I haven't", said Alice) – "and perhaps you were never even introduced to a lobster –" (Alice began to say "I once tasted –" but checked herself hastily, and said "No, never") "– so you can have no idea what a delightful thing a Lobster-Quadrille is!"

> "No, indeed", said Alice. "What sort of a dance is it?"[49]

In *Struwwelpeter*, several stories deal with the human–animal relation. One, for example, tells of a hare that takes revenge on a huntsman by stealing his weapon and glasses while he is taking a nap under a tree: "And, while he slept like any top, / The little hare came hop, hop, hop, / Took gun and spectacles, and then / On her hind legs went off again".[50] The offended mouse and the dancing lobsters in *Alice in Wonderland*, along with the sly hare in *Struwwelpeter*, show our absurd relationship to non-human animals at the same time as they are able to indicate the possibility of another kind of relation in which they are seen neither as parasites nor food.

Hebbel is, however, given some kind of restitution in another of *Minima Moralia*'s aphorisms, "Toy shop". Adorno starts by referring to a "surprising entry" from Hebbel's diary, which comments on the disappearance of "'life's magic in later years'". Hebbel goes on to attribute this to the grown up's insight

---

[49] Carroll, *Alice in Wonderland*, 100.

[50] Heinrich Hoffmann, *The English Struwwelpeter, or, Pretty Stories and Funny Pictures* (London: George Routledge & Sons Ltd., 1909), 12. The German original was first published anonymously with the title *Lustige Geschichten und drollige Bilder* in 1845. It was only with the third edition that one of the characters, Struwwelpeter, was made into the title of the book, and the previous title became the subtitle. The first English translation appeared already in 1848; the translator remains unknown, a recent article suggest that it might have been Alexander Platt, see Jane Brown and Gregory Jones, "*The English Struwwelpeter* and the Birth of International Copyright", *The Library* 14, no. 4 (2013): 383–427, https://doi.org/10.1093/library/14.4.383.

that all human activity is a mere means to "earning a living", and thus no longer joyful.[51] This gives Adorno cause to emphasise once more the connection between children and animals, and thus to point towards its utopian potential:

> The unreality of games [*Spiele*] gives notice that reality is not yet real. Unconsciously they rehearse the right life. The relation of children to animals depends entirely on the fact that Utopia goes disguised in the creatures whom Marx even begrudged the surplus value they contribute as workers. In existing without any purpose recognizable to men, animals hold out, as if for expression, their own names, utterly impossible to exchange. This makes them so beloved of children, their contemplation so blissful. I am a rhinoceros, signifies the shape of the rhinoceros.[52]

The ability to perceive the rhinoceros's own singularity, without reducing it to any human determination, demands a certain distance. Utopia "goes disguised" in animals and for this reason we need a change of perspective to be able to see it. Art, play, or children's books provide this possibility. Through such a perspectival shift, it is possible to break out of those routinised ways of relating to non-human animals, thus glimpsing what they could be were they no longer oppressed by humans, as well as what we could be were we not to repress our resemblances to them.

As indicated in the beginning of this essay, however, the future for the human species, along with many others, is uncertain. In yet another aphorism in *Minima Moralia* Adorno reflects on the discovery of a dinosaur skeleton in Utah and the fascination these traces of pre-historic animals hold for us humans: "The desire for the presence of the most ancient is a hope that animal creation might survive the wrong that man has done it, if not man himself, and give rise to a better species, one that finally makes a success of life."[53] I suggest that we should read this together with Adorno's reflection on the animal gaze in *Aesthetic Theory*: "[T]here is nothing so expressive as the eyes of animals—especially apes—which seem objectively to mourn that they are not human."[54] If we read these two statements in tandem we may question the interpretation

---

[51] Adorno, *Minima Moralia*, trans. Jephcott, 241; *Minima Moralia*, 259.

[52] Adorno, *Minima Moralia*, trans. Jephcott, 242–243; *Minima Moralia*, 260–261. See also Adorno, *Aesthetic Theory*, 112; *Ästhetische Theorie*, 171–172, where he compares the non-exchangeability of the rhinoceros to that of the artwork. For more on this topic, see my essay "In the Name of the Rhinoceros: Expression beyond Human Intention", in *Adorno's Rhinoceros: Art, Nature and Critique*, ed. Antonia Hofstätter and Daniel Steuer (London: Bloomsbury Academic, forthcoming).

[53] Adorno, *Minima Moralia*, trans. Jephcott, 123; *Minima Moralia*, 130.

[54] Adorno, *Aesthetic Theory*, 113; *Ästhetische Theorie*, 172.

of the passage from *Aesthetic Theory*, which might first come to mind, namely: animals mourn that they are not human because they would like to *become like us*—"I wanna be like you", as King Louie sings in Disney's 1967 film *The Jungle Book*. We could then reach the more sensible conclusion that it is in fact we humans who mourn, or *should* be mourning, since we are not yet human, we are *not human enough*.[55]

What Adorno is in fact implying with his wording in *Aesthetic Theory* is the following: animals seem to mourn that they are not human, because we humans always impress upon them the difference, turning this difference into something that is to their disadvantage. And so long as we continue doing this we are not living up to our potential to be human and humane. In a discussion with Horkheimer in 1956 Adorno says: "Philosophy exists in order to redeem what you see in the look of an animal."[56] This is humanity at its best, according to Adorno: *striving to be better human beings when reflected through the gaze of other animals.* Trying to be "a good animal", as he writes in *Negative Dialectics*.[57] Without the presence of other animals this would be impossible. Adorno's utopian animals incorporate the wish for a transformation of the species known as *homo sapiens*, in order that we might one day truly live up to our name.

---

[55] See also Camilla Flodin, "Afterword", in Hendrik Zeitler, *The Chosen Ones* (Stockholm: Journal, 2016).

[56] Theodor W. Adorno and Max Horkheimer, *Towards a New Manifesto*, trans. Rodney Livingstone (London and New York: Verso, 2011), 71. The original discussion was published under the title "Diskussion über Theorie und Praxis", in Max Horkheimer, *Gesammelte Schriften* vol. 19, ed. Gunzelin Schmid Noerr (Frankfurt am Main: Fischer, 1996), 32–72.

[57] Theodor W. Adorno, *Negative Dialectics*, trans. E. B. Ashton (London: Routledge, 1990), 299; *Negative Dialektik*, in *Gesammelte Schriften* vol. 6 (Frankfurt am Main: Suhrkamp, 2003), 294.

On Reification
– Some Thoughts on Benjamin, Adorno, and Honneth

GÉRARD RAULET

From his early contacts with phenomenology, in the first phase of his philosophy, Adorno kept the idea of a necessity to return to things.[1] In his later works, this injunction meets the question of reification. As a matter of fact, being under the object's mastery (*Verfallenheit ans Objekt*) is by no means a theoretical posture, nor is it a decision: it is actually the consequence of reification. As with philosophy, which in the context of a tendency towards "total administration" must acknowledge the importance of the system,[2] the subject, which is supposed to be constitutive, must accept the primacy of the object in order to oppose the general tendency towards reification. Thus only what can no more be thought becomes thinkable again. If identity is determined by reification, the object is nothing else than what the subject is unable to reflect anymore. The "second reflection" presupposes a recognition of the object's primacy. Or, to put it in Adorno's famous words, only the repeated experience of non-freedom, which brings the primacy of the object to its consciousness, can put the subject back on its own tracks. Adorno uses the same structure again in his *Aesthetic theory*, in stronger words but with comparable meaning: "Only as things can artworks become the antithesis of reified non-being".[3]

Adorno, when doing this, uses one of the fundamental patterns of Benjamin's thought. At the same time, his concern is to avoid what is uncontrollable about it, in terms of its references as well as its political strategy. The present text has no other ambition than to acknowledge this critical debt, but also to assess how far Adorno's adaptation of Benjamin's intellectual impulses might have neglected some of its essential aspects, the absence of which become painfully obvious in post-Adornian Critical theory.

Negative Dialectics constitutes a critical assessment of the judgement of identity, which claims the formal reduction of particularity and individuality to be a free act of the subject, while it is rather its logical submission to the law

---

[1] Cf. Raulet, "Verfallenheit ans Objekt: Zur Auseinandersetzung über eine Grundfigur dialektischen Denkens bei Adorno, Benjamin, Bloch und Kracauer", in Dorothee Kimmich (ed.), *Denken durch die Dinge: Siegfried Kracauer im ästhetisch-philosophischen Diskurs der 20er Jahre* (Munich: Fink, 2009), 119–134.

[2] Adorno, *Negative Dialektik* (Frankfurt am Main: Suhrkamp, 1966), 29.

[3] "Nur als Dinge werden die Kunstwerke zur Antithesis des dinghaften Unwesens". Adorno, *Ästhetische Theorie, Gesammelte Schriften* [GS] Vol. 7 (Frankfurt am Main: Suhrkamp, 1970), 250.

of exchange. In order to do justice to the particular, it seems that one should "simply" oppose, to the idea of all things being interchangeable, the pattern of the mimetic relationship. But "things" are far from being that simple. How far should Reason's self-criticism go in order for it to become "nature made intelligible through its own alienation"?[4] How far does trying to compensate the demands of dominating rationality require us to *play the object's game*? Can "mimetic power", in its phylo- and ontogenetic rooting, be the way to overcome the reification that comes as a result of the very logic which was, right from the start, embedded *in the concept itself*—without needing to resort to the capitalistic mode of relations at work in knowledge?

I

Adorno suggests, in one of his first essays, "The Idea of Natural History", published in 1932, that we should follow the path of post-Husserlian phenomenology, more specifically that of Max Scheler, who strived to "overcome the subjectivist standpoint of philosophy"[5], and that we should confront once again the ontological problem that Kant, in his *Critique of Pure Reason*, had put aside under the label of the "thing-in-itself".

Adorno's idea here can be traced back to what Benjamin had written as early as 1917 in his "Program of the Coming Philosophy", where he challenged the dualism of subject and object, hoping to "uncover the original and authentic sphere of knowledge".[6] He wrote: "It is the duty of the coming theory of knowledge to find, for knowledge, a neutral sphere, entirely detached from the concepts of subject and object".[7] This sphere, outside and beyond human subjectivity, where the foundation of all knowledge would lie, is still at the time the "divine language" he mentions in his essay on language published in 1916. But we must keep in mind that, in the texts of that period, the word "divine" does not refer to anything strictly religious, but to a metaphysical dimension beyond the dualism of subject and object that structures our concept of knowledge. According to Benjamin, the problem with Kant's critique of knowledge is that it is not emancipated from the dualism of subject and object, the upshot of which is that transcendentalism ends up confirming a conception of reality in

---

[4] Max Horkheimer and Theodor W. Adorno, *Dialektik der Aufklärung* (Frankfurt am Main: Fischer, 1988), 45.

[5] Adorno, "Die Idee der Naturgeschichte", GS 1, 346.

[6] "die ureigne Sphäre der Erkenntnis auszumitteln". "Über das Programm der kommenden Philosophie", Benjamin, Gesammelte Schriften [GS] II, (Frankfurt: Suhrkamp, 1985) 163.

[7] Ibid.

the terms of the physical sciences.[8] Against the latter conception, Benjamin urges the crossing of limits experienced in some pathological states, or the mimetic behaviour of primitive populations.[9]

This idea agrees with that of a "magic of language", which can be found in the essay on language from 1916.[10] This magic lies in the fact that through the Name, a secret pact is sealed between words and things, which excludes the subject. Explicitly in reference to that essay, in 1933, Benjamin writes two sketches on the theory of resemblance and mimetic power.[11] The idea of a "mimetic power" aims at granting an epistemological status to what, back in 1916, was mere "metaphysical" speculation.[12]

The concept of mimesis insists that we must give precedence to the materiality of the encounter before projecting on it the categories of subjectivity. To experience the world "in immediate contact with the materiality of things": such is the foundation of Benjamin's historic materialism, as Georges Didi-Huberman elegantly put it.[13] It is also the argument of Adorno's text, "The Actuality of Philosophy" (1931): the "program of all truly materialistic knowledge", Adorno says, consists in keeping in check any assumption of a hypostatic "meaning" of objects (especially religious).[14] The real source of the so-called "problem of the thing-in-itself" is actually the "historical figures of commodity and trade value", not something which would lie behind reality.[15]

Although there is no explicit reference to Benjamin, to whom Adorno was very close in his first essays, this passage from "The Actuality of Philosophy" can certainly warn us against any possible metaphysical misreading, especially the essay on language. For the name, in Benjamin's essay, is the medium of this

---

[8] An "inferior concept of experience" which has had "a restrictive influence on Kant's thought" (GS II.1, 159). See also later the fragment "Erkenntnis und Erfahrung".

[9] "We know that certain primitive populations who still belong to the so called "pre-animist" stage identify themselves with plants and sacred animals whose name they take; we know that certain mentally ill persons identify themselves partly with objects which they perceive and that these objects cease to be for them mere objects, realities lying in front of them; we know that certain sick persons do not link the sensations of their body with themselves but with others, and that certain mediums, at least according to them, are able to perceive the sensations of other people as if they were their own perceptions". (Benjamin, "Über das Programm der kommenden Philosophie" GS II.1, 162)

[10] "Über Sprache überhaupt und über die Sprache des Menschen", GS, II.1, 143.

[11] "Lehre vom Ähnlichen" (1933) and "Über das mimetische Verfahren" (1934), GS II.1, 204–210 and 210–213.

[12] In a letter he sent in 1936 to Werner Kraft, Benjamin claims that his essay on the theory of language "does not imply at all some 'metaphysics' of language". *Briefe* (Frankfurt am Main: Suhrkamp, 1978), Vol. 2, 705; GS II.3, 954.

[13] Georges Didi-Huberman, *Devant le temps* (Paris: Minuit, 2000), 107.

[14] Adorno, "Die Aktualität der Philosophie", GS I, 336.

[15] Ibid, 337.

kind of experience. It is in fact anything but an arbitrary sign; it does not belong to the category of signification, but coincides absolutely with what it designates. The child who mimics a mill or a train *is* the mill or the train.[16] Mimetic power is indeed neither *re*presentation nor is it *re*creation, it is a presentation, or even an identification. Fixed in the name, this identification constitutes a form of nominalism we can recognize as a modality of materialism. It can be found under this form in Marx's *The Holy Family* and in the preliminary reflections to *Dialectic of Enlightenment*.[17]

In the secondary literature on Benjamin, the link between the allegory and the theory of names has not been taken seriously enough, and the latter has been too hastily reinscribed in the scheme of a relationship to transcendence. Yet what the allegory strives to express, like human language, is the *break* between the dimension of divine meaning and the profane world. The end of the "writing of things" is what determines the problem of every language and, in particular, the problem of allegory. It is impossible to reconstitute that Book of Nature in which Renaissance men still read the mark of the divine. This radical mutation opens "the abyss between being and signification" by which Benjamin characterises the dialectical nature of modern (baroque) allegory[18] and which all classical and romantic conceptions aim at overcoming when they denounce allegory as a "conventional relationship between a signifying image and its signification", or even as a "playful technique of imaged figuration".[19]

On the one hand, anything profane is abandoned to arbitrary interpretation, and the relationship between the thing and the concept becomes pure convention. Indeed, for the creator the allegory's perspective, "the thing becomes something else, […] it becomes for him the key to the realm of hidden knowledge". Yet at the same time, that is precisely "what makes an allegory become writing".[20] And that is also how the allegory becomes "expression". The dialectical treatment that Benjamin imposes upon the allegory does not consist in submitting it to a "mediation" that would reinscribe it in the narrative of a *praxis* of progress throughout history. When we are confronted with such an

---

[16] The link between the theory of language and *Childhood in Berlin* is confirmed by a letter to Scholem in February 1933: "I just want to stress that it [the theory of language] has been elaborated on the occasion of sketches for the first piece of *Childhood in Berlin*" (*Briefe*, Vol. 2, 563).

[17] See Raulet, "Aufzeichnungen und Entwürfe", in Gunnar Hindrichs (ed.), *Klassiker auslegen: Dialektik der Aufklärung* (Berlin: De Gruyter, 2017), 97–113.

[18] *Ursprung des deutschen Trauerspiels*, GS I.1, 342.

[19] Ibid, 339.

[20] Ibid, 359.

uncanny (or exciting) writing (*erregende Schrift*),[21] the process of interpretation stops, mediation comes to a standstill, as if facing Medusa's *facies hippocratica*, or when facing the name itself. There is no guarantee that this halt will be the occasion of a *kairos*. The paradox about the vision of history we can find throughout the book on the *Trauerspiel* is that Benjamin thinks neither in messianic nor in apocalyptic terms. The vanishing point here is rather the architectural stratagem of the *ponderación misteriosa* that appears at the end as the only possible way out.[22]

Something similar happens in Adorno's essay on "The Idea of a Natural History", where Lukács' conception of "second nature" is explicitly opposed to Benjamin's approach, with Adorno siding with the latter. Lukács opposes a meaningful to a meaningless world, an immediate, unalienated world to the world of trade and commodity. That way, the problem of a natural history presents itself as an obstacle for the philosophy of history. Confronted with what he calls "an ossuary of dead interiorities", he is less concerned with getting to know it than with inscribing it in an eschatological perspective, and overcoming it.[23] Adorno describes this philosophy of history as "theological", and prefers Benjamin's *Origin of German Tragic Drama* and the allegorical poets' "saturnian gaze", in which the petrified face of nature and history are not mutually exclusive: "Every time, what is history presents itself also as nature".[24] What is at stake here is to go back to a conception of "second nature" that would be both monistic and dialectical, that is to say, at the same time, an act of petrification and of writing, both convention and expression. In his essay, Adorno lays the basis of his own conception of aesthetic expression that will be later developed in his *Aesthetic Theory*—an explicit reference to Benjamin's allegory.[25]

II

Despite doubt and criticism, Adorno partially includes the idea of mimetic strategy in his own thought. In fact, in the process of reification, where the two poles of subject and object merge, one pole actually takes precedence over the other: the subject thinks it is imposing its law on nature, when in reality what is happening is that it suppresses itself. To counter this dialectic, *Negative*

---

[21] Ibid, 352.

[22] See Gilles Moutot, *Essai sur Adorno* (Paris: Payot, 2010), 342–345.

[23] Adorno, "Die Idee der Naturgeschichte", 357.

[24] Ibid, 361.

[25] Ibid, 358.

Dialectics formulates two apparently contradictory demands: the primacy of the object and the injunction to "break with the lie of a constituting subjectivity by using the power of the subject".[26]

The way Adorno appropriates the concept of mimesis is illustrated by the review he publishes in 1938 on Caillois' essay *The Praying Mantis*.[27] According to Adorno's interpretation, Caillois' thesis has a "progressive aspect" in so far as it refuses to explain all psychological behaviours exclusively by the autonomous individual. Caillois' positive re-evaluation of nature, as opposed to culture and society, is interesting also from the "materialistic" point of view that, Adorno claims, "could still be dragged out of Caillois' mythologising perspective".[28] Adorno even pays careful attention to the psychophysical conception attaching psychological tendencies "not to the autonomous individual's conscious life, but to an accumulation of somatic moments" which he believes is the positive consequence of the materialistic approach.

The conclusion of this book review is crucial: it suggests that there is a form of kinship between Caillois' conception of mimesis and what Adorno later calls "mimesis of what is dead" (*Mimesis ans Tote*). Incidentally, the expression itself is more than likely to have been taken from Benjamin, its first use being, I believe, the following: "Hugo ignores the power of petrifying things which—if a biological concept is suitable—manifests itself as a sort of mimesis of death in Baudelaire's poetry".[29]

The "mimesis of what is dead" presents itself as the "materialistic" withdrawal of a philosophy that has lost all hope of thinking outside of reification. The same thing occurs with the Name—as in Benjamin's theory. In Horkheimer and Adorno's *Dialectic of Enlightenment* the proper noun prevents any judgement of identity that would operate through a copula—in the same way that mimesis deters any temptation of equating non-equivalent things. The preparatory discussions that led to the *Dialectic of Enlightenment* provide long developments on this particular question. Both Adorno and Benjamin play immediacy against mediation and support the idea of a "primacy of the object" which will be asserted in *Negative Dialectics*. The point is to thwart the logic of exchange. Without giving in to a naive form of realism, Horkheimer and

---

[26] "mit der Kraft des Subjekts den Trug konstitutiver Subjektivität zu durchbrechen" (*Negative Dialektik*, 10).

[27] Roger Caillois, *La Mante religieuse: Recherche sur la nature et la signification du mythe* (Paris: La Maison des Amis du Livre, 1937).

[28] Adorno, review of Roger Caillois, *La Mante religieuse, Zeitschrift für Sozialforschung*, 7, Vol. 3 (1938): 411.

[29] "Hugo ist das Erstarrungsvermögen fremd, das – wenn ein biologischer Begriff statthaft ist – als eine Art Mimesis des Todes sich hundertfach in Baudelaires Dichtung kundtut" (*Das Paris des Second Empire bei Baudelaire*, "Die Moderne", GS I, 587).

Adorno recognise more or less implicitly that nature has a substantial existence, for which its oppression is indeed a catastrophe: in other words, the repetition of a blind natural violence is the consequence of the rational project of a total domination of nature. The following passage oozes a feeling not quite of nostalgia, but rather of regret that "uncontrolled mimesis" was never fully accepted:

> In its magic age civilization has first substituted the organic adaptation to what is different and the properly mimetic behaviour for an organized use of the mimesis before it replaced it in the end, in its historical age, with rational practice, with the work. Uncontrolled mimesis has been banished.[30]

And yet it is precisely by repressing mimesis, by systematically subduing it to the judgement of identity, to the translation through reflection as well as to the operation of the copula, that rationality transforms itself into a "mimesis of what is dead" and that it produces forms of behaviour that both Adorno and Horkheimer (the latter in his "Theory of the Criminal"[31]) identify as the result of a death drive, with references to Freud and Caillois.

In their October 1939 discussions on language and knowledge, especially regarding "naming as an original function of language" (where the similarities with Benjamin are striking), Adorno conceives of nominalism as an alternative to subsumption. In his words: what can it mean to "talk of ontology and of a metaphysical concept of being, if being is nothing but the function of identity? Why can we attribute a substantiality to the concept of being?"[32] For Horkheimer and Adorno, opting for materialism is a consequence of the fact that, in Marx's own terms, "the representation of a thing is not the thing itself".[33] It is in this sense that Marx, in *The Holy Family*, refers to nominalism as "the first expression of materialism".[34]

In the end, Adorno agrees with Caillois not only on the diagnosis, but also on a strategy—in fact the only possible one. Except that Adorno endeavours to answer the French intellectual establishment's unfulfilled promises. When

---

[30] Adorno and Horkheimer, *Dialektik der Aufklärung*, 213.

[31] Max Horkheimer, "Theorie des Verbrechers", *Gesammelte Schriften* (Frankfurt am Main: Fischer, 1985). Vol. 12, 266–277.

[32] "Diskussionen über Sprache und Erkenntnis", 18 Oct. 1939, Horkheimer, *Gesammelte Schriften*, Vol. 12, 508.

[33] Karl Marx, *Die deutsche Ideologie*, in Karl Marx and Friedrich Engels, *Werke* (Berlin, Dietz Verlag 1959), Vol. 3, 416.

[34] Marx, *Die Deutsche Ideologie*, 416.

Kojève speaks of the end of history, and while in Bataille's thought animality and the homogenous society both express the fact that political practice has proven incapable of changing the world, already by the end of the Thirties, the authors of *Dialectic of Enlightenment* use the recurring theme of animality as the central theme of a "dialectical anthropology",[35] and Adorno is already preparing conceptual weapons for a resistance to homogenous society, from the very heart of homogeneity itself.

This means handling the myth dialectically, not rejecting it. In Raymond Aron's book review of *Myth and Man* in the *Zeitschrift für Sozialforschung*,[36] it is not so much the kinship with Freud than the risk of being assimilated to Jung's theory that is seen as a problem: "The links between Caillois' theory and Freud's theory of the death drive, but also with Jung's fashionable anthropology of a collective unconscious are obvious".[37] In saying this, Adorno rejects the possibility, suggested by Caillois, of a hobnobbing with the Freudian conception of the death drive. According to Caillois, animal mimetism illustrates "the sometimes staggering human desire to return to original insensibility".[38] If the reasons for Adorno's refusal are clear on a first level, it is nonetheless necessary to highlight the fact that it is there, precisely, that the dialectics of civilisation are set in motion, but that Adorno does not seem ready to accept it. Be this as it may, in their reflections on mimesis, Benjamin, in whose footsteps Adorno and Horkheimer follow, "rediscover" in tragic circumstances what Freud had already perfectly analysed on a fundamental level. Marcuse will later take over this line of thinking in *Eros and Civilisation*, pushing to its utmost limits his reflection on a civilisation that would reconcile the life and death drives, the principle of pleasure and the tendency of every organism to regress towards a prior state, the instinct towards indifferentiation and the desire for the non-organic.

Mimesis becomes the key to a transformation of the relationship to reality. Adorno pushes his reflection on Benjamin's concepts quite far indeed, but he keeps the idea of a need to apply dialectics: mimesis itself must be transformed if it is to become the key to a transformed experience of reality. Of course, mimesis is still a localised practice (*ortsgebundene Praktik*[39]), a "specific substitution".[40] And indeed it is true that the sorcerer, unlike the civilised man, does not consider

---

[35] See Raulet, "Aufzeichnungen und Entwürfe", 101–106.
[36] *Zeitschrift für Sozialforschung* 7 (1938): 414.
[37] Ibid, 411.
[38] Caillois, *Le mythe et l'homme* (Paris: Gallimard, 1938), 73.
[39] *Dialektik der Aufklärung*, 17.
[40] Ibid, 16.

the entire cosmos as his own private hunting ground. Nevertheless, substitution necessarily implies some kind of equivalence, and in the same way, we could go as far as to say that the fatal necessity, the implacable repetition of destiny that generalises this substitution, also implies the idea of a generalised equivalence.[41] According to Adorno, after we put a stop to the logic of unreflexive equivalence, we must introduce dialectics in the mimetic moment.

It is not certain that art, which is often hastily summoned at this point, could alone be the answer, nor that *Aesthetic Theory* could be, as we often read, the solution to *Negative Dialectics*. The utopia of art is rather a particular form of mimesis. But it does provide in itself some kind of model of what could be a critical mimesis. According to *Dialectic of Enlightenment*, "only authentic works of art have managed to avoid a mere imitation of what already is".[42] As Adorno puts it in *Aesthetic Theory*, what art offers us is an "unreconciled reconciliation".[43] And the fact that it carries out this reconciliation only in an unreal mode, "at the price of real reconciliation",[44] defines very precisely its paradoxical mission: "to bear witness of something that is not reconciled while tending towards reconciliation".[45] And that is only possible, Adorno adds, "from the starting point of a non-discursive language", that is to say through mimesis.

Adorno, in his *Aesthetic Theory*, defines "mimetic behaviour" as an action that "does not imitate something but makes itself similar to it",[46] but the opposition we might infer from this refusal of immediacy becomes impossible when we read Adorno's definition of "mimetic behaviour" until the end: "Mimetic behaviour is neither immediate nor repressed mimesis; it is the process mimesis triggers and in which it maintains itself however transformed".[47] As far as Benjamin is concerned, he refuses to distinguish a "real" and a "false" kind of mimesis. What is provoking about his position is precisely that mimesis for him is definitely both immediate and reified, that it belongs to the realm of the commodity and yet at the same time expresses a primitive, even authentic relationship to the world of things—at least in the sense that it is useless to pretend to be leaning on any exterior or superior power. The accusation of substantialism, from out of which we might be tempted to construct an opposition

---

[41] See ibid, 18 and 23.

[42] Ibid, 24.

[43] Adorno, *Ästhetische Theorie*, GA 7, 202.

[44] Ibid. 84.

[45] "Paradox hat sie das Unversöhnte zu bezeugen und gleichwohl tendenziell zu versöhnen" (ibid., 251).

[46] Ibid, 169.

[47] "ästhetisches Verhalten aber ist weder Mimesis unmittelbar noch die verdrängte sondern der Prozeß, den sie entbindet und in dem sie modifiziert sich erhält" (ibid, 489).

between Adorno and Benjamin, is actually misguided. Benjamin's "mimetic power" no more implies a return to an original, unscathed identity than reference to a transcendence does.

Adorno's doubts concerning the mimetic strategy were justified from a *political* point of view. Caillois himself did not really trust the strategy to "count on mimetism" in order to fight fascism. But Adorno felt the need to reassert more strongly than ever the doubts already expressed while reading Benjamin's *One Way Street*, about the risk of "abandoning oneself to the object until the I is literally extinct".[48] On a *philosophical* level, the opposition between Benjamin and Adorno stems from two radically different ontological conceptions. For Benjamin, the experience of reification is also a form of revelation of the world's essence—both human and cosmic, since precisely the human world goes beyond its own limits to eventually suppress itself into the cosmic world. For Adorno, on the contrary, the experience of reification is a historical experience, and will remain so. The core of their disagreement is nothing other than the ground for the relationship between subject and object. And this is where the crucial problem lies. Benjamin and Adorno offer two different answers to the question of transcendental affinity. Adorno stays true to the main argument of the Critical theory of 1937: the mystery of transcendental affinity cannot be explained unless we take into account the specific act of its completion, at one precise moment in time. (Simply put, this relationship is different for the animistic man of primitive times and in a technological, or even immaterial, age). In such a perspective, the question is to know whether or not the "mimetic moment" at work in the elective affinity between the knowing subject and the known object is authentic.[49] In other words, whether reification is "only" an accident in the subject's relationship to the world of things, a historical aberration of which capitalism could without doubt be held accountable, or if we must question the *epistemological* model asserting that the subject is always the one who sets the tone. Although Critical theory was to be profoundly revised in *Dialectic of Enlightenment* under the influence of Benjamin's work, these two positions have never been clearly distinguished and articulated.

Moreover, it is at this precise point that the question of the body steps in, that is, the question of the subject's materiality. When Adorno accuses Benjamin of insufficient dialectical mediation, he has the immediacy of bodily

---

[48] Adorno, "Benjamins Einbahnstraße", *Über Walter Benjamin* (Frankfurt am Main: Suhrkamp, 1968), 55.
[49] Adorno, *Negative Dialektik*, p. 53.

and psychic presence specifically in mind.[50] He is perfectly right, since Benjamin tends indeed to displace the enigma of transcendental affinity towards the psychophysical order of one's own body (the *Leib*).

Along with the paradigm of language,[51] one's own body is recognised, in Benjamin's conception, as a source of that superior, most authentic way of knowing, which was at stake in Benjamin's first texts on the theory of knowledge. "Perception and the body", a fragment written in 1918, was used as a starting point for exploring the paradox that our bodily existence is an immersion "in a world of perception that is in one of the most elevated layers of language", and yet is "in a blind, generally powerless fashion, like a body belonging to nature".[52] This materiality finds its theoretical expression in an anthropological rephrasing, not only of the theory of knowledge, but also of the ontology that constitutes its basis, in one way or another. Thus Benjamin's materialism does not come down to the name—which is always a proper noun: it is located in one's own body, and is based upon the "KNOWLEDGE that the first material on which the mimetic power is at work is the human body itself".[53] It is therefore not reason (let alone understanding) but one's own body that is actually the organ of mimesis.

III

Contemporary representatives of Critical theory have chosen to move away from these fundamental anthropological dimensions: Honneth for example, in his cartography of Critical theory, describes them as "marginal" and even fruitless.[54] He follows mainly Anglo-Saxon authors (especially Mead) who ignore this kind of speculation. When they read one of the fathers of French sociology, Gabriel Tarde, whose theory acknowledges the very phenomenon Benjamin wrote about, using the same name of mimetic power, they simply

---

[50] Adorno to Benjamin, 6.9.1936, in Adorno and Benjamin, *Briefwechsel 1928–1940* (Frankfurt am Main, Suhrkamp, 1994), 193. On this debate see Frank Müller, "Undialektisch, vermittlungslos und romantisch? Adornos Kritik am anthropologischen Materialismus Walter Benjamins", in Berdet and Ebke (eds.), *Anthropologischer Materialismus und Materialismus der Begegnung* (Berlin: Xenomoi, 2014), 301–325.

[51] And as a complement to it, as confirmed by the "anthropological scheme" which Benjamin sketched in 1918 (see GS VI, 64). Cf. Dennis Johannßen, "Leibhafte Politik: Zum psychophysischen Problem im Zusammenhang des anthropologischen Materialismus", in Berdet and Ebke, *Antropologischer Materialismus und Materialismus der Begegnung*, 151.

[52] "Wahrnehmung und Leib", GS VI, 67.

[53] The capitals stem from the original: "ERKENNTNIS, daß die erste Materie, an der sich das mimetische Vermögen versucht, der menschliche Körper ist." ("Zur Ästhetik", GS VI, 127, Fragment 98)

[54] Axel Honneth, "Kritische Theorie: Vom Zentrum zur Peripherie einer Denktradition", in *Die zerrissene Welt des Sozialen* (Frankfurt an Main; Suhrkamp, 1999), 93–113.

exclude his theory of suggestion. Even though this theory constitutes the centre of Gabriel Tarde's sociology, for Mead it is obvious that "social conscience [...] is the presupposition of imitation",[55] rather than the opposite. Mead embodies a sociological school of thought that refuses, as a matter of principle, any confrontation with the fundamental questions of anthropology.

Despite—or could it be precisely because of—being both descriptive and normative, the refined distinctions Honneth intends to use to rephrase the problem of reification in the terms of the theory of recognition leave aside this important aspect of anthropo-sociological thought. Honneth distinguishes for example "forms of knowledge open to recognition" (*anerkennungssensitiven Formen des Erkennens*) and "forms of knowledge in which every trace of their origin in an antecedent act of recognition has been lost" (forgetfulness of recognition, *Anerkennungsvergessenheit*).[56] These distinctions omit entirely the question of mimesis; surprising given the role they played in Adorno's thought. But this would not be of much consequence, were it not for the essay's alleged subject, namely reification.

In Honneth's writings, reification and recognition constitute two radically opposed modes of the subject-object relation. For this reason the possibility (suggested by Benjamin and Adorno) of a perspective on things that would proceed *through things* remains entirely unexplored, even in its Adornian form. Whenever Honneth refers to Adorno, he interprets his thought through his own concept of recognition: Adorno is for him a thinker of the "oblivion of a former recognition". This could be coherent with Benjamin's phylo- and ontogenetic conception, but it remains on the level of a very moderate type of psychoanalysis, where the word "former" is to be interpreted in terms of the sense of secondary processes of the consolidation of personality:

> Adorno emphasized more than any other writer the fact that the appropriateness and quality of our conceptual thought is dependent upon the degree to which we are capable of remaining conscious of the original connection of our thought to an object of desire—a beloved person or thing. He even regarded the memory of this antecedent act of recognition as providing a kind of guarantee that a given act of cognition has not constructed its object but has grasped it in all its concrete particularity.[57]

---

[55] George Herbert Mead, "Social Psychology as Counterpart to Physiological Psychology", *Psychological Bulletin* 6, vol 12, (1909): 405.
[56] Axel Honneth, *Reification: A New Look at an Old Idea*, The Berkeley Tanner Lectures (Oxford & New York: Oxford University Press, 2008), 56.
[57] Ibid, 57.

From this follows a reductive conception of praxis, which still depends on that same paradigm of consciousness Honneth criticises in Habermas. Either this practice is conscious of its own conditions of appearance, or it gives in to the instrumental way of acting, that is to say, to a process in which the "goal becomes independent of the context in which it originated".[58] This "either... or..." regularly appears in Honneth's text:

> It is clear that we are dealing here either with institutionalized practices, which cause contemplation and observation to become independent of their roots in recognition, or with socially effective thought schemata, which compel a denial of antecedent recognition. [59]

We could find in Ernst Bloch's idea of an "objective-real" possibility a concept close to Benjamin's. Bloch's dialectical conception of possibility, which does not reduce dialectics to the paradigm of consciousness, presupposes in fact a hermeneutics of natural potentialities as well as of the objective configurations in which these potentialities become reified. The absence of such a hermeneutics matches exactly what Honneth describes as a mechanism of denial and defence (*Abwehr*). Honneth proves he is perfectly conscious of the problem when he admits, at this stage in the essay, that one issue has indeed been "left on the sidelines until now": the question of whether we can draw any conclusions from our previous arguments for the primacy of recognition about humans' relation to their natural surroundings and themselves".[60] To which he adds:

> It is solely with relation to other persons that Tomasello, Hobson, and Cavell speak of the primacy of identification or acknowledgement—not at all in relation to nonhuman sentient beings, plants, or even things. Yet the concept of reification that I have attempted to resuscitate here in connection with the work of Lukács demands that we account for the possibility of a reifying perception not only of our social world, but also of our physical world.[61]

Adorno uses a very different strategy to mark his difference with Lukács, in his 1931 inaugural lecture in Frankfurt, "The Actuality of Philosophy", which almost gives us the impression that Honneth is doing his best to undo what Adorno had done:

[58] Ibid, 59.
[59] Ibid, 60.
[60] Ibid, 60.
[61] Ibid, 60f.

> Given that it would be possible to collect elements of a social analysis in such
> a way that their connection would generate a figure in which every single
> aspect would be abolished; a figure which, in fact, does not present itself as
> organic, but must be produced first: the commodity form. Of course, the
> problem of the thing-in-itself would not be solved at all; neither would it be
> solved if we exposed the social conditions that have caused the problem of the
> thing-in-itself, as Lukács still believed.[62]

What Honneth calls for next matches the direction Bloch took in moving beyond Lukács: adopting from the start an attitude towards nature that involves "interactive, recognitional dealings with animals, plants, and even things".[63] But rather than referring to Bloch, Honneth mentions Dewey and Heidegger to prove that the instrumental treatment of nature "violate[s] a necessary precondition of our social practices".[64] Significantly, he reminds us that Adorno too had appropriated the idea of "a primordial act of imitation".[65] But he makes almost no use of this passing reminder, because it is there only to support the (indubitably crucial) psychoanalytical idea that, in a child, the "act of imitating a concrete second person, which draws upon libidinal energies, becomes transmitted, so to speak, onto the object".[66] That way, the inter-subjective paradigm of the philosophy of consciousness does keep its prevalence after all. "Self-reification" is finally attributed to the subject, and must be brought back to what has been earlier described as the "oblivion of recognition".

It is only too obvious that Honneth is not one to engage in "speculations about interactive dealings with nature"—as he himself says.[67] When he speaks of a "potential reification of nature", he immediately adds that such a reification consists in the fact that the subject "[fails] to be attentive in the course of [its] cognition of objects to all the additional aspects of meaning accorded to them by other persons".[68] This merely cognitive or "recognitional" conception does not take anything away from the dominating logic of social practice, even where it leads us to cast a purely objectifying gaze towards nature. Honneth defends the philosophical oppositions of consciousness and identity with

---

[62] Adorno, "Die Aktualität der Philosophie", GS 1, 337.

[63] Axel Honneth, *Reification: A New Look at an Old Idea*, 62.

[64] Ibid, 61

[65] Ibid, 62.

[66] Ibid, 62.

[67] Ibid, 63.

[68] Ibid.

vigour: subject *versus* object, nature *versus* culture etc. His fifth chapter starts with a by-the-book declaration of faith:

> In the preceding sections, I have drawn on recognitional-theoretical considerations to reformulate two aspects of what Lukács termed reification in his classic essay. I have made clear that we can use the term reification in a direct sense only when referring to our relations to other persons, whereas our relation to nature can be called reified only in an indirect or derivative sense of the term. [69]

As readers, we might have the impression that Honneth is trying our patience when he replays once more his demonstration in his sixth chapter, claiming to have until then "left out the central piece of Lukács' analysis".[70] But he does so with a very precise intention: to claim that the "assertion that the universalisation of commodity exchange brought about by capitalism is the sole cause for these phenomena of reification" and that "subjects are compelled to conduct their social interactions primarily in the form of commodity exchange"[71] is an outdated idea. Even though it would be difficult "to raise one single, central objection" to Lukács' "compact thesis", it seems very clear to Honneth that, in the capitalist world, "the persons with whom we interact in the process of economic exchange are normally present to us, at least legally, as recognized persons"[72]—normally at least.

Against the myth of the dominating form of commodity exchange, Honneth presents the edifying fairytale of a well-meaning capitalism, anxious to peacefully set up fair contracts between equal social partners. Yet his assertions that "the legal status of the participants to an economic exchange protects them from the consequences that would result if each of them took up a merely reifying stance toward the other" and that "the other person has some minimal legal protection under the terms of the contract, which in turn guarantees him or her a minimal degree of respect"[73] are immediately contradicted by the objective observation that the labour contract increasingly tends towards the emptiness of its meaning.[74]

---

[69] Ibid.

[70] Ibid, 75.

[71] Ibid.

[72] Ibid.

[73] Ibid, 80.

[74] "The spectrum of current social developments that reflect such tendencies run from the increasing hollowing-out of the legal substance of labor contracts [...]" (ibid, 80).

The manipulation Honneth's theory undertakes is self-evident. He uses a pseudo-critique of Lukács, not to criticise the assimilation of reification to alienation, as it should, but to claim that reification must be put into perspective, or even to deny its very existence. What is at stake finally becomes clear: to cast doubt on the "assertion stating that all of society has been 'capitalized' through and through" and on the "notion of a totalization of economically based reification".[75] This means nothing less than breaking away from the basic ideas of original Critical Theory.

Adorno's key concept (and indeed, Benjamin's too) is that of the *commodity-form* rather than of economic exchange, which is only one social practice among others. One of the problems in today's critical theory is that it does not acknowledge this essential difference in re-thinking the analysis of social phenomena and the relationship to practice within a society which undeniably presents immaterial forms of reification, but which remains nevertheless subject to reification. To let ourselves be distracted by these immaterial forms quite obviously indicates a lack of theoretical coherence.

Honneth seems to consider recognition as prior to the economical sphere. He tries to prove that we do not take part in the market only as individuals, but that this taking part implies a reciprocal relationship between individuals who recognise one another as partners in a fair and equal exchange. The question that naturally follows is, of course, whether this conception that requires freely contracting subjects could be based on an illusion. Does the economic sphere really have immanent norms, which allow the market to be a relational institution of freedom, as Honneth claims in *Freedom's Right*? Or is it only a resurgence of Adam Smith?

IV

By claiming that in economic exchanges mutual recognition is "normally" the case, Honneth opens the Pandora's box of reification. With this assumption he puts Marx's critique of Hegel upside down. For Marx, capital was not only a material reality but at the same time a whole set of human relations, and in the *Grundrisse* he described the reification as the consequence of the fact that in exchange value the social relationship between persons is transformed into a relation between things. As a result of this "power of things" all relations between individuals stop being a network of reciprocal dependence and

---

[75] Ibid, 77–8.

become a general state of dependency on a domination over which individuals have no control.

In a rather strange paper delivered at the final session of our ANR-DFG common project called CActuS,[76] Honneth provided an extensive comparison of the merits of Marx's and Hegel's theories regarding the theoretical tools needed to face the new forms and social consequences of capitalism. He calls "for revisions on both sides".[77] Of course, this claim can be interpreted as an attempt to link his very long detour through Hegel to his recently published essay on the idea of socialism.[78] The essential point is the place accorded to the market economy in the Hegelian system.

In Hegel's view alienation—understood as objectification—is an inescapable process necessary for the individual's self-realisation. In the Jena version of his *Philosophy of Spirit* (1805–1806) he even characterises work as the action "of making oneself into a thing in the world" (*das diesseitige sich zum Dinge Machen*).[79] While in traditional economies, where the fundamental structure is the family, this process allows individuals to satisfy their material needs as well as their need for recognition, the increasing social diversification of labour processes makes labour and its products increasingly abstract so that the individual does not recognise in them neither himself nor ther individuals. Nevertheless, Hegel saw in the exchange process itself a means of overcoming these negative effects as far as the individual becomes conscious of being "the possession of another".[80] This is the core of the opposition between Marx and Hegel.

Honneth concedes that Hegel had great reservations about the capacity of the market to regulate itself and "therefore recommended that the threat of market excesses be held in check by regulative and cooperative institutions".[81] He even admits that Marx was completely right when he argued that

> the employment contract, one of the normative foundations of the new economic order, does not fulfill its promise of realizing individual freedom of choice, since those who depend on wage payments are forced to agree to the

---

[76] Critique – Actualité – Société (Aktualität der Kritik: Gesellschaftstheorie, Soziologie und Kritik des Sozialen in Frankreich und Deutschland), French-German research program of the Agence Nationale de la Recherche and of the Deutsche Forschungsgemeinschaft, 2013–2016.

[77] Honneth, "Hegel and Marx: A Re-Assessment After One Century", Conference on the final meeting of the ANR/DFG project CActuS. I quote the manuscript, p. 26.

[78] Honneth, *The Idea of Socialism: Towards a Renewal* (Cambridge: Polity Press, 2017).

[79] Hegel, *Jenaer Systementwürfe III: Naturphilosophie und Philosophie des Geistes*, ed. Rolf-Peter Horstmann (Hamburg: Meiner, 1987), 189.

[80] Ibid, 207.

[81] Honneth, "Hegel and Marx", 26.

contract's terms given their lack of alternative options for making a living. [...] the two central elements of Marx's analysis of capitalism – his thesis about the unfreedom of wage laborers, and his thesis about the expansionary dynamic inherent in the competitive market – have turned out to be resilient in the fact of later developments and hardly open to doubt. Especially after witnessing the so-called "neoliberal" breakdown of economic barriers over the past several decades, we can safely assume today that there is a pressure inherent in our economic system that tends to undermine individual freedom of choice both for wage laborers and in other areas of life.[82]

At the end of his text Honneth comes to the conclusion that Hegel was wrong to follow Adam Smith and to place his faith in the virtues of an economic order based on contractual relations. The model of the commercial contract cannot be transposed onto the relations between labour and capital.[83] However, while Marx and Lukács show that the laws of the capitalist economy are superimposed upon the relations between persons and give them the appearance of natural phenomena (and the same efficiency), Honneth transcribes reification back onto human relations. He shows the same confidence in the immanent mechanisms of capitalist reproduction as Habermas, who says in his *Theory of communicative action* that in order to avoid reification one has "only" to prevent the market requirements from damaging the communicative infrastructures of the life world.[84] One should, Honneth concludes, combine the negative critical approach of Marx with the critical but much more positive approach of Hegel:

> The question now is therefore how the aspects of capitalism identified by Marx might be incorporated into the framework of Hegel's social theory without destroying its inner architectonic. [...] we should adopt a much more open conception of the capitalist economic sphere which gives due place to the influence of changing social norms. Only through such a re-orientation of political economy can we do justice to the historical fact that the opportunity

---

[82] Ibid, 20.

[83] "The problematic aspect of Hegel's view lies rather in the fact that he simply transposes the features of contracts between commercial parties onto the relationship between entrepreneurs and wage laborers. His naive disregard for the influence of duress and coercion testifies to his more general tendency to neglect the phenomena of power and domination". (ibid, 25)

[84] Jürgen Habermas, *Theorie des kommunikativen Handelns* (Frankfurt am Main; Suhrkamp, 198), vol. 2, 549.

to pursue the profit principle varies with institutional and cultural circumstances, being much greater today, for instance, than forty or fifty years ago.[85]

For Honneth, Marx has failed to understand the functional complexity of modern societies.[86] Instead of the ultimately economic determination he considers the three orders of Hegel's theory of *Sittlichkeit* to be more efficient to circumscribe the normative damages caused by the overflowing intrusions of the market into the other spheres of social life. As in Hegel, the state has to play the role of a guarantor, of a regulating or repairing instance and even a therapist.

This is nothing else than a typical social-democratic accommodation with what seemed at first to be denounced: the transposition of the market laws on social and human relations,[87] which is the general trend in the capitalist world as the reform of the employment legislation by the Macron government in France has shown. (And one must add that this reform had been initiated under the presidency of the Socialist François Hollande). Against this trend Honneth is neither naïve nor cynical. His major book of 2013, *Freedom's Right*[88], draws together a basic sketch of the history and actuality of capitalism, though it tends to idealise its initial project.

Originally (and this is a sort of original myth which constitutes the base of Honneth's political thinking), the market is supposed to have aimed at "the realization and extension of social freedom".[89] The excesses (*Entgrenzungen*) we are witnessing as the output of this project (*am Ende des Weges*) must be considered as a "social failure" (*eine soziale Fehlentwicklung*) that has undermined and emptied its normative potential.[90]

Honneth's book *Freedom's Right* tries to chart a third path between the philosophy of history and normative philosophies. In order to escape the excesses as well as the powerlessness of a purely moral approach one should, according to Honneth, follow the example of Hegel's *Sittlichkeit* and elaborate

---

[85] Honneth, "Hegel and Marx", 22.

[86] "Marx lacks an understanding of the functional complexity of modern societies" – this reproach is expressed p. 23 and repeated p. 24.

[87] In so far it is completely clear why *The Idea of Socialism* was awarded the Bruno Kreisky Prize for the Political Book of 2015.

[88] Axel Honneth, *Das Recht der Freiheit* (Berlin: Suhrkamp, 2013). English: *Freedom's Right: The Social Foundations of Democratic Life (New Directions in Critical Theory)* (New York: Columbia University Press, 2015). I quote from the German original.

[89] Ibid, 320.

[90] Ibid.

the normativity on the basis of empirical experience, but at the same time determine the principles which stand up against the established order or the power of facts and which require the achievement of moral expectations. From the very first pages, Honneth stresses that the most serious defect of contemporary political philosophy resides in its disconnection from social analysis and in its concentration on purely normative principles.[91] Honneth calls for a return to Hegel's dialectics of morality, which neither accepts that norms might be imposed from outside or from above, nor that their definition might be abandoned to the empirical social sciences. He is willing to go with Hegel beyond Habermas and Rawls in order to develop a theory of justice akin to the structural conditions of contemporary societies.[92]

Overcoming the fruitless opposition of facts and ideals—that applies also to the radical and the reformist Left—is a great ambition. There is no doubt about that. But this great project is reposed on the premise that the structural conditions of contemporary societies must be accepted, so that the result is given from the beginning. Honneth is conscious of this problem and of the lasting suspicion that sticks to the idea of *Sittlichkeit*, blamed as it is for declaring only those norms and institutions as legitimate that serve the established order.[93] One can easily show that Hegel really goes through with his dialectics and that he never considers the provisional achievement of a legal form or institution as legitimising it—in § 253 of his *Philosophy of Right* he gives the example of the corporation that did not fulfil all the expectations it otherwise raised. (A very sensitive example that refers to the Fascist "third ways", such as under the French Vichy regime.)[94] For these reasons the challenge Honneth has decided to take up is very risky. It must prove that the economic activity based on the market model is also a sphere of social freedom[95] and that the conditions of free interpersonal relationship can be grounded on a capitalist economic order.[96]

This raises classical questions: one has to see whether, in a capitalist economic order, freedom is more than a mere negative liberty—the liberty of individuals fighting for their own interests—or if it can take the form of a social liberty for all concerned persons. This was, as Honneth sees it, the conviction of both Hegel and Durkheim. Hegel has shown that the interdependence of egoist interests in commercial relationship leads to a form of mutual respect

---

[91] Ibid, 14.
[92] Ibid, 17.
[93] Ibid, 25.
[94] Ibid, 29.
[95] Ibid, 317.
[96] Ibid, 318.

that is codified in contractual dispositions. From the other side, Durkheim claimed that the system of modern market economy can escape anomie and contribute to the integration of individuals only under the two conditions of equality of opportunity and an equal recognition of performances, thereby guaranteeing the general welfare of all persons.

But Hegel's and Durkheim's positions cannot be identified, for the simple reason that Durkheim affirms a normative requirement that in Hegel is supposed to result from the order of things. The gap between facts and norms is not closed. Such a common front is only acceptable from the position of a reformist social democracy that has not only already accepted the law of the market but legitimises it as a normative presupposition.

"Interest in the Body":
Art, Autonomy and Natural Beauty in Adorno

JOSEFINE WIKSTRÖM

> The love of nature and fate proclaimed by totalitarian propaganda is merely a superficial reaction to fixation at the level of the body, to the failure of civilization to fulfil itself.[1]

In the Appendix, "Notes and Sketches", to Max Horkheimer's and Theodor Adorno's *Dialectic of Enlightenment: Philosophical Fragments*, one section is intriguingly titled "Interest in the Body". Intriguing because it immediately begs the question: Whose interest in the body? Why this interest and to the benefit of whom? Like many of the other sections in the Appendix—such as "Propaganda", "From a Theory of the Criminal" and "Avalanche"—"Interest in the Body", while short and fragmentary in character, develops some of the book's main themes.[2] Written between 1944 and 1947, while in exile in the US from the Nazis in Germany, *Dialectic of Enlightenment* criticises and lays out the contradictory character of the enlightenment process—the development of civilisation and culture—that results in the perverse quasi-rationality of the heinous Hitler regime. It is in the particular section, "Interest in the Body", that this general claim is developed, but with specific focus on the role of the body in the enlightenment process as well as in fascism. Here Adorno and Horkheimer write that the repression of a human being's instincts and passions, and above all her body, was a condition for establishing civil society. This happened first through Christianity and Lutheranism; and while these belief-systems celebrated work and the working body, they also assigned to the body everything that was sinful and bad. Second the body, according to Adorno and Horkheimer, underwent repression with the development and expansion of capitalism, such that the body became reduced to work and the mere capacity to be productive. Only those bodies that willingly gave themselves over to the

---

[1] Max Horkheimer and Theodor W. Adorno, *Dialectic of Enlightenment: Philosophical Fragments*, trans. Edmund Jephcott (Stanford, California: Stanford University Press, 2002), 195.

[2] Adorno and Horkheimer write in the preface to the book that the last section consists of fragments that either found no place in the book and or were thought sketches for a future work, what they call a "dialectical anthropology". Horkheimer and Adorno, *Dialectic of Enlightenment: Philosophical Fragments*, ix. Thanks to Rose-Anne Gush who made me aware of this part of *Dialectic of Enlightenment*.

new capitalist workplaces were trusted.[3] For Adorno and Horkheimer the body reached its final degradation with the rise of fascism, where the body was subject to acute forms state control. Fascism segmented the body-mind distinction to levels before unknown. Taken together, the extent of the body's repression throughout the development of civilized modernity has resulted in a psychological and physical violence against the body; what they call a "love-hate" for the body. "The achievements of civilization are a product of sublimation, of the acquired love-hate for body and earth, from which domination has violently severed all human beings".[4]

But—and this is the crux—while Adorno and Horkheimer write that at the same time that fascism deepens the split between mind and body by controlling it to an ever-greater degree, it also expresses a strong longing for the body and for nature. The two points are in fact inseparable from each other. On the one hand, fascism celebrates the athletic body in sports competitions, white naked bodies in paintings and harmonious and synchronised bodies in gymnastics and dance.[5] On the other hand, the interest in the body leads to race biology and to the extinction of the body. Adorno and Horkheimer's brief note on the body shows how the fascists' return to nature and the body are inseparable from death. The "interest in the body" makes a direct connection between the body and extermination: "Along with the mortality rate, society is reducing life to a chemical process".[6]

Reading Adorno and Horkheimer's text around seventy years after it was written creates an interesting, if rather ominous framework through which we can approach the relation between the body, art and nature today. Three things come to mind, against which their text can serve as a backdrop. Firstly, the fact that fascism is once more strongly present in the West, and in most European countries; a frightening development intimately tied to an escalated control of the human body. This is present, for example, in the increased violation of abortion rights, in the decreased rights for workers as well as in the fenced-up

---

[3] The feminist post-Marxist Silvia Fedirici has written convincingly about the way in which unproductive bodies, like women identified as "witches", vagabonds and other people who refused to become wage-labourers, were condemned during the 16th century in the transformation from feudalism to capitalism. Federici's research is important and brings to light the many gendered problems regarding the body with the onset of modernity, aspects that are ignored by Adorno and Horkheimer. See Silvia Fedirici, *Caliban and the Witch: Women, the Body and Primitive Accumulation* (Brooklyn: Autonomedia, 2004).

[4] Horkheimer and Adorno, *Dialectic of Enlightenment*, 194.

[5] See for example Susan Manning, "Modern Dance in the Third Reich" in *The Oxford Handbook of Dance and Politics*, ed. Rebekah J. Kowal, Gerald Siegmund and Randy Martin (Oxford: Oxford University Press, 2017), 1–25.

[6] Horkheimer and Adorno, *Dialectic of Enlightenment*, 196.

refugee camps in Greece and elsewhere. Secondly, the fact that much of the last twenty years or so of theory has seen a renewed interest in the human body as well as nature.[7] In discourses such as New Materialism, Speculative Realism and related strands of thinking, the body and nature are often seen as pure and unmediated matter, reminiscent of Aristotelian ideas of materialism. These empirico-philosophical approaches to nature and the body go back to pragmatist philosophers like John Dewey as well as to philosophers of science like Alfred North Whitehead and Isabelle Stengers.

Thirdly, and the focus for this essay, is the way performance and dance, and thus the human body as an object, have recently returned to the centre of contemporary art, as well as the renewed interest in the internal functioning of the body within contemporary dance, known as Somatics.[8] Throughout the twentieth century, artistic dance and performance have represented the human body in movement as a container of truth, able to represent real unmediated presence. Choreographers like Martha Graham and Pina Bausch, as well as artists such as Chris Burden and Marina Abramović, present their own and other bodies' as "natural" and authentic.[9] But what are we to make of today's return to the interior functioning of the body in dance? Does this demonstrate a return to a naïve idea of the natural body and what similarities—if any—does it have with fascist conceptions of the body? What, if anything does this say about contemporary dance today?

Although Adorno wrote on musical performance, for example in his unfinished *Towards a Theory of Musical Reproduction*,[10] what little else he wrote on dance or performance amounted to no more than brief dismissals of 1960s art happenings.[11] He did however develop a thorough account of the relation between art and nature, primarily through the concept of "natural beauty" in the posthumously published *Aesthetic Theory*. The way in which Adorno

---

[7] See for example Diana Coole and Samantha Frost (eds.), *New Materialisms: Ontology, Agency and Politics* (Durham; London: Duke University Press, 2010), Jane Benett, *Vibrant Matter: A Political Ecology of Things* (Durham: Duke University Press, 2010) and Graham Harman, *Towards Speculative Realism: Essays and Lectures* (Winchester: Zero Books, 2010).

[8] For an overview of this field see Martha Eddy, "A brief History of Somatic Practices and Dance: Historical Development of the Field of Somatic Education and its Relationship to Dance", *Journal of Dance and Somatic Practices*, Vol 1, No. 1 (2009): 5–27.

[9] Meredith Morse shows how Martha Graham perceived her own dancing. See especially: "The Natural and the Neutral" in Meredith Morse, *Soft is Fast: Simone Forti in the 1960s and After* (Cambridge, Mass.: MIT, 2016).

[10] Theodor W. Adorno, *Towards a Theory of Musical Reproduction*, ed. Henri Lonitz, trans. Wieland Hoban (Cambridge: Polity Press, 2006).

[11] At least on one occasion he dismisses happenings and related art practices as too literal and without form. See for example Theodor Adorno, "Art and the Arts", in R. Tiedemann (ed.), *Can One Live After Auschwitz? A Philosophical Reader* (Stanford: Stanford University Press, 2003).

develops the idea of natural beauty in *Aesthetic Theory* can, alongside his and Horkheimer's brief statement on the body and fascism, provide an idea of how we might understand the role of the body in art and its relation to nature today. This, at least, is the framework through which I want to pose the broadest possible question: How can Adorno's critical theory on art, nature and natural beauty be of use currently when "interest in the body" seems to have returned in various ways, in art and elsewhere?

The aim of this essay is to first elucidate the dialectical relation between Adorno's concept of art and that of natural beauty. The purpose is also to ask what function natural beauty has in Adorno's overall concept of art and what this may indicate about the role of natural beauty and art today. Here I want to try to make two points, one that is internal to Adorno's own thought and another that goes beyond it. My first argument is that the dialectical relation between art and natural beauty in Adorno hinges on the question of separation and abstraction understood as a social form. To see the conditions of capitalism as a social form means to look at the ways in which abstraction operates at the level of social relations. The human being is separated from nature and, within capitalism, from herself, in the same way that art is separated from man. But whereas nature for man is an image of separation—an image that reveals its scar—art needs to mediate this image further within the conditions of capitalism, that is, within the process of commodification and the abstraction of labour.

I will begin by looking into Adorno's concept of art and above all what he understands as the autonomy of art. I will then show how this relates to what Adorno conceptualises as natural beauty and how this is inseparable from the autonomy of art. This will lead to the following conclusion, namely that what art takes from nature is the separation—its form—rather than its beauty, what Adorno calls "natural beauty as such". I will then connect this separation to the most central separation in contemporary capitalism, namely the separation or abstraction of the human from her labour as well as from her own body. My argument here is that art, if it wants to say something about nature needs to take this mediation of abstract labour into account as a new mediation. If it does not, then it will only appear at best as fetishistic or fascistic at worse. Towards the end of this chapter I will discuss what this might mean for the role of dance and performance within contemporary art today.

Adorno's Theory of Art: Autonomy

Adorno opens the notoriously difficult section on "Natural Beauty" by decrying that natural beauty has been repressed in aesthetic theory from F.W.J Schelling's *Philosophy of Art* (1802–03) onwards. Idealists have turned nature into art in order to favour the autonomous subject and its freedom. Considering that Schelling and other German idealists, such as Friedrich Schlegel, developed a concept of art not too far from Adorno's own (in that their concept of 'literature' is as general as Adorno's concept of art).[12] Adorno's critique was not motivated by a desire to return to a Kantian idea of natural beauty (as first nature). Instead, Adorno states, natural beauty has been repressed and eliminated from German idealism's concept of art, because it is inseparable from it. The idea of natural beauty reminded German idealism too much about the dialectics of nature and art. Adorno writes:

> Its [art's] continued presence would have touched a sore spot, conjuring up associations of acts of violence perpetrated by every work of art, as a pure artefact against the natural. Wholly man-made, the work of art is radically opposed to nature, which appears not to be so made. However, in their antithetical opposition man and nature are dependent on each other: nature on the experience of a mediated and objectified world, art on nature which is the mediated plenipotentiary of immediacy. Reflections on natural beauty, therefore, are an integral and inalienable part of any theory of art.[13]

Art for Adorno is the opposite of nature since the human being makes art. But the opposition between art and nature is nevertheless for Adorno dependent on an idea of nature as appearing natural. How is it that Adorno's concept of art is dependent on an idea of nature and an idea of natural beauty? What, more specifically, does the dialectical relations between the two look like? Or what function does the notion of nature and natural beauty have in Adorno's concept of art, at least as it is proposed in *Aesthetic Theory*? Furthermore, and if we assume that his concept of art still holds today, what might we say about the relation between art and natural beauty in contemporary art and specifically in

---

[12] For a developed argument about the proximity between Adorno's understanding of art and the concept of art advanced by the early German Romantics see David Cunningham, "Genre without Genre: Romanticism, the Novel and the New", *Radical Philosophy* 196 (March/April 2016): 4–27. This is also pointed out by Walter Benjamin in the introduction to his doctoral thesis on the romantic concept of art criticism from 1920.

[13] Theodor, W. Adorno, *Aesthetic Theory*, trans. Gretel Adorno, Rolf Tiedemann and Robert Hullot-Kentor (London, Boston, Melbourne, Henley: Routledge & Kegan Paul, 1984), 91. I will from now on use both this and a later translation of *Aesthetic Theory* and mark the year of translation in brackets after the footnote.

relation to performance and dance? Does Adorno's critical theory still hold? Here, we first need to go to Adorno's understanding of art and then return to this section on natural beauty in order to gain insight into this dialectical relation between art, nature and natural beauty.

Adorno derived his understanding of form—both in art and in philosophy—from Walter Benjamin. It was above all Benjamin's *The Arcades Project* (an unpublished work written between 1927–1949) that served as the prototype for Adorno's *Aesthetic Theory*.[14] The latter, as with almost everything Adorno wrote, is written in a so called paratactic form, meaning that it rejects all teleological ways of arguing and instead encircles different concepts in a fragmentary character.[15] This is owing to Adorno's understanding of how language and forms of writing can resist rationalisation and identity thinking and is also essential to how Adorno understands philosophy.[16] Despite the difficulty of orienting oneself in *Aesthetic Theory* a clear and distinct concept of art can be derived from it. Although aspects of Adorno's understanding of art have changed in some respects, at its core is the idea that form and thought are historical concerns. The most distinctive aspect of Adorno's concept of art is its claim to autonomy. This does not mean that art for Adorno is something placed on a pedestal, transcending life and reality. This would be a grave misunderstanding of what autonomy means for Adorno and it would fail to recognise the importance that the social has in his theory of art. By arguing for art's autonomy Adorno says that art is *fully social* but only by virtue of having separated itself from the social. "Art's double character as both autonomous and *fait social* is incessantly reproduced on the level of its autonomy".[17] How are we to understand this dialectical claim, this "social, a-sociality" of the artwork?

Following Benjamin's historico-philosophical methodology[18] as well as Charles Baudelaire's thoughts about the modern artwork, art for Adorno

---

[14] Stewart Martin, "The Absolute Artwork meets the Absolute Commodity", *Radical Philosophy* 146 (November/December 2007): 15–26.

[15] For a developed argument about Adorno's way of writing, see the chapter on style in Gillian Rose, *The Melancholy Science: An Introduction to the Thought on Theodor W. Adorno* (London: Verso, 2013).

[16] This is developed by Adorno in his essay "The Essay as Form" in which he argues for the essayistic form of writing as an example of writing that is closely related to truth. The essay form, he writes, "does justice to the consciousness of non-identity, without needing to say so, radically unradical refraining from a reduction to a principle, accentuating the fragmentary, the partial, rather than the total". Theodor, W. Adorno, "The Essay as Form", *New German Critique*, No 32. (Spring–Summer 1984): 157.

[17] Theodor W. Adorno, *Aesthetic Theory*, trans. Robert Hullot-Kentor, (London: Continuum, 1997), 6.

[18] Part of this methodology is demonstrated by Benjamin in his dissertation, *The Concept of Art Criticism in German Romanticism*, published in 1920.

should, from the nineteenth century onwards, be seen as the result of cultural and craft-like practices having untied themselves from religious and royal institutions. The historical aspect of art's autonomy is strongly present in Adorno: "The artwork's autonomy is, indeed, not *a priori* but the sedimentation of a historical process that constitutes its concept".[19] For Adorno this explicitly meant that art, in order for it to become art, had to abandon its religious and other patron-like relationships. As a result, art moved into the dominant form of production in modernity: commodity-production. This is why for Adorno, the development of capitalism as the dominant mode of production, the bourgeois subject and the emergence of art, are inseparable historical tendencies. Art, capital and the subject cannot for Adorno be thought without one another.

Autonomous works of art are autonomous for Adorno *because* they have moved to the "free market", entered the forces of production and the social techniques used in capitalist society. This is a movement from a production governed by rules within academic painting, music and sculpture to a mode of production dictated by the new forces of production in which no aesthetic conventions exist. "The aesthetic force of production is the same as that of productive labour and has the same teleology; and what may be called aesthetic relations of production—all that in which the productive force is embedded and in which it is active—are sedimentations or imprintings of social relations of production".[20] The art market takes a central role in this historico-philosophical concept of art proposed by Adorno. Autonomous art for Adorno becomes autonomous only on the condition of entering commodity-production and the social techniques driving the production of commodities.

What Adorno essentially means by the autonomy of the artwork is that the artwork's complete sociality (its entanglement in commodity-production) only appears so because it also separates itself *formally* from it. This is how the artwork's self-determining autonomy manifests itself. Adorno makes this clear from the very beginning of *Aesthetic Theory*. "Autonomous art", we read in the first chapter "Art, society, aesthetics" is characterised by its distinctness or separation from life and empirical reality. This separation, which is constitutive of the ontology of art, operates at different levels. In the broadest sense possible art is separated from empirical reality and can only come into being by claiming that it is different from the empirical reality in which it is presented. In a slightly narrower understanding, art for Adorno is also separated from

---

[19] Adorno, *Aesthetic Theory* (1997), 23.
[20] Adorno, *Aesthetic Theory* (1997), 6.

society. Therefore, art, Adorno writes, is separated from industrial production, the division of labour implied in industrial capitalist societies, the technology used in such production and the reproduction of capital more generally. The latter is key with respect to art's relation to abstraction. This separation from reality, society, industrial production (the division of labour and technological reproduction) and ultimately the value-form in modern works of art, is however, and importantly for Adorno, always a dialectical movement of negation and affirmation.

For Adorno, this ontology of art is also what amounts to art's function. By being entirely separated or autonomous from the reality and society within which it exists, art is functionless. This "dialectic of functionalism"[21] constitutive of modern art implies that the autonomous work of art is functional only in reference to itself. Art for Adorno, we might say, is autonomous from society and has no use or function, precisely because it is inseparable from the capitalist production of commodities. As Stewart Martin puts it elegantly: "Commodification produces this problem but also a solution: the distancing of the artwork from a commodified world through the abstraction of the commodity form itself".[22] What I want to stress here is that the autonomous artwork for Adorno is constructed through its epistemologically positive separation from reality and its capitalist mediations (on point of fact of it being commodified), presented as abstraction. Before looking into how art, for Adorno, can perform this double contradictory autonomy of being social and asocial at the same time, let us now move onto Adorno's understanding of natural beauty.

Natural Beauty in Adorno: Image of Separation

If we come back to the section on natural beauty in *Aesthetic Theory*, we see that natural beauty, like art, is also the result of a historical separation. If art for Adorno appears in the historical moment when art separates itself from religious, cultic and other hierarchical relationships, and finds itself in the centre of capitalist production, "the historical core", as he puts it, of natural beauty is the origin of myth: the separation of man from nature. This is why, for Adorno, natural beauty did not exist in primitive societies, in which nature was something to fear and something to be acted upon. Natural beauty in contrast is something for which everyone longs at the same time as it reveals something

---

[21] On the function and functionless of art see also Adorno, "Functionalism Today", in *Rethinking Architecture: A Reader in Cultural Theory*, ed. Neil Leach (London and New York: Routledge, 1997), 5–18.
[22] Martin, "The Absolute Artwork meets the Absolute Commodity", 20.

dark. Adorno gives the example of birds singing in the spring as something no one can resist as beautiful "yet something frightening lurks in the song of birds because it is not a song but obeys the spell in which it is enmeshed".[23] And if the function of art for Adorno is that it is separated from social reality and therefore has no function, the "function" of natural beauty is to express non-identity. If art says something about the abstract social relations of capitalism, natural beauty expresses the suffering of the separation from non-identity. Adorno writes: "The beautiful in nature is the residue of non-identity in things, in an age when they are otherwise spellbound by universal identity".[24]

Like art, natural beauty has been subject to historical change. But and in contrast to art, according to Adorno, all natural beauty expresses the memory of its "past historical suffering"[25] and presents itself as ahistorical. Neither natural beauty nor art communicates what they want to say. Adorno writes: "[N]atural beauty is defined by its undefineability, which is an aspect of the object as well as the concept thereof [...] As in music, the beautiful in nature is like a spark flashing momentarily and disappearing as soon as one tries to get hold of it".[26]

What then is the relation between art and natural beauty in Adorno? What art and natural beauty share is first of all a relation or separation which is epistemologically positive. Adorno also emphasises this when he says, for example, that one stands in front of a work of art in the same way in which one relates to nature. "Like the aesthetic appreciation of art, that of nature centres on images".[27] My suggestion here is that what art takes from natural beauty is not beauty nor nature since art cannot imitate neither nature nor specific instances of beauty. Instead my argument is that art imitates the very act of separation, both the being and contradiction of natural beauty. For Adorno, any art that tries to imitate nature through, for example, harmony in romantic music can only fail. In contrast, he says, the French impressionists succeeded, since they focused on nature's scars, and thus successfully imitated the image of the beautiful in nature. Adorno gives many other examples of natural beauty that can be found within the history of modern art. In Marcel Proust's *In Search of Lost Time* a Hawthorne hedge "figures as a fundamental phenomenon of

---

[23] Adorno, *Aesthetic Theory* (1997), 87.
[24] Adorno, *Aesthetic Theory* (1984), 108.
[25] Adorno, *Aesthetic Theory* (1984), 95–96.
[26] Adorno, *Aesthetic Theory* (1984), 107.
[27] Adorno, *Aesthetic Theory* (1984), 97.

aesthetic comportment".[28] But what does it mean to imitate a relation and a social form rather than nature as such?

Adorno writes in one of the final paragraphs on natural beauty: "If the transition from natural to artistic beauty is viewed dialectically, it reveals itself to be a transition in the development of domination".[29] Adorno's point here is that man's domination of nature increases with modernity. Natural beauty appeared with the separation of man from nature. But as nature becomes increasingly subjugated by man, art is needed to take this domination, dialectically, even further. Here I would like to propose that the function of natural beauty for Adorno's understanding of the autonomous artwork is twofold. On the one hand, natural beauty stands as a model for art in that it relates to nature in the way that art relates to reality, namely by separation or negation. Natural beauty is the result of an intensified domination of nature by man, according to which once man is separated from nature, natural beauty becomes the image of this separation. On the other hand, art needs natural beauty since art is the image or representation of *the intensification of this separation*. The implication of this is that art does not reconcile the scar that natural beauty reflects. Instead art polarises the relation between man and nature to its extreme. Art reflects the relation between man and nature only by making it the opposite of nature.

How is this separation mediated in the artwork? My suggestion is that this separation is mediated through two important aspects of the artwork. The first follows from the fact that the artwork is, for Adorno, a commodity while the second entails what Adorno calls the form or construction of the artwork. Let's first turn to the commodity aspect. Art is made through the same social forces of production by which all other commodities in a capitalist society are produced. However, for Adorno, this does not mean that the artwork functions or is like all other commodities in a capitalist society. In contrast, it is fundamental, according to Adorno, that the artwork as commodity is different from other commodities. This hinges above all on the way the artwork as a commodity is produced and how this, to a certain extent, makes it irreproducible and original. Whereas the goal for "ordinary" commodities is to make the production process of them as cheap and fast as possible, artworks are not subjected to these conditions. The main difference then between an artwork as commodity and other everyday commodities, is that although a painting can be sold on the market and in that sense is a commodity, it hasn't been produced *only* with the purpose to be sold on the market. The exchange of the painting

---

[28] Adorno, *Aesthetic Theory* (1997), 83.
[29] Adorno, *Aesthetic Theory* (1984), 113.

appears as a symptom of its production rather than being the telos of its making. We might here choose to follow Marx and say that the production of artworks has not been pushed towards the "real subsumption of labour" by which he referred to those production processes of commodities in which everything (from machinery to the use of labour) is set up with the sole purpose of making commodities for the market. Put differently, the artwork is a commodity and is part of the production of commodities. But it is also and necessarily separated from commodity production because of its exceptional character. The main point I want to make here is that the artwork's character as a commodity is dialectical, and that the separation the artwork takes from natural beauty, namely the separation of man from nature, is mediated through this ambiguous status of the artwork as a commodity.

This point requires that we turn to the second, and for us here, more important aspect of the way art is, according to Adorno, mediated *as art*. Through what he calls the *form* or *construction* of the work, art mediates the separation (and this is often glossed over in critiques of Adorno, I think). However, what Adorno means by form here should not be understood as "formalist", i.e. in the sense that we might find in someone like the American art critic Clement Greenberg who suggested that the essence of art is its purification of form. Form in Adorno is more to do with social forces and historical modes of production and therefore more akin to what we might call "social form." For Adorno, the form of the artwork is an entirely historical matter. This requires that the artwork, in order to be "new", must create new forms. Adorno develops this thought in an interesting way in a part of *Aesthetic Theory* entitled "Universal and Particular". The autonomous, or what Adorno here calls the 'nominalistic' artwork must, in order to be art, negate universals. This is specific to modern art for Adorno and stands in contrast to previous academic or classicist art. This is also why, for Adorno, the nominalistic artwork is based on "aesthetic nominalism".[30] With this he refers to "art" as something that developed alongside modernity and the formation of the bourgeois subject and as something that constituted a break with traditional genre aesthetics, i.e. so-called academic aestheticism. Adorno's point is that the relation between the universal and the particular, as it was configured in traditional genre aesthetics was broken in modernity through the development of aesthetic nominalism. Previous to modern art, particular artworks were always measured against and subsumed under universals (posed as norms and conventions). A poem had to fulfil certain standards of verse, a dance had to follow certain rules and it was a

---

[30] Adorno, *Aesthetic Theory* (1984), 262.

requirement that painting include certain *motifs* in order to pass as poetry, dance, and painting. With the onset of modernity, art began to negate these universals, and through this, mediate *new* forms. In aesthetic nominalism, the universal, Adorno argues, is dealt with through negation or separation. Expressed differently, the nominalistic artwork must—in order to be "art"—negate universals in singular and new ways. Progress for Adorno means "the negation of what exists through new beginnings".[31] Importantly, for Adorno, this dialectic between the particular and the universal is not only present at the level of a general category of art, but can also necessarily be seen as present in the *form of individual works*. The nominalistic artwork, Adorno states, is negative in relation to its form since it defines itself in relation to what it is not: the heterogeneous. The artwork, Adorno writes, "absorbs industrial technique" and "empirical reality", but does so without turning them into its laws. For Adorno then, it is the form of the artwork—where form is seen in this particular way as historical and as the breaking with universals—that enables art to mediate its "social, a-sociality". But because there is another separation or abstraction internal to the artwork as a commodity, we need to further reflect on this mediation.

We know that for Adorno the artwork is a commodity that can be bought and sold on the art market. But we also know that the commodity as artwork is not reproduced in the same way as other commodities and that this is mediated through the form of the artwork. Let's expand on this here. Adorno derived his understanding of the commodity from Marx who introduced the thought that a commodity contains both concrete and abstract labour as well as use- and exchange-value. (Although liberal economists like Ricardo and Adam Smith also had theories of the commodity, Marx always claimed that he was the first to make the distinction between concrete and abstract labour in the commodity.) The production of commodities, Marx tells us at the very beginning of the first volume of *Capital,* are at the centre of capitalism. For something to become a commodity for Marx, it must be useful. Marx gives the example of cotton. When cotton enters the market next to something else of use, a coat for example, both the cotton's and the coat's social, or "hidden labour", is quantified in the abstract. This is why for Marx the value of a commodity has nothing to do with its use-value, but only appears as something supra-sensible in the abstract. The supra-sensuous fetish character of the commodity for Marx derives from this relation in which social uses and their labour are quantified in the abstract as abstract labour. Hence he writes the

---

[31] Adorno, *Aesthetic Theory* (1984) 274.

following about abstract labour: "Tailoring and weaving are the formative elements in the use-values coat and linen, precisely because these two kinds of labour are of different qualities; but only in so far as abstraction is made from their particular qualities [...] do tailoring and weaving form the substance of the values of the two articles mentioned".[32]

In contrast to the commodity, the artwork is not useful in this sense. The artwork has, on the contrary, no specific use. Its only use is to be appreciated, an activity, which is undetermined and impossible to quantity. An artist's labour is not homogenous in the same way that a worker's labour on the conveyer belt is, and therefore it is not possible to determine in the same way. The labour of the artwork as a commodity is also difficult to quantify through what Marx termed, "socially necessary labour", i.e. the labour needed to make one specific commodity. Adorno's conception of art as functionless therefore brings Kant's thoughts on the beautiful as purposeless together with Marx's conception of the commodity and demonstrates how the artwork is a commodity with no purpose or use. In this way the artwork for Adorno accelerates and reverses the logic of the way in which commodities are made and quantified.

What does this reflect in the artwork? To elaborate on this, we might here want to come back to the section on "Natural Beauty" in which Adorno argues that the artist, in the face of an ever-increasing domination by man over nature, needs to dominate the artwork even more. The implication of this, seeing the artwork as a commodity, is that the artist needs to intervene, on every level, in the production of the artwork and therefore also in the social forces and technology through which the artwork as a commodity is produced. The artist needs to mark the material with her subjectivity at every level of production.[33] The artist, by intervening on every level of production, enables the artwork to negate and reject the abstract labour that is now formally internal to it as a commodity. This negation, or separation of abstract labour is mediated through the form of the artwork. The proposition here is that abstraction—in this two-fold sense as reflecting the abstract labour conditions of commodity production, by separating itself from it—becomes, from modernity onwards, part of the ontology of art itself. From this suggestion it follows that there can be no art that is not abstract. The suggestion is also that this abstraction might

---

[32] Karl Marx, *Capital*, Volume 1 (London: Penguin, 1990), 136.

[33] This has perhaps been best accounted by John Roberts who argues that art, if it wants to stand out as something different from other capitalist forms of production, needs to incorporate the artist's subjectivity at all levels of production. For a longer development of this see Roberts, *The Intangibilities of Form: Skill and Deskilling in Art After the Readymade* (London: Verso, 2008).

look different in different historical moments and that "abstraction" as a kind of style or genre is impossible to apprehend.

Art and natural beauty are inseparable because art takes from natural beauty a social form or a relation. But in the development of domination, natural beauty is only able to express melancholia. In order to be able to say something about the different historical ways in which this separation is mediated, art has to create new forms of negation. This means that it must also reflect the contemporary relations of commodity production of which it is a part. If art doesn't reflect on the way it is both entangled and separated from the abstract labour relations of commodities, it is unable to say something about the relation between art and nature. Such is the main argument I want to make here.

Body and Nature in Contemporary Art

Now where does all this leave us with art and natural beauty today? Adorno's essay on new music shows that Romantic music, which primes harmony, only imitates nature and as such cannot gain autonomy. It is not sufficiently rational to be able to show what rationality has forgotten, as Adorno might have put it. If art stops negating (i.e. mediating) natural beauty it is unable to mediate the key ontological condition of our modern condition: capitalist relations. Domination of nature—through abstract labour relations—have infiltrated more domains of life since Adorno. What the relationship between natural beauty and art in Adorno demonstrate is however that this does not mean that we should return to naïve ideas about nature in art, such as the natural or expressive body.

In his article "Art and the arts" from the late 1960s Adorno decried the fact that much of the then new aleatory works, such as happenings and action painting, simply ignored the aspect of form and became too literal. We know today that Adorno failed to see that these artistic tendencies actually *were new forms*, even if they might have negated other universals than the ones Adorno had in mind, including the negation of the notion of art itself.[34] I wonder though if Adorno's diagnosis of 1960s art of falling into the heterogenous without form can be redeployed in critically understanding much of contemporary art and theory today partly because of its melancholic, naïve and at times cynical relationship to nature? Might we say that much self-proclaimed art—in their lack of form—become pure imitations of nature? And is this particularly the case when it comes to dance and performance in contemporary art?

---

[34] This argument is made by Peter Osborne. See: Osborne, *Anywhere or Not at All: Philosophy of Contemporary Art* (London: Verso, 2013), 84.

And, lastly, what might the relation be to fascism and the capitalist control of the body?

I think that today we risk stumbling into two traps, though, when it comes to bodies in dance and art, the traps themselves are counterposed. Let me give you two images and two examples of art works. First, Ann Imhof's performance *Faust,* which won the most prestigious prize at the Venice Biennale 2017, the Golden Lion. For her work Imhof had rebuilt the German pavilion. The floors of the pavilion were made of panzer glass standing approximately one metre above the real floor. The walls were white and apart from the main space, there were smaller rooms with panzer glass shelves and clinically looking tools on which the dancers sometimes sat and sometimes played with. Underneath the panzer glass in the main space dancers were moving around in movements that made them look like panthers or dogs. The dancers also made fires, sang, rested and starred into their mobile phones. Instructions about what to do and when came from the artist herself and were sent to their mobile phones, which they kept with them during the whole performance. The dancers' faces were, more or less, without expressions and together with their fashionable sports outfits and skinny bodies they were reminiscent of models on a catwalk. Towards the end of the performance they escaped their "cage" under the see-through floor and began to walk as if they were on a catwalk on the same level as the visitors, blurring any previous critical distance between performers and audience.

Throughout the entire performance, which lasted approximately three hours, the dancers appeared to have no will or agency; they only followed the order from the artist. The audience were relegated to a similar feeling of being controlled by the immersive spectacle that came from all directions. The performers and the artwork, we might say, were delivered to the audience members as commodities, as pure spectacle in which the audience members became passive consumers. This cynical embracing of the commodity form was also reflected in the architecture of pavilion which was reminiscent of halls for car sales and banks in which surveillance of bodies and the exchange of capital take place under one roof.[35]

Furthermore, there is a tendency that exists among dance practitioners—both dancers and choreographers—and that is present in contemporary dance and performance educations, namely Somatics. The term was established at the

---

[35] Benjamin Buchloh made a thorough critique in *Artforum* of this performance and highlighted this resemblance between German banks and the way the pavilion was constructed. Benjamin Buchloh, "Rock, Paper, Scissors", accessed Sep 13, 2018, https://www.artforum.com/print/201707/benjamin-h-d-buchloh-on-some-means-and-ends-of-sculpture-at-venice-muenster-and-documenta-70461.

beginning of the 1970s and refers to a number of movement and bodily practices whose focus is on the feeling of one's "bodily self". For example, the aim of somatic practices such as BMC (Body Mind Centering) or Alexander Technique is to improve one's sensory and motoric capacities in order to get a better knowledge of one's body and to become free from pain. When used within dance it has become a method to produce movement that does not focus on the outside or appearance of the moving body, but rather a way of creating movements from within. An exercise might be to lie down and try to sense the weight of one's body against the floor. Another exercise could be to move in darkness as a way to heighten one's awareness of how the body feels rather than what it looks like. Within dance from the 1960s and 1970s dancers and choreographers like Steve Paxton and Anna Halprin in the US can be cited as examples. In the context of art, we can mention someone like Lygia Clark whose sensory sculptures and installations are examples where Somatics have played an important role. More recently choreographers like Jefta van Dinther and Deborah Hay, both of whom have made works for the Swedish Cullberg ballet within the last five years, use somatic techniques as a method to create movement and choreography. Philosophically and theoretically Somatics understands itself as part of a non-Cartesian dualistic way of thinking the body and mind through thinkers as different such as Alfred Whitehead, John Dewey, Gilles Deleuze and more recently, philosophers of new materialism such as Karen Barad and Donna Haraway.

The "interest in the body" within this tendency understands the body as something empirically true and as something able to resist the reification of human relations that take place through the process of commodification in capitalist society. Whereas Imhof's performance demonstrates dancer performers whose subjectivity have turned into commodity objects, dancer performers, who are preoccupied with somatic practices, appear to want to move in the opposite direction. My point here is that they reflect two sides of the same coin. *Faust* reproduces the way the body has come to be controlled under neoliberal fascist regimes by turning the body into an easily controlled commodity-object and/or consumer. This position is embraced melancholically and cynically as if there were no outside. No critical distance is made aesthetically in the artwork. The form or construction of it, to speak with Adorno, is all but new. It only copies the aesthetics of the fashion show, the car industry and the commercial emo-goth music scene. On the other side, somatic dance practices move in the opposite direction by forgetting about the objectivity of the body. They seek to move inwards towards the dancer's own inner feelings and sensations. In this way somatic dance practices demonstrate a naïve longing for a body outside of commodity relations by moving closer to nature as something unmediated and real. This is in stark contrast to Imhof's *Faust,* which performs the complete commodification of life. The problem is that neither succeed to show the contradictory aspect of natural beauty and art in modernity, which Adorno shows us in his writings. Both do however point towards the deeply uncanny and paradoxical "interest in the body", which Adorno and Horkheimer wrote about in the *Dialectic of Enlightenment* and with which I introduced this essay. An interest that seemingly remains actual in contemporary art and culture today. We now need to move from this perverse relation to the body and instead towards a dialectic of the body that captures both art in its contemporary form as well as art's complex relation to nature.

Painting in Waiting
Prelude to a Critical Philosophy of History and Art

LYDIA GOEHR

L'avenir, par définition, n'a point d'image. L'histoire lui donne les moyens d'être pensé.

> Paul Valéry, Regards sur le monde actuel (1931)

It is wise to follow a perfect epigram with a telling example. So here is one, drawn from Cervantes' last work of 1617, *The Trials of Persiles and Sigismunda*. A pilgrim poet tells of a wealthy *monsignor* in Rome who has the most curious museum in the world. It is a museum of the future comprising empty tablets awaiting persons illustrious enough to be painted. Two inscriptions indicate the persons to come: poets who through their works will declare the coming of a great political leader, in this case, Constantine. One poet is Torquato Tasso; the other Zárate. But when we learn that Tasso is named for his madness and the other for his lack of talent, suddenly something about this museum seems awry. Will not painters die of starvation waiting for the poets? Will any political leader live up to the poet's promise? And if a painting in waiting were ever to be completed, would it not necessarily enter a museum of the present, there anxiously to compete with the unsurpassable masterpieces of the past?

This essay investigates the idea of a painting in waiting by importing the idea of waiting into a critical philosophy of history and art. There is of course no one thing meant by *waiting*. It can mean to pause, hesitate, linger, falter, or to anticipate with trepidation or hope. But it can also mean to serve as ladies-in-waiting once did in courts, or as waiters once stood in readiness in restaurants, perhaps to the point of Sartrean nausea, fully prepared to accommodate the needs of others. The very idea of waiting prompts many thoughts (as it is meant to): of the relation of theory to action, of servitudes and freedoms, but of most concern here, of what waiting has to do with paintings that are imageless or blank or to books whose pages are not yet written.

My interest in waiting stems from my current book project, which begins with the very idea of beginning and seems then to keep beginning to throw doubt on any ending that suggests the final completion of the task. I stand by those who say that writing a book is like producing a painting, where finishing, in another astute observation by Valéry, is only ever a stopping on the way.

Painting, like writing, has long been construed as an endless task of patience and preparation, of repeated beginnings in the face of false starts, a constant trial and error between *what has been, what is,* and *what could be,* allowing Valéry one more quip of quite some modernist wit, that "the future is not what it used to be". It is the patience and preparation that I import into the idea of waiting for a future that, without any suggestion of regret, might be different from how things used to be or are still today.

To set the scene, I begin, as my new book does, with the thought experiment that Arthur Danto devised to open his *The Transfiguration of the Commonplace* from 1981. The experiment itself began with an anecdote he took from Kierkegaard. It spoke of an artist who, when asked to depict the biblical passage across the Red Sea, did no more than cover a surface over with red paint and, evidently needing to explain, remarked that the Israelites had already crossed over and that the Egyptians were already drowned. Beginning with this anecdote, Danto devised his famous line-up of *red squares,* asking us to engage in a passage of thought by which we come to know what art essentially *is* when nothing but blank red squares are all we are given to *see.* One evening some years ago, when I naively asked Danto why there were so few representations of the Red Sea Passage in the history of painting, he answered back quick as a snap that perhaps the subject had been too easy for artists to tackle, had it been the case that all they needed was a canvas and red paint. Beyond the wit, the question as to what more is needed for art to be art beyond a blank canvas and red paint preoccupied him as a philosophical project for fifty years. It led him to an emancipation narrative for the artworld, to declare art's end with a call to freedom aimed at exposing a politics of exclusion in the world as a whole. It was his emancipation narrative, drawn from his use of the Red Sea anecdote, which inspired me to write my own book.

My book, titled *RED SEA-RED SQUARE* is a *Passagenwerk* about passages of life, thought, and art. It offers a genealogy of freedom and an anatomy of wit to suggest with a wry smile that there is no picturing of freedom without also the liberating of wit. But what sort of wit is at work if it yields a picture with nothing to see? Seeking the many who have used the Red Sea anecdote to make much more than an anecdotal point, I draw from the work of Danto and Kierkegaard, but also Giacomo Puccini, the French poet and playwright Henri Murger, and William Hogarth. Strange bedfellows to be sure, until we discover their different contributions to what around 1800 came to be a concept standing for a life known as *la vie de bohème.* What, I ask, had the concept of bohème to do with an exodus that left the Israelites having crossed and the Egyptians drowned? We know what Moses had to do with monotheism, but what had Moses also to do with the history of the red monochrome wherein artists and thinkers sought to picture freedom and liberate wit? This question provides me with my *roter Faden*, in part by explaining why, of all colours—*Farben*—the *Faden* had to be red.

For this essay, it suffices to report only on one version of the Red Sea anecdote of consequence in post-revolutionary France, when the punch-line was revised to say not that the Egyptians had already drowned, but that they were still *yet* to come—*Ils vont venir*. When, then, it was asked what would come to France when the Egyptians arrived, everything turned on what was meant by *the Egyptians—Egyptiens*. Was France eagerly awaiting the import of a wisdom of the once great empire of the Pharaohs or in horror for the so-named *lesser-Egyptians* who, through extraordinary confusions of history, theology, and myth, were falsely believed to have travelled as vagabonds in divine punishment all the way from the biblical Red Sea? Viewed on the long path as undesirable emigrants, these *lesser-Egyptians* picked up many names: *Gypsies, Zigeuner,* and in France, *les bohémiens*, meaning that they were seen as having come from the German lands of Bohemia without any *right* of passage. When, then, they arrived in Paris, many (and most famously Karl Marx) demanded that they be swept away like a plague upon the streets, and strikingly under the rubric of *La Bohème*. But what had this *la bohème* to do with the artists living *la vie de bohème*? And why did Puccini's *La Bohème* open with a painter trying but failing to paint a Red Sea—*Questo Mar Rosso*? As intriguing as these questions are, it is enough here to note only the confusion of the passage of the *lesser-Egyptians* with the other migration from the Red Sea, of the sometimes named *Red Jews*, partly so-named or misnamed for their alleged shame in never having shed themselves of the idle worship of idols inherited from their enslaved ancestors. If some believed that the red of the Red Sea signified the blood of the drowned Egyptians, others eagerly spread the red to the Jews who, for centuries thereafter, were declared incapable of understanding what freedom in the Promised Land really meant.

The Jews of exile and diaspora would be declared many times *False Prophets*, architects, as Kant would put it, of their own fate, for having wrongly waited for freedom's promise. Without paradox, to wait wrongly meant both waiting too long and not waiting at all. For assuming they knew too much or, worse, trusting too well what the future would bring, they were said to have foreclosed the possibility of their prophecy changing with the times, rendering it redundant for the future or as an outdated prophecy of the past. Leaving space for history to play its proper part encouraged the critics of false prophecy to propose a waiting game on corrected terms, where, at the centre of the game, facing the future meant making only a limited claim upon it.

This essay focuses on the limit [*Grenze*] in this claim. What has it meant, as a negative injunction of critique, to leave the canvas of the future blank, unpainted or withdrawn from sight? In the background, I will retain the thought of a waiting room with blank walls, which, from a past perspective, remembers a bloody history of oppression and tyranny, while, from a new perspective, gestures towards the blood of life and freedom.

When I first began thinking about waiting, I mistakenly believed that, as a philosophical motif, it had been insufficiently addressed. Soon, however, I found waiting everywhere, in proverbs such as "time and tide waits for no man" or in the *hesitant openness* brilliantly theorised by Siegfried Kracauer in *Die Wartenden*. And then in the endless endgames of waiting for only God knows what in the dissonant theatre of the absurd, which in turn influenced Joseph Kosuth's depiction of everything that *nothing* could mean once written onto a black surface, and whose musical score would surely have been performed as John Cage's *Waiting* of 1952. And then the countless images and stories about people in transit, or standing in queues, or living in some sort of witness protection program, as suggested by Walt Whitman in his poem about the *fog* of the *mockings and arguments* of the *linguists and contenders*: "Both in and out of the game, and watching and wondering at it", he wrote, "I witness and wait". Or T. S. Eliot's waiting between "Birth, copulation, and death, That's all the facts". Or the lonely waiting game of Dr. Seuss in "The Places You'll Go":

> Everyone is just waiting.
> … I'm afraid that some times
> you'll play lonely games too.
> Games you can't win
> 'cause you'll play against you.

Offered as an antidote to expose and halt the conceits of false prophecy and false positivity, many have engaged what I think about as a *philosophical furniture art*, so that, with chairs in rooms with bare walls, one may ask after the true posture of waiting whether it is an active standing, an in-between sitting, or a resigned lying down. Many have declared waiting as hard a task as living an emancipated life; perhaps it is the same task. One difficulty, *apropos* Nietzsche's untimely thoughts, turns on the phenomenology and hermeneutics of subjective time, consuming the mind with fearful feelings that one's past is but one's future, or that the future will never come, turning one's life into a lying down in an empty cask or hollow coffin. Another difficulty, *apropos* Kafka, turns on how sitting or standing *before the law* has meant waiting for the equality promised by the idea of justice, while cognisant of the lack of perfect justice in the reality that is always already ours. A third difficulty, *apropos* Beckett, is whether every waiting is a waiting *for.* Is it possible to wait in an intentionless mental space for nothing as though one's mind was or has become a blank canvas? But when we say that we are waiting for nothing, are we not meaning a nothing in particular, where we know not for what we wait specifically, or that we are conscious of waiting for something but cannot put our finger on what it is? Can one wait as an existential mood, and would we say there was a benefit to being in this mood if the mood yielded no more than a *mere* or *bloßes* nothing?

Waiting has submitted to necessarily impossible instructions, to stop short but not too short, to believe but not with false conviction, to doubt but not in order to lead to the impotence of inaction, to risk and improvise but not for their own endless sake. It has been invested with healthy and unhealthy scepticisms, between procrastination and leaping, stasis and movement, forgetting and remembering, idle satisfactions and the idyll of contemplation. It has been made into a lost and found office, sometimes coloured with all the blandness and alienation of the reduced *grau* of Goethe's *alle Theorie*, but thereafter rescued as a twilight zone or a site for a threshold experience with all the hues of life returned. Spatially, the waiting room has also been pictured as nomadic and monadic, fourth walled yet not windowed, if this would tempt anyone to forget the inside of their mind by focusing only on the offerings coming from the outside. Temporally, it has been invested with sustained thoughts of eternity or of the *here and now*, or with transformational glimpses of messianic truths, revealed and concealed, seen darkly or in the light, given and withheld in discourses of speech and silence. And then there are all those tragi-comedies made from the frustrated waitings in games of power or submission, or from the daily waitings for the traffic to move, for a dentist to call you to the chair, for the executioner's blade to fall, or for Wagner's operas to end, or for potentially didactic lectures like my own never properly to begin. But then again, we are told that beginning is always also a starting in the middle, if not also at the end. So, in a waiting room, it is often unclear where we are or where we are going.

Subtitling my own essay by reference to a prelude, I have in mind what Nietzsche achieved by prefixing his *Philosophie der Zukunft* with a *Vorspiel.* By the prefix, he aimed to undercut the conceits of those who had pictured the future not as a sketch of limited norms or principles, but with too dangerous a positivity of speculative content and conviction. Nietzsche aimed to *prelude* readers into *precluding* a blind enthusiasm for a *new man* who would arrive naked and emancipated with a pure ego, to reoriginate in a rebirth the lost spirit of humanity against those who, populating the streets, were described as living with a false egoism defined by petty bourgeois (often Jewish and womanly) self-interests. If a new person for the future was to arrive, the message would better come from the *stuttering* mouth of a Zarathustra, Moses, or ironic Socrates, allowing Nietzsche to declare with a mouth half open of him having "learned to wait—thoroughly" but only, he then added, for *myself—aber nur das Warten auf mich.*

To "wait for myself" meant, for Nietzsche, the conquering of one's impatience to prove one's honor in a duel or one's inclination to live in the ease of forgetting the present as though, suddenly timelessly, one could assume a Christ-like posture of being *not of this world.* Surveying the long nineteenth century, Nietzsche looked to *die Kinder der Zukunft* who, listening to *die Zukunfts-Sirenen des Marktes,* were taken in by the foolish hopes piped out by the *rat-catchers*: that one's miserable enslavement would soon pass if only one was prepared *from this day to the next* endlessly to wait *for something to come from outside.* He described how this waiting could lead to a feverish thirst until, jumping up as a *triumphant beast,* one proclaimed oneself already free. He warned against falling prey to the antiquated reflections of those who, gray-haired, offered only a poison to encourage "the doubting drive, the denying drive, the waiting drive, the collecting drive, the disintegrating drive—*der anzweifelnde Trieb, der verneinende Trieb, der abwartende Trieb, der sammelnde Trieb, der auflösende Trieb*".

He further considered a mass exodus in Europe of workers whose situation was not of possibility but of impossibility, reasoning that their social sickness, far from being cured, was only falsely being consoled by leaders whose self-interests favoured, contrary to their words, the perpetuation of injustice. If once a futurity of vision had liberated a people from one sort of slavery, the new Europeans had entered another, a new *Sklaverei* to a promise of principles or ascetic ideals that had nothing to do with living life now, or to a submission to a world-history that construed the present only as an ever-fleeting stage towards a not-yet existing future.

Nietzsche's critique was shared by many, including Richard Wagner, and this despite the strong case Nietzsche made against him. Looking for a model not of conceit but of courage, Wagner had concluded his treatise on the *artwork of the future* with a striking image for the emancipated mind of both artist and the German *Volk.* Rather than following the proud and haughty

Egyptians into the Red Sea, one should borrow, he had insisted, the courage of the Old Israelites who had shed their skins as enslaved beasts of burden by crossing over. In crossing over, one would become a person of true pride, capable of singing in the new land the authentic *Volklieder* of praise of the *Minne* and *Meistersinger*. In the era around 1848, looking back to the Old Israelites was a very familiar way to praise the Old Testament that had led to the New, so as to condemn a society that had become overrun by a modern Jewry which, not keeping up, had turned true into false pride, and which once had led Yahweh to drown the hardhearted Pharaoh of the Egyptians. But when the case was made against Wagner, one complaint hoisted him high on his own petard: that in so capitulating to false pride, his own words and works increasingly demonstrated an insufficient courage to think in a truly emancipated way.

Yet long before any case was made against Wagner, the perpetuation of unfreedom and injustice concealed behind loud claims to the contrary was diagnosed as a pride of superiority, even a hard-headed *trumpery* cast over a society by those who exhibited every sort of failure to wait. To exhibit *every* sort of failure is, one would think, quite a feat for a single individual, hard to fathom until, we might think, today—but then perhaps the always-today. Many are presently discussing *trumpery via* the authoritarian personality or the one-dimensional man, and the analysis fits scarily well. But I'm interested in the particular hubris of impatience to which waiting has always been offered as the antidote. To speak of an antidote is to seek a cure for a sickness, but where the cure must prevent itself becoming part of the problem. And this prevention is done through the labour of the negative, as when one *stops short* of letting injustice have the last word. In the nineteenth century, the historian Macaulay said that Francis Bacon would have been a second Moses had he been better able to wait. But far worse were the tyrants who, in oppressive regimes, made citizens wait in lines strung out day after day by false promises.

This brings me to an old joke from the Soviet Union, about a queue where everyone waits the first day for the promised bread. As the promise decreases, persons are sent home according to their value to society: the lowest first, the Jews, then women, then non-party members third, leaving the party-faithful to stand alone, only to discover on the fourth day that no bread will arrive. And the punchline coming from the most bitter mouth: "you see, the Jews have all the luck!" If, now, we add to this joke Kant's anecdote about the doctor of speedy cures, our message is almost perfectly delivered. For consoling every patient *von Tag zu Tag* with promises of imminent recovery, the doctor is outwitted when a new patient turns up complaining of the most fatal illness of all, *Ich sterbe vor lauter Besserung*! The word *lauter*—*louder*—is repeated end-lessly in the critique of false prophets, but the usual English translation—"I'm dying from *sheer* recovery" picks up also on one connotation of the word *sheer*, that all that glitters in a house painted white is not gold.

In the waiting game, even when our thoughts in an *essai* or *Versuch zur* lead to something *beyond [Jenseits]* or *infinite [Ewig]*, they cannot forgo the mediat-ed labour of history's time and tense. Nor can they forgo the preparation that tends more to unseat than unsettle expectations as to what freedom and justice really mean. But where in this labour does one begin?

In his museum of the future, Cervantes used the word *tablet*—*tablos*—to allow his readers to consider not only blank paintings, but also books with empty pages. He had in mind not the art-history of artists and writers filling in their tablets with visions of the Garden of Eden or the afterlife of heaven and hell, but the *Tabula Rasa* tradition that, raising questions of *innatism*, had asked whether at birth a child's mind was empty, or, with Plato, full of forgotten remembrance, or what it meant, as for Locke, to await first experiences from which then one abstracted the first *ideas*. Before Locke, Aristotle in *De Anima* likened the naked mind to an *unscribed tablet,* inspiring many thereafter, including the German Idealists, to refuse a mind conceived of as a passive container awaiting external stuff to fill it up. In a popular essay on the human vocation, Fichte added the word *mere—bloß* —to the *empty pages [leere Blätter]* to capture the mind that falsely suspends its capability to engage reason as a practical activity of mediation between the outer and inner. Hegel differently called upon the empty pages to mark the "periods of happiness"—*die Perioden des Glücks*—which, lacking the requisite antagonism, meant that nothing in world-history was happening. In this use, the empty pages represent the *un-historical present* without consequence for spirit's advance of reason into the *future.*

To say that the history of empty pages is today full to the brim would be no exaggeration. Long before one could see empty paintings in the modern museums of the twentieth century, one could read about them as witty and serious *ekphrases* of the pen. Consider just the examples from seventeenth century experiments, inspiring those of the *Tabula Rasa* tradition to negotiate the terms of modern science through emblemata and *parerga:* the blank tablet in Otto van Veen's *Theologicae Conclusiones,* Robert Fludd's cosmological black page *ad infinitum,* and Saavedra Fajardo's blank canvas on an easel, where with "the pencil and colors of art", he saw persons "born without any manner of knowledge ... being left to draw the lineaments of Arts and Sciences on [their minds] as on a blank Canvas". Or Cornelius Gijsbrechts' issuance of the back of a framed painting as part of the *trompe l'oeil* tradition, where the deception implied by the term *trompe* encouraged the wit of inversion that later inspired Jacques Derrida to reveal the philosophical import of the parerga shown as a gap or emptiness in the frame.

Waiting has often been called upon to sustain the dialectical arrest of time deemed essential to artworks that await a history to unfold for their interpretation or social truth content to come to timely and untimely articulations. Adorno wrote of the *afterlife* of artworks in a reception room caught between a refusal and a wanting to be understood. Mostly, however, the waiting served for him as an antidote to a contrary conceit. "The greater the artist", he explained, "the stronger the temptation of the chimerical. For, like knowledge, art cannot wait, but as soon as it succumbs to impatience it is trapped". He unpacked the thought by exposing the vanities in Aldous Huxley's not so brave world or anywhere else where he saw a reconciliation effected through extortion, or an *angedrehter*—translated as a *trumped-up*—realism of utopian phantasy. He described the counterfeit of positivity that concealed the suffering of people, but refused to let the suffering, as the trace of humane content, serve as a guarantee that in the future the counterfeit would be exposed. The idea of suffering was not to be pocketed as a safe possession alongside life's accumulated wares. Sustained as remembrance, suffering opened up an *insight* through negation into the falsity of an art that had renounced all difference in the name of a social reconciliation with what exists for *sight* in the *here and now*. Writing about a jazz performed by the white men of Paul Whiteman's orchestra, he found that no longer was anything allowed to exist that was not *like the world as it is*. He saw this jazz capitulating to one-dimension, to a *false liquidation,* the more it forced gestures towards a different world to *disappear* from the *picture*. The greater the success of this liquidated art, the more the refused gestures were placed into safe-keeping in an art of an uncompromising *image-less image* awaiting a world that coming tomorrow might not be the same as today. Whenever endorsing the erasure of appearance, Adorno stressed the capability of artworks to refuse a mimetic verisimilitude to the *what is*, retaining thereby a utopian, even messianic, *mimesis in waiting* for the *what of the not yet*. This stress tallied with a modernist aesthetic theory favouring blind spots, gaps, limits, and profiles, variously theorised under the rubric of *die Bildlichkeit der Leerstelle* or the *absurd* or *dissonant disabling of representation.* But it also played into the waiting game, as exemplified, say, as an aesthetic of psychological *intensification*, where, in Arnold Schönberg's *Erwartung*, the woman's *moment* of torment is drawn out to the extreme. Or as an endless frustration in his *Von Heute auf Morgen*, when *der Mann* strikes out at *die*

Frau's siren-song by asking: "*Glaubst du wirklich*—Do you really think you can scare me through pictures of the future—*erschrecken durch Zukunftsbilder*—which [only] alienate me coming from your mouth?"

Let me turn now to how the disabling of representation has come to correspond to a limited political provision of ideals, principles or norms, limited because the provision stops short of the design or colour that would count as the filler or substance of the desired realisation—*Verwirklichung*. A single passage is most helpful, drawn from an interview between Habermas and Michael Haller published in 1991 as *Vergangenheit als Zukunft, Das alte Deutschland im neuen Europa*. Discussing what philosophical theories can and cannot accomplish, Habermas criticises the tendency of arguments to become both highly improbable or heavily presuppositioned. (Modifying Max Pensky's translation), the passage reads:

> The 'emancipated society' is in fact an Ideal that suggests misunderstandings. I prefer to speak of the idea of the undamaged intersubjectivity. This idea can generally be derived [or won] from the analysis of necessary conditions for communication [for reaching an understanding/consensus]. It signifies something like the appearance of symmetrical relations of a free reciprocal recognition amongst communicatively acting subjects. Of course this idea must not be pictured into the totality of a reconciled form of life and cast into the future as utopia. [*Die Idee darf allerdings nicht zur Totalität einer versöhnten Lebensformen ausgemalt und als Utopie in die Zukunft geworfen werden.*] It contains nothing more, but also nothing less, than the formal characterization of necessary conditions for the not-anticipatable forms of a non-damaged life. 'Socialism,' likewise ought never—and this well might be the greatest *philosophical* mistake of this tradition—to have been conceived of as the concrete whole of a determinate future form of life. I have always said against this: 'Socialism' is useful only for referring to the quintessence of necessary conditions for emancipated forms of life, about which the participants *themselves* would have to reach an agreement.

Putting aside the conversation demanded of a good socialism, let me note Habermas' negating terms, of what is not damaged and not anticipatable, echoing Adorno's image of a damaged life lived at so catastrophic a moment that Adorno would declare life no longer liveable at all. Habermas was less extreme, though he resisted any turn of the negative into an empty positive, and this in recalling Hegel's description of the greatest philosophical error, when an ideal of truth or freedom is posited as a timeless, merely or unmediated formal or *a priori* ideal. Or when, according to Hegel's critique of the one-sided monochromatic formalism from his *Vorrede* to the *Phänomenologie*, one speaks wrongly of the absolute as a night when *all cows are black.* Hegel criticised those who "start straight off with absolute knowledge, as if shot from a pistol", or those who dogmatically affirm what they think they already know, thereby precluding the dialectical labour, the thinking through of our concepts, that would lead to genuine knowing. Habermas likewise insisted that working through the past in the present for the sake of a better future, one must never assume the conceit, by use of the term *ausgemalt,* to picture the future as a reality before its time.

Everything turns on what is meant by picturing. Hegel used the term *ausgemalt* in his *Vorrede/Preface* to his *Grundlinien der Philosophie des Rechts* to pick up on meanings ranging from *imagining, envisioning, intensifying* but also *picturing* and *painting* by means of *sketch, design,* and *colour.* There is too much to say here about how Hegel connected his critique of *monochromatic formalism* to his declaration from the *Philosophy of Right,* that philosophy, coming too late, pictures the form or *Gestalt* of life that has receded into the past *mit Grau in Grau,* allowing in the gathering clouds of twilight the Owl of Minerva then to begin its flight. (I treat this connection in detail in my book.) Here, let it be enough to pose an intriguing question as to why Hegel made philosophy do its *picturing* not with a *mere-bloßes* Grau but instead by reference to a monochromatic technique that for centuries had gone by the description *mit Grau-in-Grau.* I will return briefly to this question below.

When Habermas described the future as coming to appearance, he used the term *Vorschein* to suggest an intuitive *glimpse* or *sketch* of a future awaiting its actual appearance—*Schein.* To wait for the future was for him to acknowledge the cognitive limits in the coming to "appearance of symmetrical relations of a free reciprocal recognition amongst communicatively acting subjects". The waiting was offered without guarantee that the *Schein* comes as hoped for or expected. Refusing the guarantee countered the conceit of anyone who thinks the *totality* of a *reconciled form of life* can be cast in advance. Avoiding the conceit, he *pluralised* the forms of a future that is not anticipatable, and issued *necessary* formal conditions that together are not *sufficient.* Only if philosophy retains its commitment to necessary conditions that stop short of reaching sufficiency does the picture remain *critical.* I think this is key to the argument. For set between necessity and sufficiency is the space for history (the mediation of reality or the concrete), a space wherein one might be given signposts towards freedom, even a form or some principles, but where still a future normatively *forecast,* even *predicted,* must not trip over into false prophecy. In this picturing, the formalism is necessary, but it is not enough.

Danto also maintained a comparable critical gap when offering his definition of art. If the definition was to accommodate a radical pluralism of art's appearance, one could not close the concept down according to what art had been or now was in the present. Specifying the necessary conditions that art must have *meaning* and *embodiment*, he refused to substantiate the conditions in any way that would restrict how art might come to appearance, even to the point where art may come, as in conceptual or abstract art, somehow to no appearance at all. Wanting to keep the future open, he brought his philosophy of art into accord with his philosophy of history, the latter having been written to liberate claims of history from substantive, totalitarian conceits. Once the liberation was philosophically in place, all the hard work and choices for persons or artists began (as for the Israelites having crossed the Red Sea).

Habermas used the term *allerdings* in a sentence that insisted on not *picturing* the reconciled form of life. One wonders whether his *of course* signalled a repetition of what philosophers have long done when maintaining that they ought never to step over the line as an antidote to what politicians do, and arguably must do, if it is true that nobody with a quiet or stuttering voice wins votes. This brings me to a pressing question, whether the waiting game should or can really preclude philosophers getting their hands dirty. Before Marx's theses on Feuerbach or Sartre's plays of dirty hands, Heine quipped that a philosophy of a history of life made, as by Kant, from formal principles alone would suffer from having neither history nor life. A practical philosophy without the mediation of practice renders a philosophy of principles empty, or, as Goethe put it, *bloßes* grey. For freedom, it is not enough to be guided by the pure form of lawfulness or respect. But as soon as we think about practice, are we not involved with social conditions that are, can, and should be painted not merely with colour but also design? Do we not use the paint brush to blot out false visions? Many have said, going back to Socrates, that philosophy has not the metaphysical or epistemological tools to paint, and that painting damages the more images play into the hands of those with the *louder* sophistic voices. So a strategic silence becomes the name of the game, a game of essential *reserve, a reserve* that becomes a non-picturing picture of freedom.

When Kracauer described the modernist alienation of the urban waiting room, he pictured people in grey suits standing unaware of each other, though with a common fate. He saw an *emptying out* of all relations of attachment. Their autonomy awarded by modern rationality situated them, he said, between the extremes of an empty timelessness and the extreme arbitrariness of daily existence. After this, he worked through every modern *either-or* attitude of rootlessness, homelessness, skepticism, and nihilism, as well as through every sort of inclination to take *short-circuits* or *shortcuts*. But he never gave up on the idea of waiting. He rather rescued it from its dangers with the utopian and gestural *perhaps* of critical theory: *Übrig bleibt vielleicht nur noch die Haltung des Wartens,* he wrote. He saw waiting as a *zögerndes Geöffnetsein,* which, he added, had *allerdings* a sense that was difficult to clarify. The *of course* brought waiting into contact with the irony of a critical theory wherein it has long been acknowledged that matters like freedom and wit cannot be made fully explicit without erasing precisely what is to be explained. Not wanting to explain waiting away, all the questions then remain as questions-in-waiting. We might ask whether "hesitancy" or "reserve" would not be the better terms; why award priority to "waiting"? And does waiting really stop one from saying much about the future that has not yet happened? A quick glance at the *Oxford English Dictionary* lists several connotations for "waiting", one of which is keeping guard, not as a soldier, but as a biblical shepherd or as a thinker in Plato's republic. Without any guarantee, guardianship perhaps offers a sense of safety in a wilderness or wasteland of history that feels so unsafe.

In the same waiting room, one has the chance also to hear the voice of Charles Sanders Peirce, not because of what he said about the firstness of redness, but because, in his essay on "how to make our ideas clear", he separated by reference to a state of hesitation the doubting that serves one from a self-defeating doubt. He described the *hesitancy* when, in a waiting room in a railway station, one passes the time reading advertisements on the wall, engaging fantasy or entertaining oneself as to where one might alternatively travel. He made the hesitancy then serve his scientific enquiry, when images and thoughts come and go slowly and quickly until one reaches a belief on the basis of which one can commit oneself—and act.

Many critical film theorists have with great insight drawn from Kracauer's essay, but not, I believe, in connection with David Lean's classic British wartime film *Brief Encounter.* The film is about a waiting room at a railway station where two lovers meet and part, experiencing an interruption of the truth that hell is other people when mostly women gossip with words that flow as pointlessly as the watery tea. Being at once a safe and unsafe space, the waiting room mirrors in a dialectical play two more spaces: the home of a marriage temporarily interrupted and a borrowed, prefabricated space interrupted when the lovers try to consummate their desire. Were one to view this film only along Tolstoy's lines about the happiness and unhappiness of families, accompanied by Rachmaninoff's music, one might overlook what Adorno captured so well in his *Minima Moralia,* when he described a public rooflessness of a city rained on by bombs coming ruthlessly to penetrate the private home, so that the homeliness became a war-ridden homelessness.

With Kracauer, Adorno wrote that however comfortable the appearance of the interior space, it has become emptied of meaningful relations of communication or design, cut now from prefabricated models to produce a *tabula rasa* for modern disenchanted occupants. For Adorno, adultery was less the issue than a marriage contract that had done away with the possibility of what he termed an *Intermezzo der Freiheit.* Drawing from the French *nostalgie du dimanche,* he envisaged a couple or an entire family feeling homesick in the false sea of satisfaction of weekend days. Like Marx before him, he saw a contradictory anxiety: on the one hand, a guilt implicit to the emerging modern work ethic—that, when not at work, one feels as though one were merely idling one's time away—and, on the other, a sheer exhaustion at spending one's free time not living the moment, but wishing that the workday tomorrow would be a day as free as today. Adorno turned many an *intermezzo* of freedom into bored chords of a modernist unfreedom, to be rescued for married couples only by the hope of a little infidelity to the contradiction that was turning their lives to a *bloßes* grey.

This brings me to a last example, the waiting room of a modernist home that contains a painting, back to front, that shows all *and* nothing. Much has been written about Samuel Beckett's *Endgame,* in and out of relation to his *Waiting for Godot.* Readers have focused on the waiting game, which, without a winner, asks whether the beginning and ending only keeps everyone where they always are, suspended like the "hung verdicts", sometimes catastrophic, of human history. Stanley Cavell finds in *Endgame* Nietzsche's last man who "would rather take the void for his purpose than to be void of purpose", but also Camus' rescue of a humanity in its relinquishing of its aim to play God. Christoph Menke has more recently read the game as a negotiation of an emancipation narrative, writing about the promised freedom as *un-plotted,* so that the lordship-bondage dialectic or the telling of a joke can find no resolution, but only an expiration in sheer exhaustion. He reads *Endgame* "as a play about the end of play", but the play specifically of aesthetic strategies that leaves the faltering struggle for liberation always only in a *deuce.* The *faltering* is evidenced in every crippled gesture or invocation of a blindness or deafness that is reinforced, in my own reading, by the many pauses and hesitations written into a script that stops and starts with all manner of disconcerting and liberating puns of rhythm and rhyme.

Everything in Beckett's *Endgame* counts in a waiting game that tells you that you are damned if you do and damned if you don't, including the opening stage directions of a *tableau* of a philosophical furniture art that Beckett insisted should not be overlooked. "Bare interior", his list begins, followed by "Grey Light". Now observe his inversions that name the objects last: "Left and right back, high up, two small windows, curtains drawn. Front right, a door. Hanging near door, its face to wall, a picture". The instructions continue: "*Front left, touching each other, covered with an old sheet, two ashbins. Center, in an armchair on castors, covered with an old sheet, Hamm*". Until finally we read, "Motionless by the door, his eyes fixed on Hamm, Clov. Very red face".

What does a grey room with a red face have to do with a picture/painting which, face to wall, is not turned around even when Clov takes it down in order to replace it with a clock threatening to set off an alarm, and an alarm following his declaration that the pill box is now empty of pills to kill the pain? Much has been asked about the picture. Does the not-showing matter more than the not-seeing? Does any member of the family know, or did they ever know, what it showed, if ever it showed anything (after *Corinthians*) face to face? Did it once show the time when God was not dead or before God's back was turned on humanity? Or did it only ever have a backside, making the back the front? Or if once a family portrait, did it face the wall like a punished child? Or because whoever designed it found no way to finish it? Or was its point only ever to raise such philosophical *questions* as *questions in waiting*, so that when the answers came, the questions were immediately replaced, like Cervantes's tablets, by new ones that were forever the same ones?

A precursor episode from Walter Scott's *Woodstock* shows, amidst old furniture, the narrator Wildrake stumbling over "*several paintings in massive frames, having their faces turned towards the wall.*" When one is turned around, we are introduced to *the* idea *of* how one looks into a painting to anticipate *the future* as a way to unburden oneself of a terrifying or terrorising past. Is there or can there be this unburdening in Beckett's play? Or is the fact that the picture is not turned around indicative of the fear, as Menke suggests, namely that, were we to turn it around, we would only find an artist or thinker so committed to failing to paint, that all we would see would be a waste comparable to the waste that comes from the ash-can, where even the oldest joke in the world cannot be delivered? "Nothing is funnier than unhappiness", Nell remarks from the ash-can to bring out the comedy of the tragic truth that if this family has obliterated its happiness, then indeed *nothing* is the funniest unhappiness of all.

To make more of the wit that is meant to liberate nothing from nothing, recall the moment when Clov picks up the telescope to take a view through the window. I hear here an echo of Achilles' *red-faced* gaze over the *wine-dark sea* to the glory that never dies. With no more glory on the horizon, Hamm and Clov negotiate each day as a repetition of *any other day. Looks like it*, says Clov. In his reading of the play, Adorno noted the repeated inversions that turned the *anything* into a *nothing on the horizon.* Lowering his telescope, an exasperated Clov declares: *What in God's name would there be on the horizon?* Hamm answers: *The waves, how are the waves?... And the sun?... But it should be sinking.* Looking again, Clov sees nothing, provoking a *damn the sun*, allowing Hamm to presume the night to have arrived. Clov denies this, remarking not once, but twice, and with increasing intensity that it is still grey. *Grey ... GRREY!*

One possible way of interpreting this episode would be to unpack the relation of the wine-dark sea to the Red Sea from which so many have produced intoxicated visions of the past and future of rising and setting *suns* that are also rising and setting *sons*: from Moses to Christ. Here, however, it is more relevant to observe how, in the grey room tinged with red, Adorno stressed the *colourlessness* of a modern wit that was as damaged—*beschädigt*—as the modern selves trying but failing to deliver it. Looking through the telescope, Clov frightens Hamm with the word *grey*, though quickly corrects himself, *a light black.* Adorno saw the correction as smearing the punchline first delivered in Molière's *L'Avare.* Adorno had in mind the spat staged between the miserly master Harpagon and his servant Jacques. Jacques asks what colour a casket is, whether it's *a certain colour* and whether such a colour can even be named. He suggests *red*, to which Harpagon replies *No, grey*, leading Jacques to oblige him with *gris-rouge!*

Here, in my view, is the *grey-red* of an older *monochromatic* palette of painting *mit Grau in Grau*, which, applied to wit, allowed early writers like Molière and Cervantes to use the marrow in the bone to deliver a wonderfully digestible and indigestible humour. Adorno then remarked that Beckett's genius was precisely to have sucked the marrow from the bone, leaving, we now say, nothing but a mere grey grit that kept the family, in Beckett's words, always in "the middle of the steppe".

In the middle, we are compelled back to my own beginning for this essay and to the very first lines of Beckett's play when Clov *tonelessly* says: "Finished, it's finished, nearly finished, it must be nearly finished" and then after a pause, "Grain upon grain, one by one, and one day, suddenly, there's a heap, a little heap, the impossible heap", so that, toward the end, we learn that "all life long you wait for that to mount up to a life." A mountain waiting to be made from a molehill, made from mere grains, can make much ado about a grey grit, which, when interrupted by a single reference to red, allows Hamm with *modesty* to say that nothing gets one very far, but still that this *nothing* is *better than nothing*. Asking after the possibility of something being better than nothing, Clov turns what perhaps is the red shame in his face into the red (sea) of a horizon that gestures toward the only *possibility* left: that the future will not be as things stand today.

I have merely scratched the surface of a picturing of freedom that is liberated by wit. But I give the last laugh literally to the French philosopher Hélène Cixous who, when face to face with the horrifying head of Medusa, sees a woman, as though for the first time, declaring her freedom with words that draw us back to the first song of the sea. "Ah, there's her sea", she writes: "But look, our seas are what we make of them, opaque or transparent, red or black". If the seas are what we make of them, then making is also our freedom to rewrite the history handed down to us, only a tiny part of which I have told here, so that we may begin again in a room, which even if painted grey has a single red line: a horizon of possibility that *nobody*, who still has a will to be *somebody*, can do without.

* An earlier version of this essay was printed in German in a Festschrift, for Christoph Menke: Thomas Khurana, et. al. (eds.), *Negativität: Kunst, Recht, Politik* (Frankfurt am Main: Suhrkamp, 2018). I thank Julia Peters for detailed comments, as well as the many with whom I had the opportunity to discuss the themes.

Adorno's Aesthetics Today

SVEN-OLOV WALLENSTEIN

Adorno in the Present

In many respects, Adorno's *Aesthetic Theory* seems to belong to a past that is moving away from us at increasing speed. Adorno himself acknowledges this belatedness, for instance when in the draft introduction he says that already the very term philosophical aesthetics "has an antiquated quality".[1] In this particular passage his suggestion is tied to what he sees as the nominalism of modern art, whose emergence he locates in Croce and Benjamin, but we may also think of Duchamp's "pictorial nominalism", which would render the observation even more acute.[2] But while aesthetics must acknowledge that it no longer can subsume its objects, it can just as little opt for mere particularity; there is an inescapable antinomy between empty universality and the contingency of particular judgements. And from the vantage point of the present, this seems only to have been exacerbated: no theory appears to be able to delimit a priori what counts as artistic practice, as a work, and as an aesthetic experience—an emptying out that, at the same time as Adorno's reflections on art were drawing to a close, was registered both in the arts themselves and in many strands of philosophy, notably in institutional art theory, although without the historical depth and socio-political urgency that we find in Adorno.

If we add to this his infamous resistance to popular art, his highly selective canon of works drawn from an equally selective idea of tradition, and the fact that as time went by he became increasingly remote from the avant-garde of his own present, his obsolescence seems to be confirmed. Furthermore, while

---

[1] Theodor W Adorno, AT, 493/422. Page references given directly in the text are henceforth to Adorno, *Ästhetische Theorie* (Frankfurt am Main: Suhrkamp, 1973), followed by *Aesthetic Theory*, trans. Robert Hullot-Kentor (London: Continuum, 1997): AT German/English; *Negative Dialektik, Gesammelte Schriften* (Frankfurt am Main; Suhrkamp, 1997), vol. 6, followed by *Negative Dialectics*, trans. E. B. Ashton (London: Routledge, 1973): ND German/English.

[2] Marcel Duchamp seems to have eluded Adorno, no doubt because the decisive role he is ascribed today is a retroactive phenomenon that occurs from the late 1950s onwards. His "pictorial nominalism" (*nominalisme pictural*) relates to painting, which he declares to be a thing of the past while yet affirming it, when he suggests that the readymade should be seen as a painting precisely because it negates everything that painting has ever been. The expression "pictorial nominalism" appears in a note in the White Box; see Marcel Duchamp, *Duchamp du signe: Écrits*, ed. Michel Sanouillet (Paris: Flammarion, 1976), 111, and Thierry de Duve's detailed tracing of this idea in *Nominalisme pictural: Marcel Duchamp, la peinture et la modernité* (Paris: Minuit, 1984).

the integration of art into the culture industry since the 1960s, which transformed both in a way that some time ago could be theorised as "postmodernism" and the "cultural logic of late capitalism",[3] was acutely perceived by Adorno, his own philosophical and artistic preferences made it difficult for him to discern the positive features of what was emerging.

And yet, in spite of all these caveats, he wrote an aesthetic theory, summarising decades of intense engagement with the arts. In a certain way it is obviously a retrospective work, looking back at the experience of modern art, and especially at his far-reaching involvement with the musical avant-garde between the wars and in the post-war period. On another level, he refuses to look back: what art *is*, its limits and potentials, must be determined in the present, and with a view to its future transformations. As Adorno often stresses, it is present works that unlock the past, that prise open the smooth surface of masterworks; it is the critical power of Schönberg that renders the inner tensions in Beethoven visible, and any aesthetic theory that settles for merely regretting the loss of traditional works lacks binding force.

The relation between past, present, and future is thus anything but linear, as seems to be presupposed when critical theory is sometimes understood as an impediment to emerging practices. We should rather see it as a recursive loop: it is present works that make it possible to approach the monuments of the past beyond mere passive admiration, just as it is such a reinterpreted past that in turn strikes back at the present, because both of them, in their respective ways, come towards us from the future. The activity of critique, in keeping with the Greek etymology of the term, would be a *splitting* that tears apart the three dimensions of time; it is an unhinging of time from its axes, which I think was there in Adorno's understanding of how contemporary works burst open past ones and let us glimpse that which did not add up in them, but was concealed underneath their seemingly unbroken surfaces.

Our question, then, must be: what is our present, from which we look back at Adorno? To what extent are his problems still ours, and in what way could they be rethought? In the following, I will present some of the key concepts at

---

[3] It must be noted that neither of the two most influential theories of the postmodern, Fredric Jameson and Jean-François Lyotard, ends up disavowing Adorno. See: Jameson, *Late Marxism: Adorno, or the Persistence of the Dialectic* (London: Verso, 1990), where it is argued that it is precisely today, at the moment where all pockets of resistance seem to have been emptied out, that Adorno acquires his full relevance. Lyotard's comments shift from his early phase, where Adorno is mostly seen as the quintessential enemy, to the later writings from the mid-eighties onwards, where Adorno becomes an ally in the project to resist an all-embracing idea of communication. For a discussion of Lyotard's different readings, see Daniel Birnbaum and Sven-Olov Wallenstein, *Spacing Philosophy: Lyotard and the Idea of the Exhibition* (Berlin and New York: Sternberg Press, 2019), 99–103, 100f.

stake in Adorno's two main late works, *Negative Dialectics* and *Aesthetic Theory*, and then suggest four points I think may be fruitful to consider further, and where a continuation of Adorno's line of thinking in the present might require a rethinking that, once again, in fact remains loyal to him.

The Claims of Negative Dialectics

First, the claims of *Aesthetic Theory* must be seen in conjunction with his other major work, *Negative Dialectics*. The two books are, he writes to Rolf Tiedemann, "what I have to throw in the scale" ("was ich in die Waagschale zu werfen habe").[4] But how are they linked? We must avoid seeing the first book as proposing a general theory that then would find an application, categories that subsequently could be projected onto a certain type of objects called artworks; rather, the two books are the mutually implicative sides of the same project—and yet they remain apart, and cannot be brought together into a whole. Perhaps, paraphrasing Adorno's famous letter to Benjamin commenting on the latter's Reproduction essay, and substituting "philosophy" for "freedom", we might say: Both are the torn halves of an integral philosophy, to which, however, they do not add up ("beide sind die auseinandergerissenen Hälften der ganzen Freiheit, die doch aus ihnen nicht sich zusammenaddieren lässt").[5] The true is not the whole—a figure that Adorno will constantly elaborate from his dense formula in *Minima Moralia* onwards, that the whole is the *untrue*—but the *whole as differing from itself*, split in two halves that can just as little be reconciled as one of them can be simply discarded in favour of the other.

The first claim, then, is to show the priority of the object (*Vorrang des Objekts*), how it escapes subsumption while still not being simply independent of it. If there is always something more in experience than what can be captured by our categories, then at first sight this might be construed as a traditional empiricist or nominalist claim.[6] But, for Adorno, there is no immediacy to be

---

[4] Cited in Rolf Tiedemann's postface, AT 537/459.

[5] Adorno and Benjamin, *Briefwechsel 1928–1940*, ed. Henri Lonitz (Frankfurt am Main: Suhrkamp, 1996), 171.

[6] The idea of nominalism is dealt with differently in *Negative Dialectics* and in *Aesthetic Theory*. In the first, nominalism is somewhat of a philosophical temptation that must be resisted, but also given its due; in a note from an earlier lecture series on ontology and dialectics, Adorno writes: "Not jump over nominalism. Transcend it from out of itself". See *Ontologie und Dialektik (1960/61)*, *Nachgelassene Schriften*, 4/7, ed. Rolf Tiedemann (Frankfurt am Main: Suhrkamp, 2002), 425. In *Aesthetic Theory*, nominalism forms the ineluctable condition of modern art, and it bears on the relation between artistic conventions and genres, and individual works, and while the two sides of the problem are obviously related, they cannot be treated in the same way.

regained outside of conceptual mediation, just as the subject itself would be nothing without an exterior that eludes it. The two sides form a non-identity, which he opposes to idealism's claims about the priority of the subject; idealism and empiricism are, as it were, played against each other, each infiltrating the other without achieving a stable third position.

The second claim is that we must use the power of the subject to dispel the illusion of a constitutive subjectivity. This involves all the dimensions of the subject that cannot be absorbed by its rationality, and yet remain indispensible for knowledge in its fullest extent. Here Adorno retrieves crucial features of psychoanalysis, but also elements from anthropology and the study of religion: in the formation of the subject and its rationality there are always vestiges of magic and mimetic relations to things, an archaic indiscernibility of subject and object, which are features that can never be fully eradicated, just as little as they can be opposed as an alternative to instrumental rationality and its domination over nature.

Subject and object can thus neither be sublated into a higher unity nor posited as merely external, but form a mutually implicative, historically changing constellation. Both sides correct each other; there is something more in the object than what can be held in cognition, and something more in the subject than cognitive acts, even though to make this present in the form of philosophical theses would be to betray it, which is, as we will see, one of the reasons why negative dialectics and aesthetic theory presuppose each other. The truth that philosophy demands is something other than the truth of art, and yet it is not entirely without it.

Both of these sides, the objective and the subjective, are implied in what Adorno calls the non-identical, which is the key to the negative moment in negative dialectics. This however immediately poses a problem: in what way can we think or speak of the non-identical, if thinking, as Adorno stresses, always means to identify ("Denken heisst identifizieren")? On the theoretical and discursive level this can only be done indirectly, through a critique of the insufficiency of subsumption, otherwise it would once more turn the non-identical into something identical, absorbing it into its concept—which might have been Hegel's critique *avant la lettre* of the very idea of a negative dialectic: to speak and to make *sense* is already to enter into the movement of sublation. Adorno too emphasises the necessity of linguistic mediation, but his task is rather to make the non-identical felt in language without becoming an object, like a trace; it is, we might say, the *limit* of sense, not its simple cessation or fall into non-sense. It is what makes sense possible. At least in this respect, the influential critique directed against Adorno by Habermas and his followers seems unwarranted: he does not advocate a different rationality of an aesthetic kind that would lack clear criteria and eventually end up embracing irrationality, but instead proposes to explore a tension within rationality itself, without which it would not be fully rational. It is to this inner difference and incompletion that aesthetic experience testifies, even though it too, as Adorno always cautions us, must be thought by philosophy in order for it to unfold as an internal unrest in reason itself, rather than just remaining an exterior force. Philosophy in this way places itself at the margin of rationality, and if it wants to transcend the concept, it must do so through the concept, so that it constantly pushes up against its own inner limit.

This is also why philosophy's own form of presentation—its *Darstellung* in the Hegelian sense—must reflect something of the non-identical, which for Adorno implies a writing composed of "constellations" that bring together terms and concepts from many fields, and for which Benjamin's Arcades project is the great model (even though Adorno was far from uncritical of what he perceived in Benjamin as an undialectical "magical positivism"). Philosophy can never settle for pure *a priori* concepts, but is always related to the matter at hand, the specific content of the thing; it is *sachhaltig*, which means that no singular method can be specified in advance. However, this stress on empirical content and historical givens does not mean that epistemological questions would simply vanish and be dissolved into any of the sciences. Adorno holds onto the truth content of idealism and, I would argue, in spite of some of his comments, to the analysis of transcendental conditions, even though—and this is the precarious balance he has to strike—they can never be pure. The transcendental itself has a history, to be sure not one reducible to empirical events, but more like a movement separating and articulating the empirical and the transcendental in the inherited Kantian sense; they are like the two sides of history, neither identical nor simply separate.[7]

Hegel's critique of Kant, which introduces movement in thought on all levels, is obviously decisive here for Adorno, with the difference that negativity must have the last word, and no identity of subject and object can be achieved. This non-identity is however not just a theoretical claim, but fundamentally practical: what motivates philosophy is *suffering* as the condition of all truth.

---

[7] These formulations may seem simply wilfully paradoxical, but here – as well as elsewhere – Adorno is moving the same direction as many French philosophers of the period. So, for instance, both Maurice Merleau-Ponty and Michel Foucault in their respective ways attempted to rethink the transcendental as situated and historical, as a "concrete a priori" (Merleau-Ponty) connected to the body, and then, in a more expansive fashion, to the "flesh of the world", or as a "historical a priori" (Foucault) located in the rules of discourse that determine what counts as a meaningful object of knowledge in a particular historical epoch.

But at the same time, in order for this practical side not to relapse into mere hopelessness, thought must be guided by the possibility that here beyond the ubiquity of suffering would exist another state, neither negative nor dialectical: utopia as free relation between the particular and the general, or the "being together of the diverse" (*Miteinander des Verschiedenen*) (ND 153/150) in knowledge as well as in society, for which thinking at present can only be a "placeholder" (*Platzhalter*). This utopia at present remains impossible to determine, it is outside of direct linguistic expression, and it even evades the language of negative dialectics, which can be no more than the "ontology of the false state" and thus always needs to remain vigilant so as not to fall into the trap of becoming yet another metaphysical system.

The Claims of Aesthetic Theory

As we know, *Aesthetic Theory* was by the time of Adorno's death far from having arrived at a definitive form, and the text that was published is the result of the efforts of the editors, Rolf Tiedemann and Gretel Adorno, to provide the manuscript with a systematic order. In this way, the book is not a work in the same sense as *Negative Dialectics*, and yet it has achieved the status of a philosophical testament.

But even though much of the actual structure of the book is due to the editors, there are important comments by Adorno himself with respect to the compositional problems that occupied him to the end. If *Negative Dialectics* obeys a fairly recognisable philosophical architecture, taking us from general reflections on the character of philosophical experience, via a series of "models", and up to the concluding meditations on what remains of metaphysics today, at the moment of its downfall, then *Aesthetic Theory*, as Adorno writes in a letter to Rolf Tiedemann, in a more radical fashion would have accepted that there is no "first principle" from which the rest would follow. Thus, he continues, one can no longer "build an argumentative structure that follows the usual progressive succession of steps, but rather one must assemble the whole out of a series of partial complexes that are, so to speak, of equal weight", so that the book must be written in "paratactical parts that are arranged around a midpoint that they express through their constellation" (AT 541/462).

In this way, *Aesthetic Theory* can be said to integrate something of aesthetic experience into its own composition, without thereby ceasing to be a philosophical reflection on art. The theory bears on the aesthetic sphere, but it can no longer dominate its object from the outside, which always entails the risk of the "pseudomorphosis" that he rejected in the introduction to *Negative Dialectics*.[8] Thought must find a way to think *in* and *through* artworks—which also means coming back to them from a certain outside, a place that is neither that of the artworks themselves nor a readymade philosophy, and which *Aesthetic Theory* not only needs to locate, but must also invent.

In order to at least circumscribe this place, I will extract three concepts (many others could no doubt be selected) from the book: *autonomy*, *mimesis*, and *truth*.

Autonomy, Adorno proposes, must be understood as a social fact, which does not entail that it would in any way be illusory. Rather, it is a concept that names a constantly shifting relation, and it must be seen in relation to the circulation of commodities, services, rationalities and forms of information in society at large, which always condition art, while the latter works over them, reflects on them, and displaces them. Autonomy is always double-edged, and in the section that the editors have subtitled "Art's double character: *fait social* and autonomy; on the fetish character", Adorno stresses that the modern phenomenon of art's emphatic opposition to society is what gives it a social content, not its use of technologies or the empirical stuff that enters into it: art is something "crystallizing in itself as something unique to itself" (AT 335/296), and yet its seeming asociality is in fact the determinate negation of a determinate society. On the other hand, this opposition requires that art partake in the structures that it questions, not least fetishism, which is both a force that threatens to overtake art, and something that it itself needs to deploy in order to have a critical purchase on reality.[9]

This doubling leads to a series of paradoxes: art's only function is to be functionless, its enchantment is disenchantment, and its essential quality is to contradict itself. While it is true that works seal themselves off from what they truly are, i.e. determinate negations of society, and this turns them into ideology to the extent that they inevitably are led to posit something spiritual

---

[8] So Rüdiger Bubner, who argues that this places Adorno in a position that allows the theory of aesthetics to itself become aesthetic; see Bubner, "Kann Theorie ästhetisch werden?" in Burkhardt Lindner and W. Martin Lüdke (eds.), *Materialien zur ästhetischen Theorie: Theodor W. Adornos Konstruktion der Moderne* (Frankfurt am Main: Suhrkamp, 1980). This objection is then echoed in Habermas, *Theorie des kommunikativen Handelns* (Frankfurt am Main: Suhrkamp, 1981), vol. I, 489ff. The aesthetic dimension, as Adorno often notes using a musical analogy, lies in philosophy's need to be *composed*, even though this is not carried out in the same way in *Negative Dialectics* and *Aesthetic Theory*. The best study of Adorno's mode of writing is still the remarkably overlooked thesis by Antje Giffhorn, *In der Zwischenzone: Theodor W. Adornos Schreibweise in der "Ästhetischen Theorie"* (Würzburg: Königshausen & Neumann, 1999).

[9] For a discussion of the various sense of fetishism in Adorno, see my "The Necessary Fetishism of the Work of Art", in Anders Burman and Anders Bartonek (eds.), *Hegelian Marxism: The Uses of Hegel's Philosophy in Marxist Theory from Georg Lukács to Slavoj Žižek* (Huddinge: Södertörn Philosophical Studies, 2018).

outside of society, at the same time, this spiritual dimension—*Geist* now understood not as a sphere outside of the material, but as the *facture* of works, the interplay of their constituent parts that takes them beyond the world of *facts*—is what gives them their critical power. Their distance from the real opens a space for freedom that still remains unreal, imaginary, and even compensatory, which is why autonomy is just as much false as it is true.

If art, as Adorno famously suggests against a long tradition of Marxist theories of art, does not relate to society by depicting its contents, but by internalising its antagonisms as tensions and contradictions in its inner form—linguistic, musical, painterly etc.—then the concept of autonomy needs to invoke a certain formalism, though not at all in terms of aestheticism or a doctrine of *l'art pour l'art* (or better, it requires the extraction of a truth content from aestheticism, as is indicated when Adorno in his letter on Benjamin's Reproduction essay calls for a study of Mallarmé as a "counterpoint" to the claims about the decay of the aura in mechanical reproducibility). Art addresses society at the deepest level where its own "logicity" (*Logizität*) intersects with the instrumental rationality that permeates the social world, grafting itself onto it while also twisting it around, parodying it, and in this opening up towards a different, free order, or a "violence-less synthesis", as Adorno sometimes says.

Mimesis is the movement by which art internalises, reflects and transcends the given. Mimesis is for Adorno not primarily imitation, depiction, or any kind of mirror relation between an original and a copy, but first of all has its roots in an archaic and magic relation to the object that characterises prehistory, and remains as a trace in art after it has disconnected from myth. Mimesis thus precedes the movement of spiritualisation; it is absorbed into it, which does not mean that it is repressed, but that it is preserved as an inner tension in artistic form. This relation to something that precedes history in a structural sense—as is indicated by the prefix "*Ur-*", the domain of the originary, the *arche* in the archaic—is one of the aspects that gives art its *methexis*, its participation, in redemption, although Adorno stresses that there is no way of returning to a state that would have preceded rationality, otherwise than through regression to myth.

At the other end of the historical spectrum, in the modern world of enlightened rationality, the mimetic relation bears on the developed antagonisms of society. Antagonisms relate to particular social forms and are as such always historically specific. Beyond this, the fundamental antagonism, I think, is the one that also echoes the archaic origin, i.e. the tension between mimesis as a moment of dispersion and a descent into affective and corporeal impulses, and the need for rational construction. In the administered world, from which art cannot escape by some magic trick, its rational constructions are nevertheless permeated by something else—as we have seen, their logicity is a doubling both of the social logic and the logic of identifying, discursive ordering, turning them back on themselves in order to set something else free; it prefigures something of the non-identical. The artwork in this shows something to philosophy, in its way of letting particulars come together without subsuming them, and yet creating a unity, although of a different kind.

Here one must once more note the important criticism that has been levelled at Adorno's claims, specifically by Habermas and his followers, and which has become almost a standard objection in the literature. In this line of reasoning, the concept of mimesis must be rejected, since it allegedly sets itself up as an alternative to discursive rationality without being able to supply any normative criteria for its application.

These criticisms, first of all, seem to me misguided in relation to Adorno, but, furthermore, they lead in a direction opposed to what I am proposing here: to push Adorno's idea even further. Mimesis, Adorno often underlines, can just as little replace instrumental reason or identity thinking as it can be suppressed by it. Rather, as I have suggested, it is better understood as an inner corrective, a reminder of what this thinking can never exhaust, since its conceptual domination is built upon the repression of the mimetic, which nevertheless leaves scars or traces in experience that art and philosophy register, each in their own way, without being simply mapped onto each other.

This criticism of Adorno's use of mimesis is then connected to the second and more far-reaching claim to which Adorno would have remained oblivious, i.e. the turn from a philosophy of consciousness to a philosophy of language, and thus would have remained trapped in "metaphysical thinking". This we see in, for instance, Albrecht Wellmer, who speaks of Adorno's failure to attain a "post-metaphysical aesthetics of modernity"[10] that shifts the focus to the communicative role of art, and suggests that he remained entrenched in late modern strategies of refusal and negation, which in turn would be based in unnecessary paradoxes derived from an outdated philosophy of consciousness.

Now, it seems clear that the idea of art as communication, which this argument takes as the solution, is what in fact *Aesthetic Theory* opposes from beginning to end, rather than being something Adorno would have overlooked or failed to grasp. Communication is what is demanded of art not only by the culture industry, but also by those who opt for a culinary highbrow aesthetic,

---

[10] See Wellmer, "Adorno, die Moderne und das Erhabene", in Franz Koppe (ed.), *Perspektiven der Kunstphilosophie* (Frankfurt am Main: Suhrkamp, 1991), 190.

precisely because they defuse art and turn it into a specific sphere of experiences to be placed alongside the other spheres, eventually endowing it with a compensatory function. In addition, while Adorno in many contexts insists on the constitutive resemblance of art to language, its *Sprachähnlichkeit*, he adds that language becomes art precisely as "writing", i.e., through a moment of self-reflection, opacity, and refusal of meaning that transforms it into an enigma and calls for a particular type of interpretation—the basis also for his (perhaps unjust) rejection of hermeneutics as a theory that claims to simply dissolve the enigma. "The task of aesthetics", he writes, "is not to comprehend artworks as hermeneutical objects; in the contemporary situation, it is their incomprehensibility that needs to be comprehended." (AT 179/157)

Furthermore, and most generally, there is the assumption that a philosophy of consciousness would be metaphysical, whereas a philosophy of language would somehow escape this condition, and constitute an unequivocal and assured progress, since it would once and for all solve the problems posed by its predecessor. Irrespective of how one understands the term "metaphysics", it seems obvious that none of this can be taken for granted. Finally, regardless of whether refusal and negation are sufficient concepts to grasp artistic work, other means are equally available that just as little give in to the idea of communication, which probably is, as Heidegger once said of the notion of *Erlebnis*, "the element in which art dies".[11]

Third, then, the idea of *truth*. What Adorno calls the "truth content" (*Wahrheitsgehalt*) of a work is not a propositional content that can be extracted (or communicated), and cannot be identified with intentions or themes; truth belongs to movement of the "intentionless" (*das Intentionslose*), which passes through the subject, and is neither simply without it, nor can it be reduced to it. Truth is mediated through all of the work's particular sensuous moments, whose transcendence in relation to the factually given occurs through their facture, how the work is put together and organised through artistic technique; its objectivity or quality as a thing or object (*Sachlichkeit*) and its truth are inextricably intertwined, Adorno writes.

The relation to truth is not simply historical in a straightforward sense, as in the claim that a work provides us with the truth about an epoch or a social formation, but above all, and more profoundly, it is a relation between the historical and the *Ur-* or archi-historical, the threshold that separates and joins the archaic repetition of myth from the movement of history; the moment of

---

[11] *Der Ursprung des Kunstwerkes*, in *Holzwege, Gesamtausgabe* (Frankfurt am Main: Klostermann, 1977), vol. 5, 67. In a handwritten marginal note (b) Heidegger adds that the true task is to "attain a wholly different element for the becoming of art" ("ein ganz anderes Element für das Werden der Kunst zu erlangen")

natural beauty in art echoes this, at once a reified image and the bearer of a hope of reconciliation. Because of its mediated distance from this first nature, art is able to recollect it, it can preserve the "shudder" that belongs to the archaic without ceding to regression, by transposing it into the parallel world of imagination. Art is in this sense a critique of myth and as such always part of the enlightenment, but also a way to save its truth content and turn it into a corrective against a thought that aspires to seal itself autonomy. In modernity, this is played out as the tension between mimesis and construction, which includes all those technological means that have been absorbed into art, without as such having a direct causal influence, as Adorno often objects to Benjamin.

This utopian moment has often, together with mimesis, been understood as the main problem with Adorno's aesthetics, and it has been suggested that the idea of redemption, which holds artworks hostage to a preconceived theory, must be left behind if Adorno is to be saved from himself. Just as in the case of mimesis, I would like to follow a different direction. First, the problem with this salvation is, as I see it, that it saves Adorno by cutting off his head, i.e. it evacuates his basic claim, without which the different elements that are disengaged from the redemptive horizon would appear as a set of perhaps interesting remarks on formal problems in modern art, but in the end run the risk of saying the opposite of what was intended. If art is deprived of its capacity to internalize, reflect on, but also point beyond the administered world, then it becomes little more than an object of judgements of taste in the Kantian sense, and the relation not just to truth, but also to the enigma of truth, simply disappears.

It is true that there is a constant risk that artworks become merely a mirror that philosophical thought holds up to itself, and in which it sees its own unity and fulfilment achieved, although in a form that yet lacks the kind of conceptual reflection that philosophy is called upon to supply. "The truth of discursive knowledge", Adorno writes in a compressed sentence that summarises the force of this logic, "is unshrouded, and thus discursive knowledge does not have it; the knowledge that is art, has truth, but as something incommensurable with art" (AT 191/167). This chiasma (neatly expressed in the semicolon that splits Adorno's sentence into two reflecting parts) just as much embraces a certain "aestheticising" of philosophy—for instance when Adorno claims that philosophy must always refer to the singularity and monadic dimension of the work as the "*organon* of truth" (AT 338/298)—as it implies a becoming-philosophy of art, when he claims that the "progressive self-unfolding truth of the artwork is none other the truth of the philosophical concept", and that [a]esthetic experience is not genuine experience unless it becomes philosophy"

(AT 197/172). On the one hand, this sets up a tension that surely can become immensely productive, as Adorno's own detailed analyses of musical works show abundantly, but, on the other hand, it obviously also entails a risk of reductionism and a violence done to the singularity of the work. The allegation that this generally blocks the approach to the individual work of art is however not warranted in the case of Adorno. It is true that his aesthetic would collapse (or at least would have to be substantially rethought, as for instance Albrecht Wellmer proposes) if the idea of reconciliation was dispensed with; and yet this idea would mean little were it not ceaselessly developed out of the actual substance of works from Beethoven to Schönberg's dodecaphony, Webern's proto-serialism and beyond, and it can hardly be argued that Adorno would remain indifferent to musical detail or formal analysis, only that these empirical features, for him, as a *philosopher* (and not a musicologist) must always be related to a philosophical task.

Four Points

Finally, there are four points I would like to make. Rather than conclusions, they are guidelines for future thinking, with and against Adorno.

The first concerns the status of *interpretation*. We noted above the ambivalence of Adorno's take on this concept: on the one hand, he insists on reception as a "freedom towards the object" (*Freiheit zum Objekte*), in which the subject abandons itself to otherness, and on works as "things of which we do not know what they are" (AT 174/149); on the other hand, he sometimes claims, as we have seen, that the truth of art is nothing but the truth of the philosophical concept. In fact, I would argue, interpretation should be seen as a second work of a particular kind, rather then something merely grafted onto the first object. If the object embodies contradictions, and these can be read out of it by an interpretation, the latter nevertheless remains an invention of theory. While these contradictions do originate in society, which for us inevitably means the world of contemporary capitalism, and are reflected in the work, this reflection is not a simple mirroring that has a bearing on content or the "objective moment", as Adorno says, but occurs through an act of mimesis that in turn generates tensions and contradictions within the construction, form, or immanent structure of the work. Teasing out these contradictions from the object is itself a different form of mimetic creation, neither superior nor inferior to the first work, and in this sense interpretation produces a second work alongside the first, which cannot avoid embodying contradictions that it, in turn, itself cannot master. Thus, neither work nor interpretation is the key to the other; instead, both have multiple intersections in common, although without being reducible to a third underlying matrix. This inevitably entails a crumbling of the hierarchy between the muteness and opacity of the work and the eloquence of interpretation that Adorno, notwithstanding his many precautions, sometimes ends up reproducing. If artworks, as he sometimes writes, appear to be saying something, but that it is impossible to say what they say, we should not believe that philosophical interpretation succeeds in saying it, only that it provides a different take on this impossibility as such, traversing the divide between language and "resemblance to language" without ceasing to be language and concept.

Second, our concept of *autonomy* must be articulated differently from the articulation of the concept available to Adorno, since the idea of closure that guided him is no longer the same as ours. This does not mean that it has simply evaporated, but rather that it has been transformed along with the development of technologies of both production and distribution. These shifts are indicated by, for instance, the inverted constellation of concepts and particulars in conceptual art and everything that would follow in its wake, or by the open or processual artwork that Adorno indeed glimpsed but attempted to enclose within the negative concept of the "informal",[12] by the incessant interrogation (both theoretical and practical) of the status of the art object that understands it as more of a product of discursive conditions than a perceptual given, and a host of other shifts, all of which belong to a phase of aesthetic reflection that emerged in the sixties just as Adorno's work was drawing to close. Autonomy is more like a result of the "knight's move" of the work, its "swerve", to use a term borrowed from Shklovsky and Russian formalism.[13] The work's distance from reality is itself conditioned by reality, it is the way in which reality is taken up and deflected, which does not make the distance that it sets up any less real; conversely, the work could be said to inject this distance into the real itself (which could also allow us to glimpse a different sense of *realism* in Adorno than the petrified forms of nineteenth-century art and their continuation in socialist realism).[14] If in Skhlovsky's view the sideways move of the knight occurs because the direct road ahead is blocked, then this move is itself not just a leap into the imaginary, but rather introduces a different spacing of the board

---

[12] See Adorno, "Vers une musique informelle" (1961), in *Quasi una fantasia, Gesammelte Schriften* 16; *Quasi una fantasia: Essays on Modern Music*, trans. Rodney Livingstone (London: Verso, 1992).

[13] Se Viktor Shklovsky, *Knight's Move*, trans. Richard Sheldon (Norma, Ill.: Dalkey Archive Press, 2005).

[14] For further discussions of realism in Adorno, see my "Adorno's Realism", *Baltic Worlds* Vol. IX, no 4 (2016).

itself. Autonomy must not be taken as an objective property that some things may have while others simply lack, but as a kind of limiting or framing condition that determines what belongs to the inside of the work and what to its outside. Autonomy is the effect, the *work*, of a *beside-the-work*, a *parergon*, or a *frame*, as Derrida noted already in Kant's aesthetics,[15] and in this sense it cannot be eliminated without the work ceasing to exist. The process underway since Adorno's time might be analysed as the gradual introjection of such framing conditions into the work itself, so that they now can become its explicit and thematic material instead of passively assumed outer boundaries.

Third, *contradiction* must be rendered more fluid so as to incorporate a more expansive sense of difference. This need to rethink the idea of contradiction signals that negative dialectics, in its dependence on the Hegelian legacy, ought to be loosened from its fixtures (which obviously does not rule out that this could also be carried out through a more attentive reading of Hegel himself, which Adorno sometimes sketches). It needs to confront other traditions that understand difference in another fashion—the task could be to cross-read Adorno's *Negative Dialectics* with, say, Deleuze's *Difference and Repetition*, a task that I here, by way of conclusion, will briefly indicate. Two years after *Negative Dialectics*, Deleuze points to Heidegger's ontological difference, structuralism, the *nouveau roman* and role of repetition in language, in the unconscious, and in art, and suggests that "[a]ll these signs may be attributed to a generalized anti-Hegelianism: difference and repetition have taken the place of the identical and the negative, of identity and contradiction. For difference implies the negative, and allows itself to lead to contradiction, only to the extent that its subordination to the identical is maintained".[16] For Deleuze this points to a "transcendental empiricism" that, notwithstanding the

---

[15] See Derrida, "Parergon", in *La vérité en peinture* (Paris: Flammarion, 1974); *The Truth in Painting*, trans. Geoff Bennington and Ian McLeod (Chicago: University of Chicago Press, 1987). Derrida starts out from the legal distinction that organizes Kant's critical philosophy – the difference between *quid facti* (what are the facts relevant to the case, the actual features of our experiences and judgments) and *quid juris* (by what right can they lay claim to their respective places in reason's general architectonic) – and shows that this in the aesthetic sphere entails an entanglement of both sides. Kant's attempt to frame aesthetic judgment cannot avoid having recourse to instruments drawn from theoretical reason, which are always foreign to and yet related to the aesthetic, and when he needs to establish the connection to the critical system at large, this produces a movement of (de)framing, a frame that continually breaks up and opens an intermediate zone of undecidability. It is in this zone that Derrida locates the parergon, something beside (*par-*) the work and yet essential to its working, to the *energeia* of the *ergon*. Derrida's analysis of the frame in many ways intersects with Adorno's comments on the logicity of the work and on how it mimes yet distances itself from instrumentality.

[16] Deleuze, *Différence et répétition* (Paris: PUF, 1968), 1; *Difference and Repetition*, trans. Paul Patton (London: Continuum, 1994), ix.

differences in vocabularies, in many respects intersects with Adorno's negative dialectic.[17] Both of them address the question of how to approach the singular or the "monadic", of difference as the limit of the non-identical and the sensible as a differential, of the limits of conceptual subsumption, although they reach results that at first may seem opposed to each other, or perhaps just simply unrelated. Both of them could in fact be taken as the heretic heirs of Hegel's logic of essence, where the movement of difference (*Unterschied*) leads from diversity (*Verschiedenheit*) via opposition (*Gegensatz*) to contradiction (*Widerspruch*), and then returns to the ground (*Rückgang in den Grund*), but also founders (*zu Grunde gehen*). Both want to intervene in the first step of this movement, but then take off in different directions: Adorno wants to halt the dialectic, or rather force it to ceaselessly return to a ground that it can never master; for Deleuze, difference is a dispersal that occurs already within the sensible as such, and antedates all ordering in opposites, and the ground that is reached is an un-grounding (*effondement*),

Now, while a reconstruction of a space in which such different claims could communicate might seem like an excessively abstract and even abstruse proposal, it will have an impact on the very vocabulary of critical theory. For Adorno, it was necessary to retain traditional concepts like subject and object, self-consciousness, identity, etc., and he always insisted on their double nature. As sediments of a reified tradition, they also contain petrified mediations that could once more be set free; just like artworks, concepts have an inner historicity that does not seal them within the confines of the past, but rather makes it possible for them to take on new meanings in other contexts. It may be the case, however, that the unquestioned presuppositions that many of these terms carry with them today may block thought rather than open it; the passage from the language of critique to the critique of language—which, to stress this once more, is not the same as a linguistic turn towards communication—is however always a tenuous one. The antinomy between philosophy as a "creation of concepts" (Deleuze) and as a de-sedimentation of older ones is no doubt as such too simplified, and yet it cannot be simply dismissed: the creation of concepts does not take place in a void, but presupposes a matter that it transforms; negative dialectics wants to be a memory of that which has always resisted integration, but it can only do this by creating something that has never been fully said or thought.

---

[17] The connections between *Difference and Repetition* and *Negative Dialectics* are still largely unexplored. The only systematic treatment seems to be Wu Jing's thesis *The Logic of Difference in Deleuze and Adorno: Positive Constructivism vs. Negative Dialectics* (Hong Kong: The University of Hong Kong, 2009, online).

Fourth, *the critical and utopian work of the work must be pluralised*. Because the work is not simply a reflection, but fundamentally a working over or working through (and in this it is akin to Freud's *Durcharbeitung*), it liberates a singular transcendence that allows us to perceive particulars in a way that releases them from conceptual subsumption without simply bypassing it—the being-together or togetherness of the diverse, which for Adorno was the moment of utopia or reconciliation, albeit veiled, ungraspable, and only accessible in a negative mode. For Adorno, the possibility of a togetherness that escapes identificatory binding together in oppositions and contradictions would be the *utopian limit* of negative dialectics where it ceases to be both negative and dialectical; for Deleuze, this state of a free difference in the sensible need not rely on a projection of the future, but determines the place to be reached as a site constituted in a now-and-here that is also a *now/here*, or, if we read this term backwards, as Samuel Butler once proposed (with a minor transposition of letters to reflect the backwards pronunciation), as an *erewhon*. The ideas invented by philosophy—which here seem almost indistinguishable from artworks—are, Deleuze suggests, "neither universals like the categories, nor are they the *hic et nunc* or *now here*, the diversity to which categories apply in representation. They are complexes of space and time, no doubt transportable but on the condition that they impose their own scenery, that they set up camp there where they rest momentarily: they are therefore the objects of an essential encounter rather than of recognition. The best word to designate these is undoubtedly that forged by Samuel Butler: *erewhon*. They are *erewhons*."[18]

While the moment of utopian reconciliation cannot be simply erased, as some would like to do,[19] if the entire edifice of Adorno's aesthetic theory is not to mutate into a series of formalist analyses of modern art, perhaps it is possible to break it up, spectrally, in the sense of refraction as well as that of a haunting. From Adorno's point of view, the spectralisation of reconciliation might suggest that its basis in an interpretation of natural history needs to look different in the age of modern technology: how can we think a philosophy of nature when the difference between nature and the artificial has, as Deleuze once proposed, disappeared?[20] In what sense would a non-coercive, non-violent rela-

---

[18] Deleuze, *Différence et répétition*, 364f; *Difference and Repetition*, 285.

[19] So for instance Wellmer, who suggests that Adorno's failure to recognise that he already possesses all the elements of a post-metaphysical aesthetic is due to the fact that he sees them in the "distorted" optic of reconciliation; see Wellmer, "Adorno, die Moderne und das Erhabene", 190.

[20] See the interview with Raymond Bellour and François Ewald, on the occasion of the publications of *Le Pli: Leibniz et le baroque*, "Sur la philosophie", *Pourparlers* (Paris: Minuit, 1990), 212: "On Philosophy", *Negotiations*, trans. Martin Joughin (New York: Columbia University Press, 1995), 155.

tion between inner and outer nature be possible in a world that on one level seems to have erased the last vestiges of otherness, while on another level reproduces it as immanent "risks" that proliferate precisely because of the domination of nature?

Interpretation, autonomy, difference, and utopia—to these four points others could no doubt be added. To pursue the task of critical theory as bequeathed to us by Adorno means to think through them, with and against him, in order to come back to him from a vantage point that belongs to the future.

Orientation Towards the Concrete

ANNE BOISSIÈRE

The future of Critical Theory is not "After Adorno", notwithstanding certain claims that have been advanced,[1] but "Forevermore with Adorno". Indeed, in matters of art and aesthetics, the critical potential of Adorno's thought has not as yet delivered all its content. This is specifically so regarding the reception of Adorno's musical writings. Here there has been much talk about evaluating ideas, theses and arguments, but little or nothing about another and decisive aspect, i.e., a philosophical *gesture*, the manner of philosophising within this domain.

While the tendency to discourse *on* art *in general* is becoming increasingly more strong and dominant, for his part Adorno invents another style, the philosophical importance of which is pivotal: he orients his thinking *towards the concrete*, faithful to that experiential core without which dialectics would not only be an empty word but would also produce the worst effects of seizure and domination. With him, the non-identical, that is, the aptitude of not only turning towards alterity but of considering details, does not only constitute a theoretical or apodictic positioning, it implies a different *manner* of philosophising. It is by virtue of this gesture—which is rigorous, demanding and, to be sure, most rare—that Adorno's philosophy is, especially today, a resource without equivalent.

Close to art, thought cannot simply proceed by argument, all the more so when experience is upsetting, when it brings with it a world of dreams, of childhood or just of an "elsewhere" breaking with the mechanisms manipulating life towards self-preservation. A certain *passivity* or *relaxation* arises, conferring upon music a quite different status from that of an *object* of discourse. Adorno *lets himself go* to music, not content with merely analysing it in terms of history or progress: experience is crucial, and one even observes that it takes an ever more significant place in his approach, including the questioning of established positions—even those of Adorno himself. Orientating thought towards the concrete does not solely amount to turning to art or even artworks—that would be trivial. It is the aptitude to deepen experience where it is most irreducible

---

[1] I am alluding to an article collection edited by Rainer Rochlitz, *Théories esthétiques après Adorno*, (Arles: Actes Sud, 1990), generally in favour of a remaking and overcoming of Adorno's aesthetics as represented notably by the contributions of Albrecht Wellmer and Peter Bürger. I discussed these positions in my book *Adorno: La vérité de la musique moderne* (Villeneuve d'Ascq: Presses Universitaires du Septentrion, 1999).

and where it may even run counter to conceptuality—especially when the latter falls back into "positivism", as Critical Theory conceives of it. Unless Adorno's philosophy is to be rashly reduced to theses or unquestioned schemes of reading, it becomes possible to consider and to welcome its experiential core, at the very least in the case of music, which presents itself as the truly active and critical focus of Adornian thought.

The Constellation of "Beautiful Passages"

Let me begin with the 1965 talk "Beautiful Passages" ("Schöne Stellen"). This text is quite astonishing, since it goes against many of the common ideas that surround Adorno's reception: one discovers a philosopher speaking on the radio, being careful to communicate in an understandable language, above all defending a praxis of extracts or fragments. Adorno is perfectly aware of doing something new compared to what he had said or written elsewhere. He adjusts his thinking in accord with the demands of the historical situation, thus reminding us that critical theory must move with its object. Adorno puts to work some themes present in his philosophy. On the one hand, there is the notion of regressive listening—a subject that in its turn belongs to wider themes surrounding the cultural industry—and on the other hand, there is the issue of musical form, and how the totality connects to particular details.

When placed within the dual contexts of the radio and the idea of the fragment, Walter Benjamin seems to constitute the horizon of Adorno's text. Besides, Benjamin had already introduced the notion of "Beautiful Passages" regarding writing in *Denkbilder*. Incidentally, Adorno makes an explicit reference to *Einbahnstrasse* in order to speak about the subversive role of "citation". The musical extracts termed "Beautiful Passages", which Adorno presents for audition and commentary, would thus have in themselves an explosive force apt to tear them away from the dire and morbid destiny of the cultural industry.

Without any doubt Adorno situates himself in a Benjaminian horizon, but only to go in a direction proper to himself: firstly, because he deals with music, secondly because the dialectic he introduces is not in fact present in Benjamin.

"Beautiful Passages" is inseparable from the *experience* of music, listening included, and accordingly Adorno accepts to relate a dimension of this experience to childhood, that is, to *his* childhood. Far from introducing the arbitrary, this fills the experience of "Beautiful Passages" with a unique substance. One notices that Adorno's taste for so-called "grand music", from Bach to Schönberg and Webern, is not contradicted given that all the examples come from this area. But the experience Adorno wants to discuss is not determined by this social-didactic dimension; or if it is, it is so only to be overcome. The beauty in question is not conventional; nor is it the beauty connected to Kantian contemplation, which is reflective, supposing at any rate a distance from the object. On the contrary, immersion is both total and ephemeral. "In order to be assured of such beauty, it is needful to lose oneself without reservation to singularities for which there is no substitute in anything else whatever; and it is of such details that I want to talk."[2]

This lecture "Beautiful Passages" is important, since Adorno makes himself the speaker of a musical experience irreducible to socio-historical determinations, for which nevertheless he fights in his philosophy. "The singular element" is not the detail linked to the whole, according to a dialectical logic that one could apprehend in terms of either matter or the composition. "In it, there accumulates *substantiality*, as much as music itself, according to its own idea, *exceeds culture* or, synthesis."[3] Adorno, while seemingly closest to sensualism, which in a certain sense he is, indicates an experience of a quasi-metaphysical nature; experience of the absolute, unspeakable in certain ways, which he here relates to an "exact imagination" (*exakte Phantasie*). It is crucial to become attentive to what appears as a break—a sort of interruption and suspension— with respect to the dialectical reflection, organising itself about history, culture and society, that we know constitutes the core of his philosophy. Yet to bring his thought down to this level would amount to depriving it of its deep life, of its pulsation, that is, its experience. It would condemn it to getting lost in gossip.

With "Beautiful Passages", music is no longer an *object* of a conceptual and reflective study, in terms of the withdrawn point of view that organises most of Adorno's socio-historical approach, and of which a book like *Philosophy of New Music* would be emblematic. With the singular element, this distance does not exist anymore. What can philosophy do, then? What can be said at this point?

It would be an error to think that the experience of "Beautiful Passages" is something singular and thus of little importance. This would be rash and prejudicial, short-circuiting developments which would otherwise incline us instead to uphold its significance, even though it seems to go against a certain number of other ideas one also finds in Adorno. Through the reception of

---

[2] Theodor W. Adorno, *Gesammelte Schriften* vol. 18, 700, ("nur bedarf es dazu, dass man solcher Schönheit sich versichert, dessen, dass man an Einzelnes, durch nichts anderes Substituierbares ohne Vorbehalt sich verliert, und von solchen Einzelheiten will ich reden").

[3] Theodor W. Adorno, *Gesammelte Schriften* vol. 18, 699, emphasis mine ("In ihm sammelt sich soviel Substantielles, wie Musik selber, ihrer Idee nach, mehr ist als Kultur, Ordnung, Synthesis").

Freud, he nevertheless invites a grasping and deepening of details, chiefly when such details introduce a false pitch, a disparity with respect to an established totality. Detail is not only what is small; it is a smallness out of which one is wholly able to revisit the conception of things, to acquire a different idea of reality, thus of thinking—since thinking equally belongs to reality.

One may pay attention to the fact that the experience of "Beautiful Passages" is taken further through other experiences of the same sort—there are equivalent openings in Adorno's musical thinking. Even if these passages do not lead to elaborate developments, they ought not to be neglected or held to be of little weight. It is not my intention to present them fully. Rather, my aim here is chiefly to shed light upon a constellation—in the sense that Adorno understands the term, namely as a structure of moments that share an affinity with one another and thus form a non-systematic coherence.

The first fragments[4] of the unfinished work on Beethoven are of this kind. Adorno begins what was supposed to become his philosophical masterpiece by recalling the way in which, as a child, he saw and lived a score: not as a text with notes to read the music, but as a magical site, peopled with living creatures, starting with the instruments; for him, Waldstein, the name of Beethoven's sonata, was a "knight venturing into a thick forest". To recall music's magic is not a rhetorical, or an introductory artifice. Rather, Adorno insists on the fact that his entire future relationship to music is carried by this primal sensation, which he says he felt for the first time, and has felt ever since, when reading the Pastoral Symphony. One part of this remembrance is certainly a construction, and the "Beautiful Passages" themselves partly issue from such a construction. But this construction holds its truth through what it draws from the initial experience. Here what is initial is magic. Initial does not mean that one stands at the beginning; precisely, there is no start, no beginning. Magic is for the child a *given*: without cause, it gives impulse to everything else; it is in this sense that it is primal.

Music, before being an object of study, is a dream, not in a psychical or psychological sense, i.e. subjectively, but in the sense of a dream taking us to a different and objective reality, one that is perhaps truer than the real in which we live. Music does indeed take us elsewhere. As in the experience of the singular element to which the "Beautiful Passages" correspond, it has a quasi-metaphysical turn; at any rate, it is a complete form of *existence*.

---

[4] Theodor W. Adorno, *Beethoven: Philosophie der Musik*, Fragmente und Texte herausgegeben von Rolf Tiedemann (Frankfurt am Main: Suhrkamp 1993), fragments 1–4, 21–22.

Childhood, dream, magic belong to the experience of "Beautiful Passages". This experience is synonymous with a letting-go to the point of losing oneself. One must accept that there exists no further goal, except letting us be carried away by the music, giving ourselves over to it, placing ourselves within the flux, within the transition, in a sort of a limit state that necessarily defies words. Adorno's last two musical monographs, on Mahler and Berg, do feature this idea of relaxing, of passivity and of abandon, and which belong to the experience of "Beautiful Passages". The conception of lingering becomes, in the book on Mahler, one of the central axes around which the œuvre of the Austrian composer coheres: "duration is spread out as composed".[5] This means that Mahler's music still offers the possibility of abandoning oneself to the experience of a temporality that has broken with quantitative and measured time; one can simply be there, letting oneself go in the lengths that are no longer lengths. On this point Adorno develops technical considerations, introducing the idea of a musical time of the "extensive type". This time is not far away from the "Beautiful Passages": it concerns those moments where the music opens itself to the kingdom of an "exact imagination"—where music is dream or narration.[6] In the book on Berg, Adorno's last work, everything converges at once towards childhood[7] and abandon, to the very point of disappearance. It is as if Adorno was pushing the experience of beautiful passages even further: the very fact of existing is transformed into a mortal disappearance.

Presenting the constellation linked to "Beautiful Passages" in this way must not, however, lead to the conclusion that we have the equivalent of a concealed metaphysics that should be rejected. Adorno introduces childhood and dreams precisely insofar as he incessantly thematises their disappearance and destruction. Therefore "relaxation" must be related to a sense of "rigidness" and "mechanism", from now on innervating most of the gestures placed under the

---

[5] Theodor W. Adorno, *Gesammelte Schriften*, vol 13, 221–222, "The epic type of symphony relishes time, leaving itself to it, wishing to concretize physically measurable into living duration […] duration is spread out as composed" ("Der epische Symphonietypus aber kostet die Zeit aus, überlässt sich ihr, möchte die physikalisch messbare zur lebendigen Dauer konkretisieren […] Dauer wird auskomponiert")

[6] I comment on this aspect extensively in my book *La pensée musicale de Theodor W. Adorno: L'épique et le temps* (Paris: Beauchesne, 2011).

[7] Theodor W. Adorno, *Gesammelte Schriften*, vol. 13, 334, "Among the leaders of New Music, he least of all represses aesthetic infancy, the Golden Book of music. He used to make fun of the cheap objectivity which is built upon such repression. His concreteness and human breadth he owes to his tolerance with respect to things past which he lets permeate, yet not literally but as recurrent in dream and involuntary memory" ("Unter den Exponenten der neuen Musik hat er die ästhetische Kindheit, das goldene Buch der Musik, am wenigsten verdrängt. Über die wohlfeile Sachlichkeit, die auf solcher Verdrängung beruht, spottete er. Seine Konkretion und humane Breite verdankt er der Toleranz gegen das Gewesene, das er durchlässt, aber nicht buchstäblich, sondern wiederkehrend in Traum und unwillkürlicher Erinnerung").

"shock ", as the essay on Stravinsky in *Philosophy of New Music* attempts to show in attacking the "motorism" and the "sewing-machine" style of that composer. Similarly, childhood has nothing to do with a state of origin, as understood in Romanticism. Adorno brings it closer to the animal, inquiring into the pathologies surrounding childhood when art glides into "infantilism", as it always seems to do with the Russian-born composer. The dream constitutes the ground, or the margin, of a thought that analyses, more than any other, the nightmare of the epoch and of history.

Reading Adorno Against the Grain

How to read Adorno? A question that he himself posed in relation to Hegel. On this matter Adorno left an instructive text, entitled "Skoteinos, or how to read", that provided not reading recipes but suitable orientations to accompany those reading his own philosophy. Here he emphasises the need to read Hegel "against the grain", that is to say, not to fall into the trap of a system that crushes singular analyses, which, nonetheless, by the logic of the system itself are necessary. He suggests that one stands close to those singular moments in order to receive them in themselves, and not only as steps in a process of incorporating or overcoming them. He outlines a reading of resistance. Instead of the forward movement that accompanies synthesising logic, he invites us to linger within the singular and to penetrate it, so as to liberate what is contained within it: "Hegel must be read against the grain, in such a manner that each and every logical operation, however formal it may present itself, is brought back to its core of experience."[8] To escape the traps of the system, to dive backwards into singularity, to explore the opacity of the latter and to give it another life by fostering a perspective that with reference to Benjamin, is qualified as "micrological": such would be the orientation of a reading attentive to not yielding to the trap of the affirmative or synthetic moment of dialectical logic, even when granting to this latter the privilege of a unique relation to experience. However, Adorno shows himself to be more precise. He makes himself attentive to the literary or written forms of thought, insisting that the decision to dwell in the microstructure affords a new angle for considering the logical status of singular moments. Far from this being viewed as belonging to a discursive logic placed in the service of a thesis—following a distinction between thesis and argument that Hegel himself puts in question—those moments are approached as

---

[8] Theodor W. Adorno, *Gesammelte Schriften*, vol. 5, 368 ("Hegel ist gegen den Strich zu lesen, auch derart, dass jede logische Operation, und gäbe sie sich noch so formal, auf ihren Erfahrungskern gebracht wird").

belonging to another, quasi-rhythmical, logic; Adorno talks about them as moments when thought "relaxes", thereby making possible a "relaxed" reading.

> The ideal is nonargumentative thought. His philosophy, which, as a philosophy of identity stretched to the breaking point, demands the most extreme efforts on the part of thought, is also dialectical in that it moves within the medium of a thought freed from tension…. Relaxation of consciousness as an approach means not warding off associations but opening the understanding to them. Hegel can be read only associatively. At every point one must try to admit as many possibilities for what is meant, as many connections to something else, as may arise. A major part of the work of the productive imagination consists in this.[9]

Adorno's methodological reflection concerning Hegel perfectly applies to his own philosophy and to our way of reading it, especially with respect to aesthetics and music: how to read Adorno "against the grain", i.e., liberating the experiential core contained within his thought? Nothing is less easy. Very quickly we fall back into the traps we should or would hope to avoid. On the side of aesthetics, readers prefer to view it from the exclusive angle of general theory, even though Adorno himself maintained that aesthetics could no longer evolve independently from the experience of objects. In other words, one tends to privilege theses that are easily transformed into doctrines. On the side of music, either one speaks in a general fashion, or one makes of it a domain that stands apart, preferably attended to by specialists who are best suited to consider the technical range of those writings—indeed written by one of the most competent men in the field. Thus, in the reception of Adorno, commentators tend to recycle oppositions, separations, and hierarchies that the philosopher himself always denounced. Where does Adorno's aesthetics begin and where does it end? Why not include in his "aesthetics" the singular analyses he wrote at the same time as he was engaged in elaborating a general theory? His insistence on the value of an immanent analysis or singular moments in the process of thinking, should on the contrary encourage this approach. Moreover, what should we mean by a "philosophy of music"? The

---

[9] Theodor W. Adorno, *Hegel: Three Studies,* trans. Shierry Weber Nicholsen, (Cambridge: MIT Press, 1994) 141–42; *GS*, vol. 5, 370–371, ("Das Ideal ist nichtargumentatives Denken. Seine Philosophie, die als eine der zum höchsten gespannten Identität äusserste Anspannung des Gedankens fordert, ist dialektisch auch insofern, als sie im Medium des entspannten Gedanken sich bewegt. Ihr Vollzug hängt davon ab, ob die Entspannung gelingt […] Entspannung des Bewusstseins als Verhaltensweise heisst, Assoziationen nicht abwehren, sondern das Verständnis ihnen öffnen. Hegel kann nur assoziativ gelesen werden. Zu versuchen ist, an jeder Stelle so viele Möglichkeiten des Gemeinten, so viele Beziehungen zu anderem einzulassen, wie irgend sich aufdrängen. Die Leistung der produktiven Phantasie besteht nicht zum letzten darin")

term is ambivalent and is a source of misunderstandings, to the extent that it suggests that music is an object or a field of study among others. Now nothing of the kind is true for Adorno; or more exactly, if music does in fact present itself on the one hand as a field of philosophical investigation among others—the publication of a book like *Philosophy of New Music* bespeaks this, as well as do many other writings, the majority to be precise—on the other hand, it is irreducible to this kind of presentation. This is crucial. As the constellation of "Beautiful Passages" reveals music is not simply a local affair, it is not even a question of an object or a work to be studied; it engages a dimension of experience removed from all socio-historical, cultural and psychological determinations, which nevertheless constitute it.

Experience, then, encompasses the whole; it has a quasi-absolute, metaphysical dimension. It is a *given* not deducible from anything and is neither justified nor explained by anything; this *given* would rather seem to be the source of the need for explanation and rationality. If this content of experience is not directly thematised in Adorno, this does not mean that it is not present and active, at work, in his musical thought.

However, this experiential content is only attainable on condition of avoiding the prejudices of reading that in fact separate the general and the singular, philosophy and music.[10] One must voluntarily suspend those kinds of presuppositions and try to rely on a musical thought for which one does not, not yet or *a priori*, know its contours. Without this, one must perforce sacrifice what is the most precious part of Adorno's work of thinking, i.e., that which puts us in contact with singularity and experience. This contribution is all the more precious since it is rare, even unique, in the current contexts of aesthetics and the philosophy of art. Moreover, in being non-thetic, Adorno's contribution constitutes what is properly speaking impossible to sum up: it resists the theft of information that transforms everything into a product of consumption or trade, including thinking. Above all, the potential of a negative dialectic lies in wait.

Adorno invites us to read his musical thought against the grain, indissociable from taking an unhesitating plunge into singular moments. This kind of reading emphasises continuities or webs of connections where others might tend to fix and separate, and it dissolves the poor and artificial coherence that rests on unquestioned divisions. One must take the risk of immersion in a thought which has no identifiable beginning: one advances little by little,

---

[10] Even if one seeks to reunite them subsequently, promoting for instance relations of "elective affinities", as is the case with Lydia Goehr, *Elective Affinities: Musical Essays On The History Of Aesthetic Theory* (New York: Columbia University Press, 2011), 1–44.

finding references linked to its internal movement and seeing certain trajectories emerge.

The discovery of "Beautiful Passages" shows such trajectories in Adorno's musical thinking. But amazingly these are silenced by most commentators, who content themselves with the philosopher's socio-historical component. This latter component has, of course, its moment of truth, and it is crucial; but this truth reveals itself to be neither unique nor ultimate. One must accept to link it to that other component, which the "Beautiful Passages" incarnates, and which inscribes into Adorno's musical thought according to "vanishing lines" (*Fluchtlinien*). This concerns what one might think, following Miguel Abensour's analysis of the utopian,[11] as indicating a "way out" of dialectical logic, a way out independent of a negative dialectics, freed from its affirmative moment that proves itself to be aporetic. Adorno himself indicates those vanishing lines in section 100 of *Minima Moralia* ("Sur l'eau"), refusing any determination of utopia in terms of activity or a project. By way of an opening, it would interrupt and suspend a spatio-temporal reality without equivalent: "*Rien faire comme une bête*, lying on the water looking up peacefully into the sky, 'to be, nothing else without further determination and fulfillment' might take the place of process, activity, fulfillment and thus truly keep the promise of dialectical logic, that of ending up in its origin".[12] The gist of this experience has its equivalent in music. Or perhaps more, what if one supposes that the content of this experience first finds expression when one starts from music, where it becomes itself a beautiful passage, and where the immersion into the flux is no longer hindered and relaxation reaches its summit. This relaxing "sur l'eau" has nothing to do with a pleasurable well-being attributable to music. If sensuality is at its peak, it reveals at the same time a relationship to the whole which goes back to what is initial, or something like an origin first felt in music, before it becomes an object of philosophical thinking. Far from short-circuiting music, this experience on the contrary calls for music more than ever; music becomes its beginning and its end, by this interruption of the course of things and by the priceless suspension it offers; and all that without willing it, as a *gift*.

---

[11] See especially Miguel Abensour, *Utopiques II: L'Homme est un animal utopique*, (Paris: Sens &Tonka, 2013), 243–244. Concerning music, the notion of utopia is a delicate one, given that it refers to Ernst Bloch who employs it pivotally in his philosophy, in a perspective that Adorno does not share.

[12] Theodor W. Adorno, *Gesammelte Schriften*, vol 4, 179 ("Rien faire comme une bête, auf dem Wasser liegen und friedlich in den Himmel schauen, sein, sonst nichts, ohne alle weitere Bestimmung und Erfüllung könnte an Stelle von Prozess, Tun, Erfüllen treten und so wahrhaft das Versprechen der dialektischen Logik einlösen, in ihren Ursprung zu münden").

The Effort to Say that which One Cannot speak

Drawing the vanishing lines that pass through Adorno's musical thought in favour of this "substantial" dimension of music that, in the parlance of "Beautiful Passages", indicates it is "more than culture", is not, however, enough. It does not suffice if we are to take seriously the idea of a reading "against the grain" aiming at coming close to, and liberating, the core of experience. It is indeed in this sense that the Adornian claim of the concrete is not a vain and sterile prescription but becomes a praxis at once of reading and of thinking. In Adorno's own words, "it is not *about* but *out of* the concrete that one ought to philosophize".[13]

This requires more than one would wish—since the job is not an easy one. It means progressing and penetrating the musical writings, in terms of criteria of reading we might qualify as "immanent", freed from the prejudice, obstinate after all, that what is philosophical must be proffered at a level of generality. Adorno's dialectical approach calls this prejudice into question and thereby opens up a new way to write and to think in philosophy. But as long as one remains within the general exegeses, one fails to seize this countermovement. The idea would basically be to bet on the philosophical content of the musical writings, including those which do not look like it; that is, where orientation towards the concrete and the non-identical, essential to Adorno's philosophy, is being constructed. In other words, the task is to go on a quest for a philosophy not *on* or *of*, but *out of* music. This leads furthermore to abandoning the point of view of music "in general", for the sake of the work of art, and more precisely of its experience. The project in Adorno of thinking music philosophically must be taken to this crucial and delicate point, according to which music—surely a domain of history and culture—brings *to experience* another dimension: should it be called metaphysical? Utopian? Indeed, it is not necessary rashly to put words where Adorno, himself, tries hard to work out a concrete thought.

The musical writings constitute a rather heterogeneous domain, marked by diverse intentions and circumstances of publication; they do not form a monolithic block. They are sustained by rhetorical and also theoretical registers which would deserve to be distinguished or differentiated more than we are used to do. For my part I would like to point out an evolution within this corpus, which sees the part of experience that I have sought here to define, increase and affirm itself to the point of being the organising focus of this

---

[13] Theodor W. Adorno, *Gesammelte Schriften*, vol. 5, 43: "Nicht über Konkretes ist zu philosophieren, vielmehr aus ihm heraus".

musical thought. Otherwise said, and with regards to the two components I have identified, i. e., the socio-cultural, well-known in Adorno, and that more "substantial" or metaphysical, less directly accessible component. Here it may be observed that the second of these elements takes precedence over the first. This shift is significant if one considers the book on Mahler (published in 1960) and the book on Berg (Adorno's last, submitted for publication in 1968), both of which have a content and a form of thinking different from the others (chiefly *Philosophy of New Music* and *Essay on Wagner*). Childhood and dreams appear to structure a thinking which can no longer be satisfied with making music a simple *object* of analysis or of polemics: music becomes like a visage. In his preface to the French translation of the *Berg*, Jean-Louis Leleu emphasizes this constitutive dimension of the approach linked to the idea of a "physiognomy" that no longer separates the artwork from the human being. The fact that a photograph of Berg's face should have been placed at the beginning of the original edition corroborates this intention to situate the book under the sign of a relation which is of another kind than pure and simple socio-cultural diagnosis. In the features of a visage, it is music as a whole that emerges in its alterity, profoundly expressive and not attainable by words. For instance Adorno, when evoking the smile of Mahler's death mask, sees in it the expression of the cunning of a whole life of composition haunted by ill luck and despair about the course that the world had taken, but that eventually the overcame them; the cunning of music is "the ruse of hope and not of reason". It is as if the composer said: "I have finally led you down the garden path…"[14]

In these books Adorno approaches experience at its most subjective and unspeakable. This does not mean falling back into the arbitrariness of taste. Against the positivist tendency, the philosopher emphasises in *Negative Dialectics* the extent to which "in sharp opposition to the current ideal of scientificity, the objectivity of dialectical cognition demands not less but *more subject*".[15] This "surplus of subject "is not the one of individualism. It belongs to the experience of one abandoning oneself to the singular element, with the possibility of an "elsewhere" that it offers. It falls to the activity of the imagination to touch upon the concreteness of music. When music becomes a face, an emotion beyond the individual and all its intentions arises, sweeping momentarily away the discourses linked to rationality. A "détente" or relaxation

---

[14] Theodor W. Adorno, *Gesammelte Schriften*, vol. 16, 349–350.

[15] Theodor W. Adorno, *Gesammelte Schriften*, vol. 6, 50, emphasis mine ("In schroffem Gegensatz zum üblichen Wissenschaftsideal bedarf die Objektivität dialektischer Erkenntnis nicht eines Weniger sondern eines Mehr an Subjekt").

imposes itself, which may or may not cause tears, but in any case, it is a vehicle of an emotion impossible to name otherwise than *qua* encounter in experience. A link between the face and relaxation is implicitly formulated[16] in *Philosophy of New Music*, where it is used to emphasise the gestural character of music in causing tears. In the books on Mahler and Berg, this link between face and relaxation appears more present, even becoming the very principle of Adorno's approach: the book on Berg, anchored in the personal relationship Adorno had with the composer, his teacher, is particularly moving—"one of the more captivating ones", says Jean-Louis Leleu—and it bears, for this reason, a content of experience which has no equivalent in his other musical writings. This content irradiates in its own style, disarming all attempts to reduce it to theses. Here we learn something about Adorno's relation to music that is not to be summed up and cannot provide the object of a doctrine. We must read the book and open ourselves to its "tone", which, in communicating and transmitting itself, colours experience.

Adorno unceasingly pursues and weaves the socio-cultural part of music, doing this in a way that remains independent of a philosophical approach to music, something that does not concern him directly. But at the same time he strives, in discourse and for the sake of thought, to give shape to an experiential content that situates music within in a "substantial" dimension, "outside of culture", the one which in fact precedes and follows philosophical argument. A crucial characteristic of his approach is not only to introduce this content of experience but to treat it philosophically. Adorno takes up the challenge— echoing the Wittgensteinian formula which he is up against—of refusing to silence that of which one cannot speak, but striving on the contrary to say it: "Philosophy might be defined, if at all, as the effort of saying that of which one cannot speak: of bringing the non-identical to expression, even though expression ever yet identifies it".[17] Adorno does not cede to the idea of an unspeakable element of music, even if experience might attest to it. True to his philosophical project of liberating experience, he invents another manner of philosophising, of which he says with Benjamin, with and against Hegel, that its ideal would be not to argue. The impossibility of argument does not lead him to forbear saying and thinking: it engages him to mobilise other means, those already found in the midst of Hegel's philosophy in moments of relaxation of thinking conveyed

---

[16] Theodor W. Adorno, *Gesammelte Schriften*, vol. 12, 122.

[17] Theodor W. Adorno, *Gesammelte Schriften*, vol. 5, 336 ("Philosophie liesse, wenn irgend, sich definieren als Anstrengung, zu sagen, wovon man nicht sprechen kann; dem Nichtidentischen zum Ausdruck zu helfen, während der Ausdruck es immer doch identifiziert").

in immanent singular analyses, and close to which stands experience at its most irreducible.

The Book on Mahler: Thinking in Models?

Structured around singular analyses, the book on Mahler belongs to this other mode of philosophising. One might say—taking up the expression Adorno coined while in touch with what he judged to be the part of Hegelian dialectic logic worthy of being saved—that the book moves within the "medium of relaxed thinking". This work enjoys a particular status to the extent that Adorno here attempts to bring to language what otherwise escape words. More than in other texts, the philosopher seeks to articulate in discourse the content of experience that confers to music its irreducibility to socio-cultural determinations. This book is neither an orthodox book of musicology nor is it a work of critical sociology in Adorno's sense. Rather, music is approached as a visage, in a dimension of experience or alterity that disarms all scientific pretension, all objectivation. But neither is it, obviously, a work of philosophy in the conventional sense of the term, by virtue of its relation to the "non-conceptual". Mahler's music is here considered in and of itself, and not only as a reference illustrating a predominantly general or conceptual argument. To be sure, these classifications have something inadequate in this context and do not allow one to take the measure of the writing and thinking work it accomplishes, making the *Mahler* text probably the most original and promising part of Adorno's musical thought. This book does not advance arguments and yet— or perhaps for that very reason—it is philosophy; it stands by experience, not abdicating before the unsayable. Comprehension is engendered in contact with the work, in a direction that, as remarked by Adorno with regards to Hegel, constitutes a "means to open up intelligence to associations rather than fending them off".

A few more precise elements may also be presented on account of this major orientation of musical thought towards the concrete and the non-conceptual. First, this book possesses a real unity, it is thoroughly composed. If it does not make a system, it answers to the definition Adorno gave of the "constellation" *qua* relation of an unregulated and inexhaustive unity between diverse moments; its chapters arrange themselves according to a constellation. Above all, it relativises the historico-philosophical concepts of material and form for the benefit of a thought organising itself around the category of "tone"—as is the case also with the book on Berg. Tone (*der Ton*) is here the echo of what was characterised in "Beautiful Passages" as the "singular element", which tears music away from its historic and cultural contingency, and by virtue of which music would find its authenticity: "a colour that does not dissipate into the whole". Its text would be comparable to a "name", following the semantic network running through that same text, "Beautiful Passages". We are here referring to the dimension of experience we described before, which finds its correspondence in the few reflections concerning relations between music and language, in the shape of certain fragments of *Quasi Una Fantasia*: music speaks not in the fashion of semantic language but through the singular element, comparable to a "name". This moment when music speaks, without any intention of meaning, is nothing other than the experience of music as an "elsewhere", like a "vanishing line", if we privilege the utopian inflexion that Miguel Abensour proposes. "The light of the beauty of details, once apprehended", continues the author of "Beautiful Passages", "deletes the illusion that culture lays over music and which agrees only too well with the latter's dubious aspect: as if it were already the blissful totality which refuses itself to humankind until this hour".[18]

The remarkable aspect of the book on Mahler consists in promoting a thinking *out of* that dimension of music rather than letting it fall into what is outside of philosophy. In this text, Adorno's philosophical requirement to "say that of what which one cannot speak" reaches its highest degree. From this perspective the matter is very different from the more directly socio-cultural approaches—e.g. in *Philosophy on New Music*, which serves as a kind of appendix to *Dialectic of Enlightenment*—even if in Mahler the socio-cultural perspective remains present and even crucial. Nevertheless, it does not have its end in itself and nor does it constitute the organising principle for the whole. Above all, Adorno seeks to describe this irreducible dimension of experience, and he invents to that effect a set of formal categories which he qualifies as concrete: accomplishment (*Erfüllung*); breakthrough (*Durchbruch*); suspension (*Suspension*) and breakdown (*Einsturz*)—these are the main ones. They are distinctive not only by virtue of being specific and entirely adapted to Mahler's music, but also by being answerable to experience. They come to determine in what music is a visage; they articulate the traits of this face and give flesh to its physiognomy. Adorno chose as the subtitle to *Mahler*, "A musical physiognomy", in order to situate this philosophical effort, the most

---

[18] Theodor W. Adorno, *Gesammelte Schriften*, vol. 18, 700, ("Das Licht der Schönheit von Einzelheiten, einmal wahrgenommen, tilgt den Schein, mit dem Bildung Musik überzieht und der mit ihrem dubiosen Aspekt nur allzugut sich versteht: sie sei bereits das glückliche Ganze, das der Menschheit bis heute sich versagt").

concrete and accomplished, to make music speak beyond semantic language, simply in its apparition as music.

Close to experience, thought does not argue. By means of concrete categories, the book on Mahler proposes to *describe* that same music as one would describe the features of a face. In certain ways, one might even say, still following Adorno in "Skoteinos" on singular analyses in Hegel, that they are all about "descriptions of meaning implications" (*Deskriptionen von Sinnesimplikaten*).[19] Notwithstanding that the reference to Husserl is here polemical, this allows us to focus on an aspect of Adorno's philosophical work that is most astonishing and insufficiently considered: were it not a vanishing line, the work of description and of meaning constitution through categories intrinsic to Mahler's music would mark the point of dialectical fulfillment. Thus, the book in question stands apart: in a situation of extra-territoriality, it overthrows all parallels or affinities one may conceive between music and philosophy—something that, by the way, Adorno himself does not fail to evoke.

But the effort to determine musical experience, in its specificity, remains most important for us who read Adorno today, where the philosopher moves in the direction of a thinking in models, towards the concrete and the nonidentical: "The model hits the specific, and more than the specific, without dissipating it into its more generic class concept. Thinking philosophically is tantamount to thinking in models; negative dialectics to a set of model analyses".[20] In that sense, Mahler is an analysis of models. Between *Negative Dialectic* and *Aesthetic Theory*, Adorno in his musical writings pursues a philosophical work of which we have hardly begun to take the measure.

Acknowledgements

An earlier version of these reflections has been published as "Orientation vers le concret" in C. David and F. Perrier (eds.), *Où en sommes-nous avec la* Théorie esthétique *d'Adorno* (Rennes: Pontcerq, 2018). The author wishes to thank Holger Schmid for his help with the English text.

---

[19] Theodor W. Adorno, *Gesammelte Schriften*, vol. 185, 369–70. "Hegel may be understood solely when and if one reads the singular analysis not as an argument but as descriptions of "meaning implications"; only the difference those are not conceived after the fashion of Husserlians, as fixed meanings, ideal units, invariants, but as moved within themselves" ("Verstehen lässt er darum sich nur, wenn man die Einzelanalysen nicht als Argumentationen, sondern als Deskriptionen von « Sinnesimplikaten » liest. Nur werden diese nicht, wie in der Husserlschule, als fixierte Bedeutungen, ideale Einheiten, Invarianten vorgestellt, sondern als in sich bewegt").

[20] Theodor W. Adorno, *Gesammelte Schriften*, vol. 6, 38 ("Das Modell trifft das Spezifische und mehr als das Spezifische, ohne es in seinen allgemeineren Oberbegriff zu verflüchtigen. Philosophisch denken ist soviel wie in Modellen denken; negative Dialektik ein Ensemble von Modellanalysen.")

Arendt on Aesthetic and Political Judgement
Thought as the Pre-Political

CECILIA SJÖHOLM

The Politics of Critical Thought

In present times, around the globe, we are witnessing a public sphere in crisis, distorted through fake news, lies, threats of violence and call for constraints. This has occurred not only in states of authoritarian rule, but also in liberal societies. Thus, one of the great challenges for critical thought today is to be able to maintain sound methods of reflection when the public space, which since the enlightenment has been called upon to maintain a legacy of critical reflection and freedom, appears undermined. For Kant, Arendt, Habermas and others the public sphere was expected to sustain a measure of soundness of thought. But when the public sphere can no longer do so, and thought retreats into itself, what means do we have to engage in the world and develop a thought that is congruent with political possibilities? The concept of "critical thought" in this context refers not to the school of critical theory, but to the kind of thought that Arendt advocates—a thought that is socially, ethically and politically astute. It means to scrutinise opinions and beliefs and to practice a certain "Socratic midwifery".[1] It is in this context that the inner voice is heard. The first site of truth in Western philosophical history appeared in the form of a dialogue, and Socrates may be read as an internal voice. In *Theaetetus*, Plato writes: "the soul when thinking appears to me to be just talking—asking questions of herself and answering them, affirming and denying".[2] But how are we to conceive of the validity of the inner voice? Is thought not merely cementing "what is", reflecting a state of things that it is unable to change?

For Slavoj Žižek, the problem with Arendt's philosophy is that she lacks a notion of transformation proper. In representing a position of resistance against utopian ideologies, she becomes a right-wing intellectual "knave"; Arendt is as incapable of producing challenges as the utopian "fool", according to Žižek.[3] She is merely confirming "what is".

---

[1] Hannah Arendt, *Lectures on Kant's Political Philosophy*, ed. Ronald Beiner (Chicago: University of Chicago Press, 1992), 36.

[2] Plato, *Theaetetus*, trans. Benjamin Jowett (Cambridge: Cambridge University Press, 2010), 416.

[3] Slavoj Žižek, *In Defense of Lost Causes* (London: Verso, 2009), 29.

Such a charge may well refer to the weight given to thought, and to the function of judgement in the thought of the later Arendt. The domain of the political is not altogether relegated to the world of action. Although this was the primary presumption of *The Human Condition,* and by far the most well-known doctrine in her work, her later writings disproved it. In the lectures on Kant, the political becomes a concept more involved with judgement.[4] The lectures on Kant provided the groundwork for a volume that was never completed; it was meant to comprise the third of a trilogy on thinking, willing and judging. The first two are explored in *Life of the Mind.* Here Arendt's reflections on thinking in *Life of the Mind* lay out a groundwork for the work on judgement. As Arendt explains towards the end of "Thinking" in *Life of the Mind,* thought is the ground for judgement: judgement "realizes thinking" and makes it manifest in the world of appearances.[5]

Arendt does not equate thought with judgement, nor does she equate judgement with political activity. Rather, she defines judgement as integral to political action. As for thought, one could argue, then, that she gives to thought the dignity of being pre-political. It is a dignity that today, in so-called post truth societies, is not easy to uphold; one can retort to Žižek that it is not easy to affirm "what is".

For Arendt, political judgement depends on what she calls a sense of realness, a sense that is formed in and through the public sphere. "What is", a sense of realness, is precisely what was distorted in totalitarian society. And I believe that most of what Arendt ended up writing was conceived against the backdrop of her experience of and work on totalitarian society; hence the insistence on a sense of realness, the sustenance and weight of the public sphere.

Critical Theory and the Two-in-One

Arendt's agent of thought in *Life of the Mind* is what she calls a two-in-one. It is an individual who thinks about him- or herself, as reflected not only in the history of philosophy but also in literature and art. The thinking individual who is in dialogue with him- or herself is an aspect of plurality and replaces the transcendental subject as the agent of experience.[6] Arendt's famous argument in *Life of the Mind* of thought-processes taking on a figure as a "two-in-one"

---

[4] Hannah Arendt, *The Human Condition* (Chicago: Chicago University Press, 1998), 7: action is the only true correspondent to plurality. As Rudolph Beiner has shown in his postscript to Arendt's lectures on Kant, Arendt's endeavour was to repoliticise judgement, see Hannah Arendt, *Lectures on Kant's Political Philosophy.* 106–107.

[5] Hannah Arendt, *Life of the Mind I* (London: Harcourt, 1978), 193.

[6] Hannah Arendt, *Life of the Mind I,* 179–97

incorporates reflections on Shakespeare's *Richard III*. This is no coincidence. What is interesting with these plays, and this is perhaps why they have together with for instance *Hamlet* drawn so much interest in the last few years, is that they point to the fragility of that last resort of democracy: thought itself. When opinions cannot be advocated in the open, thought can still withdraw and lay the ground for political judgement.

This has also been staged at the theatre. Shakespeare's play with internal voices has been used for the immanent critique of authoritarian rule. Shostakovich's opera *Lady Macbeth of the Mtsensk District* (1934), for instance, uses a novel by Leskov in order to conjure up a Shakespearian motif, and to stage a critique of Stalin. Written in exile in Finland after a stay in Stockholm, Bertolt Brecht's *The Resistible Rise of Arturo Ui* (1941) is itself an allegory on National Socialism based on *Richard III*. These critical theatrical adaptations, along with others, formed a background against which a significant amount of philosophical reflection dedicated itself to Shakespeare during and after the war. Such reflections focused on the capacity of the individual to reason, reflect and judge. These capacities are also in focus in two of the most talked about performances in Germany in recent years, Thomas Ostermaier's staging of *Hamlet* and *Richard III* at the Schaubühne in Berlin. Engaging with contemporary right-wing populism, Ostermaier refers to a long tradition of critique of authoritarian rule. Ostermaier's target is the neoliberal destruction of democracy, the commodification of power, and rule through fear.

The Shakespearean form of monologue from *Richard III*, directly delivered towards the audience, is a theatrical means of staging the inner voice of a Machiavellian player. As we overhear the inner voice of the king in *Richard III*, authoritarianism is underscored while his symbolic authority is undermined. To Arendt, the play stages the undoing of conscience, an aspect of the process of thought that precedes the capacity to make political judgements.

To many post-war European intellectuals, such as Arendt, Adorno and Brecht, one of the most problematic features of their own time was that conscience had become bankrupt. In 1966, Adorno discussed this in the radio program, "Education after Auschwitz". There is, says Adorno, no conscience in our time.[7] What should be internalised in the form of fundamental laws preserved by each individual has travelled out into a patchwork of contingent rules upheld by external authorities. While exiled in the US, trying his best to succeed the film industry, Brecht writes in his journal: "Shakespeare's grand motif, the

---

[7] Theodor Adorno, "Education After Auschwitz", *Critical Models: Interventions and Catchwords*, trans. Henry W. Pickford (New York: Columbia University Press, 2005), 194

fallibility of instinct (indistinctness of the inner voice) cannot be renewed".[8] The little people, as Brecht put it, were defenceless against a moral codex that had gone berserk. The problem of the corruption of conscience could not be relegated to grand tragic figures. It was to be found, rather, on a universal scale, in the form of a deafening of an inner voice that should have symbolised the possibility of conscience; there was nothing to hold onto as persecutory and racist ideals took the place of conscience.

The reflections on Shakespeare's staging of the inner voice became a point of reference for negotiations of self-reflexivity, and questions of compromised forms of contemporary subjectivity for Adorno, Brecht, Arendt and others. Plays such as *Macbeth* and *Hamlet* were seen to deal with issues of power, delusion and madness while problematising the possibilities of action.[9] But they were, above all, seen to stage fundamental problems inherent in contemporary subjectivity.

Arendt's Reading of *Richard III*

Richard III, as is well known, murders his adversaries in his ascent to power. He is plagued by an inner voice of doubt that pushes through in instances like the monologue quoted by Arendt:

> What do I fear? Myself? There's none else by:
> Richard loves Richard: that is, I am I.
> Is there a murder here? No. Yeas, I am:
> Then fly: what! From myself? Great reason why
> Lest I revenge. What! Myself upon myself?
> Alack! I love myself. Wherefore? For any good
> That I myself have done unto myself?
> O! no: alas! I rather hate myself
> For hateful deeds committed by myself.
> I am a villain. Yet I lie, I am not.
> Fool, of thyself speak well: fool, do not flatter.[10]

---

[8] Bertolt Brecht, Journal Entry, sept 20 1945, quoted in James K. Lyon, *Bertolt Brecht in America* (Princeton: Princeton University Press, 1980), 80.

[9] Cf. Zdenek Stribny, *Shakespeare and Eastern Europe* (Oxford: Oxford University Press, 2000); Agnes Heller, *The Time is Out of Joint: Shakespeare as Philosopher of History* (Boston: Rowman & Littlefield, 2002), and Marta Fik, "Shakespeare in Poland, 1918-1989", *Theatre Research International*, 21: 2 (1996).

[10] Hannah Arendt, *Life of the Mind I*, 189.

Here, the inner voice appears as the two-in-one, literally speaking. Richard the murderer speaks and thinks to himself. The monologues communicate through an inner voice. The two-in-one of the thought-process is, for Arendt, dramatically different from being in the world of appearances, where "the outside world intrudes upon the thinker and cuts short the thinking process".[11] In private, Richard sees the ghosts of all those he has murdered. In public, he rejects them. The ghosts are dismissed to the cellar of non-consciousness. But the inner discord, nevertheless, interferes with the capacity of judgement.

The scene with Richard III is mentioned in conjunction with Arendt's negotiations of the two-in-one, her reflections on thought as internalising some kind of alterity. According to Arendt, thought proper strives towards a certain congruence with itself, it strives to accommodate the other in such a way that discord is replaced with differentiation: I become the two-in-one, I accommodate the internal friend "at home".[12] As Richard is alone, the ghosts are present in his mind. As he meets with his army later on, he forecloses this process of negotiation.

The question of conscience was important also in Arendt's report on Eichmann in Jerusalem, which moreover is the work in which *Richard III* was mentioned for the first time. Eichmann, Arendt notes, surprisingly, did not deny the call of conscience—he was in fact obsessed with it. He did not need to "close his ears to the voice of conscience", because his conscience did not, unlike Richard III's, speak with the voices of his victims. It spoke, instead, with a "respectable voice", with the voice of what Eichmann regarded as the respectable society around him.[13] Eichmann's actions, then, were not the result of a denial but a perversion of the call of conscience. But it was never rooted in fundamental laws of morality. Eichmann's conscience was not founded on the prohibition against killing the other.[14] Again we hear again of an absence of fundamental laws, which resounds in Adorno's analysis of "cold thought" as well as in Brecht's display of the perversion of moral laws on a universal scale.

In *Richard III*, thought comes across in the form of voices, bringing us beyond the idea of a self that is self-contained and self-reflective. The inner voice is a trace inscribed in consciousness that appears to give witness to another consciousness. Although that consciousness is never fully represented, it appears as the trace of something or somebody. The monologue resounds

---

[11] Ibid, 185.
[12] Ibid, 190–91.
[13] Hannah Arendt, *Eichmann in Jerusalem* (New York: Viking, 2. ed. 1964), 61.
[14] Ibid. See in particular chapter 4.

with "the standpoint of somebody else", and it evokes an internal voice that may guide our sense of the real, an internalised presence of alterity that "assures us of the reality of the world and of ourselves".[15] An aspect of plurality manifests itself in the thought of Richard III to begin with, but then is cut off.

It is this sense of the real that has been cast off in the testimony of Eichmann, offering us instead a dead language of bureaucracy. If there is an inner voice in Eichmann, it is a commander who talks to a "knave", submissive to any kind of demands, an invisible master rather than the trace of an alterity to whom I owe my conscience and my consciousness. It is clear that to Arendt, it is impossible to detach these issues from what she regarded as the political proper, the functioning of the public sphere.

The Ear of Critical Thought

The Human Condition conceived of freedom in conjunction with a model of the public space that is no longer applicable.[16] Recently, Arendt's analysis of the totalitarian tendency to suppress public spaces through lies, distortions and suppression, has garnered considerable attention. There are several ways in which public spaces have been perforated also in democratic societies, for instance through political lies,[17] the commodification of politics, the threat of violence etc. In times of short-sighted economism and individualism, finding new models for judgement is one of the greatest challenges for critical thought.

Something that may contribute to this problematic is widening the scope of the conception of the public sphere. We need to understand not only the role of free speech and action, but also thinking and judging. For this purpose, Hannah Arendt has much to offer; although, alas, her work on these issues was never completed. In *Life of the Mind*, she develops a distinct theory of thought, which can be linked to a notion of plurality inherent to the very definition of the public sphere. And her notion of judgement, as has been argued, plays a distinct political role.

For Arendt, the public sphere represents plurality, for instance through the interaction of institutions, but also through individuals gathered in various forms of collectivity. Although they appeal to different modes of discourse and action, both Habermas' and Arendt's notion of the public sphere, elaborated

---

[15] Hannah Arendt, *The Human Condition*, 50.

[16] Ibid. 12. This is made clear by Arendt who notes the exclusion of slaves etc. if one sticks with an ancient model of free political life.

[17] As noted by Arendt in "Lying in Politics", in *Crisis of the Republic* (Orlando: Harcourt, 1972), 1–49.

after Kant, can be regarded as normative models of how an open society was supposed to function, in the wake of the totalitarian state.

Many have questioned the current relevance of Arendt's post-war notion of the public sphere.[18] According to Bruno Latour, political issues are no longer motored by public debates but by concerns invested in by multiple individuals. These concerns may find an outlet in sites that constitite a network binding together a hidden geography, for instance through works of art, sites on the Internet, and clusters of groups. Latour's notion of hidden geographies identifies political concerns that are negotiated on sites often not public in and of themselves, but merely semi-public. Real political issues are no longer fuelled by ideas and ideologies. They have to do with particular issues that give rise to feelings: it could be the melting of the polar icecaps, writers in prison, the depletion of cultural institutions. We no longer gather around ideas that found "realpolitik" at the cost of the concern of living beings. We gather around objects that are immediately linked to the big questions of our time. Here, we find the existence of an alternative public space that no longer is a space of free speech but of engagement. We find a politics based not on freedom but on bonding. It is here that a hidden geography comes to the fore, on virtual spaces and cultural spaces.[19] The concept of what is public must then be widened: it must refer to all possible places for engagement that can even be considered— the question is no longer what the physical conditions are for publicness. It applies rather to the networks behind the engagement. In an exhibition called "Making Things Public", performed in Karlsruhe 2005, Latour created a simulation of the invisible flows and movements that create public spaces today.[20]

In many ways, however, Latour's idea of new forms of publicness only emphasises the kind of complexities that existed already before; as Kant noted, not only opinions and action but also affectivity of engagement belongs to public cultures.[21] And for Arendt, not only actions and opinions, but also thought, must be considered crucial for democratic practices. As Arendt has shown, thought is not abstract, it is embedded in a variety of practices, and it has several

---

[18] Cf. Chantal Mouffe, "Art and Democracy: Art as an Agnostic Intervention in Public Space", *Open 14: Art as a Public Issue: How Art and Institutions Reinvent the Public Dimension,* eds. Jorinde Seijdel and Liesbeth Melis (Amsterdam: NAI, 2008)

[19] Cf. Bruno Latour, "Emancipation or attachments? The different futures of politics", In *Modernity, Postmodernity, Contemporaneity,* eds. Terry Smith, Okwui Enwezor, and Nancy Condee (Durham: Duke University Press, 2008), 309–24.

[20] Cf. Bruno Latour, "From Realpolitik to Dingpolitik, Making Things Public", *Atmospheres of Democracy,* eds. Bruno Latour and Peter Weibel (Cambridge: MIT, 2005), 14–31.

[21] Immanuel Kant, *Critique of Judgment,* trans. James Creed Meredith (Oxford: Oxford University Press, 2007), § 29.

functions; art for instance. Just as speech, art is embedded in a context. Thought is not autonomous.

What marks the crisis of the public sphere is the experience of the senses—for instance, the affect of "enthusiasm" is replaced with the overruling imaginary structures of ideology. Thought and experience become disconnected. Rather than negotiating reality as a ground for the feasibility of action, the agent of the public sphere becomes someone who has many opinions. When opinions rule over experience, reality becomes distorted. Experience is no longer a measure that may point to the coming together of a sense of the real, a *sensus communis*. The undoing of experience produces not only fake news but also fantasies. The responsibility that accompanies thought is replaced with the attachment to fantasies that may be more or less persecutory. Instead of acting in a make up of society where differences are accepted, persecutory fantasies about the other come to reign.

This has resulted in the loss of the inner voice, the tonality of alterity. It is replaced with the voice demanding submission of the "knave", the subject that thinks but who merely affirms "what is" in the language of Slavoj Žižek. The voicing of readymade opinions, often construed in and through virtual collectives, replaces thought. In contrast, can the internal voice of thought, or what Kant calls "the voice in the belly", serve as a site for pre-political forms of negotiation in times when public space in the post-war sense has been compromised?

What Is the Inner Voice?

Philosophy has often been conceived through a concept of *theoria*, an idea of overview or spectatorship. There is an awareness of this in the critique of western logo- and visual-centrism, as we can find for instance in Jacques Derrida, Jean-Luc Nancy, Mladen Dolar, and others.[22] The first site of truth in Western political history appeared in the form of an internal voice. Socratic consciousness appeared through a fictional character without body, character, or face. This has continued in the tradition of philosophy, where the voice comes forth as a tonality that appears in metaphysics, ethics, politics and physics. The Socratic voice may be an invisible voice of consciousness, but it also serves the injunction of laws and moral concepts in a more formalised manner.

---

[22] Cf. Jacques Derrida, *The Ear of the Other: Otobiography, Transference, Translation*, trans. Peggy Kamuf (Nebraska: University of Nebraska Press, 1988) and Jean-Luc Nancy, *A L'écoute*. (Paris: Broché, 2002).

To quote Jean-Luc Nancy, the subject of vision is always given as an angle, a point of view. Listening, on the other hand, penetrates, but at the same time, the locus of its call is unclear.[23] Sounds are not something we act upon. They are something that break down our defences, they run deep into us. Whereas vision is framed, listening exposes us to a lack of limit. From such a perspective, the inner voice of thought can be described as a kind of sensorial encroachment. The voice through which we think, the moods that accompany thoughts, impinge upon us from both the outside and the inside, transcending the division between private and public, the intimate and the collective.

In times of authoritarianism, might the inner voice escape ruination? Hannah Arendt reflects on the tonalities of the inner voice from two points of view. The primary question is how actions "in concert", collective actions that carry their own specific mood, are made possible. The second, of principal interest for us here, is how thought carries its own tonalities.

From the first point of view, collective action is best formulated through a notion of attunement. It is something that happens, something around which we simply wrap ourselves without noticing how or why. The verb *hören* (to listen) also carries the connotation of: *gehorchen, hörig, gehören,* words that, in English, are translated as to *obey, be in bondage, to belong.* In *gehören* (to belong), the "listening" implies not just a sense but also a relationship of power. The one who listens is exposed; sound is more penetrating than visual sights. Through sight, we can orient ourselves in space and locate our position. Sound, however, is not always easy to follow towards its source. It may surround us and pierce through our shields more easily. Sound may be experienced as lacking the kind of shape that makes it objectifiable and possible to locate.

Arendt's notion of mood, which accompanies her conception of actions in concert, can be compared to the Heideggerian term *Stimmungen,* a form of unveiling that is non-discursive and non-conceptual. It is also not perceptible or sensible; it is a mood that sticks to phenomena of experience without being properties of them. To Heidegger, moods such as fear and the sense of the uncanny disclose predicaments of human beings. At the same time, moods are conveyed in music, literature and art in general. In this sense, *Stimmungen* belong to those aspects that cut across the limit between art and philosophy.[24] Moreover, an aspect of mood overruns the distinction between the collective and the individual, between public action and the tonality of individual thought.

---

[23] Jean-Luc Nancy, *A L'écoute,* 44.

[24] Martin Heidegger, *Being and Time,* trans John McQuarrie and Edward Robinson (Oxford: Wiley Blackwell, 1978), 230–35.

Relating *Stimmungen* to politics, however, is not unproblematic. In Slavoj Žižek's film *The Pervert's Guide to Ideology*, one scene depicts Beethoven's ninth symphony as a suggestive device; not only is it used as a signature for the European Union, it was a symbol in Nazi Germany, the China of the cultural revolution, Stalinist USSR, etc., an empty shell into which all ideologies can be poured. In the negotiation of a theory of listening that can be related to political action, therefore, we need to separate the notion of the collective, and the kind of ideology produced in a collective, from the kind of attunement Arendt relates to political action, properly speaking.

Here, the notion of plurality is crucial; attunement is a figure that begins with plurality. From this point of view, we need to consider plurality as something more than the collective. Here, I think that Arendt's notion of thinking, and the kind of inherent plurality that it may represent, is helpful. It is a plurality illuminated by way of the notion of the inner voice, presenting the two-in-one, the plurality present in thought itself.

The inner voice, in this way, may orient us towards a horizon that supports a common grasp of the world. Thought may offer a site of truth that resists assaults on our senses of the real in other compromised forms of discourse.

How Do I Listen?

From the notion of the inner voice as a kind of integration of the other, and from the notion that thought has a kind of tonality, a subset of questions follows: is the inner voice private, or does it engage and direct us to a community? Is the inner voice related to corporeal desires and intimate relations, or can it, in contrast, offer a means to better understand community?

In his *Anthropology*, Kant writes that thought is not devoid of communicable language, it is not simply silent or abstract. It is communicable language directed to oneself. Thinking, he comments famously, is *speaking* with oneself. Figuratively it would correspond to "speech in the belly".[25]

This means for Kant that thought is accompanied by an I of apperception that is tangible through an inner tonality. To think, therefore, is to listen to oneself. This is a conception of thought that, for Kant, is not contrary to a metaphysical notion of reason. On the contrary, for Kant, the tonality of the belly can be encountered in the movement towards humanity's venture to think for itself, i.e. to use reason. Here, another element is added, a form of extension: thought, among other criteria, should be reflective and consistent. But it must

---

[25] Immanuel Kant, *Anthropology from a Pragmatic Point of View*, trans. Robert Louden (Cambridge: Cambridge University Press, 2006), 86.

also apply a certain universal command. For Kant, this is not simply abstract. His formula for the command—and this intrigues Arendt—is the following: to use reason is "to think for oneself (in communication with human beings) into the place of every other person".[26]

Critical thought, Arendt argues, becomes in principle "anti-authoritarian"[27] from such a point of view. The subject must be capable of thinking by itself and not in accordance with inherited and imposed views or ideas. It must negotiate the capacity of putting oneself in the place of the other.[28] Ever since Socrates, thought has been a silent dialogue with oneself, directed towards the public. What Kant negotiates distinctly is precisely that direction, the transient leap towards the public, which should from the very beginning be inherent in the process of thinking itself.

Thought itself, as Arendt notes in her diaries, may be guilty of the mistaken leap towards a humanist metaphysics that occurs when thought is conceived as an inner, silent dialogue with a representative of reason that has no tone and no self. When thought fails to appear in the form of a tone, or when it appears in a way that is not distinct enough, the thinking self appears to be ageless, without qualities: "It is", Arendt writes, "as if I am not a human being, but *the* human being".[29]

The very attachment to the idea of thinking as a kind of toneless inner dialogue may mean that I can *only* be myself when I am thinking, Arendt writes. But this is a grave mistake. Heidegger, Arendt notes, could not deal with the fact that thought might not only be complicit with, but in fact also dependent on, the manifestation of plurality. But it is not only Heidegger who is unable to hear not only the call of conscience but the actual space from where it derives. The sterility of the thought of Hegel and Marx, Arendt argues, lies in their understanding of thought as pure consciousness.[30]

As a reader of Kant, Arendt picks up the idea that to think is to speak to oneself, and to hear oneself *"innerlich"*.[31] This "inner" motion of thought is not only inner in the sense of beng incorporated. It is *innerlich*, a tonality that is intense, when the voice from the belly suggests a doubleness of agency. The doubleness of the thinking individual is added to Arendt's notion of plurality.

---

[26] Ibid, 124.

[27] Hannah Arendt, *Lectures on Kant's Political Philosophy*, 38.

[28] Ibid, 42.

[29] Hannah Arendt, *Denktagebuch*, 2 vols, eds. Ursula Ludz and Ingeborg Nordmann (Munich: Piper, 2002), 723.

[30] Ibid, 695.

[31] Kant, *Anthropology from a Pragmatic Point of View*, 86.

Thought does not have an object. It is not congruent with judgement, which has an object, but traces, rather, a relation to the world. Judging, Arendt argues, deals with thinking, deals with absences: absent friends, the negative, a world that is not present.

Thought is not the universal reflection of reason, although it can be that. Most of the time, however, it is embedded in a mood that carries as much meaning as do connotations of words flowing in a conscious train of thought. The mood of the thinking ego, she writes, is serenity, melancholy even, and intensely involved with recollection.

The subject that thinks does so from a position in which its reflections are intertwined with the tonality of its inner voice. What is "inner" to Arendt comes to the fore as a mood. Through this mood, language is not only pointing to phenomena, but also to itself. Language, therefore, does not communicate emotions to the exterior world as much as it transposes thought through moods.[32] Thought becomes embedded in moods and tonalities of language. Action is also encompassed by "moods", the happiness of the revolution for instance. The concept of mood transcends the differentiation between individual and collectivity; it encompasses the thinking individual in larger movements of action.[33]

The capacity to think involves an "enlarged mentality".[34] This means that inner thought is not a detached ego-less and universalistic abstraction, it is attached to a form of representation, though it may be a vague one. As one can argue by reading Arendt, the inner voice can be imbued with tasks that point in a direction where the inner voice of critical thought acquires a tonality that pushes the limits of the I of apperception. Thought points to the primacy of alterity through the use of imagination. Through our imagination, we "go visiting".[35] That means, when we abstract from the particular we are not merely set in a colourless and airy room of the mind. We imagine places and people with which we are unfamiliar. The inner voice, in this way, pushes us in directions with which we are unfamiliar.

Sometimes we may hear ourselves thinking. We may hear our own voice, as in an echo. Sometimes, thoughts appear, as voices in a cave. They strike us, as

---

[32] Arendt, *Denktagebuch*, 690.

[33] It is, in this sense, as Artemy Magun has put it, a form of rhythmic and reasoned coordination, with other things, beings and with the internal splits within oneself. See Magun, *Unity and Solitude* (London: Bloomsbury, 2013), 41.

[34] Immanuel Kant, *Critique of Judgment,* § 41. See also Hannah Arendt, *Lectures on Kant's Political Philosophy,* 73.

[35] Hannah Arendt, *Lectures on Kant's Political Philosophy,* 43.

from the outside. We hear them, from an invisible point that we cannot see, and yet they are structuring our perception and our apprehension of space.[36] When we hear our own thoughts, we experience ourselves not as estranged from ourselves, but somehow as naturally double, as reflecting beings capable of reflecting in the world internally and silently, in our own minds. When the voices appear as foreign, as the voices of angels or devils, or simply as belonging to other people, this would be a sign of psychosis.[37] When we hear our own thoughts internally, however, as aspects of ourselves, we experience ourselves as integrated in the world, as capable of reflecting, and although we may be alone, as capable of engaging in vivid internal reasoning with ourselves, and with the world.

To Arendt, then, we can only really think when others are encroaching upon us. Only in a world of plurality can we truly reflect on ourselves and our actions. For Arendt, the truly interesting forms of thought manifest themselves in the engagement with internal voices. It is certain that thinking and action are two separate activities that can never be viewed as interchangeable. But thinking, although it is conducted in solitude, manifests itself precisely through the encroachment of others not only on our horizon of perception but also in our minds.

Thought, Arendt suggests, may appear to put us close to the neutral manifestation of a non-self: "It is because the thinking ego is ageless and nowhere that past and future can become manifest to it as such, emptied, as it were, of their concrete content and liberated from all spatial categories". But this neutrality is only an illusion. Thinking, in fact, takes place in a "time-space", in which the thinker is reflected and deflected. Time can come into being "only with [the thinker's] self-inserting appearance".[38] Neither philosophy, nor literature, may exist outside of the "time-space" in which the activity of thinking, writing or listening takes place; producing the deflection of those that think, tell or listen. This is precisely what philosophy may learn, when it listens to literature. There is no place outside of time that can be emptied of this deflection.

It is this challenge that the inner voice of critical thought needs to meet; gathering voices, in order to listen, rather than return to the same, and thus straying errantly, ever further away from the web of voices. It is this challenge, also, that we need to face as we look for new models for critical thought, and I believe that this is what Arendt allows us to do.

---

[36] Michel Chion, *The Voice in Cinema* (New York: Columbia University Press, 1999), 21.

[37] Cf. Jacques Lacan, *Le Sinthome* (1975–76) (Paris: Broché, 2005)

[38] Hannah Arendt, *Between Past and Future* (New York: Viking, 1961), 10–11.

The Future of Saying No
The Non-Identity and Incompatibility of (Critical) Theory

ANDERS BARTONEK

For the Critical Theory of the Frankfurt School, at least for the first generation of Max Horkheimer and his co-members, the question of theory and praxis was essential. And subsequently, in his text on "Traditional and Critical Theory" from 1937, Horkheimer fashioned the concept of Critical Theory precisely as consisting of the ambition of theory not to stay within its own abstract realm and borders, but to lead to a change of the false society of capitalism and fascism. In the words of Horkheimer, Critical Theory therefore is a theory "dominated at every turn by a concern for reasonable conditions of life".[1] Horkheimer continues:

> Traditional theory may take a number of things for granted: its positive role in a functioning society, an admittedly indirect and obscure relation to the satisfaction of general needs, and participation in the self-renewing life process. But all these exigencies about which science need not trouble itself because their fulfillment is rewarded and confirmed by the social position of the scientist, are called into question in critical thought. The goal at which the latter aims, namely the rational state of society, is forced upon him by present distress. The theory which projects such a solution to the distress does not labor in the service of an existing reality but only gives voice to the mystery of that reality.[2]

Critical Theory is not identical with or a defendant of existing reality, and unlike traditional theory should not copy and imitate the falseness of this society, but make visible its problems and hopefully lead to its fundamental transformation.

The Frankfurt School had no direct connections to political parties or organisations. It seeks, first of all, to address and localise the problems of society theoretically, so as then, secondly, to provide openings and possibilities for radical action. The early members of the Frankfurt School are therefore no political activists, though they are political and theoretical thinkers of political problems and possibilities. They are more akin to theoretical activists. This

---

[1] Max Horkheimer, *Critical Theory: Selected Essays* (New York: Continuum, 1972), 199.
[2] Ibid, 216–217.

sounds like a contradictory, maybe even a ridiculous, formulation. However, as we will see, it takes much courage and strength to resist the societal coercion to act practically in certain pre-given forms. And this coercion comes both from capitalistic dimensions of society as well as from the left itself, e.g. Theodor W. Adorno's confrontation with the students, who condemned theory for not obeying the need for praxis. According to this general view, the only thing that matters is what one does. In this, capitalism and the student movement were allies. An important characteristic of the early Frankfurt School is precisely the double nature of, on the one hand, designing a theory that has as its ultimate goal the transformation of society, and, on the other hand, criticising the pressure to act within existing society—actions that are parts of the society in need for change.

Adorno is the member of the Frankfurt school who to the greatest degree represents this double-sided attitude. This essay will accordingly be about Adorno and his understanding of theory and of its relation to praxis and society. In Adorno, the relation between theory and praxis is even more cautiously formulated than within the tradition of Critical Theory generally construed. Indeed, Adorno is very ambivalent on the matter of praxis, and much of his work can be seen to dwell on the tension between, on the one hand, the absolute necessity of a transformative praxis, and, on the other, his analysis of how society blocks every form of such praxis, reducing it to mere forms of pseudo-activity. The necessity of social transformation does not make praxis possible, while the difficulty of reaching a genuine political praxis makes it no less needed. And the cunning dimension of society is precisely its character of simultaneously forcing human beings to be practical as it blocks radical and liberating praxis.

Here, one can refer also to Herbert Marcuse (another of the most famous early members of the Frankfurt school) on society's ability to block as well as render harmless political praxis. In his late and maybe most famous book *One Dimensional Man* from 1964, Marcuse distinguishes two central but contradictory tendencies in industrial and capitalist societies. First, as Marcuse writes, "advanced industrial society is capable of containing qualitative change for the foreseeable future". But on the other hand he claims that "forces and tendencies exist which may break this containment and explode the society".[3] This points towards a general problem surrounding radical action, broaching its very possibility. There are possibilities for change in society, but society also has methods for undermining this change. In general, I think, Adorno would agree

---

[3] Herbert Marcuse, *One Dimensional Man: The Ideology of Industrial Society* (London: Sphere, 1968), 13.

with Marcuse's sentiment, even if Adorno is more cautious about the possibilities for social transformation. He is more focused on not giving in to the temptation of pseudo-activities, which, precisely because they are pseudo-activities, appear more fruitful and effective than they actually are. Such actions do not change anything. Adorno is not saying that political praxis is impossible. Were this the case he would have refrained from writing entirely. Rather, Adorno is critical towards anything that can be understood as the wrong way forward, and that would strengthen the existing state of things because it suggests that change, or the possibility for it, is already here. The list of such missteps is long: pop music, jazz music, some classical music (for example Stravinsky); the practical ambitions of the student movement in Germany, as well as Heidegger's philosophy. Adorno's thinking can be seen as highly politically motivated even when addressing themes not immediately of a political nature, and I agree with Espen Hammer's claim that Adorno "invented a form of philosophical reflection that at every step is politically oriented and critical".[4]

Adorno's principal object of critique is, as already mentioned, modern capitalist society. But it is decisive that Adorno adopts a critical stance from the viewpoint of capitalism's identity principle, something he originally diagnoses and criticises within both the scientific and philosophical traditions of the west.[5] Both in society and in science the principle of identity is all-pervasive. It consists in the activity of reducing all individual human beings and things to a common denominator and an all-embracing system as well as conforming them and robbing them of their uniqueness. Therefore, Adorno criticises capitalist society with help from his critique of identity within philosophy, and he uses the concept of identity in order to describe the problem of capitalist society, mainly as a system of exchange. And this would then be the task of theory: to transcend this principle through thinking and to create a platform for thinking beyond this conforming principle of identity. Theory seeks to reject identity.

And although political praxis is in many ways the main goal for Adorno's thinking, the problems of society and the difficulty of praxis lead him to a certain understanding of Critical Theory. What is required for Adorno is not an abandonment of theory in the struggles for praxis, but rather a deepening of theory. The existing state of society makes the need for theory even more acute, and the theory required is not simply the servant of praxis, but is acknowledged as an activity in its own right. Adorno writes:

---

[4] Espen Hammer, *Adorno and the Political* (London: Routledge, 2006), 178.
[5] Theodor W. Adorno, *Negative dialectics* (London: Routledge, 1990), 146.

> Praxis is a source of power for theory but cannot be prescribed by it. It appears in theory merely, and indeed necessarily, as a blind spot, as an obsession with what is being criticized.[6]

So, the distance between theory and praxis is again essential. Theory can only indirectly lead to praxis by not immediately trying to prescribe what is to be done. Theory is obsessed with the objects it criticises, and precisely in this critical reflection on society Critical Theory has it potential. Adorno thus protects theory from becoming instrumentalised by political actions while at the same time he seeks to turn it into a powerful source for future praxis. Praxis is always an issue within theory, but only as a "blind spot", indirectly deriving from the critical and negative work of theory.

The concept Adorno uses in order to bring forth the position of theory is the concept of non-identity. As non-identical, theory is connected to society and yet not entirely subsumed by it. While theory is not identical with society, not entirely consumed by it, it nonetheless has a critical connection to it, and is thus not isolated from it. The precise mode of this connection between theory and society—connected to and mediated by society, and yet with a critical distance to it—is essential for Adorno's understanding of Critical Theory. The distance represents its relative freedom and its contact represents the very possibility for critique. And it is because Adorno constructs his critique of capitalist society through the concept of identity that he can understand theory as being potentially non-identical.

However, there seems to be a risk inherent in Adorno's theory. The ambition not to accept any of the problematic and false dimensions of society, in combination with the difficulty of generating a true praxis in capitalist society, risks ending up in an incompatibility between theory and society.[7] Thus theory loses its critical contact with society. But the positive dimensions of such an incompatibility must be understood from within Adorno's own refusal to deliver some constructive critique in order to improve capitalist society, which would delimit the possibilities of Critical Theory.

And it is this tension between theory's non-identity and its incompatibility with society that I want to discuss. I will criticise both an understanding of Adorno as resigning from political hope altogether and the view of Adorno's emphatic negativity, which, in those moments when it seems to dominate his

---

[6] Adorno, *Critical models: Interventions and Catchwords* (Columbia: Columbia University Press, 1998), 278.
[7] See also Stefano Giacchetti Ludovisi, "Adorno as Marx's Scholar: Models of Resistance Against the Administered World", in Giacchetti Ludovisi (ed.), *Critical Theory and the Challenge of Praxis* (Farnham: Ashgate, 2015).

argument, judges it to be an easy way out or a form of resignation. To give an example: in Robert Lanning's book *In the Hotel Abyss: An Hegelian-Marxist Critique of Adorno* one finds both. According to Lanning, Adorno does not expect any change to happen within capitalist society and therefore "a perspective on actual politically-driven change is absent in Adorno's work".[8] And later in the book, Lanning argues that when he abjures from becoming involved in actual political activity, Adorno chooses a safe and easy path. According to Lanning, political action for Adorno "do[es] not yet have the capacity to result in a full-scale development of revolutionary and conclusive possibilities".[9] Lanning then goes onto write: "in Adorno's case, such rigidity—the sense so often of absoluteness—is a point of departure toward safer sailing away from the shop and street wars of the actual proletarian struggle, with an approach that affirmed the separation of theory from practice".[10] Even if this critique of Adorno's absolute demand might have plausibility, my argument is that Adorno is not abandoning the hope for political change. Rather, he is doing everything possible and fruitful for its prospect. And even in formulations that seem most pessimistic, this is not to be understood as an easy way out. It is never easy to say no under such circumstances.

Against this background, the first part of this text will deal with the non-identity of Critical Theory in accordance with Adorno's thinking. In the second part, I will address the risk of Adorno's thinking ending up in a position of incompatibility with society, according to which the distance to society as an object of critique becomes so big that any critical contact tends to get lost. For this purpose, I will refer to Adorno's late philosophy, mainly his book *Negative Dialectics* from 1966 and the text "Marginalia to Theory and Praxis" from 1969.

Theory as Non-identical

In this section I will address what Adorno meant by the concept of non-identity, in what way theory is non-identical, and what it means for theory to be non-identical regarding the possibility of praxis. To begin with, what is non-identity and the non-identical in Adorno's philosophy? Adorno's concept of non-identity has three main dimensions.[11]

---

[8] Robert Lanning, *In the Hotel Abyss: An Hegelian-Marxist Critique of Adorno* (Chicago: Haymarket, 2014), 2.

[9] Ibid, 23.

[10] Ibid.

[11] See Anders Bartonek, *Philosophie im Konjunktiv: Nichtidentität als Ort der Möglichkeit des Utopischen in der negativen Dialektik Theodor W. Adornos* (Würzburg: Königshausen & Neumann, 2011), 57–88.

First, we have non-identity between subject and object, between thinking and reality, or the non-identity between theory and praxis. This aspect of non-identity underlines the fact that subject and object are not identical, at the same time as it contains a critique of certain philosophical and political traditions that claim they are one with their objects. In reality such positions only turn objects into slaves under their own mastery. Thus, this dimension of non-identity has the purpose of defending reality from theory. And this of course is an integral part of Adorno's reflections on the possibility of radical action: theory must not be instrumental, not even for the sake of freedom; it must develop a self-critical stance towards its oppression of reality in order to think beyond a stagnated society.

Second, we have non-identity within the subject or theory itself, highlighting that the subject is not a closed unity or system, but rather in itself contains this conflict between subject and object. Horkheimer and Adorno's discussion of Odysseus in *Dialectic of Enlightenment* is a good example of this when they show how Odysseus' subjectivity depends on his control over his inner nature.[12] Along with this, capitalist society forces human beings to instrumentally suppress their inner nature in order to be functioning members of society. Subjects become non-identical with themselves.

Third, we have non-identity within the object and reality with itself. In this case Adorno points to how reality and individual things are hindered in capitalist society, due to its domination over nature, to develop themselves on their own terms. For example, the inner nature of Odysseus is blocked from developing and flourishing. As a consequence, the object, or in this case, inner nature, is not identical with itself, it wants to become something else.

Here, the first two dimensions of non-identity are of most importance. According to the first, theory, as a subjective dimension of society, is non-identical with the objective reality of society, meaning that it is a part of society but also ungraspable for society. If theory is critical, it is non-identical. Regarding the second dimension of the non-identity of the subject itself, one can highlight the possibility for the subject to become aware of its domination over nature and thus realise how deeply connected it is to nature, although this inner split of the subject is initially what makes the mastery of nature possible. But ultimately this non-identity within the subject is what accounts for the subject's ability to transcend society whose principle is the domination of the natural world.

---

[12] Adorno & Horkheimer, *Dialectic of enlightenment* (London: Verso, 1997), 43ff.

This makes clear how theory is connected to society at the same as it has a critical distance to it. And this is the "positive" aspect of the domination over nature: it has created a distance to objective reality which now can be used in a critical sense against capitalist society. But might it even achieve more? As I have argued in another context, non-identity is the place for thinking the possibility of the utopian, although there are of course no guarantees for practical success.[13] But by reaching a position of being non-identical, I think this is what Adorno is trying to say: theory has the double role of criticising itself and society; of being the place for thinking and for opening up the possibility of the utopian. Adorno's theory is mainly negative, but contains also this more positive dimension, which undoubtedly has political and emancipatory ambitions.[14]

But this possibility is a very fine line. And, as Sullivan and Lysaker put it in their "Between Impotence and Illusion: Adorno's Art of Theory and Practice": "The question is: how is thought to function in the attempt to overcome alienated life without becoming a co-conspirator in the practice of domination?"[15] For Pickford, in "The Dialectic of Theory and Praxis: On Late Adorno" the critical activity of Adorno can be viewed as an "intervention by problematisation".[16] And the experience of theory "consists in the awareness of the negativity between the emphatic concept and its present unfulfillment". Sangwon Han understands Adorno's thinking as a philosophy of saying no and tries to give the radical negativity of Adorno's thinking a "constitutive" function for a true future positivity, which transcends the mere destructive dimension of negation.[17] But maybe this is to go too far: can negativity really transcend its character of parasite-like criticism and thereby create a negative void for a possible better future—a position I would personally subscribe to—or can it even by itself be constitutive of this positivity? I would precisely question this alternative. Han's argument is more affirmative than my suggestion, namely that the non-identical is a negative place for an indirect possible development

---

[13] Bartonek, *Philosophie im Konjunktiv*.

[14] See also Joan Alway, *Critical Theory and Political Possibilities* (Westport: Greenwood, 1995) and Russell Berman: "Adorno's Politics", in Nigel Gibson & Andrew Rubin (eds.), *Adorno: A Critical Reader* (Oxford: Blackwell, 2002).

[15] Michael Sullivan & John T. Lysaker, "Between Impotence and Illusion: Adorno's Art of Theory and Practice", *New German Critique* 57 (1992): 94.

[16] Henry W. Pickford, "The Dialectic of Theory and Praxis: On Late Adorno", in Gibson & Rubin (eds.), *Adorno: A Critical Reader*, 333 and 327.

[17] Sangwon Han, *Konstitutive Negativität: Zur Rekonstruktion des Politischen in der Negativen Dialektik Adornos* (Bielefeld: Transcript, 2016), 14–15, 29ff, 255.

of a better future, but not that negativity in itself can secure a constructive function within such a development.

The utopian possibility must therefore not be overestimated. This was, for example, according to Adorno, the case with the Student movement in Germany. The students, according to Adorno, turned the idea of radical action into a compulsion to act. This only resulted in pseudo-praxis that turned into a denunciation of theory and made the problems worse and harder to identify. Fabian Freyenhagen also defends Adorno's critique of the actionism of the student movement in his text "Adorno's Politics: Theory and praxis in Germany's 1960s", referring to how "Adorno suspects that actionism is actually a vain attempt to compensate for both (1) the fact that revolutionary activity is blocked and (2) the disintegration and paranoia of individuals by engaging in largely blind activities for their own sake".[18] Adorno himself writes about the danger of desperate action and how it tends to make things worse:

> The dialectic is hopeless: that through praxis alone is it possible to escape the captivating spell praxis imposes on people, but that meanwhile as praxis it compulsively contributes to reinforcing the spell, obtuse, narrow-minded, at the farthest remove from spirit.[19]

Although the need for radical action and change is extremely acute, according to Adorno "[f]alse praxis is no praxis".[20] And the denunciation of theory becomes a weakness in praxis, because desperate action is irrational. The students again are an example of this:

> Today once again the antithesis between theory and praxis is being misused to denounce theory. When a student's room was smashed because he preferred to work rather than join in actions, on the wall was scrawled: 'Whoever occupies himself with theory, without acting practically, is a traitor to socialism.' It is not only against him that praxis serves as an ideological pretext for exercising moral constraint. The thinking denigrated by actionists apparently demands of them too much undue effort: it requires too much work, is too

---

[18] Fabian Freyenhagen, "Adorno's Politics: Theory and praxis in Germany's 1960s", *Philosophy and Social Criticism* 40 (2014): 882; see also James Gordon Finlayson, "The Question of Praxis in Adorno's Critical Theory", in Giacchetti Ludovisi (ed.), *Critical Theory and the Challenge of Praxis*.
[19] Adorno, *Critical models*, 262.
[20] Ibid, 265.

practical. Whoever thinks, offers resistance; it is more comfortable to swim with the current, even when one declares oneself to be against the current.[21]

Theory as such is already a praxis of resistance. Accordingly, we do not need less theory, but more. And also, in Adorno's view, on those occasions where he himself had any impact on society, it happened through theory alone. This notion of theory, which is non-identical with reality and which refuses to engage in praxis for the sake of it, turns theory into a saved and unrealised promise. In the beginning of *Negative Dialectics*, Adorno formulates his diagnosis of the state of philosophy:

> Philosophy, which once seemed obsolete, lives on because the moment to realize it was missed. The summary judgment that it had merely interpreted the world, that resignation in the face of reality had crippled it in itself, becomes a defeatism of reason after the attempt to change the world miscarried. [...] Perhaps it was an inadequate interpretation which promised that it would be put into practice. Theory cannot prolong the moment its critique depended on. [...] Having broken its pledge to be as one with reality or at the point of realization, philosophy is obliged ruthlessly to criticize itself.[22]

Theory is seemingly waiting for its moment to have an impact on society. And this might be the dilemma of theory: it needs to become identical with reality at the same time as it must protect itself from becoming realised in the wrong way. So, Adorno needs to seek openings for action, but also to close itself off, in order to survive as long as radical action is not possible. This is the dilemma of the all or nothing. In this sense Adorno risks becoming entirely incompatible with existing reality, losing the non-identical contact with it. This may result in a mutual lock-out of theory and reality. But maybe this is not entirely bad? Is the future of Critical Theory a future of incompatibility? Is it a future of saying no?

The Incompatibility of Theory

As non-identical, theory conquers a position from out of which the critical view on society and on itself is made possible. Moreover, as non-identical, this critical position, which for the most part is a negation, also represents the possibility of creating a space for thinking the utopian, what in the subjunctive mood would be a better society, for instance a society in which it would be possible to

---

[21] Ibid, 263.
[22] Ibid, 3.

live together without fear. Now, for Adorno the choice between being too close or too far away from the criticised society seems easy—if he must choose. Rather than formulating a constructive critique towards society and its way of life and seeking to achieve "Anschluss" to society and it discourses, therefore arguably keeping more than just the baby when emptying the bathwater, Adorno would choose to avoid any form of conciliatory approach to society. But the reason for this "choice" is, in Adorno's eyes—and I have mentioned this before—that society is largely blocking the possibility of its fundamental transformation. In "Marginalia" he writes that "[w]hereas praxis promises to lead people out of their self-isolation, praxis itself has always been isolated; for this reason practical people are unresponsive and the relation of praxis to its object is a priori undermined".[23] At the same time this creates hate towards those not accepting the offered platform, and forces critical thought, in order to suffocate it, to choose between the inside or outside: you are either in or out! In "The Essay as Form", Adorno describes the choice in these words:

> The person who interprets instead of unquestioningly accepting and categorizing is slapped with the charge of intellectualizing as if with a yellow star; his misled and decadent intelligence is said to subtilize and project meaning where there is nothing to interpret. Technician or dreamer, those are the alternatives.[24]

In German the words being used are *Tatsachenmensch* and *Luftmensch*, between which one has to choose, that is, between being a human being of facts or a human being of air. So, either one accepts the rules and platform of established society and sticks to the facts, or society will try to exclude you and turn your transcending and critical thoughts into nothing else but air, seeking to rob it of its critical contact with reality. Because of this, Critical Theory becomes incompatible with society, for society it is nothing but air. But for Adorno's thinking it is no option to become a theory of facts in order to overcome this air-status of critical thinking. Of course, it may be a problem if the theoretical task is reduced to writing air theory. In Freyenhagen's *Adorno's Practical Philosophy: Living Less Wrongly*, Adorno's attempt to connect negativity and indirect utopian claims without having to ground them in hard facts seems to be defended, when Freyenhagen, in Adorno's favour,

---

[23] Ibid, 259.
[24] Adorno, "The Essay as Form", *New German Critique* 32 (1984): 152.

questions the necessity of grounding normative claims in the positive knowledge of the good.[25]

One can say that Adorno oscillates between being more optimistic and more pessimistic about the possibilities of theory. In those moments when he appears more optimistic, and acknowledges theory's own critical (and non-identical) contact with society, Adorno sees how he has had an effect on it, though only through theory itself. I have already mentioned this, but now I quote:

> Wherever I have directly intervened in a narrow sense and with a visible practical influence, it happened only through theory: in the polemic against the musical Youth Movement and its followers, in the critique of the newfangled German jargon of authenticity, a critique that spoiled the pleasure of a very virulent ideology by charting its derivation and restoring it to its proper concept.[26]

Other remarks about the possibilities of theory, however, strike a more pessimistic tone. Adorno develops images of theory as an expression of desperate action in a world entirely closed off from its influence—this is what I describe as the incompatibility of theory. One example of this is in "Marginalia", where Adorno describes theory with the following words: "Despite all of its unfreedom, theory is the guarantor of freedom in the midst of unfreedom".[27] In German, Adorno uses the word *Statthalter*, arguably saying that theory is defending a sanctuary of freedom in a state of unfreedom, without the direct possibility of expanding this limited realm. Theory is defending its minimal access to oxygen.

Another example of this desperate and incompatible understanding of the role of theory in capitalist society is the image of the "message in a bottle", a *Flaschenpost*. Adorno does not use this concept frequently, but when for example writing on new music, he employs this metaphor. For Adorno, no one wants to have anything to do with new music; it remains unheard, without echo. It finds its only happiness in recognising unhappiness. And for Adorno, due to it not being acknowledged properly, it is the true message in a bottle.[28]

---

[25] Freyenhagen, *Adorno's Practical Philosophy: Living Less Wrongly* (Cambridge: Cambridge University Press, 2013), 10; see also Freyenhagen: "What is Orthodox Critical Theory?" (http://www.worldpicture journal.com/WP_12/pdfs/Freyenhagen_WP_12a.pdf) and João Pedro Cachopo, "Disagreeing before acting: The paradoxes of critique and politics from Adorno to Rancière", *Theoria and Praxis* 1 (2013).
[26] Adorno, *Critical models*, 278.
[27] Ibid, 263.
[28] Adorno, *Philosophie der neuen Musik* (Frankfurt am Main: Suhrkamp, 2003), 126.

In other texts, for example the aphorisms from *Dialectic of Enlightenment*, Horkheimer and Adorno discuss who, in an (almost) wholly alienated society, is the addressee for Critical Theory, broaching this matter in a way closely related to the idea of the message in a bottle:

> It is not the portrayal of reality as hell on earth but the slick challenge to break out of it that is suspect. If there is anyone today to whom we can pass the responsibility for the message, we bequeath it not to the 'masses', and not to the individual (who is powerless), but to an imaginary witness – lest it perish with us.[29]

Theory is written without any direct and immediate addressee. Yet, it has to be written for it not to "perish" along with its authors. Critical Theory therefore aims at an "imaginary witness", who it tries to reach by means of messages in a bottle, the destination of which is dependant on the arbitrariness of the sea. But at the same time, in the preface to a later edition of *Dialectic of Enlightenment* from 1969, Horkheimer and Adorno seem to have a more ambiguous view on the possibilities of theory. One must, according to them, defend the existing "residues of freedom", and this would answer to the more pessimistic view. But they also, and this seems more optimistic, describe such residues as "tendencies towards true humanism", seeing in them a movement towards more.[30]

In her book, *The Highway of Despair: Critical Theory after Hegel*, which partly deals with Adorno, Robyn Marasco is interested in "the forms that critique takes at the heights of despair"[31] and affirms the critical potential of Adorno's aporetic negativity. In the despair of negative dialectics she finds the possibility for "hope" to "find indirect expression".[32] However, it might be problematic to formulate the pessimistic dimensions of Adorno's thought (i.e. despair) as hopeful, to the exclusion of the optimistic dimension from the scope of his thinking. If what I call the incompatibility of theory addresses a similar problem as Marasco's notion of despair, then I think that Marasco's interpretation misses out on the promising dimension of the non-identical. Still, having to rely on messages in bottles offers only a modicum of hope, though for Adorno, if this transpires to be the only option available, then this is how it must be. With little by way of public recognition, even from those initially allied

---

[29] Adorno & Horkheimer, *Dialectic of Enlightenment*, 256.
[30] Ibid, ix–x.
[31] Robyn Marasco, *The Highway of Despair: Critical Theory after Hegel* (New York: Columbia University Press, 2015), 85.
[32] Marasco, *The Highway of Despair*, 86.

with him, Adorno does what he can passionately. Adorno chooses incompatibility before constructive critique and thereby risks to lose contact with society and to appear as a querulant, not letting go of his mystical and utopian goals. But as we have seen, Adorno sees the role of Critical Theory as holding onto the little amount of freedom that is inherent in theory and trying to keep it alive. If there is nothing else to hold onto, Adorno must stick to this non-identical theory, which boils down to society-incompatible residues that contain almost forgotten images and promises of something other and better.

Conclusion: Possibilities and Limitations

I believe that the future of Critical Theory and the possibility for changing society must acknowledge Adorno's understanding of the problem of theory and praxis. There will be no shortcut to circumvent it. If it wants to take the possibilities and problems of theory and praxis seriously, it must not neglect Adorno's reflections. Therefore, in this situation, where it seems distant from a radical theory to establish a link to radical action (and capitalism arguably is even stronger than during Adorno's lifetime), the future of Critical Theory might be stuck in the activity of saying no. It is hard to decide in what ways current theories are non-identical in the fruitful critical sense discussed above or incompatible in the more limited way, but nevertheless, Critical Theory, as a heritage that comes from Adorno, contains the risk of becoming non-constructive and incompatible with the object it criticises, since Adorno would never choose a path in which he saw the confirmation of the false. For Adorno, it is better to keep theory from being realised rather than engaging with reality in an acquiescent and false way.

But does this mean that the future of Critical Theory is a future of saying no? Is this what Critical Theory will, from here onwards, have to be about? If so, would this constitute a problem? Yes, because it would have to put on hold its programmatic ambitions to have practical effects in society. Or, at best, the only way of trying to produce societal effects would necessarily be through blind messages in bottles, that is, nothing more than enveloped ideas without an addressee. But if Critical Theory sustains itself solely as a negative attitude of saying no, mainly in order to prevent itself from engaging in pseudo-free activities, then this would come across as taking the easy way out. Would Critical Theory then entirely abandon the imperative of radical action, with its theorists becoming self-sufficient meditators? Is it really just a betrayal of its program, or even a weakness as well as an easy way out? I don't think so. Here I shall offer two points:

1) The reason for turning its back on direct political praxis derives from a differentiated reflection on society and on the relation between theory and praxis; this is done for the sake of society. Adorno and other critical thinkers hold onto the promise of happiness in order for it not to be destroyed. For Adorno, the last way of holding onto a minimal chance for societal change is to block society out as much as possible and become incompatible with it.

2) It is not a sign of weakness to say no.[33] It is not easy to say no and at the same time avoid giving in to the prospect and fame of delivering a practical theory. But Adorno refuses to be constructive; he would have rather endured the fact of inaction. And this effort is immense. Weakness would rather be to say yes. In line with this, Freyenhagen states that, defending Adorno, "[t]o face up with this, to assign critical reflection priority, is not a sign of resignation, but the only way to keep the flame of resistance alive".[34]

So, one can say, depending on his different interpretations of society, in his various texts and formulations, Adorno is more or less pessimistic. But none of the options are completely hopeless. If theory is non-identical it has a critical contact with its object and can be the place for a thinking that transcends society towards possible futures. If theory instead only sees itself as conserving the promise of a better future for another time and receiver, *this* society, if interpreted adequately, makes theory incompatible. The worst-case scenario for Critical Theory would of course be if even these critical residues were themselves eliminated. Notwithstanding this, the minimal criterion for Critical Theory is that it should, at least for future generations, continue sending out messages in a bottle. One could say that positive and constructive engagements in existing society—I think this would be Adorno's position—should never be betrayals of or avoidances of the priority of saying no in Critical Theory. Or, Critical Theory can only become constructive when at the same it has not betrayed the imperative of saying no. And every action trying to escape or denounce this critical and negative priority, in order to act constructively within society, risks deceiving precisely its critical motivation. Critical Theory might want to reach further than this, but if it can only get there by sacrificing the critical activity of saying no, then it probably is the wrong way forward.

---

[33] See also Eric Jarosinski, *Nein: A Manifesto* (Frankfurt am Main: Fischer, 2014), and Stefan Müller-Doohm, *Adorno: A Biography* (Cambridge: Polity Press, 2005), 325ff.
[34] Freyenhagen, "Adorno's Politics: Theory and Praxis in Germany's 1960s", 883.

What is a Revolutionary Subject?
Activism, Theory, and Theodor W. Adorno's Conception of the Subject

SVEN ANDERS JOHANSSON

2018: Activism and Critical Theory

In July 2018 a short film clip, shot on a plane about to take off from Gothenburg to Istanbul, goes viral. The film consists of a close-up of a young Swedish woman who, crying, refuses to take her seat. While recording herself with her phone, she explains that there is a refugee on the plane, about to be sent back to Afghanistan. Through her actions, the young woman tries to stop this from happening: she refuses to take her seat and disembark the plane until the refugee is also allowed to leave the plane and stay in Sweden. In the background one can hear the crew trying to convince her to sit down, while angry fellow passengers begin attacking her verbally; still, she refuses to back down. Finally, her actions have the desired effect: once it is verified that the man has been escorted safely off the plane, she also leaves.[1]

The reason for drawing attention to this video is that it raises several questions central to our theme; questions regarding activism, politics, and the possibilities for an individual subject to protest against the situation at hand. Was the action of the young woman, Elin Ersson, successful? Why did the film clip attract so much attention? What kind of subjectivity is staged here? Is this what a revolutionary subject looks like in 2018?

A direct response to these questions is the secondary aim of this essay; the primary focus is Theodor W. Adorno, and more precisely his critique of activism and, above all, the faith he places in its antipode, theoretical thinking or—with the label that has almost turned into a trademark—Critical Theory. Almost half a century before Ersson's intervention, Adorno states: "Today [...] one clings to interventions [*Aktionen*] for the sake of the impossibility of action".[2] This remark appears in the essay "Resignation"; originally a radio talk, it was written as an answer to accusations that had been directed at the Frank-

---

[1] See David Crouch, "Swedish student's plane protest stops Afghan man's deportation 'to hell'", *The Guardian*, July 26, 2018.

[2] Theodor W. Adorno, "Resignation", *Critical Models: Interventions and Catchwords*, trans. Henry W. Pickford (New York: Columbia University Press, 2005), 290 ("Heute [...] Man klammert sich an Aktionen um der Unmöglichkeit der Aktion willen". "Resignation", *Kulturkritik und Gesellschaft I/II. Gesammelte Schriften*, vol. 10.2, ed. Rolf Tiedemann (Franfurt am Main: Suhrkamp, 1977), 795.

furt School from the radical student movement, that its members were too far removed from reality, resigned, even conservative. Adorno's defence takes the shape of a counterattack, arguing that the interventions of the activists are affirmed and tolerated not because they make a difference, but on the contrary because they lack real consequences.

What are the grounds for this decisive attack? And fifty years later how relevant is Adorno's critique of activism? What would he have said about Ersson's intervention, for example? My claim is that the crucial aspect of Adorno's critique lies in understanding that which is hardly visible in the quote above: the *one* behind the action. Or more accurately, the category of the subject. The crucial question is thus how Adorno understands *the subject* of activism and, correspondingly, theoretical thinking. I will try to demonstrate that his idea of the subject breaks with a common liberal conception of the individual, and that this break is decisive in his critique of activism. If agency, control, consciousness and reason, have been the basis for the constitution of subjectivity since Descartes, Adorno brings passivity, corporeality and frailty to the fore. This, I would argue, is a somewhat neglected aspect of Adorno's thinking, and it leads to a need to rephrase the question of what a revolutionary subject may be. Put differently, the future of Critical Theory depends on how the subject is to be understood.

But critique or critical thinking is not a transcendental possibility, according to Adorno and the early Frankfurt School; critique is something that may or may not be extracted from a historical situation.[3] If we want to understand the current status—or even the future—of Critical Theory, we have to look not only at Adorno's work, but also at today's problems. The same goes for activism and the possibility of political action: it is not a given. If there is a possibility to intervene or protest through direct political action, then this possibility must be extracted from the historical situation at hand.

In order to understand Ersson's intervention for example, we have to relate it to what came to be called the "refugee crisis". When this label first appeared it is hard to say. What we do know is that it became frequently used by European media during the summer of 2015. It was during this time that, as a result primarily of the war in Syria, the number of refugees arriving into Europe reached new heights. At this point the publication of the image of the drowned child, Alan Kurdi, gave rise, all over Europe, to a wave of solidarity as well as a general eagerness to help. Suddenly celebrities and politicians competed in

---

[3] Max Horkheimer, "Traditionelle und kritische Theorie", *Gesammelte Schriften 4: Schriften 1936–1941*, ed. Alfred Schmidt (Frankfurt am Main, Fischer, 1988), 203.

showing their more "humane" credentials in receiving refugees. At the same time the extreme right parties gained support for their nationalist, very restrictive refugee policies. Both the debate and the activists' reactions were indeed polarised.

Sweden was one of the countries that received the most immigrants per capita, at least for a short period in 2015. If Sweden started out with a very generous asylum policy, which was supported by both the media in general and the majority of the population, this changed very rapidly during the fall of 2015. Almost overnight the country was considered "full", and a more restrictive policy, including harsh border controls, replaced the initial attitude of generosity.

Three years later, the situation has not changed much. The war in Syria still continues. Refugees still drown in the Mediterranean in their desperate attempts to reach Europe, while the political attitude towards immigrants in Sweden becoming harsher with every passing day. One issue for debate has been the young Afghan men waiting for their asylum applications to be processed. Should they be deported to a very insecure future in Afghanistan, a country that in many cases they have never seen? Or should they be allowed to stay, a decision that would probably be a welcoming signal to more refugees?

This was the background to Ersson's intervention. It took place just a few months before the Swedish election in which the extreme right wing party looked as though it would be the big winner. In that light her intervention expressed both despair and hope. And that partly explains why it garnered much attention. Maybe things could be changed? Maybe all of us could actually do something to change the course of events?

1969: Adorno vs. the Students

There is a widespread image of Adorno as the incarnation of the academic locked away in his ivory tower. There are certainly reasons to question this image. Above all since it does not fit very well with the role Adorno actually played as a public intellectual in post-war Germany. As Detlev Claussen puts it in his biography, when after the war Adorno returned to Germany he "had had enough of a marginalized existence. He now pushed his way into the West German public sphere".[4] Apart from his duties at the university, he contributed

---

[4] Detlev Claussen, *Theodor W. Adorno: One Last Genius*, trans. Rodney Livingstone (Cambridge, Mass.: Harvard University Press, 2008), 225. See also 176.

to newspapers, gave numerous radio talks and public speeches—hardly what you would expect from someone turning his back on society.

At the same time, there is, in Adorno's work, an undeniable reluctance to support all revolutionary ambitions to change society.[5] On the whole, Adorno seems to be dismissing all revolutionary praxis and political activism as futile or misdirected, arguing that "politics has migrated into the autonomous work of art".[6] Not only is revolutionary practice blocked, but politics as a means of changing society has shrunk to nothing—ironically the autonomous realm of art has become the only place where it might linger. In this situation, theoretical thinking needs to be defended, since "[d]espite all of its unfreedom, theory is the guarantor of freedom in the midst of unfreedom".[7] Adorno's critical theory is simply not aimed at igniting some kind of revolutionary change, but rather to uphold the possibility of thinking, since this—if anywhere—is where freedom may still exist. Or with the famous beginning of *Negative Dialectics*: "Philosophy, which once seemed obsolete, lives on because the moment to realize it was missed".[8] The unrealised character of philosophy, its missed moment, has become its very reason to exist.

It is interesting to compare this statement with the critical remark I quoted earlier: "Today [...] one clings to interventions [*Aktionen*] for the sake of the impossibility of action".[9] Indirectly Adorno seems to be saying that *both* philosophy and activism live on because of their impossibility. Neither of them can extend beyond themselves and change society. Their predicament is in that respect similar: they are both marked by the division of labour upon which modern society is based.[10] Why then does Adorno praise one and dismiss the other? Why does the afterlife of philosophy imply freedom, while activism does not?

---

[5] For a thorough account of Adorno's critique of political activism, see Fabian Freyenhagen, "Adorno's Politics: Theory and Praxis in Germany's 1960s", *Philosophy & Social Criticism*, vol. 40(9), 2014.

[6] Theodor W. Adorno, "Commitment", in *Notes to Literature*, vol. 2, trans. Shierry Weber Nicholsen (New York: Columbia University Press, 1992), 93 ("In die autonomen [Kunstwerke] ist die Politik eingewandert". "Engagement", GS 11, 430). Cf Espen Hammer, *Adorno and the Political* (London & New York: Routledge, 2005), 122–143.

[7] Theodor W. Adorno, "Marginalia to Theory and Praxis", *Critical Models*, 263 ("Trotz all ihrer Unfreiheit ist sie im Unfreien Statthalter der Freiheit". "Marginalien zu Theorie und Praxis", GS 10.2, 763).

[8] Theodor W. Adorno, *Negative Dialectics*, trans. E.B. Ashton (New York: Continuum, 1973), 3 ("Philosophie, die einmal überholt schien, erhält sich am Leben, weil der Augenblick ihrer Verwirklichung versäumt ward". *Negative Dialektik*, GS 6, 15).

[9] Theodor W. Adorno, "Resignation", *Critical Models: Interventions and Catchwords*, trans. Henry W. Pickford (New York: Columbia University Press, 2005), 290, translation modified ("Heute [...] Man klammert sich an Aktionen um der Unmöglichkeit der Aktion willen". "Resignation", GS 10.2, 795).

[10] Ibid. 289 (794).

If we start with the former, the short answer is that theoretical thinking, as Adorno conceives it, implies a possibility to cope with or even transcend the false condition according to which reason is functionalised into a "purposiveness without purpose".[11] To think is to identify, as Adorno states at the beginning of *Negative Dialectics*; thinking is thus bound to that which exists. But thinking is also "enlightenment conscious of itself".[12] This self-consciousness may also be described as an acknowledgement of that which is non-identical to conceptual thinking. On a more concrete level this manifests itself in a theory operating by means of conceptual constellations rather than definitions.[13] In that manner philosophy may actually still broach something true, from its position within the false. What may appear as inactive resignation is thus "actually a force of resistance" as he puts it in "Resignation".[14]

This is a force that the activism of the student movement in its turn lacks. If the division between theory and activism is a consequence of the capitalist division of labour, the activists not only confirm this division, but also transform it "into a prohibition on thinking", Adorno argues.[15] In this respect the activists' call for action is not only naïve, but also repressive. The very point of theoretical thinking—the utopian aspect, the possibility to "find an exit"—is thrown away, while discussions that are actually held "degenerate into tactics".[16] Another way to formulate the problem is that activists do not really engage with objective problems; they are engaged primarily in the interventions themselves. Contrary to what it aspires to, activism thus becomes its own goal. Adorno characterises their activism as pseudo-activity: "actions that overdoes and aggravates itself for the sake of its own *publicity*, [...] elevating itself into an end in itself".[17] Activist's actions are hence reduced to a kind of a commercial for the activist subject's own agency, a subject who simply appears more narcissistic than revolutionary.

---

[11] Max Horkheimer & Theodor W. Adorno, *Dialectic of Enlightenment: Philosophical Fragments*, trans. Edmund Jephcott, Stanford: Stanford University Press, 2002, 69 (*Dialektik der Aufklärung: Philosophische Fragmente*, GS 3, 103).

[12] Theodor W. Adorno, "Resignation", 291(GS 10.2, 796).

[13] See Theodor W. Adorno, "The Essay as Form", in *Notes to Literature*, vol. 1, trans. Shierry Weber Nicholsen (New York: Columbia University Press, 1991), 12–13 ("Der Essay als Form", GS 11, 20–22).

[14] Theodor W. Adorno, "Resignation", 293 ("Eigentlich ist Denken [...] die Kraft zum Widerstand", GS 10.2, 798).

[15] Ibid, 290 ("wird daraus fix ein Denkverbot", GS 10.2, 795).

[16] Ibid, 291 ("in Taktik ausarten", "Einen Ausweg [...] finden", GS 10.2, 797).

[17] Ibid ("Tun, das sich überspielt und der eigenen publicity zuliebe anheizt, [...] sich zum Selbstzweck erhebt". GS 10.2, 796). Slavoj Žižek later makes a similar distinction between *act* and *activity*, but his argument is grounded in Lacan, not in Adorno. Slavoj Žižek, *The Ticklish Subject: The Absent Centre of Political Ontology* (London & New York: Verso, 1999), 374–75.

For Adorno, this aspect becomes most evident in what he labels the do-it-yourself-attitude of activism: "activities that do what has long been done better by the means of industrial production only in order to inspire in the unfree individuals, paralyzed in their spontaneity, the assurance that everything depends on them".[18] Here he touches upon an aspect that is arguably even more important for the understanding of today's activism: the faith in the agency of the individual; the assurance that everything is up to you and me. This ideology was doubtless especially strong during the refugee crisis. Huge mass media campaigns addressed the issue on an individualised level: "what have *you* done?" A complicated political problem was thus transformed into a moral question for the individual to solve. This is arguably also why Ersson's video left its mark: it confirms the power of the liberal individual that the mainstream media tends to highlight. All structural problems, geopolitical factors and political solutions are put to one side, while an image according to which everything is up to you circulates far and wide.

Objections to Adorno's Critique

But even if one acknowledges that Adorno's critique of activism is to some extent still relevant, one may certainly object to his argument, especially considering how the "Resignation" essay concludes. Against the pseudo-activity of the activists, Adorno places "the uncompromisingly critical thinker, who neither signs over his consciousness nor lets himself be terrorized into action".[19] What's strange in this is that the individual act, which was discarded as futile in the case of activism, is heralded as heroic and uncompromising in the case of thinking. If "[t]hinking is a doing", as he puts it in another context, should not the reverse also be the case: doing is a thinking?[20] Could not activism be just as conscious and uncompromising as theoretical thinking? If thinking "points beyond itself", why would that not be the case for action? If thinking "has sublimated the rage", could not the same be said of action?[21] On this point it is tempting to direct Adorno's favourite objection against his own reasoning: he is (or so it seems, at least) not dialectical enough.

---

[18] Adorno, "Resignation", 291 ("Tätigkeiten, die, was längst mit den Mitteln der industriellen Produktion besser geleistet werden kann, nur um in den unfreien, in ihrer Spontaneität gelähmten Einzelnen die Zuversicht zu erwecken, auf sie käme es an". GS 10.2, 797).

[19] Ibid. 292 ("der kompromißlos kritisch Denkende, der weder sein Bewußtsein überschreibt noch zum Handeln sich terrorisieren läßt". GS 10.2, 798).

[20] Adorno, "Marginalia to Theory and Praxis", 261 ("Denken ist ein Tun", GS 10.2, 761).

[21] Adorno, "Resignation", 293 ("weist über sich hinaus", "hat die Wut sublimiert" GS 10.2, 798–9).

Here a further question is to be raised: why should the doing that thinking partakes in be understood as something *individual*, an act belonging to "the thinking person", or respectively, why should activism be tied to unfree *individuals*?[22] Adorno appears to be unwilling or incapable of understanding the subject as something that may be collective, nonhuman, or in any way not identical to the bourgeois Western individual. Would it not, for example, be possible to understand Elin Ersson's intervention as just a small part of a bigger struggle? Is there necessarily an opposition between her act and political change? Could not the former lead to the latter, rather than contradict it? After all, it is difficult to tell where a thought ends and an act begins—neither exist in a vacuum.

All this was addressed already by Peter Sloterdijk, in his *Critique of Cynical Reason* (1983): "Adorno's theory", Sloterdijk writes, "revolted against the collaborative traits embedded in the 'practical attitude'".[23] Even though he follows Adorno a long way, the problem, he argues, is that Adorno was too eager to ensure that his own critical subject (on a theoretical level, that is) remained unharmed: "what is called subject in modern times is, in fact, that self-preservation ego that withdraws step by step from the living, to the summit of paranoia. Withdrawal, distancing, self-displacement are the driving forces of this kind of subjectivity".[24] To what extent is this true of Adorno? If one looks at his confrontation with the activists, and the argument he advances in "Resignation", it is hard to deny that Sloterdijk has a point.[25] It becomes more important for Adorno to keep the subject intact—as the locus of thinking— than to really address the objective situation. Espen Hammer also points out this danger: "there is always a danger for Adorno's negative dialectics that it becomes a means to secure purity and inner certainty at the expense of engaging with realms in which the acceptance of political responsibility is both costly and unavoidable".[26] From this perspective, it is better to do nothing at all, than to run the risk of becoming involved in praxis and tactics, where one is not really in control of one's own subjectivity.

An interesting implication of this critique is that, from this perspective, Adorno ends up pretty close to the narcissism he discerns in activism, even if they may appear opposed. If there is a certain narcissism in activism, the same

---

[22] Ibid. 293 ("der Denkende", 799).

[23] Peter Sloterdijk, *Critique of Cynical Reason*, trans. Michael Eldred (Minneapolis: University of Minnesota Press, 1987), xxxv.

[24] Sloterdijk, 355.

[25] Cf Louisa Shea, *The Cynic Enlightenment: Diogenes in the Salon* (Baltimore: The Johns Hopkins University Press, 2010), 152–6.

[26] Hammer, 179.

applies to the "cynical" theorising Adorno stands for. They are both primarily preoccupied with the self, their own subjectivity, rather than with objective circumstances. In fact, they may both be understood as two self-centred means of ensuring that subjectivity remains intact.

This is, I would argue, not the full picture. The crucial question is how this subjectivity or subject is to be understood. When Adorno, at the end of the "Resignation" essay, states that "[t]he happiness that dawns in the eye of the thinking person is the happiness of humanity", it may appear to confirm the critique referred to above: thinking is there to strengthen the individual subject, the thinking person. However, the translation is in fact slightly misleading: there is literally no "person" in the original, only *someone* who is thinking ("Das Glück, das im Auge des Denkenden aufgeht, ist das Glück der Menschheit").[27] If this is a small difference, it is nonetheless quite telling. Even though there is a (male) thinker implied in "des Denkenden", it makes a difference if this act is tied or not to *personhood*.[28] If we read the original, thinking is neither there to give joy to the person behind it, nor is this person to be understood as the locus of happiness. It is rather the case that the act of thinking is opened up to something *non- or pre-personal*.

A passage from the short text "Marginalia to Theory and Praxis" is illuminating in this regard: "To the extent that subject, the thinking substance of philosophers, is object, to the extent that it falls within object, subject is already also practical".[29] What is interesting here is that the distinction between subject and object breaks down at the same time as the difference is maintained dialectically. The "difference between subject and object slices through subject as well as through object", as it is formulated in the essay "On Subject and Object".[30] More concretely, the act of thinking is not a capacity controlled by the individual. And even the most theoretical thinking is on some level something material; the thinking substance—that which thinks—is a praxis within the subject, so to speak. And this is a praxis that dissolves rather than defines the person where it takes place. It must be understood as a dialectical movement between subject and object, substance and praxis.

---

[27] Adorno, "Resignation" 293 (GS 10.2, 799).

[28] The *person* and the idea of *personality* is criticized extensively in Adorno, for imstamce in *Dialectic of Enlightenment*, 125–6 (GS 3, 178–79).

[29] Adorno, "Marginalia to Theory and Praxis", 261 ("Soweit Subjekt, die denkende Substanz der Philosophen, Objekt ist, soweit es in Objekt fällt, soweit ist es vorweg auch praktisch". GS 10.2, 761).

[30] Adorno, "On Subject and Object", in *Critical Models*, 256 ("Differenz von Subjekt und Objekt schneidet sowohl durch Subjekt wie durch Objekt hindurch", "Zu Subjekt und Objekt", GS 10.2, 755).

What is the Aim of Everything?

What in that case is so good about thinking? Was not Critical Theory supposed to provide an opportunity to change the wrong state of things? Is the uncompromising thinking an end in itself, and if not to what is it supposed to lead? The beginning of an answer may be found in the talk about happiness in the quote above: "The happiness that dawns in the eye of the thinking is the happiness of humanity". The individual act of thinking is connected to something bigger, to "the happiness of humanity". How is this connection and this happiness to be understood?

To answer this we have to look beyond the short "Resignation" essay, and turn, for example, to the aphorism *"Sur l'eau"* in *Minima Moralia*. Here Adorno raises a question about the aim of the emancipated society; that is, what is the goal of both activism and theoretical thinking? He immediately dismisses utopian answers such as "fulfilment of human possibilities or the richness of life", since they are connected to an existing ideal of "production as an end in itself". These answers are actually shaped by the system they are trying to leave behind, and hence are not utopian at all. Put differently, we cannot imagine a happiness or utopia that is not a reaction to—and hence an expression of—the unhappy circumstances at hand. Therefore, Adorno demurs from the most pretentious answers regarding the question in what an emancipatory society is to consist. At the end of the day, "fulfilment of human possibilities" means nothing else than fulfilment of the ideals pertaining to the false condition we are stuck in. Instead he states that only the crudest demand would be tender enough: "that no-one shall go hungry anymore".[31]

If this stands out as a low-key answer, it does not serve as the last word. A little later in the same aphorism Adorno develops his argument, and states that "[a] mankind which no longer knows want will begin to have an inkling of the delusory, futile nature of all the arrangements hitherto made to escape want, which used wealth to reproduce want on a larger scale".[32] Exactly the same progress, which has obliterated hardships, has actually caused *more* suffering, and the latter is impossible to keep separate from progress itself. The idea here is familiar to every Adorno reader: the dialectic of enlightenment once again. Our best intentions cannot be separated from the worst consequences.

---

[31] Adorno, *Minima Moralia: Reflections on a Damaged Life*, trans. E.F.N. Jephcott (London & New York: Verso, 2005(, 156 (*Minima Moralia: Reflexionen aus dem beschädigten Leben*, GS 4, 178).

[32] Adorno, *Minima Moralia*, 156–57 ("Einer Menschheit, welche Not nicht mehr kennt, dämmert gar etwas von dem Wahnhaften, Vergeblichen all der Veranstaltungen, welche bis dahin getroffen wurden, um der Not zu entgehen, und welche die Not mit dem Reichtum erweitert reproduzierten." GS 4, 179).

Progress is real, but unfortunately so is its dialectical counterpart. Or rather, as Thijs Lijster succinctly puts it, "[p]rogress, in other words, is neither necessary nor impossible".[33]

With the student protests and the spirit of 1968 in mind ("Be realistic—demand the impossible!"), this may certainly sound a bit resigned or cynical. Adorno's answer is what one would expect from someone who has withdrawn to the ivory tower and given up on the possibility of creating a more just society. The attitude may appear even more problematic in relation to the situation we are facing today. For is there not something disturbingly Eurocentric in equating the enlightened subject of Critical theory with humanity, or in the talk of "[a] mankind which no longer knows want?" And does not the comment about the "futile nature of all the arrangements hitherto made to escape want" stand out as cynical if we relate it to the theme, with which I began, namely the refugee crisis? Of course, this is not the question Adorno was addressing, but if we address it anyway (after all, is this not what theories are for?), the implications appear to be rather negative: all efforts and good intentions will only result in more suffering.

Even if there is some truth to this (if we look at how the Aid Industrial Complex works for example), it is hardly a satisfying response from whatever understands itself as Critical theory. This becomes all the more evident once we formulate this in more concrete terms: there is nothing the Europeans and North Americans can do to stop the suffering of the refugees from Syria, Libya, Afghanistan or Somalia. From this perspective, Adorno is perhaps not the thinker to turn to if we want to find arguments for more humane asylum policies. Or if we want to do that anyway, it appears that we would first have to "decolonise" his critical theory, as Amy Allen has argued.[34]

A Revolutionary Subject

This impression is certainly strengthened if we return to Adorno's clash with the students in 1969. On one occasion, on 31 January, when the students appeared to be occupying a room at the university, Adorno felt obliged to call the police; 76 students were arrested.[35] Adorno describes the incident in a letter

---

[33] Thijs Lijster, *Benjamin and Adorno on Art Criticism: Critique of Art* (Amsterdam: Amsterdam University Press, 2017), 192.

[34] Amy Allen, *The End of Progress: Decolonizing the Normative Foundations of Critical Theory* (New York: Columbia University Press, 2016).

[35] Esther Leslie, "Introduction to Adorno/Marcuse Correspondence on the German Student Movement", *New Left Review*, 233 (1999): 120.

to Herbert Marcuse, but to his surprise and big disappointment Marcuse sides with the students.

In retrospect it is striking how hard the incident appears to have hurt Adorno (one almost gets the impression that it provoked not only depression, but also the heart attack he died from a few months later). One explanation is that the episode touched the very heart of Critical Theory: the possibility of change, the insistence on thinking. It is also significant that Adorno was accused from two directions: from the left for being conservative and from the right for having provided the students with their theoretical weapons. It is perhaps understandable, then, that he is incapable of seeing the situation from no other perspective than his own.

In Marcuse's argument in contrast, there is a widening of the focus:

> This isolation [of the concept "Democracy" from capitalism] permits repression of the question: "better" for whom? For Vietnam? Biafra? The enslaved people in South America, in the ghettos? The system is global, and it is its democracy, which, with all its faults, also carries out, pays for, and arms neo-colonialism and neo-fascism, and it obstructs liberation.[36]

Whereas Adorno, in his attempts to win Marcuse's understanding, is preoccupied with the publication lists of the Institute for Social Research, on the one hand, and, on the other, the risk that its facilities might be demolished, alongside the concrete physical threat the activists themselves carried, Marcuse tries to place the significance of the student protests within a wider global perspective.

This seems to confirm the widespread image, expressed for example by Joan Alway, of "Marcuse continuing to search for a revolutionary subject and Horkheimer and Adorno tending to turn away from politics altogether".[37] One may object that this comment is a simplification, that it misses the point both with respect to Horkheimer's idea of Critical Theory and to Adorno's interest in art and aesthetics. And yet there is a certain truth to the comment: yes, Adorno turned his back on "politics" in Marcuse's sense, but not—and this is crucial—on the "revolutionary *subject*", with emphasis on the last word. It is just that Adorno approached these matters in an entirely different manner,

---

[36] Theodor W. Adorno & Herbert Marcuse, "Correspondence on the German Student Movement", *New Left Review*, 233 (1999): 134 (letter from Marcuse to Adorno on 21 July 1969).

[37] Joan Alway, *Critical Theory and Political Possibilities: Conceptions of Emancipatory Politics in the Works of Horkheimer, Adorno, Marcuse, and Habermas* (Westport: Greenwood Press, 1995), 135

through other conceptual constellations. The crucial question to him is not "better for whom?" but rather "what is a subject?"

As Espen Hammer notes, there is an ambivalence in Adorno's account of the freedom of the individual subject.[38] I would argue that this ambivalence is actually conceptualised in terms of the distinction between the "individual" and the "subject" in his thinking. Although Adorno is not fully consistent here, *the individual* rarely has positive connotations in his work, while for the most part the *subject* does.[39] The individual is a product of capitalism, merely an ideological function; the subject, on the other hand, is the locus of experience, and the condition of both critical thinking and happiness. This difference is often disregarded, for example by Jürgen Habermas when Adorno is criticised for being seduced by simplified interpretations, such as the "thesis of the end of the individual".[40] But to Adorno the individual, or the "self-identity" about which Habermas speaks, has never been anything but the reified version of the subject—to mourn "the end" of it, as Habermas wrongly accuses Adorno of doing, does not make sense. If there is freedom, it pertains *not* to the individual, whose self-identity and freedom is an illusion,[41] but to the subject, "the thinking substance", to draw once more on a formulation from "Marginalia to Theory and Praxis".[42]

But if individuality is an illusion, it is also a reality—we cannot avoid it, inasmuch as we cannot avoid the false condition that modern society is. Subjectivity, on the other hand, is harder both to grasp and maintain. It is in crisis, dissolving, Adorno argues; this dissolution serves also as a possibility: "the subject's dissolution presents at the same time the ephemeral and condemned picture of a possible subject".[43] The meaning of a "possible subject" is important to my line of argument. I would argue that it is this possibility, rather than a changed society, that accounts for Adorno's faith in theoretical

---

[38] Hammer, 112.

[39] See Anders Johansson, *Självskrivna män: Subjektiveringens dialektik* (Göteborg: Glänta produktion, 2015), 111–120.

[40] Jürgen Habermas, "Moralentwicklung und Ich-Identität", in *Zur Rekonstruktion des Historischen Materialismus* (Frankfurt am Main.: Suhrkamp, 1976), 65.

[41] Horkheimer & Adorno, *Dialectic of Enlightenment*, 125–6. (GS 3, 178–9); Theodor W. Adorno, "Reading Balzac", in *Notes to Literature*, vol. 1, trans. Shierry Weber Nicholsen (New York: Columbia University Press, 1991), 130 ("Balzac-Lektüre", GS 11, 149); Adorno, *Negative Dialectics*, 312 (GS 6, 306–7).

[42] Adorno, "Marginalia to Theory and Praxis", 261 (GS 10.2, 761).

[43] Adorno, *Negative Dialectics*, 281 ("so ist die Auflösung des Subjekts zugleich das ephemere und verurteilte Bild eines möglichen Subjekts", GS 6, 277). For a thorough discussion of the different aspects of the dissolution of the subject, see Alastair Morgan, *Adorno's Concept of Life* (London and New York: Continuum, 2007), 119–137.

thinking as well as for his dismissal of activism. Ultimately this subject is constituted not by its own actions, nor by its independent judgements, clear vision or distinct thoughts, but rather by its corporeality.

Not everyone will agree on this point though. According to J. M. Bernstein, Adorno identifies constitutive subjectivity with "rationalized reason". Consequently "the modern subject [according to Adorno] *is* abstract, an abstraction". With regards to thinking, this implies a non-identity "between the empirical subject and the I that thinks".[44] In developing this argument, Bernstein emphasises the Kantian aspect of Adorno's theory; the transcendental subject becomes the matrix of understanding his notion of the subject. What this disregards, I would argue, is that not even the act of thinking can, according to Adorno, be abstracted from the corporeal or somatic aspect of subjectivity. It is not only the case that "[t]here is no sensation without a somatic moment", but this moment is a part of all knowledge:

> The somatic moment as the not purely cognitive part of cognition is irreducible, and thus the subjective claim collapses at the very point where radical empiricism had conserved it. The fact that the subject's cognitive achievements are somatic in accordance with their own meaning affects not only the basic relation of subject and object but the dignity of physicality. Physicality emerges at the ontical pole of subjective cognition, as the core of that cognition.[45]

When Bernstein, from his Kantian—or even Cartesian—perspective argues that the subject, for Adorno, has its basis in thinking and reason, he fails to see that thinking is grounded in a corporeality, something somatic—indeed, in that which is not subjective within the subject—which, on the other hand, is brought together and given form through cognition, experience, sensation, thinking. In other words, the subject is nothing but a moment in a constant dialectical exchange with its opposite, and hence just as material as abstract.

Let us return now to the passage in "*Sur l'eau*" which we discussed earlier. Against this background another aspect becomes visible:

---

[44] J. M. Bernstein, *Adorno: Disenchantment and Ethics* (Cambridge: Cambridge University Press, 2001), 212–13, 216.

[45] Adorno, *Negative Dialectics*, 193–94. ("Keine Empfindung ohne somatisches Moment" GS 6, 194 "Irreduzibel ist das somatische Moment als das nicht rein cognitive an der Erkenntnis. Damit wird der subjektive Anspruch dort noch hinfällig, wo gerade der radikale Empirismus ihn konserviert hatte. Daß die cognitiven Leistungen des Erkenntnissubjekts dem eigenen Sinn nach somatisch sind, affiziert nicht nur das Fundierungsverhältnis von Subjekt und Objekt sondern die Dignität des Körperlichen. Am ontischen Pol subjektiver Erkenntnis tritt es als deren Kern hervor." GS 6, 194–95). Cf. Alastair Morgan, *Adorno's Concept of Life*, 136.

> A mankind which no longer knows want will begin to have an inkling of the delusory, futile nature of all the arrangements hitherto made to escape want, which used wealth to reproduce want on a larger scale. Enjoyment itself would be affected, just as its present framework is inseparable from operating, planning, having one's way, subjugating. *Rien faire comme une bête* [sic], lying on water and looking peacefully at the sky, "being, nothing else, without any further fulfilment", might take the place of process, act, satisfaction, and so truly keep the promise of dialectical logic that it would culminate in its origin. None of the abstract concepts comes closer to fulfilled utopia than that of eternal peace.[46]

At the beginning of this passage we find the autonomous, active human individual—"rationalized reason" to speak with Bernstein—with the power to eliminate all suffering, all want. But this power also brings forth a sense of disillusionment or futility. In the end, what are all these arrangements good for? Even enjoyment as such, which is bound up with all our efforts, stands out as futile. "Progress occurs when it ends", as Adorno formulates it in the essay "Progress".[47]

The continuation of the passage, with the body floating on the water, "comme une bête" (the quote here is taken from a short story by Maupassant), like a beast, points in another direction, however. What we are facing here is no longer an autonomous active individual, but a body passively letting itself be carried by the water. An object just as much as a subject. Why does Adorno affirm this? It might sound like just another version of cynical resignation, but this time one cannot accuse Adorno of inwardness and stubborn self-defence. Instead we are dealing with a subject that is totally open, defenceless, almost blurred, not really defined by its own actions but by the actions of the circumstances, the water. The point is that this subjectivity, not constituted by agency or self-realisation, but by passivity and loss of control, opens up towards another ideal of happiness and freedom—"fulfilled utopia". Hence it is an answer to the earlier question: what is the goal of all our efforts? To be a subject.

"Do something!"

But why highlight this passive ideal today? As we are becoming all the more painfully aware, humanity faces acute problems. Here, now: streams of refugees; climate change, and the dissolution of democracy. How should we

---

[46] Adorno, *Minima Moralia*, 156–57 (GS 4, 179).

[47] Theodor W. Adorno, "Progress", in *Critical Models,* 150 ("der Fortschritt ereigne sich dort, wo er endet". "Fortschritt", in *Kulturkritik und Gesellschaft I/II,* GS 10.2, 626).

cope with it? Does Adorno's Critical theory have any answers? Is not the situation so desperate—for the refugees on the Mediterranean, for example—that we need to take more direct action?

Unlike the student protests Adorno faced in the 1960s, there is nothing immediately revolutionary about this activism. The aim is not to overthrow the existing world order, but to help suffering refugees in a difficult situation. Does this difference make Adorno's critique less relevant? Not necessarily. What he criticises in "Resignation" is above all the reification of actions and the overestimation of the power of the individual; individuals "paralyzed in their spontaneity" in the illusion "that everything depends on them". This idea, this ideology and this reification have arguably only gained in strength since Adorno wrote his essay. In fact, the pressure to "do something", the individual's responsibility and desire to *act*, is something that appears relentlessly in the media today, both as a subjective desire and a moral imperative, not least during the most acute phase of the refugee crisis.

"After the summer tour this year I was able to take it easy back home. But all the images and reports about desperate refugees trying to get to Europe gnawed inside me more and more. *I felt I wanted to do something more concrete.* I wanted to be there in the famine with love, clothes and money" Carola Häggkvist, a popular Swedish singer, declared.[48] She was not alone—an entire cavalcade of celebrities expressed their eagerness to "do something". "What have *you* done?" the media repeatedly asked, as if it was up to the individual European newspaper reader to end the war in Syria.

That, three years later, Elin Ersson's intervention fits into the same pattern becomes even clearer if we listen to her own posterior explanation: "This Monday I could do something, and that's why I did it. No one can do everything, but everyone can do something, Elin Ersson said".[49] Just like in Häggkvist's case, the focus in the comment is not on the circumstances that should be changed, but on the very act itself. Häggkvist's wish to do something "concrete"—not just to help in an indirect way (by donating money for example)—may point in another direction. But this concreteness is abstract, so to speak; what she asks for is not a specific concreteness ("I want to help *that* refugee who I met on the street yesterday"), but concreteness in general. There is something similar in Ersson's answer: she decided to do something, not for a particular reason ("this particular person needs help"), but *because she could.*

---

[48] Thomas Lerner, "Carola fick nog – reste till Grekland och hjälpte flyktingar", *Dagens Nyheter*, 2015-09-29 (italics added).

[49] Madeleine Bäckman, "Elin Ersson, 21, stoppade utvisning – blev världsnyhet" [Elin Ersson 21, stopped deportation – became world news], Expressen, 2018-07-26.

What unites the two cases is hence the focus, not on the needy, but on the benevolent act. The subjective possibility of action, of doing something concrete, is thus more or less taken for granted—"everyone can do something".

One may argue that, on the concrete level on Häggkvist talks, Ersson's action was nevertheless a failure: the 25-year old individual she intended to save was not on the plane (he was on another flight). Her intentions then switched to another man who just so happened to be on her flight (afterwards it turned out that he was convicted for domestic violence). She did indeed obstruct his deportation, but in the long run it changed nothing—the deportation was only postponed for a while.

But this objection misses the point. All that mattered was the enormous media attention it garnered; the video went viral. Why did it? For the same reason as Adorno dismissed activism: because it performed individual action, courage, commitment, compassion, and agency. It made it clear that, with Ersson's own words, everyone can do something. In this respect the intervention was a huge success. In fact, it did not matter at all who the deportee was, what he had done, if he was allowed to stay in the long run, etc. The intervention was its own purpose. All that mattered was the very performance of agency, commitment, and compassion, or rather the mediation of it via the mobile phone. (It is significant that the most dramatic moment in Ersson's video occurs when a fellow passenger takes the phone away from her, and hence makes the recording impossible. If one of the crew members had not quickly returned it to her, the actions would have been a true failure, since the documentation of the intervention *is* the act. Hence one may argue that the true subject here is Ersson's mobile phone.)

Of course, one might argue that the real purpose was to encourage other individuals to act, and in the strategy to apply pressure on politicians to open the borders, and let refugees stay. However, one may also turn this causality around: the command to "do something" may be understood as an interpellation in the Althusserian sense. In that case Häggkvist's and Ersson's initiatives are just manifestations of a grander ideology.[50] More precisely the individual intervention is a ritual that turns the idea of the free individual into something real. From that perspective, the crucial thing is not the concrete outcome of the intervention, but the idea that reality—"the concrete"—is there to be reached— yes, that it is actually *produced*—by the individual in action.

---

[50] Louis Althusser, *On the Reproduction of Capitalism: Ideology and Ideological State Apparatuses*, trans. G. M. Goshgarian (London & New York: Verso, 2014), 259–72.

It is not far-fetched to see this reification of the individual as a phenomenon produced by the logic of digital social media and the technical devices for communication,[51] but it may also be understood as a symptom of a larger crisis of the modern subject. It was not only the goodness of the subject that was brought to the fore during the refugee crisis, it was subjective *agency* as such. This clearly relates to Adorno's critical remark about "action that overdoes and aggravates itself for the sake of its own *publicity*", but the question is if the problem has not been amplified since the late 60s.[52] An explanation of this is that the reification of agency is a symptom of a general *lack* of subjective agency. Perhaps the insight that is most unbearable, almost taboo to Western society today is that the individual may actually be powerless. That we, enlightened, rich, democratic Europeans are just as powerless as the Syrian refugees themselves. Why is this unbearable? Because it threatens the very form of the liberal subject: the individual constituted by its free choices, free will, independent actions—in short, by its agency. This explains the desire and demand, in the mass media, for people to perform actions, individuals enacting commitment. They prove that there is freedom, that individual action is possible, and that action is the way to touch reality. Hence the individual "is spared from recognizing his powerlessness", as Adorno puts it.[53]

As we have already seen, Adorno argues in *"Sur l'eau"* that this active individual is modelled on an idea of production as an end in itself. The individual—cherished as the origin of free actions, free speech and free feelings—is just a function of the capitalist logic that it believes that it has have created. This is the content of the remark I started out with: "One clings to interventions for the sake of the impossibility of action". That is: one attempts performatively to demonstrate one's power, the more impossible it proves to be. There is an ideological pressure on the individual to act, since the possibilities to do so are increasingly unequally distributed and in a general sense are being rapidly attenuated. By inducing in us the faith that everyone has the power to act, the rather frightening and—to the western European mind—scandalous fact that we, on the contrary, lack this power, may be concealed.

One problem with this desire or ideology is that, if what matters is the higher meaning of the life of the helper, everything outside of the subject becomes

---

[51] See Elliot T. Panek, Yioryos Nardi & Sara Konrath, "Mirror or Megaphone? How relationships between narcissism and social networking site use differ on Facebook and Twitter", in *Computers in Human Behaviour*, 29 (2013); Christopher J. Carpenter, "Narcissism on Facebook", *Personality and Individual Differences*, 52 (2012).

[52] Adorno, "Resignation", 291 ("Tun, das sich überspielt und der eigenen publicity zuliebe anheizt", GS 10.2, 796).

[53] Ibid., 292 ("Ihm wird erspart, seine Ohnmacht zu erkennen", GS 10.2, 798).

irrelevant or contingent—near extinct tigers may serve just as well as Haitian earthquake victims or Syrian refugees. One may of course argue that it does not matter *why* people want to help refugees—what matters is that they do. But in the long run, an activism that is not really concerned with the objective situation, only with the subjective commitment itself, is dangerous, since in the end it does not matter if I act to *help* the refugees or act to *stop* them, the only thing that matters is that I appear to be active, that I do something, i.e. that I perform activity.

Another problem is the undialectical distinction between helping activists and helpless victims that is reproduced through these actions: agency belongs to "me", passivity belongs to "the other". In this way "the subject of the West, or the West as Subject" is preserved, as Gayatri Spivak famously puts it in "Can the Subaltern Speak".[54] Yes, maybe this is even the sole purpose of this activism: to confirm this distinction, to keep activity on one side (the considerate western intellectual or activist), thanks to the passivity of the Other (the drowning refugees, or the asylum seekers waiting to be deported). When Adorno introduces passivity as an ideal, this dialectic—and this is crucial—is actually skewed, it is twisted.

The failure to understand the young Europeans who go to Syria to join the IS, or who kill themselves along with as many innocent victims they possibly can in Europe or wherever, is revealing in the following sense: are not their reasons exactly the same as the ones offered by the Swedish artist Carola to go to Greece or by Ersson when attempting to stop the flight? The feeling that there must be more to life than this? The desire to "do something concrete", to do something, to make a difference? The need to step out of the mediocre life one is living, and really make one's mark? And yet *their* activism is treated as totally alien, evil, impossible to understand.

Interestingly enough, in this postcolonial perspective, Adorno's cynicism actually hits its mark. For it is exactly *the agency* of the Western subject that is questioned in the end of "*Sur l'eau*". Against the seemingly active, operative, planning, efficient individual, Adorno places the body passively floating upon the water. In this context, one can hardly avoid associating this floating body with the refugees drowning in the Mediterranean. This parallel may sound vulgar and ill judged, but perhaps this is actually a viable point to make: what constitutes us is, in the end, not our deeds, actions and free thoughts—our ability to "do something"—but a corporeal passivity, a somatic quality, which

---

[54] Gayatri Chakravorty Spivak, "Can the Subaltern Speak?", *Can the Subaltern Speak? Reflections on the History of an Idea*, ed. Rosalind C. Morris (New York: Columbia University Press, 2010), 22.

links us to other living beings, or even to dying beings. "Rien faire comme une bête"—the quote from Maupassant catches it.

This is not only a description of a utopian state, it is also a means of establishing a ground for solidarity and political action. At the most basic level, as living beings, we are all just as helpless, just as fragile. It is in this state of corporeal passivity, and not in some presumed power to act, that an argument for generous asylum policies and an activism focused on helping refugees should start.

If critical thinking is possible at all depends on objective circumstances. There is always agency; every subject is indeed involved in possibilities to act, think, interact and communicate. But these possibilities are always conditioned and limited, and perhaps it is these limitations that unite us more than the possibilities. And that applies to critical *action* as well. From such a perspective one might argue—perhaps slightly, but only slightly, against the grain of Adorno's general argument—that thinking and action are both parts of the same event, of which the subject is *the medium* rather than the origin. This may be a modest point, but maybe this modesty is just what is needed today.

Adorno's *Minima Moralia:*
Malignant Normality and the Dilemmas of Resistance

SHIERRY WEBER NICHOLSEN

The logic of history is as destructive as the people it brings to prominence; wherever its momentum carries it, it reproduces equivalents of past calamity. Normality is death.

("Out of the firing line", 56)[1]

"Malignant normality" is a term coined by Robert Jay Lifton, a psychiatrist who researched situations of mass murder in their historical and social contexts. It refers, he says, to a social actuality that is "presented as normal, all-encompassing, and unalterable" but is nevertheless conducive to inhumanity.[2] Lifton coined the term in his study of Nazi doctors, with specific reference to Auschwitz. But it is not as though the fall of the Third Reich has meant the end of situations of malignant normality. "[E]quivalents of past calamity", as Adorno puts it, can be produced in different contexts. In his foreword to *The Dangerous Case of Donald Trump*, Lifton cites as instances of malignant normality within contemporary United States the participation of American psychologists in the construction of the CIA's torture protocol and how the Trump administration has threatened the viability of democratic institutions of American democracy, all the while operating more or less within the norms of the American presidency.[3]

Adorno's *Minima Moralia* is a key document for the future of critical theory precisely because it addresses and describes the workings of malignant normality both within a specific historical context and in the dynamics that recreate, and in different guises, are continuing to recreate it. Written during and immediately after the second World War, its context is the malignant normality of the Nazi regime within the larger historical trajectory of advanced capitalism, as Adorno experienced it in his exile in Southern California. At the same time, intrinsic to *Minima Moralia* is a reflection on the slight possibilities of resistance within the totalising nature of this malignant normality. The diagnosis of malignant normality and the possibility of resistance cannot be

---

[1] Unless otherwise indicated, quotations are from the NLB edition of *Minima Moralia* (1974), trans. E.F.N. Jephcott.

[2] Robert Jay Lifton, "Foreword" to *The Dangerous Case of Donald Trump* (New York: St. Martins, 2017), xv.

[3] Ibid, xvi.

separated. In this way too *Minima Moralia* is a key document for the future of critical theory.

The attempt to formulate this conjunction of a malignant normality and the possibility of resistance is by no means unique to *Minima Moralia*. It is in the nature of studies of mass murder and malignant normality to imply the possibility of, and hope for, resistance—and I will sometimes refer to other works on the subject in order to exemplify or highlight the contributions made by Adorno in his text. If *Minima Moralia* does not immediately strike us as belonging with historical or social-psychological studies of genocide, holocaust, or mass murder and resistance to them, this is because it takes articulations of and reflections on individual experience, and the individual experience of only one person—Adorno himself—as so to speak its data and its method of research. Nor, however, is *Minima Moralia* a personal memoir of suffering, resistance and survival but rather a set of short texts on a wide diversity of historical, cultural and personal topics. As its subtitle, "Reflections on damaged life", indicates, in *Minima Moralia* experience is intrinsically linked to critical thought.

Adorno would argue that his choice of individual experience as the basis for the analyses undertaken in *Minima Moralia* follows from the specific phase of the broader historical trajectory in which he is living: the illusion of the individual's absolute autonomy has disintegrated, but the remnants of the individual remain enough outside the malignant levelling of contemporary society to reflect on it. Against Hegel's notion of an overarching objective *Weltgeist*, Adorno asserts in his dedication to *Minima Moralia* that "social analysis can learn incomparably more from individual experience than Hegel conceded [...] In the period of his decay, the individual's experience of himself and what he encounters contributes once more to knowledge, which he had merely obscured as long as he continued unshaken to construe himself positively as the dominant category".[4] In other words, it is precisely the decayed—but not yet fully eliminated—status of the individual that allows the malignancy of contemporary normality to be read in his experience.

Malignant Normality: All-Encompassing and All-Penetrating

If we ask what is malignant about the malignant normality Adorno addresses, in one sense the answer is simple: it is inhumane and brutal; it promotes suffering. And if we ask what is normal about it, the answer is also simple, but less so: it is normal because the brutality is couched, at least in superficial ways,

---

in accepted social norms. It is also normal because this conjunction of brutality and social norms does not describe a state of affairs in which norms are routinely violated by non-conforming individuals or groups. Rather, the state of affairs is experienced as all-encompassing, without exceptions or loopholes. The term "all-encompassing" reflects the claim that social actuality is total, without exit of any kind.

While Adorno refers frequently, if briefly, to the economic basis of malignant normality, *Minima Moralia* is in no way an analysis of global capitalism. Rather, the impact of *Minima Moralia* depends on its very precise articulation of the experience of this encompassing malignancy. The diversity of the facets of experience addressed in *Minima Moralia* reflect this all-encompassing quality. "All-encompassing" means precisely that. One is surrounded, literally, by malignancy; wherever we look there is an aspect of malignancy and there seem to be no exceptions. The all-encompassing aspect of conventional reality includes not only the world of social relations and the concrete details of everyday life but the material world of man-made products as well—witness Adorno's discourses on the unsatisfactory quality of both contemporary and restorationist housing, or on the failure of contemporary doors to indicate privacy. But when Adorno complains that "dwelling [...] is now impossible",[5] ("Refuge for the homeless", 38), that is, that houses as such are finished—in that new ones are not oriented to human comfort and the imitations of old ones are fake—he is not so much waxing nostalgic for what once was but rather noting the uniform absence of humaneness in the built environment.[6]

The all-encompassing malignancy works inwards as well as outwards, penetrating as well as encompassing, and destroying the distinction between internal and external experience. In this regard, the effect of malignant normality on sleep and dreams is telling. Adorno cites a German magazine proposing that modern man wants to sleep on the ground, in effect "abolishing with the bed the threshold between waking and dreaming," Adorno states. He continues, "[t]he sleepless are on call at any hour, unresistingly ready for anything, alert and unconscious at once".[7] From 1933 to 1939, when she left Germany for the USA, Charlotte Beradt, a psychoanalytically informed journalist, collected protocols of those dreams that the dreamers identified as depicting their experiences of the Third Reich. These dreams evidence the penetrating force of

---

[5] Adorno, *Minima Moralia*, 38.

[6] Cf. Matt Waggoner *Unhoused: Adorno and the Problem of Dwelling* (New York: Columbia University Press, 2018).

[7] Adorno, *Minima Moralia*, 38.

terror in life within a malignant totality. Here, for instance, is the dream of a 45-year-old doctor, dreamt in 1934:

> Around nine in the evening, after my office hours, as I am about to stretch out peacefully on the sofa in my apartment with a book about Matthias Grunewald, my room and my whole apartment suddenly become wall-less. I look around, horrified, and all the dwellings around, as far as the eye can see, no longer have walls. I hear a loudspeaker blaring out: "according to the decree of the 17th of the month, regarding the elimination of walls...." The doctor wrote the dream down the next morning and then dreamt of being accused of writing down dreams.[8]

The elimination of walls signifies the elimination of the distinction between the inner and the outer. The dreams in Beradt's book are a vivid complement to Adorno's experience of life in America. "Dwelling [...] is now impossible",[9] which can also be rendered as "the house is past", as Adorno writes, while Beradt's doctor dreams of an existence without walls. The distinction between reality and nightmare is eliminated along with the walls. Here too Adorno's experience complements Beradt's dreams: In a *Minima Moralia* aphorism from 1935 Adorno describes the way his childhood memories of being mocked and bullied prophesied Fascism. "Now that the [tormentors] have stepped visibly out of my dream and dispossessed me of my past life and my language", he comments, "I no longer need to dream of them. In Fascism the nightmare of childhood has come true".[10] "Society has, as it were, assumed the sickness of all individuals", he writes in another *Minima Moralia* aphorism, "and in it, in the pent-up lunacy of Fascist acts and their innumerable precursors and mediators, the subjective fate buried deep in the individual is integrated with its visible outward component".[11] Individual nightmare and collective malignancy are thus two sides of the same coin. The surface of social relations and ordinary sociability then becomes the normality of those whose individuality has been eliminated, sucked up into collective madness, which under capitalism also takes the form of commercial relations in the marketplace. Hence Adorno can write that "[n]othing is innocuous any more [...] All collaboration, all the human worth of social mixing and participation, merely masks tacit

---

[8] Charlotte Beradt, *Das Dritte Reich des Traums.* (Munich: Nymphenburger, 1966), 25 (my translation).
[9] Adorno, *Minima Moralia*, 38.
[10] Ibid, 193.
[11] Ibid, 59–60.

acceptance of inhumanity".[12] Everything becomes a matter of "connection" or "relationship", in contemporary corporate jargon. Adorno lays out the brutality of this deformation in a text called "Health unto Death".[13] Neurosis and sexual repression seem to have disappeared, he writes, but those who seem "healthy"—we might also say "normal"—are already dead. These are the ones who are unremittingly ready for anything.

The ingratiating qualities of these apparently healthy, connection-seeking people make them both temptingly attractive and confusing. Lifton devotes a chapter of his book *The Nazi Doctors* to Dr. Ernst B., a paradigmatic instance of what Adorno is talking about here. Lifton interviewed Ernst B. for many hours and was confused and suspicious when he initially found something likable in him. Indeed, Ernst B., who worked in a section of Auschwitz not directly engaged in killing, and as we shall see, did not engage in selections, was thought by some prisoners to be an exception, a "good Nazi". Much later, when Ernst B. was brought to trial for his wartime activities, he was acquitted, in part because of testimony by some of the Jewish prisoners that he had been nice to them. For Lifton, Ernst B.'s defining characteristic was his ingratiating sociability. He wanted to be liked and knew how to go about it. He was unusual in being on good terms with both his fellow SS doctors and the prisoner-doctors of whom he was in charge. He managed to get the prisoners on his side by calling them by name, and he was liked by his fellow SS officers because he actively socialised with them. Indeed, he had joined the SS, believing it to be a good social club. By the end of his interviews with Lifton, Ernst B. had apparently given up trying to ingratiate himself with him, instead waxing nostalgic about the good times of idealism and solidarity with his fellow Nazis.[14]

Vulnerabilities and Temptations

If nothing is innocuous, everything represents a temptation to acquiesce in inhumanity. Much in *Minima Moralia* speaks to the particular difficulties of intellectual life in an all-encompassing malignant situation and to the particular difficulties of an *émigré* intellectual. "Every intellectual in emigration is, without exception, mutilated and does well to acknowledge it to himself", Adorno writes.[15] There is a sense of being hampered by isolation, by unfamiliarity, or financial need, of constantly working against the grain, of becoming

---

[12] Ibid, 25–26.

[13] Ibid, 58–60.

[14] See Robert Jay Lifton, *The Nazi Doctors: Medical Killing and the Psychology of Genocide* (New York; Basic Books, 1986), 303–36

[15] Adorno, *Minima Moralia*, 33.

exhausted, and then in one's exhaustion being tempted to abandon one's own standards for work: "Bustle endangers concentration with a thousand claims, the effort of producing something in some measure worthwhile is now so great as to be beyond almost everybody. The pressure of conformity weighing on all producers further diminishes the demands on themselves. The centre of intellectual self-discipline as such is in the process of decomposition".[16]

The iconic dream with which Beradt begins her book speaks to this process of being worn down until one's resistance is broken. This is the dream of a factory-owner in his sixties, a lifelong Social Democrat. He dreamt it three days after Hitler took power:

> Goebbels comes into my factory. He has the employees line up in two rows, right and left. I have to stand between them and lift my arm in the Hitler greeting, Heil Hitler. It takes me half an hour to lift my arm, one millimetre at a time. Goebbels watches my exertions as though he were at a play, without applause and without any expression of displeasure. But when I have finally raised my arm, he says five words: "I don't want your greeting", turns around and goes to the door. So, I stand, in my own business, among my own employees, pilloried, with my arm raised. I am physically able to do so only by keeping my eyes on his clubfoot while he is limping away. I stand this way until I wake up.[17]

As Beradt notes, this dream represents the dreamer's humiliation and deprivation of identity—the "mutilation" to which Adorno refers.

> With exhaustion comes also the temptation of self-mutilation – to stupefaction or self-confusion, the destruction of our own mental capacities – as a defence against the pressures of the malignant situation. The dream of a German cleaning woman from the summer of 1933 illustrates this: "I dreamt that as a matter of caution I speak Russian in my dream (a language I don't know at all, and besides I don't talk in my sleep), so that I won't understand myself and so no one can understand me, in case I say something about the state, because that is of course forbidden and has to be reported".[18]

The stripping of the intellectual's professional self corresponds to the perversion of the professions themselves. Lifton's book, *The Nazi Doctors*, is a study of the perversion of the medical profession, which, grounded on the

---

[16] Ibid, 29.
[17] Charlotte Beradt, *Das Dritte Reich des Traums*, 8 (my translation).
[18] Ibid, 56 (my translation).

Hippocratic Oath to preserve life, comes to define its duty as killing during the Third Reich. Lifton, himself a psychiatrist, emphasises the vulnerabilities of professionals of all kinds; they can be tempted by money, by fame, by closeness to those in power, and as we will see, by the opportunity for scholarly "contributions". In *The Nazi Doctors* Lifton details the recruiting of professsionals as heads of agencies engaged in a variety of forms of medicalised killing, and, in his foreword to *The Dangerous Case of Donald Trump*, he notes tellingly that "nothing does more to sustain malignant normality than its support from a large organisation of professionals".[19]

A colleague of the sociable Nazi doctor Ernst B. can serve as an example of such a temptation for the professional. Ernst B. did not want to perform "selections"—the process of deciding which Jews arriving at Auschwitz would be sent immediately to the gas chamber. He convinced one of his superiors in Berlin to send another SS doctor to take over this particular duty. It is the story of that other doctor, Delmotte, that interests me in this context. As Ernst B. told Lifton, Delmotte, an idealistic SS man, had wanted to be sent to the front but had agreed to go to Auschwitz because he had been assured that he could work on his doctoral dissertation there. After his first shift at selections, however, Delmotte became nauseous, got drunk and went into a catatonic state. When he emerged from this state he said that "he didn't want to be in a slaughterhouse. As a doctor his task was to help people and not to kill them". Delmotte was offered a "therapeutic" program if he chose to stay on at Auschwitz, and as part of this agreement he would be assisted by an esteemed older Jewish prisoner-doctor in researching and writing his dissertation. He accepted.[20]

For Adorno, as an intellectual and philosopher, both thought and language offer temptations to acquiesce in the inhumanity of malignant normality. The intellectual has no choice but to use language, even though language can be co-opted in the service of maintaining the semblance of normality in a malignant situation. In his *States of Denial: Awareness of Atrocities and Suffering*, Stanley Cohen details some of the ways language can be perverted in accounts that serve to justify or excuse and thereby deny atrocities. It can be used to deny responsibility for actions, to deny that any injury was inflicted, to deny that victims are victims and not perpetrators. Moreover, language can be used as a condemnation of those who condemn the atrocities along with an appeal to alleged higher ends that would justify the actions.[21] For the émigré intellectual

---

[19] Robert Jay Lifton, "Foreword" to *The Dangerous Case of Donald Trump*, xvi.

[20] Robert Jay Lifton, *The Nazi Doctors: Medical Killing and the Psychology of Genocide*, 309–11.

[21] Stanley Cohen, *States of Denial: Knowing about Atrocities and Suffering* (Cambridge: Polity Press, 2001), 60–1.

who hopes that writing can serve as a refuge—then, "for the man who has no homeland, writing becomes a place to live"—this itself is an illusion, a form of denial. Writing can no more provide a refuge than the house does for the refugee. The difficulties that beset the émigré intellectual—isolation, pressures for conformity, the need to survive—can serve as a pretext for indulging in writing that would otherwise be rejected as trash[22] or can lead to a weariness that stifles the free flow of energy necessary for serious writing.[23] In either case language becomes infected with social control and serves the purposes of denial through stupefaction; as is the case with the German cleaning woman's effort to protect herself by dreaming in a language she did not understand.

Resistance

Inherent in a situation of malignant normality is a claim to represent the totality of reality. Indeed, much of Robert Jay Lifton's work is dedicated to showing how totalisation, the claim to absolute totality, is the hallmark of genocidal dynamics. But the all-encompassing and therefore total nature of malignant normality is an illusion propagated by the forces of malignancy. Absolute totality is not possible; a system based on destructiveness cannot become by definition totally cohesive. This is one meaning of Adorno's dictum "the whole is the false",[24] and the crux of *Minima Moralia*'s argument with Hegel's notion that a rational *Weltgeist* culminates in the end of history, ultimately completely subsuming the individual under the general.

Lifton characterises malignant normality as not only all-encompassing but also unalterable, implying that there is no recourse against it. If nothing can be done, how is resistance possible or meaningful? As Stanley Cohen remarks, the question may not be so much why we resort to denial but why do we ever not do so?[25] Meanwhile, *Minima Moralia* directs the same question towards resistance of any kind: the question is not so much how entanglement in malignant normality comes about but how is it ever possible to resist it?

The question of resistance is pervasive in *Minima Moralia*. If one of its subtexts is Adorno's argument with Hegel, the other is his argument with Nietzsche. If with Nietzsche we accept that a universal moral law is no longer tenable, for Adorno the *amor fati* (embracing one's fate) that Nietzsche counsels represents acceptance of the status quo in the form of resignation.[26] If there

---

[22] Adorno, *Minima Moralia*, 29.

[23] Ibid. 86–7.

[24] Ibid. 50.

[25] Stanley Cohen *States of Denial: Knowing about Atrocities and Suffering*, 249.

[26] Adorno, *Minima Moralia*, 97.

can be no absolute totality, then resistance, as that which is outside or different from the totality, is always possible, at least in principle. In fact, precisely because of the all-encompassing nature of malignant normality, in *Minima Moralia* the question of resistance arises everywhere: in the actions of everyday life; in the social relations of the émigré intellectual; in the activities of thought and writing. The possibility of resistance arises within the context of malignant normality. But this means that to imagine that resistance can itself be wholly untouched by malignancy is as much an illusion as the idea that resistance is completely impossible. Hence the dilemmas and paradoxes of resistance to which much of *Minima Moralia* is devoted.

What then are the bases on which resistance, however problematic and embattled, remains possible? Let me begin not with *Minima Moralia* itself but with some propositions and anecdotes from other writers on the subject of inhumanity and one's resistance to it. In his book *Humanity: A Moral History of the Twentieth Century*, Jonathan Glover addresses the question of what kind of "moral resources" might be available to people once it is clear that the idea of a universal moral law is untenable? Glover suggests three kinds of "moral resources" available to people in the face of inhumane forces: (i) rational self-interest; (ii) what he calls the "human responses" of sympathy and respect, and (iii) one's "moral identity", that is, the sense of the morality necessary for one's self-respect.[27] Glover's book attempts to show how these resources become overwhelmed in various kinds of extreme situations but nevertheless may break through in individuals.

An example of such a breakthrough, and thus an act of individual resistance, is detailed in Lifton's book, *The Nazi Doctors*. Taking place in Auschwitz, the quintessential atrocity-producing situation of malignant normality, a survivor imparts to Lifton the story of Marie L., a prisoner doctor in Auschwitz who was ordered to perform harmful surgeries on other prisoners. Having initially complied, she then refused, absolutely and repeatedly. Like others, Marie L. believed that none of them were likely to survive Auschwitz. "So the one thing [...] left to us is to behave for [...] the short time that remains to us as human beings", she said. When confronted, she explained that the activities she was being ordered to perform were "contrary to my conception as a doctor".[28] Marie L was a devout Protestant, but in her refusal she emphasised what Glover would call her moral identity as a physician and a human being.

---

[27] Jonathan Glover, *Humanity: A Moral History of the Twentieth Century* (New Haven: Yale University Press, 2001).
[28] Robert Jay Lifton, *The Nazi Doctors: Medical Killing and the Psychology of Genocide*, 297–8.

The question of the motivations for individual acts of resistance was addressed in a social-psychological study by Samuel and Pearl Oliner.[29] The study focused on individuals identified as "rescuers" by Yad Vashem in Israel, that is, non-Jews who were reliably confirmed to have offered help to Jews in Nazi Europe at risk to themselves and without promise of material gain. Although most of the rescuers were assumed to be acting from a mixture of motives, the Oliners identified three motives that might have taken priority, depending on the individual: (i) an empathic response to the needs and suffering of the other; (ii) a "normocentric" response based on the norms of a group with which the rescuer identified, whether imposed by the group or internalised by the individual; and (iii) an autonomous principled response. Regardless of the specific motives, what emerged was an ethics of care, what the Oliners called "extensivity"—a concern not limited to specific groups but extending generally to human beings.

Another instance of individual resistance in an atrocity-producing situation can be found in Lifton's book about the Vietnam Veterans against the War.[30] The breakthrough on this occasion is based on what the Oliners call "normocentric" motivation. An American soldier who Lifton interviewed had been present at the My Lai massacre but did not participate in the killing. Instead he walked around with his gun pointed at the ground and was heard muttering, "It's wrong, it's wrong". Lifton suggests three factors that helped the man to resist engaging in the massacre. First, he was a loner and thus less subject to the group pressures operating on the other men in his company. Second, while no longer a practicing Catholic, he had been brought up in a religious family and was susceptible to feelings of guilt and hoped to avoid them (nevertheless, he was left feeling guilty that he had not actively intervened to try to stop the massacre). The third factor may be the most telling. The man had gone through a difficult time during adolescence and young adulthood, using drugs and feeling lost. He had "found himself" when he joined the army and became inspired by military ideals. He considered the massacre a revolting affront to those ideals.[31] The key to this man's capacity to resist, we might say, was a refusal to violate a deeply internalised moral code that entailed respect for the lives of civilians.[32]

---

[29] Cf. Samuel and Pearl Oliner, *The Altruistic Personality: Rescuers of Jews in Nazi Europe* (New York: Free Press, 1988).

[30] Robert Jay Lifton, *Home from the War* (New York: Simon and Schuster, 1978).

[31] Ibid, 57–8.

[32] Cf. Michael Walzer's analysis of just and unjust actions in various wartime situations in Walzer, *Just and Unjust Wars: A Moral Argument with Historical Illustrations* (New York: Basic Books, 1977).

The Individual as the Site of Resistance

If the individual is the site of resistance in the above accounts, this does not mean that it is simply a matter of individual personalities determining whether some will be resisters while others will be complicit in malignancy. Rather, for Lifton as well as the others I have cited, it is a question of the interaction of many factors—historical and socio-cultural as well as individual; individual dispositions, perhaps, but also cultural norms, ideological justifications, and so on. Lifton for instance is intent on showing the interaction between socio-historical forces and the differing adaptations of individual personalities to those forces. For their part the Oliners point to the very different chances Jews had of being rescued by individuals with different resources in different countries with different cultural attitudes towards Jews and different degrees of close surveillance by Nazi occupiers. In his book, *Becoming Evil: How Ordinary People Commit Genocide and Mass Killing*, James Waller presents multiple studies debunking the myth of "the mad Nazi".[33] Likewise, Adorno is scornful of attempts to analyse the individual psychopathology of mass murderers. Hitler may be pathological "in himself", he says, but what he is *in* the whole is what matters.[34] Analogously, Charlotte Beradt considered the dreams she collected to be portrayals within individual psyches of the collective terror under which the dreamers were living rather than as symbolic representations of individuals' personal conflicts.

Adorno's account of the basis for resistance, insofar as it can be gleaned from the many references to resistance in *Minima Moralia*, is not incompatible with Glover's or the Oliners'. It too takes the individual as the site of resistance, though as we have seen, it takes account of it in ways they tend not to, i.e. the individual resister's inevitable complicity in collective malignancy. Adorno's account differs in being, it is explicitly based on the possibility of a standpoint which both allows and depends on hope. "Finale", the last text in *Minima Moralia*, condenses Adorno's argument for and against the possibility of resistance. It begins by naming the hope of redemption as the *sine qua non* of resistance: "The only philosophy which can be responsibly practiced in face of despair is the attempt to contemplate all things as they would present themselves from the standpoint of redemption".[35] The possibility of that standpoint is the crux of the possibility of resistance. The text continues: "perspectives

[33] James Waller, *Becoming Evil: How Ordinary People Commit Genocide and Mass Killing* (New York: Oxford Universiry Press, 2002).

[34] Adorno, *Minima Moralia*, 56–7.

[35] Ibid, 247.

must be fashioned that displace and estrange the world, reveal it to be, with its rifts and crevices, as indigent and distorted as it will appear one day in the messianic light".[36] The dilemma of resistance is that it presupposes these perspectives. Not only is it a struggle to achieve a standpoint removed "even by a hair's breadth"[37] from what is, but what one gains is distorted by the status quo, that is, the all-encompassing malignant normality from which it has been wrested. The individual is also the site of resistance because it is the individual who has the capacity to struggle for this virtually unattainable standpoint.

Adorno frames this understanding of the individual in terms of his anti-Hegelian understanding of the trajectory of history. "In the age of the individual's liquidation, the question of individuality must be raised anew", Adorno writes.[38] In his account, during the height of the bourgeois era, the individual was touted as the apex of civilisation, the site and beneficiary of autonomous moral principles and freedom. But now the forces of sameness produced by global capitalism have made the individual in that sense obsolete and have revealed the ideological core of the old notion of the individual. On the one hand, the individual's capacity for experience shrinks under the onslaught of the forces of malignant normality; on the other, to the degree that it survives in the form of a castoff waste product, the capacity for experience falls outside the norms and thereby becomes relevant for its critical potential. Though virtually obsolete, the individual is not ahistorical. In fact, "the individual is so thoroughly historical that he is able, with the fine filigree of his late bourgeois organization, to rebel against the fine filigree of late bourgeois organization".[39] As historically obsolete, then, the individual "becomes the custodian of truth, as the condemned against the victor".[40] The individual and reflection on individual experience thus become the crux both of complicity in malignant normality and of resistance to it.

Experience and Self-Reflection

The critical potential of the obsolete individual's experience depends on the capacity for self-reflection intrinsic to experience. There may be no way out of entanglement, as Adorno acknowledges, but awareness of entanglement represents the "hair's-breadth" of a perspective on it. If the intellectual in exile is

---

[36] Ibid.
[37] Ibid.
[38] Ibid, 129.
[39] Ibid, 145.
[40] Ibid, 129.

mutilated and isolated, a detached observer, still "the detached observer is as much entangled as the active participant; the only advantage of the former is insight into his entanglement, and the infinitesimal freedom that lies in knowledge as such".[41] Insofar as the individual is capable of experience, self-reflection on experience within a situation of malignant normality is at the same time an exercise of thought, thought that unfolds the intrinsic dialectic of what it reflects upon. In Hegelian terms, this self-reflection is an exercise of determinate negation. "Consummate negativity, once squarely faced", writes Adorno in "Finale", "delineates the mirror-image of its opposite".[42]

Fundamentally, the individual's experience contains the potential for resistance because it represents difference, a difference from the status quo. Experience, to the extent it is possible, is both individual and complex. Arguing against the demand that writers "honestly" trace the logic of their thought processes, for instance, Adorno points out that even if one tried to do so, no linear progression would be evident. "Rather, knowledge comes to us through a network of prejudices, opinions, innervations, self-corrections, presuppositions and exaggerations, in short through the dense, firmly founded but by no means uniformly transparent medium of experience.[43]

It is experience as this complex of psychic activities and indeed eccentricities that is the target of obliteration in what Adorno calls the health unto death. At the same time its eccentric complexity is what renders experience unpalatable, indeed ultimately indigestible, to the health unto death, that is, to standardisation. Everything that seems to be nostalgia for the good old bourgeois days on Adorno's part ("the last bourgeois") can be understood as an exercise of the capacity to note that things can be otherwise. This apparent nostalgia for the way things were, distorted as they were by the malignancy that is always at work, is nevertheless a protest against malignant normality's claim to be unalterable. It is only when the various aspects of experience are mediated through self-reflection as dialectical thought that they win their value for the perspective of redemption and become carriers of hope and thus resistance. Hypostasised as the key to resistance, each alone is vulnerable to colluding with malignant normality by engaging in denial and self-deception that constitute stupefaction. For Adorno, this is true for all the factors that can be cited as the bases for resistance—for truth, knowledge, rationality, morality, as well as the irrational in its various forms. Of thought in its relation to feeling, for instance,

---

[41] Ibid, 26–7.
[42] Ibid, 247.
[43] Ibid, 80.

Adorno writes: "the assumption that thought profits from the decay of the emotions, or even that it remains unaffected, is itself an expression of the process of stupefaction".[44]

Morality itself in its true form is for Adorno precisely this mediation of thought and emotion, feeling and understanding: "Intelligence is a moral category. The separation of feeling and understanding, that makes it possible to absolve and beatify the blockhead, hypostasises the dismemberment of man into functions [...] It is rather for philosophy to seek, in the opposition of feeling and understanding, their—precisely moral—unity".[45] Consider, in contrast, Jonathan Shay's account in his *Achilles in Vietnam* of the unmediated moral outrage expressed in berserk violence.[46] For Adorno such rage is itself a form of enacting collective malignity. "The almost insoluble task", he writes, "is to let neither the power of others, nor our own powerlessness, stupefy us".[47]

Even dialectical thought is vulnerable to collusion with malignant normality insofar as it claims objectivity. ""it is the cardinal untruth, having recognised existence to be bad, to present it as truth simply because it has been recognised".[48] The vulnerability of even dialectical thought attests to the potency of the notion that malignant normality is unalterable. In the form of Nietzsche's *amor fati*, it tempts us into resignation, which, as Adorno says, bows down before the powers that be. Resistance to *amor fati* requires hope. True objectivity, or genuine truth, depends not purely on thought but on the hope that flows from and constitutes the perspective of redemption. Resistance can base itself on truth only when truth takes the form of hope. "In the end", writes Adorno, "hope, wrested from reality by negating it, is the only form in which truth appears. Without hope, the idea of truth would be scarcely even thinkable".[49]

The specificity of experience, its relatedness to the actual matter at hand in its uniqueness, is the complement of hope. This becomes clear when Adorno unfolds the dialectic of objectivity and subjectivity. Whereas power reverses objectivity and subjectivity, according to which objectivity is the propriety of the status quo while the subjective is dismissed merely as that which "engages the specific experience of a matter", the genuinely objective is available only

---

[44] Ibid, 122.

[45] Ibid, 197–8.

[46] Jonathan Shay, *Achilles in Vietnam: Combat Trauma and the Undoing of Character* (New York: Scribner, 1994).

[47] Adorno, *Minima Moralia*, 57.

[48] Ibid, 98

[49] Ibid, 98.

through subjective experience—engagement with the specificity of the object—which "substitutes relatedness to the object for the majority consensus of those who do not even look at it, much less think about it".[50]

As the complement of this kind of specific experience, the utopian hope that Adorno invokes as the crucial element in resistance does not spell out utopia in pragmatic or conceptual terms. To even ask the question of the goal of an emancipated society is illegitimate, he writes.[51] Rather, the utopian promise is present as a kind of aura of freedom from regimentation and coercion accompanying the weak resistance made possible by self-reflection—not a paradise of unrestrained production and abundance, or indeed realisation of potential, but rather a lack of compulsion. "*Rien faire comme une bête*, lying on water and looking peacefully at the sky, 'being, nothing else, without any further definition and fulfilment", Adorno writes in "*Sur l'eau*", "might take the place of process, act, satisfaction...."[52] Something of this vague hint of freedom from constraint is already present in our ordinary experience if we can allow ourselves to be aware of it through self-reflection. Thought is not able to provide a coherent picture of experience, Adorno writes, but this inadequacy "resembles that of life, which describes a wavering, deviating line, disappointing by comparison with its premises, and yet which only in this actual course, always less than it should be, is able, under given conditions of existence, to represent an unregimented one".[53]

Finale

Hegel may have been wrong about the cumulative rationality of the whole, but for Adorno after the Holocaust he was not wrong about history having a trajectory. For Adorno, and for us today and no doubt into the future, the turn of the historical screw continues in the direction of greater suffering. It is not that things are always the same: "What is constant is not an invariable quantity of suffering but its progress toward hell.... Not only in the developments of forces of production but also in the increasing pressure of domination does quantity change into quality."[54] If, as Adorno says in his introduction to *Minima Moralia*, those who speak of the individual in the face of unspeakable

---

[50] Ibid, 69–70.
[51] Ibid, 155–56.
[52] Ibid, 156–57.
[53] Ibid, 81.
[54] Ibid, 234.

collective events are complicit,[55] as the individual becomes ever more complicit and resistance becomes even less possible, resistance nevertheless still depends upon hope, which still resides in individual experience. "Beside the demand thus placed on thought", Adorno concludes, "the question of the reality or unreality of redemption itself hardly matters".[56] Engagement with this demand is what *Minima Moralia* offers to the future of critical theory and to the future itself.

[55] Ibid, 18.
[56] Ibid, 247.

“In many people it is already an impertinence to say ‘I’”
Some Critical Observations

ANKE THYEN

Rather than a coherent moral theory, *Minima Moralia* presents miniatures from a damaged life or, as the subtitle explains, anxious *reflections from damaged life*. Perhaps, within its pages, we find no theory at all. The aphorisms “express the melancholy and despair that their emigrant author attributed to his own experience of homelessness”.[1] In a way Adorno’s *Reflections* present themselves as modest. Nonetheless, fired with ideological criticism, they are accompanied by a high moral standard that leaves many behind. According to Adorno, in the false life, within the system of delusion (*Verblendungszusammenhang*), (almost) everyone is equal, equal in terms of being made identical to one another, reduced to a quality-lacking function within the system. Adorno’s critique of life within the false life applies to (almost) everyone,[2] those who are deformed through a failed civilisation process, the morally and cognitively incapacitated. The individual is only a caricature, an “exhibition piece, like the foetuses that once drew the wonderment and laughter of children”.[3] It is not powerlessness from which this critique speaks. The critique sees itself placed sooner on an irreproachable ground: the morality of thinking, which can escape the totality of the false life by at least thinking correctly about the impossibility of the true life within the false. This may be an impossible task for those “drowning at five o’clock in the morning on the commuter train”, but presumably not for those who, like Adorno, “patiently unfold the sweat-cloth of theory” and “teach in the name of the unteachable”, as Hans Magnus

[1] Stefan Müller-Doohm, *Adorno: Eine Biographie* (Frankfurt am Main: Suhrkamp, 2003), 464; *Adorno: A Biography* (Cambridge: Cambridge University Press, 2004), 305.

[2] Theodor W. Adorno, *Minima Moralia* (Frankfurt am Main: Suhrkamp, 1951), 42; *Minima Moralia: Reflections from Damaged Life*. trans. E. F. N. Jephcott (London: Verso, 2005), §18. (In all subsequent references to this text, German pagination is stated first and then corresponding reference to English translation.)

[3] “To think that the individual is being liquidated without trace is over-optimistic. [...] The present situation is very different. The disaster does not take the form of a radical elimination of what existed previously; rather the things that history has condemned are dragged along dead, neutralized and impotent as ignominious ballast. In the midst of standardized, organized human units the individual persists. He is even protected and gaining monopoly value. But he is in reality no more than the mere function of his own uniqueness, an exhibition piece, like the foetuses that once drew the wonderment and laughter of children”. (*Minima Moralia*, 176f; *Minima Moralia*, 144.)

Enzensberger puts it.[4] Here, Enzensberger may well express Adorno's self-understanding. Yet, this self-understanding does not correspond to Adorno's philosophical approach, which, as we will see, does not shy away from deriding the drowning and unteachable, along with their damaged lives. Adorno does not count himself as one of the unteachable, the deformed, but rather as one of those who managed to preserve true individuality in the false life. "What enables him [the individual] to resist, that streak of independence in him, springs from monadological individual interest and its precipitate character".[5] Critique and reflection are "temporarily withdrawn to the individual sphere"; "if critical theory lingers there, it is not only with a bad conscience."[6] The critique of the false life is "not fully encompassed by the prevailing system and is still happily surviving".[7] If this ends up being the normative ground of critical *reflection*, do we not then have to ascribe to Adorno an elitist view, one that is articulated in an openly aggressive way?

In his critical review of *Minima Moralia*, Karl August Horst notes that two things belong to the moralist—a label he ascribes to Adorno: "loneliness and aggression"; "loneliness is increasingly noticeable in the destiny of the emigrant, who as a victim of societal processes punishes society. Aggressivity, which, as for all moralists, needs the medium of solitude to reflect it in a fractured way, operates with weapons of the sociological dialectic—the rigorous consequence of which was already indexed in his collaborative work with Horkheimer in Adorno's *Dialectic of Enlightenment*—makes the voice of the caller sound from the desert".[8] The rigorous consequence here is a form of slander perpetrated against those individuals, i.e. the deluded ones, entirely ensnared within the system. Even if there is much talk about them in *Minima Moralia*, one does not have to accept the extent of their ridicule.

Whether one wishes to follow Habermas, who in his review of *Minima Moralia*, elevates the book to the status of a masterpiece, is quite another matter. Anyway, the book is a work of philosophy. The first sentence of the dedica-

[4] Hans Magnus Enzensberger, "schwierige arbeit (für Theodor W. Adorno)", *Blindenschrift* (Frankfurt am Main, Suhrkamp, 1965), 58f.
[5] *Minima Moralia* 195; 158.
[6] "part of the social force of liberation may have temporarily withdrawn to the individual sphere. If critical theory lingers there, it is not only with a bad conscience". Ibid. 11/18.
[7] "The radically individual, unassimilated features of a human being are always both at once: residues not fully encompassed by the prevailing system and still happily surviving, and marks of the mutilation inflicted on its members by that system". Max Horkheimer and Theodor W. Adorno, *Dialektik der Aufklärung* (Frankfurt am Main: Fischer, 1971), 216; *Dialectic of Enlightenment: Philosophical fragments*, ed. G. Schmid Noerr, trans. E. Jephcott. (Stanford: Stanford University Press, 2005) 200.
[8] Karl August Horst, "Minima Moralia", *Merkur*, no. 41 (1951): 695.

tion clarifies what it is about. Adorno tells us that it concerns "a region that from time immemorial was regarded as the true field of philosophy, but which, since the latter's conversion into method, has lapsed into intellectual neglect, sententious whimsy and finally oblivion: the teaching of the good life".[9] What this means is that the book has to accept being critiqued. *Minima Moralia* is a question of truth, and "he who wishes to know the truth about life in its immediacy must scrutinize its estranged form, the objective powers that determine individual existence even in its most hidden recesses".[10]

Adorno's conceptual tool is ideology critique,[11] philosophically, sociologically and psychologically charged. We have in front of us a philosophical text whose ambitions are, however, attenuated in the last sentence of the dedication, where Adorno writes that the "parts do not altogether satisfy the demands of the philosophy of which they are nevertheless a part".[12]

Even if *Minima Moralia* does not claim to be a moral theory, the book nonetheless stands for a critical theory with a practical intent. Under these circumstances we must examine whether its practical intentions can be achieved with the conceptual instruments deployed in the text.

The "weapon of criticism",[13] to use Marx's words, is not arbitrary; this choice demands justification. Only in this way can critical theory prove itself an instance of philosophical discourse; only in this way can it have its say on the question of the correct teaching of the right life. But do the conceptual means that Adorno harnesses in his "reflections of the damaged life" endure beyond their own time? One can doubt that, since in *Minima Moralia* the characteristic of an unwavering ideology critique misleads by leaving one significant question unanswered: how can the criticism of the damaged life contain the subject of this critique under the conditions of a system of total delusion? It is insufficient to state that the system of delusion, the whole untruth, is not as total as the criticism suggests; neither is it enough to make reference to the quietistic way out into the "sphere of the individual", where critical "autonomy" is still possible.

---

[9] Adorno, *Minima Moralia*, 7;15.

[10] Ibid.

[11] Cf. Robin Celikates, (2009): *Kritik als soziale Praxis: Gesellschaftliche Verständigung und kritische Theorie* (Frankfurt am Main: Campus, 2009); Herbert Schnädelbach, "Was ist Ideologie? Versuch einer Begriffsklärung", *Das Argument* 50 (1969): 71–92; "Zum Ideologiebegriff – 20 Jahre nach der Wende", in G. Raupach-Strey and J. Rohbeck (eds.), *Philosophie und Weltanschauung* (Dresden: Thelem; 2011).

[12] Adorno, *Minima Moralia*, 12; 19.

[13] Karl Marx, "Zur Kritik der hegelschen Rechtsphilosophie: Einleitung", in Karl Marx and Friedrich Engels, *Werke* (Berlin: Dietz 1956), vol. 1, 385.

Of what abilities exactly are societal actors actually deprived? What would be the basis of a faculty of critical judgement, in a system of total delusion? Who can exercise autonomy? These questions are directed to *Minima Moralia*—and also to this sentence: "In many people it is already an impertinence to say 'I'".[14] This sentence too does not help in light of what Adorno once asserted about the "new categorical imperative"[15] after Hitler: "When we want to find reasons for it, this imperative is [as] refractory [...]. Dealing discursively with it would be an outrage".[16] Neither the claim that it is already an impertinence to say "I" nor the categorical imperative are immune against discursive treatment. How could they be if they want to be taken as philosophical sentences! It is no small and pardonable matter to criticise persons saying "I" when referring to themselves. After all, this criticism aims at the personal status of human individuals. Therefore, it should prove itself discursively and be able to reason for its normative standards. When rejecting this expectation, critical theory is not in good shape. For, from case to case, when claiming auto-immunity against discursive philosophising, it loses its right to be "critique". Discursivity, the immanent principle of all philosophising, cannot—not even occasionally—be suspended and by no means is the discursive treatment of philosophical judgements an "outrage" (*Frevel*). Whoever, like Adorno, defends the suspension of philosophy's principle of discursivity withdraws into the elitist "sphere of the individual", from whose intellectualised viewpoint the "many people" are only objects of self-satisfied observation, and not subjects. Which is to say, they are to be understood not as the agents of social praxis, which, if critique and critical theory are to be possible at all, generally includes the possibility of criticism. Under these circumstances, can critical theory cope with the moral verdict upon saying 'I'? Basically not, since this verdict fundamentally contradicts the essence of philosophical critique. Does this mean that it is indeed legitimate to "unfold" the "sweat cloth of theory" "in the name of the others who don't know anything about it",[17] considering those "drowning at five o'clock in the morning on the commuter train"? It is doubtful.

In what follows, within the context of the twenty-ninth aphorism of *Minima Moralia,* there are three aspects on which I would like to elaborate. These are:

---

[14] Adorno, *Minima Moralia*, 57; 54.

[15] "A new categorical imperative has been imposed by Hitler upon unfree mankind: to arrange their thoughts and actions so that Auschwitz will not repeat itself, so that nothing similar will happen. When we want to find reasons for it, this imperative is as refractory as the given one of Kant was once upon a time. Dealing discursively with it would be an outrage". Theodor W. Adorno, *Negative Dialektik* (Frankfurt am Main: Suhrkamp, 1973), 358; *Negative Dialectics* (London: Routledge, 1997), 365.

[16] Ibid, 358;365.

[17] Hans Magnus Enzensberger, "schwierige arbeit", 58f.

(i) the use of a psychoanalytically informed theory of society; (ii) the concept of nature, and (iii) a notion of linguistic reference, which becomes relevant in the context of the use of the term 'I'.

I

Who are these "many people" about whom it is already an impertinence to say "I"? The closest answer to be found in psychoanalytic theory is the "weakness of the ego" (*Ich-Schwäche*). Freud's psychoanalysis, a pillar of critical theory besides Marxist theory and *Kulturkritik*, provides a psycho-social approach to the diagnosis of the damaged life. From psychoanalysis Adorno borrows conceptual tools that are supposed to explain a socially prefabricated but seemingly natural deformation of the ego-structure. In order to explain this deformation, along with the manipulation of the ego-structure, Adorno persists in speaking of the primacy of the domination of nature. This confirms Honneth's thesis that a theory of the social does not really exist in Adorno's own theory of society; it has been ousted in favour of the paradigm of domination of the natural world.

However, the explanation that the deformation of the ego-structure goes back to this mastery of nature, i.e. understood as a naturally evolving process, leaves no room for the potential of the inner human nature to resist its complete integration into the system. Adorno's construction is itself inconsistent. On the one hand, when Adorno assumes that there is a core of natural human drives that resist the system, he argues *naturalistically*. On the other hand, when he speaks of how the natural drives are social, and thus infinitely adjustable constructions, he argues *socio-theoretically*. However, in the first case, the theorem of the system of delusion and, in the second, the motif of reconciliation of the unregulated individual are rendered obsolete. All the same, Adorno persists with the perspective, from which the ego-structure can be systematically neutralised by the apparatus of mastery. If then no ego exists, it is therefore an impertinence to say I. It also follows that it would be hubris for the many who say I to claim for themselves a mode of individual existence that resists this total control, since this very mode of existing consists of being an ego.

How, then, does this radical de-structuring of the ego happen, which not only leads dramatically to the weakness of the ego, but also, and finally, to the very "liquidation" of all individuality?[18] Adorno's deduction of the loss of the

---

[18] Adorno, *Minima Moralia*, 168; 138

ego is based on the premise that instrumental reason's mastery over nature can only be understood adequately if one sees the logic of its totalising intentions. Here it becomes clear that for the free self-preservation of the individual, i. e. the preservation of the self through the self itself, there is no space under the condition of instrumental reason. This is because, once it has become socially effective, instrumental reason creates a totalitarian—in a way mythically regressive—system of coercion from which the individual has no way of escaping. In Adorno, self-preservation through instrumental reason becomes the self-preservation of instrumental reason. The consequence of this vicious circle is the hollowing out of the particular individual and the enforced conformity of all individuals, thereby resulting in the individual's liquidation.

The products of the culture industry promise compensation. Their system stabilising function is supposedly guaranteed by the fetish character of a uniform individuality of the consumers. Under such conditions, the proper development of the ego is impossible, since in a way there is no I that, as the agent of socialisation, could create the space for connecting and disconnecting, for dependent and independent experiences, for conflict and harmony. Here, in short, the authoritarian character compensates for the weaknesses of his ego, which, by means of narcissistic regression, is not modelled on any strong super-ego. The psychodynamic situation surrounding narcissism and the loss of the father provides Adorno with an explanation for how there is an ideological susceptibility for both cultural-industrial and political mass idols. The creation of an inner super-ego is unsuccessful, it remains external and, from the beginning, the ego is systematically replaced with a mass-I. Under these circumstances the ego cannot remain itself as itself and accordingly disintegrates. On Adorno's account, the more advanced this ego-disintegration, the bigger the narcissistic mimicry of the apparatuses of mastery.

When individuality is only the reflection of the system then—at least from the critico-ideological viewpoint—it is a presumption, an impertinence to say "I". The I is dispensable. "The social power-structure hardly needs the mediating agencies of ego and individuality any longer. [...] The truly contemporary types are those whose actions are motivated neither by an ego nor, strictly speaking, unconsciously, but mirror objective trends like an automaton".[19]

Adorno's way of expressing things here is more reminiscent of amphibians than humans; it is contemptuous and betrays the humanistic *Geist*, and this from a viewpoint that Adorno does not say how it is possible to occupy. How

---

[19] Adorno, "Zum Verhältnis von Soziologie und Psychologie", in Adorno, *Soziologische Schriften I, Gesammelte Schriften* 8.1 (Frankfurt am Main: Suhrkamp, 1972), 83.

is it possible that there exist "types" of human beings that say I without it being an impertinence?

This question touches on the inconsistencies and conceptual confusions of the psychoanalytically inflected ideology critique of the mass-I and thus on Adorno's social psychology. Its nucleus, fundamental for Adorno's theory of society, allows him to build the thesis that the destructuring of the super-ego and finally of the ego can be explained by means of the model of the mastery of nature and not by any theory based strictly on social and historical conditions. Adorno extends the model of mastery of nature to all areas of the individual's development. The mastery of inner nature is the result of the model of external nature. The destructuring and then finally the loss of the ego not only precludes the appropriation of *moral* norms of action, but, as Honneth works it out, it leads generally to a "loss of the cognitive capacities of the self".[20] However, there are no credible reasons for conceptually mixing moral and cognitive socialisation, even if precisely it is this mixing that explains the "impertinence" of saying "I". Because those individuals for whom the appropriation of a morally effective super-ego has failed are equally cognitively deformed. It is for this reason that Adorno sees it as a *moral* error for humans to say "I". The correlation that Adorno makes here is not convincing; he is lacking the theoretical basis as well as proven conceptual tools. The social psychological construction, which is meant to show that individuals are not only in some but in all respects fundamentally damaged, fails to convince; the less so because some escape the deforming manipulations that the system metes out to individuals. The mechansisms of social integration remain entirely underdeveloped. In Adorno's social theory monads are interrelated with the system while no social interaction takes place between individuals. The neglect of the social has dramatic effects on critical theory. Not least this neglect accounts for the conceptual inertia within the founding generation of critical theory. Its status seems to be preserved in *Traditional and Critical Theory* (1937) and *Dialectic of Enlightenment* (1947). After Horkheimer had diagnosed the "disintegration of reason",[21] once philosophy had "basically resigned",[22] and after Adorno's judgement of "a

---

[20] Axel Honneth, *Kritik der Macht: Reflexionsstufen einer kritischen Gesellschaftstheorie* (Frankfurt am Main: Suhrkamp, 1985) 102f; *The Critique of Power: Reflective Stages in a Critical Social Theory* (Cambridge, Mass.: MIT, 1991), 88.

[21] Max Horkheimer, "Vernunft und Selbsterhaltung", in Hans Ebeling (ed.), *Subjektivität und Selbsterhaltung* (Frankfurt am Main: Suhrkamp, 1984), 57.

[22] Max Horkheimer, "Pessimismus heute", in Horkheimer, *Sozialphilosophische Studien*, ed. Werner Brede (Frankfurt am Main: Fischer, 1972), 142.

practice indefinitely delayed",[23] one has possibly to speak of a "postponement of theory".[24]

II

The socio-psychological concept of the drive (*Trieb*), which also plays a role in *Minima Moralia,* is based on a concept of nature not always seen in its full theoretical and strategic scope.[25] The influence of the concept of nature on Adorno's theory of society is immense. This becomes evident once one raises the question about *what exactly* the mechanisms of coercion operating upon and within individuals and upon their lives deform and liquidate. Adorno's response does not emphasise the intersubjective structures of communication, nor the social network that carries individuals. The logic of instrumental reason's mastery, as developed by Horkheimer and Adorno in the *Dialectic of Enlightenment,* "does *not* provide the explicative tools needed to explain what the instrumentalization of social and intrapsychic relations means from the perspective of the violated and deformed contexts of life. [...] So the appeal to social solidarity can merely indicate *that* the instrumentalization of society and its members destroys something; but it cannot say explicitly *wherein* this destruction consists"[26]—at least not in socio-theoretical concepts; rather, as *Dialectic of Enlightenment* seeks to show, instrumental reason destroys human nature in the sense of a first nature. The critique of dehumanisation is however a critique under the colours of the Romantic—one should say an updated Marxist romantic here[27]—according to which the human through social imperatives is alienated from itself, its work, its generic nature and from nature as such. This view is not unproblematic, since it seems to be based on a psychologistic fallacy, according to which civilisation is to be understood as the history of alienated man, just as it is the history of the authoritarian character. *Dialectic of Enlightenment* and also Adorno's moral philosophical reflections are testament to this. The repressive moment always outweighs the moment of

[23] Theodor W. Adorno, *Negative Dialektik*, 15; *Negative Dialectics*, 3.

[24] Anke Thyen, "Pessimismus und Kritik: Perspektiven der Vernunftkritik in der späten Philosophie Max Horkheimers", in Helmut Holzhey and Georg Kohler (eds.), *In Erwartung eines Endes: Apokalyptik und Geschichte* (Zurich: Pano, 2001), 100.

[25] An exception to this is Friedemann Grenz, *Adornos Philosophie in Grundbegriffen: Auflösung einiger Deutungsprobleme* (Frankfurt am Main: Suhrkamp, 1975).

[26] Jürgen Habermas, *Theorie des kommunikativen Handelns* (Frankfurt am Main: Suhrkamp, 1981), vol. 1. 522: *Theory of Communicative Action* (Boston: Beacon Press, 1984), 389.

[27] Karl Marx, "Ökonomisch-philosophische Manuskripte" (1844), in Karl Marx and Friedrich Engels, *Werke*, vol. 40 (Berlin: Dietz, 1990).

freedom, as it is stated in his lectures on *The Problems of Moral Philosophy*:[28] Kant's moral law is criticised as the "pure principle of the domination"[29] of inner and outer nature. It is a "model case of fetishism"[30] that ultimately derives its idea of self-legislation from "renunciation of instinct into an absolute".[31]

And civilisation: is it the principle of repression of human nature? It is clear that, sticking with the distinction in the German language, Adorno plays "civilisation" and "culture" off against one another.[32] Civilisation is what humans are afflicted with—as the paradigm of Odysseus shows. Culture, on the other hand, is meant to be or become an indicator of humanity never losing sight of the human in development. For Adorno, though, the problem is that, in a society riven with antagonism, people are "a priori damaged".[33] The thesis surrounding culture's failure results from the mixing together of "society" and "nature". This thesis had already been advanced by Walter Benjamin in *The Origin of German Tragic Drama* from 1928, and had inspired Adorno's essay, the "Idea of Natural History"—thoughts that were further developed in *Dialectic of Enlightenment*. What results from this admixture is the historicity of nature, whereupon the resultant historical action is still natural in terms of a "pre-history as always the same mastery".[34] Culture, which is meant to de-barbarise, has yet to show its effect; it has not "been able to migrate into humans".[35] Rather, since the culture industry reproduces barbarism, culture anthropologically describes the regression to mythic naturalness and "tends to revert the human capacity for experience [...] to that of amphibians".[36]

But if domination is inevitable—i.e. if delusion is total and culture principally fails—then how is a culture possible in which Adorno sees humanity

---

[28] Theodor W. Adorno, *Probleme der Moralphilosophie* (1963), ed. Thomas Schröder, *Nachgelassene Schriften*, Abteilung IV: Vorlesungen, vol. 10, 199: *Problems of Moral Philosophy*, trans. Rodney Livingstone (Cambridge: Polity Press, 2000), 133.

[29] "I may remind you that we had defined the moral law or rational principle as the pure principle of the domination of nature, and by this we meant the domination of our inner nature as well as nature outside us". Ibid, 202; 136.

[30] "We might say – and this appears to me to be the decisive criticism to be made of Kant's moral philosophy – that we are faced here with a model case of fetishism". Ibid, 207; 13.

[31] "This casts a curious light on Kant's widening of the renunciation of instinct into an absolute in the shape of the categorical imperative". Ibid, 206; 139.

[32] Grenz, *Adornos Philosophie in Grundbegriffen*. 21.

[33] Theodor W. Adorno, "Zum Verhältnis von Soziologie und Psychologie", 69.

[34] Grenz, *Adornos Philosophie in Grundbegriffen*, 162.

[35] Adorno, "Zum Verhältnis von Soziologie und Psychologie", 140.

[36] "The elimination of qualities, their conversion into functions, is transferred by rationalized modes of work to the human capacity for experience, which tends to revert to that of amphibians". Max Horkheimer and Theodor W. Adorno, *Dialectic of Enlightenment*. 28.

placed? And if there never was a state to which the human could long to return, then what makes all the talk of a multifaceted alienation plausible? The nature of the human is neither alienated nor unalienated. Thus, Adorno cannot answer the question from what man is alienated or unalienated. Adorno's reconstruction of history as natural history results in a historicisation of nature in a way that naturalises Marxist social theory. The objectification of Man is in Marx the social nature of Man, apart from which there is no first nature. For Marx the principle of domination results from the social conditions of work and exchange, that is, from the contradiction between relations and forces of production. In contrast, and according to Adorno, one can speak about a conceptual primacy of domination over relations of exchange. The conceptual primacy of domination over exchange has its origins in so-called identity thinking.[37]

With *Dialectic of Enlightenment*, mastery of nature becomes the central concept. This conceptual transformation of the Marxist theory of reification is inspired by Nietzsche, the Spiritus Rector of *Dialectic of Enlightenment* and inventor of the critique of identificatory thinking: "All thought, judgement, perception, regarded as an act of *comparing* has as a first condition the act of 'equalizing', and earlier still the act of 'making equal'."[38] And "the concept originates from equalising the non-equal. [...] The equal is taken for granted because one presupposes *identity*; therefore because of false perceptions".[39] Social theory thus becomes an *ontology of the damaged life*. Adorno does not answer the question regarding an originary condition of unalienation, since it is obviously possible for only a few to escape this condition of damaged existence, at least insofar as the demand for an ego-identity is maintained.

That it can be regarded as an "impertinence" to say "I" results from the principal failure of culture, from the natural-historical deformation of humanity. Only in this way can the barbarism of national socialism be understood both as a consequence and an expression of the historical decay of civilisation and culture, and not as a break or rupture within civilisation. This diagnosis is fatal; it is akin to stabbing enlightenment in the back. Since, understood from within the frame of natural history, Fascism's barbarism appears as a natural pheno-

---

[37] Cf. Thyen, *Negative Dialektik und Erfahrung*, 225.

[38] Friedrich Nietzsche, *Sämtliche Werke, Kritische Studienausgabe*, eds. Giorgio Colli and Mazzino Montinari (Munich, Berlin, New York: de Gruyter, 1980), vol. 12, 209: *The Will to Power: An attempted transvaluation of all values* trans. Anthony M. Ludovici, in *The Complete Works of Friedrich* Nietzsche, ed. Oscar Levy (Edinburgh and London: T. N. Foulis, 1909–1913), vol. 15, 23.

[39] Friedrich Nietzsche, *Sämtliche Werke*, vol. 7, 542; trans in Peter Bornedal, *The Surface and the Abyss: Nietzsche as Philosopher of Mind and Knowledge* (Berlin and New York: de Gruyter, 2010), 76.

menon. Only under these circumstances can the whole be seen as untrue. That Auschwitz should not be repeated presupposes, of course, that individuals reach social agreement about this fact. If one follows Adorno, however, they are blindly exposed to the historical decay of civilisation.

In this history of decay, a series of Lukácsian motifs remain implicit, namely history as pre-history as well as the "place of a skull", which Adorno uses in "The Idea of Natural History".[40] But where within this inescapable natural history is the moment of discontinuity that could explain how escape is possible, and that furthermore could justify why it is admissible for the "many" to say "I" to others—are they few?—or not? The motif of an anthropogenetic decline in natural history[41] precludes individuals from finding any way out of their history in order to critique this very history of decay.

III

While linguistic analyses of Adorno remain rare, they raise interest and make accessible what with some exceptions is a lesser appreciated aspect of his philosophy. When Adorno criticises those who say "I", he ties together psychological, grammatical as well as semantic perspectives. It is as though in the sentence "for many people it would already be an impertinence to say I", what is of central concern is the linguistic reference at stake in the expression "I".

In fact we are dealing with something else: a conceptual mingling of the social psychology of the individual with the epistemological subject or critique of the subjective "I". Only in this way can Adorno come to a normative judgement that the reference behind the use of the "I" would be an impertinence and is thus morally inadmissible.

Adorno does not differentiate between questions of semantics, social psychology and moral philosophy; such differences were not especially important for him anyway. Rather, Adorno understands the use of the expression "I" as a moral-practical act. The semantics here are normatively loaded, but there is no theoretical basis for the claim he is making, at least none that is visible. But Adorno alleges that there is indeed a normative content in saying I. Otherwise the moral verdict surrounding its impertinence would make no sense at all. It lacks, as already mentioned, all theoretical foundation. From the viewpoint of grammar, the "I" expression refers to the speaker of the utterance as a morally substantive fact. Here the distinction between grammatical and normative

---

[40] Adorno, "Die Idee der Naturgeschichte", GS 1: 360.
[41] Grenz, *Adornos Philosophie in Grundbegriffen*. 169.

rules blur, and Adorno cannot answer why any reference to oneself through the use of the personal pronoun "I" is automatically a normative-moral matter.

The reference to oneself through the linguistic indicator "I" (or, in other languages, different related grammatical structures) is the *conditio sine qua non* of any language use. We would not have a language were we not to refer to ourselves as the speaker *in* language. Therefore, the use of personal pronouns (or equivalent grammatical structures in other languages), which reflect the personal relationships between speakers, are indispensable. In German, we do not capitalise "ich". Kant had already criticised this fallacy in his paralogisms in the *Critique of Pure Reason*. Whoever uses "I" in direct speech refers to herself as the speaker of the statement. Whoever uses "I" refers to *herself,* but not to any "meaning" nor to the object of "I". With "I" we make current fleeting acts of self-reference; we do not refer to ourselves by identifying a special object attached to the "I". First of all, "I" is used without criteria, i.e. I do not have criteria for the correct use of "I" when I refer to myself as "I". Secondly, the use of "I" is immune against any false identification, i.e. I cannot be mistaken when I use "I". In direct speech, it is me to which the "I" contained in a statement refers. Thirdly, the use of "I" is *not normative-practical.*

The assumption of a morally laden, practico-normative use of the "I" would have to respond to the following objections: the *first* refers to a substantialist view of the 'I', which Adorno holds. According to this, 'I' refers to a substance to which properties are assignable, for example, the impertinence of the 'I'. If Adorno assumes a capitalized 'Ich' (and not "ich"), then a substantialist semantics is implied. The ego becomes substance through the substantiation of the corresponding personal pronoun. The substantivised personal pronoun that, from a grammatical point of view, could be accompanied by an article or pronoun—the I, an I, my I—is accepted as substance. Wittgenstein reflects on this process when he speaks of a "bewitchment of our understanding by the resources of our language"[42]. One of the great sources of philosophical bewilderment is, for Wittgenstein, precisely when "we try to search for a substance that corresponds to a substantive".[43]

In Adorno's use of "I" one can well speak of a bewilderment of the mind by means of philosophy. The article that the substantivised "I" carries suggests a thing, a substance that inclines one to engage in a—futile—search. In the para-

---

[42] Ludwig Wittgenstein, *Philosophical Investigations,* trans. G. E. M. Anscombe, P. M. S. Hacker, J. Schulte, revised fourth edition (Chichester: Wiley-Blackwell, 2009) § 109.

[43] Ludwig Wittgenstein, *Das Blaue Buch, Werkausgabe* vol. 5 (Frankfurt am Main: Suhrkamp, 1984), 15; *The Blue Book* (Oxford: Oxford University Press, 1958), 1.

logisms from *The Critique of Pure Reason,* Kant showed that 'the' I does not correspond to a thing; the soul cannot be a substance. "The consciousness of myself in the representation 'I' is not an intuition, but a merely intellectual representation of the spontaneity of a thinking subject".[44] As such 'I think' is part of a transcendental explanation how it comes that I am the subject of my utterances: 'I think' is an index of representations which I can understand as my representations. I don't have to worry whether a representation is my representation or not. A representation is my representation in so far as it is, as Kant says, "accompanied" by 'I think'. The sentence 'I think' is a transcendental-philosophical construct, with which Kant wanted to demonstrate the conditions of possibility for a unity of consciousness in time, which means the possibility of me as a thinking being; 'I think' is the explanation of the condition of the possibility of being a conscious thinking being. It is not a sentence by an empirical speaking-subject, who says 'I think' in terms of 'I think *p*'.

The "I" in the sentence 'I think' is not an example of the transcendental-empirical philosophical doublet. Or, to put the matter otherwise, it is not the empirical individual who refers to itself with the personal pronoun "I". The unity of consciousness has as little an 'owner' as the 'I' does.[45] One can have "a representation of his I or of his person",[46] but this does not mean that one has or possesses an I.

A second obvious objection relates to the normative-practical use of the capitalised 'I' (that is, in German, "Ich" not "ich"), and the possibility of it being employed in the same way as a name, such as with proper names, to put the matter restrictively and thus to avoid making the matter even more complicated. To use the "I" as if it were a name is nonsensical; in any case it would not work, since it would not be clear to whom or to what the name is referring.[47]

---

[44] Immanuel Kant, *Critique of Pure Reason*, trans. N. K. Smith (London: Macmillan: 1968), B 278

[45] Wittgenstein, *Philosophical investigations*, § 398. Cf. § 293: The use of the term "I" does not function according to the pattern "object and name".

[46] Kant, *Anthropologie in pragmatischer Hinsicht*, in *Schriften zur Anthropologie, Geschichtsphilosophie, Politik und Pädagogik, Werkausgabe* vol. XII (Frankfurt am Main Suhrkamp, 1968), 407; *Lectures on Anthropology, The Cambridge Edition of the Works of Immanuel Kant in Translation*, eds. Paul Guyer and Allen W. Wood (Cambridge: Cambridge University Press, 2012), 50. "Lecture of the Winter semester 1784–1785 Based on the Transcription Mrongovius, Marienburg", trans. R. R. Clewis: "Of all creatures on earth, the human being alone has a representation of his I or of his person (Person)", 348. And, of course, of *her* I and *her* person.

[47] Cf. Gertrude Elizabeth Margaret Anscombe (1981), "The first person", in S. Guttenplan (ed.), *Mind and language* (Oxford: Oxford University Press, 1981); Sidney Shoemaker, "Self-reference and self-awareness", *The Journal of Philosophy* 65 (1968): 555–567; John Perry, "The problem of the essential indexical", in Perry, *The Problem of the Essential Indexical and Other Essays* (New York: Oxford University Press, 1993); Wolfgang Künne, "First person propositions: A Fregean account", in W. Künne, A. Newen, M. Anduschus

Moreover, there would be no clear use of the personal pronoun "I". After all, "I" is an indexical, irreplaceable expression the use of which, unlike names, does not require self-identification. With respect to names, this may be the case: let us assume someone's name was changed when she was a child. If the person concerned discovers she was previously called a different name, she could say: 'A. B. – so that's me?' If 'I' was used as a name, no such criteria exist to prevent misidentification. After all, everyone also deploys 'I' with respect to themselves. The point is that by using "I" one does not identify oneself *as* oneself, but refers to oneself as the utterer of a sentence, which (in direct speech) contains "I". In the company of others, one cannot with the use of "I" identify who one is. Neither can this be accomplished through "I" as a name; for example, the person who says "I" when answering the phone cannot guarantee that they will be recognised.

A third objection is to assume that the speaker's reference to herself by the use of "I" can either be true or false. This for Adorno is probably the key point. However, were this the case any reference with respect to the "I" would be unreliable, i.e. not immune from errors of misidentification. It follows that there would be no use of "I" at all. Whether or not somebody using "I" is actually referring to herself would thus be impossible to decide. She could refer to herself or at the same time not refer to herself; she could truthfully refer to herself or in fact be mistaken. Under these conditions, sentences like this would be possible: "Someone has a headache at the moment. Is it I?" We would neither know from ourselves nor from others to whom we refer when we say "I". The "I"—and by extension all other personal pronouns—would lose their sense, or as Wittgenstein would say, their use. The grammar of the expression would cease to work correctly; it would be used only in private language games. The difference between normative, descriptive, evaluative and explicative references would not make sense anymore either. And, precisely, it is this consequence that above all else Adorno's sentence suggests. He understands the referential use of "I" semantico-ontologically, *and* then normatively charges this use in terms of a moral thinking that he then attributes to the subject. There is here a misunderstanding at the level of a theory of signification, a grammatical illusion. This is to say, "I" has no normative meaning. And yet Adorno insists on this point, and thus his critico-ideological intention turns out to be nothing short of a defamation. In a way the "workings of our

(eds.), *Direct Reference, Indexicality, and Propositional Attitudes* (Stanford: Stanford Unversity Press, 1997), Anke Thyen, *Moral und Anthropologie: Untersuchungen zur Lebensform "Moral"* (Weilerswist: Velbruck, 2007).

language"[48] is, from an ideology-criticism point of view, instrumentalised. But the use of "I" cannot be epistemically true or false, contrary to what Adorno wants us to believe; it can only be semantically true or false (for example when someone has not learned the use of the personal pronouns properly or, in the case of small children, when they mix up the pronouns).

A quite elitist Platonic gesture holds sway in Adorno's understanding of language. The nerve of Adorno's *Negative Dialectic*, which, like no other work, depends on a robust theory of language, is struck when Albrecht Wellmer reproaches Adorno that his understanding of signification is caught up within the model of a meaning constitutive subject and a name theory of reference. He uses "basic philosophy of language [...] naively, as if Nietzsche's openly paradoxical unmasking of the conceptual thinking comprising traditional philosophical theses could be taken literally". The generality of the terms means "not even an *eo ipso* violence against the non-identical".[49] For Adorno the critique of identity and the magic of the non-identical remain in a dialectical balance. The negative dialectic veils in a way what it wants to say. It is interested in the non-identical, criticising the falling apart of both concept and thing, of subject and object. And this eludes all discursive treatment. From where can this falling apart be registered? Clearly not from the viewpoint of the Hegelian dialectic. Adorno refuses this possibility, since it targets the whole, which is the untrue. Seen in this way, the negative dialectic seems to be a method that holds concepts in abeyance and leaves them there. It is questionable whether a discursive, exoteric, critical philosophy can connect to this. "To proceed dialectically means to think in contradictions, for the sake of the contradiction once experienced in the thing, and against that contradiction."[50] But in what sense is it a question of a general practicable procedure? To this question we can, from Adorno, probably expect Platonic answers to follow, i.e. that it depends on the right consciousness, if and when the dialectic meets the non-identity of the thing. Because the dialectic is "the consistent consciousness of non-identity."[51]

This kind of dialectic can always be sure of its truth. It is immune against critique, insofar as it can refer to contradictions in the thing, in thinking and finally to the non-identity between the thing and thought. It slips away from discursive thinking, which aims at knowledge. From the dialectic itself no

---

[48] Wittgenstein, *Philosophical investigations*, § 109

[49] Albrecht Wellmer, *Zur Dialektik von Moderne und Postmoderne* (Frankfurt am Main: Suhrkamp, 1985), 156.

[50] Theodor W. Adorno, *Negative Dialektik*, 148; *Negative Dialectics*, 144f.

[51] Ibid 17; 5. Translation modified.

cognition (*Erkenntnis*) results, no knowledge (*Wissen*). Knowledge is not increased by means of the dialectical method. For this, additional assumptions and hypotheses regarding the purpose of investigations employing dialectical techniques are necessary.

The dialectical 'method' deployed in *reflections from the damaged life* does not on its own ensure knowledge. In his review of *Minima Moralia*, Hermann Krings makes the following comment: "Paradoxical as it may seem when judging a work written in such a carefully constructed and precise language, there is a sense in which this can be called romantic; that is to say, it makes an absolute claim, but one that does not emerge from the terrain of dialectics".[52] This is because, understood as a method, the negative dialectic cannot of itself provide the correct knowledge. The 'absolute claim' to know that the life we are living, which operates under the condition of delusion, is the wrong life needs a discursive justification for the normative standards it adopts, and accordingly cannot retrieve its right directly from the dialectic itself.

That it should be an impertinence to say "I" is not an insight that derives from the dialectic. As a method it cannot serve as the ground for moral judgements. That Adorno makes this correlation results from a—*eo ipso* normatively rich—*utopia*. Which is to say, Adorno's idea of the negative dialectic is in the end a romantic idea: "The cognitive utopia would be to use concepts to unseal the *non-conceptual with concepts, without* making it their equal."[53] It evades any strict discursive treatment. But can one allow philosophy to get away with this, and if so what kind of philosophy would this imply? Adorno's indignation about saying the "I" in the twenty-ninth aphorism from *Minima Moralia* is not at the discretion of a philosophically correct consciousness. Rather it has to be insisted that the reference to the "I" ("ich") and "I" ("Ich") is morally neutral.

It is incomprehensible whence Adorno assumes the entitlement to his outrage that it is an impertinence for many to say "I". Adorno himself would have seen the source of this legitimacy grounded in a substance-ontological concept of subject or ego respectively, implying that only in the system of delusion, in the scattered and isolated consciousness of the right in the false, is it permissible to describe oneself as "I". One can contest his entitlement with good reasons. Understood as a private expression of opinion, the aphorism would still remain an imposition for all who know how to distinguish the critico-ideologically motivated ridicule from the critique of inhumane action without denying that agents are persons.

[52] Hermann Krings, ""Grenze der Dialektik" Zu Th. W. Adornos Minima Moralia", *Hochland* 45 (1953): 362–366; Stefan Müller-Doohm, *Adorno: Eine Biographie*, 519; *Adorno: A Biography*, 342.
[53] Theodor W. Adorno, *Negative Dialektik*, 21; *Negative Dialectics* 10.

However, this sentence was written in a philosophical book and therefore cannot be excluded from discursive argumentation. This is the expectation that Adorno's sentence does not fulfil. For he holds truth-claims for a form of contempt. When the saying of "I" turns, according to Adorno, into a moral category, being a person becomes subject to negotiation. This is not up for negotiation; nor can philosophy after Adorno follow his path. The morally correct use of "I" remains ultimately reserved to an unregulated thinker, the critic of the administered world and its deforming mechanisms. Such mechanisms finally lead to the de-substantialisation of the individual.

Morality is thus only a limited possibility: "such things as moral philosophy or virtue are only possible in a circumscribed universe [...] because it is only where our universe is limited that something like Kant's celebrated freedom can survive".[54] This is claimed by Adorno in 1963, in a lecture on the *Problems of Moral Philosophy*. The 'famous Kantian freedom', under the condition of these limitations, is also not possible anymore—at least not for everyone.

Adorno has abandoned the universal claim of morality, thereby dispensing with the reflexive claim of his own critical theory. He relinquishes an explanation of its normative bases *in* society.[55] Not only practice, as Horkheimer and Adorno stated in *Dialectic of* Enlightenment, but obviously theory is postponed. It is alive only in the threatened sphere of the individual. The awareness of negativity is not a basic moral-philosophical concept that could be universalised. "[I]n second nature, in the universal dependence in which we stand, there is no freedom; and therefore there is no ethics in the administered world; and therefore the prerequisite for ethics is the criticism of this administered world".[56] Except, however, in some "spheres of the individual". Adorno's humanism of the unregulated thinker is a monological ethics of the individual that distrusts the reason of others. If, though, no reason is believed and

---

[54] "What this means, I believe, is that such things as moral philosophy or virtue are only possible in a circumscribed universe, in contrast to the immeasurable expanded universe of today which is incommensurable with our experience. This is because it is only where our universe is limited that something like Kant's celebrated freedom can survive. In the immeasurably expanded world of experience and the infinitely numerous ramifications of the processes of socialization that this world of experience imposes on us, the possibility of freedom has sunk to such a minimal level that we can or must ask ourselves very seriously whether any scope is left for our moral categories". (Theodor W. Adorno *Probleme der Moralphilosophie*, 147; *Problems of Moral Philosophy*, 98f)

[55] Cf. Anke Thyen, "'Es gibt darum in der verwalteten Welt auch keine Ethik': Moral und Moraltheorie", in D. Auer, Th. Bonacker. St. Müller-Doohm (eds.), *Die Gesellschaftstheorie Adornos: Themen und Grundbegriffe* (Darmstadt: Primus, 1998).

[56] "But what appears in Kant as the intertwining of man and nature is also the intertwining of man and society. For in that second nature, in our universal state of dependency, there is no freedom. And for that reason, there is no ethics either in the administered world". (Theodor W. Adorno, *Probleme der Moralphilosophie/ Problems of Moral Philosophie*, 261/176).

expected of individuals, if it is not possible for the damaged to use their own minds under conditions of systemic delusion, then Adorno's critical theory has no future. Because its task would be to show how it is possible for the many to escape the state of immaturity by reason. But Adorno gave up this task a long time ago and suspended every idea of practical reason. It can be doubted whether, under these conditions, philosophy can still connect to Adorno's philosophy, in general, and to *Minima Moralia,* in particular.

—Translated by Dana Schmidt.

Critical Theory and the Good Life:
Do All Good Things Go Together?

HELENA ESTHER GRASS

"[A]nd there is no longer beauty or consolation except in the gaze falling on horror, withstanding it, and in unalleviated consciousness of negativity holding fast to the possibility of what's better."[1]

Thinking about the good life from a critical perspective is not very popular in contemporary philosophy. Of course, there are many approaches and authors addressing the good life in a broader sense (such as Martha Nussbaum, Alasdair MacIntyre, Philippa Foot, Ronald Dworkin or Ursula Wolf)[2], but what we miss nowadays is an explicit *critical* perspective on the good life. Why is this so? I think that there are two reasons. On the one hand, critique as such is still perceived to be primarily *negative*, while articulations of the good life self-evidently take the form of a strong positive gesture. But somehow with critical approaches it seems to be much easier to determine what is wrong than talk about what should be the case because it is considered right. The discourse about the good life is no exception here: it is much more popular to tackle aspects of life that are judged to be normatively wrong and therefore in need of change.[3] And apart from that, it is a widespread opinion that the good or successful life cannot be determined. According to Jürgen Habermas—the most prominent representative of the so-called second generation of the Frankfurt School as well as its most popular representative—it is not possible to make any assumptions about the right life at all.[4] Instead, only the wrongness of life can be determined as such.

---

[1] Theodor W. Adorno, *Minima Moralia*, (London: Verso) 25.

[2] See Martha Nussbaum, *Creating Capabilities: The Human Development* Approach (Cambridge: Harvard University Press, 2011); Alasdair MacIntyre, *After Virtue: A Study in Moral Philosophy*, 3rd edition (Notre Dame: University of Notre Dame Press, 2007); Philippa Foot, *Natural Goodness* (Oxford: Clarendon Press, 2001); Philippa Foot, *Moral Dilemmas: And Other Topics in Moral Philosophy*, Oxford: Clarendon Press, 2002); Ronald Dworkin, *The Tanner Lectures on Human Values* (Salt Lake City: University of Utah Press, 1990); Ursula Wolf, *Die Philosophie und die Frage nach dem guten Leben* (Reinbek bei Hamburg: Rowohlt, 1999).

[3] Martha Nussbaum and her "capability approach" can be regarded as an exception here. Nevertheless, talking about capabilities the way Nussbaum does, is – compared to what I call Critical Theory – not a genuine part of it. See Martha Nussbaum, *Creating capabilities*.

[4] See Jürgen Habermas, *Moralbewußtsein und kommunikatives Handeln* (Frankfurt am Main: Suhrkamp Verlag, 1983), especially 53–126 and 198–119.

I do not agree with Habermas' thesis or the overall liberal doctrine that the question of the good life belongs ontologically to the individual or private sphere instead of the general or the public sphere and thus can only be answered individually. Nor do I agree that the question is no longer part of philosophy, which concerns itself with the general rather than the particular. Furthermore, I do not agree that critique and a positive gesture are incompatible. In contrast, I shall talk about what I call Critical Theory on the one hand and the good life on the other hand as two subjects whose relationship can be fruitful for each other. More specifically: I will tackle the question whether Critical Theory can provide any kind of tools for elaborating on the good life in contemporary society.

The question I would like to discuss is whether Critical Theory, especially the writings of Theodor W. Adorno, provide a form, a kind of method, and furthermore any substantive content to develop a concept of the good life from a critical perspective. Against this background two questions arise. The first is: what does Critical Theory mean today in this context? Or what do we mean when we talk about Critical Theory as such? The second question is: what is the good life? What does this very broad term stand for? Can these two terms somehow go together—or is it *not* a good idea to mix up critique and the rather negative gesture of Critical Theory with the prescriptive concept of the good life, with its entirely positive connotations? My thesis is that a critical theory is capable of capturing the notion of the good life, and I will refer to the writings of Theodor W. Adorno in order to show how this is so. I will argue that the critique of given social contexts can indicate a path to a utopian idea of how things might be better. I do think that ethics and Adorno go together quite well—albeit in a fairly unique manner. Furthermore, I contend that Adorno provides us with instruments or tools to elaborate upon the good life from a critical perspective. Thus we can consider Adorno in particular as the enabler of ethics in the middle of the twentieth century, a time whose circumstances made it strictly impossible to talk about the good life at all. In a way it was morally forbidden to mention the good life while people vanished in gas chambers and while the individual was obliterated. Adorno managed to do so nonetheless by reintroducing this topic into the philosophical and intellectual discourse implicitly, by presenting it in the rather negativistic form of *Minima Moralia. Reflections from Damaged Life*, written in the 1940s and first published in 1951.

First, I will talk briefly about what the term Critical Theory stands for today. I will try to sketch out some aspects that are helpful in sharpening our understanding of Critical Theory, without saying that there is a fixed set of criteria defining critical approaches.

Second, I will quickly outline what has been called "the good life", and Adorno's specific perception of it. Afterwards, I will talk about Adorno's particular form of philosophy. In doing so, I will talk about the dialectics of content and form we find most significantly in *Minima Moralia* or *Negative Dialectics*[5]—even though they are crucially important for all of Adorno's writings.

Third, I will look into Adorno's methodology, namely his general understanding of critique and of determinate negation, and also what he calls "immanent critique."

Fourth, I will talk briefly about a vision of the good life as a utopian idea without overstretching the concept of utopian thinking—something I do not think is so easily done when focusing on the good life from a critical standpoint.

And fifth, I will sketch out what this rather positive reading of Adorno might mean for Critical Theory today.

What is Critical Theory Today?

The question of what Critical Theory actually is cannot be answered easily. It may even be impossible to do so, since we find a huge variety of scholars who announced themselves as doing Critical Theory or critical theorising during the last 90 years. This includes the first generation of critical theorists—Walter Benjamin, Leo Löwenthal, Max Horkheimer, Herbert Marcuse and Theodor W. Adorno—but also includes scholars like Jürgen Habermas, Axel Honneth, Rainer Forst and Rahel Jaeggi, all of whom are perceived to belong to the critical tradition. This is not to forget the so-called great-grandfathers of Critical Theory: Immanuel Kant, G. W. F. Hegel, Karl Marx, Friedrich Nietzsche and Sigmund Freud, who are also extremely important figures when talking about critical thinking and the roots of Critical Theory that emerged during the twentieth century. So, under the umbrella of Critical Theory we find a great diversity of thinkers. I would like to mention some examples: Horkheimer is a materialist thinker, Adorno's starting point is the suffering of the individual, in Marcuse's writings we find the crucial role of fantasy alongside a strong utopian moment, Habermas talks about the decentralisation of reason, and Honneth about social freedom, drawing on Hegelian resources in order to do so. We also find a great variety of topics in what is called Critical Theory, such as epistemology, moral philosophy, aesthetics, ethics, political

---

[5] Theodor W. Adorno, *Negative Dialectics,* translated by E. B. Ashton (New York: Continuum Publishing, 1990).

theory—and everything in between. Moreover, we find different ways of philosophising. It is reasonable to say that Critical Theory is as much part of idealist philosophy as it is the materialist tradition; it is, of course, an important part of so-called continental philosophy, but it should not be forgotten that some scholars are engaged in strands of analytic philosophy.

In short, then, bringing together all these different perspectives requires that the research programme remains open towards its methods, its objects and its outcomes. Since there is no distinct criterion that could define Critical Theory stringently, and owing to its obviously multifaceted character, we cannot speak of one uniform Critical Theory. What we find instead are three generations of what is labelled the Frankfurt School that I have just mentioned. But furthermore, we also find approaches in feminist theory (e.g. Judith Butler), political theory (e.g. Antonio Gramsci), postmodern theory (e.g. Robert Walker), and also postcolonial studies (e.g. Tarek Barkawi and Mark Laffey), neo-marxist theories (e.g. Immanuel Wallerstein), and International Relations Theory (e.g. Robert W. Cox) that can all somehow be captured by this label.

So my question is: is there any common ground among all these approaches? Or do we have to give up the concept because in fact Critical Theory has already become nothing but a floating, or maybe even an empty signifier with no substance left? I want to claim that we do not have to give up the idea of Critical Theory. Instead we should take a close look at all its different forms and manners/aspects and figure out what critique and Critical Theory really *is* about, how it works, how rich it actually is, and how it can serve us in doing our research today. In doing so, we might find a new and maybe even better understanding of it.

But apart from that, I want to highlight that Critical Theory is nothing but a concept, and conceptual thinking leads inevitably to the well-known problem of non-identity raised by Hegel and sharpened by Adorno: what we try to grasp with a concept is necessarily identical as well as *non*-identical to the concept.[6] There will always be a part of the object which is non-conceptual as such and which therefore cannot be identified with the concept (or concepts) we make use of. However, that the concept does not properly fit the object does not mean that the object with all its parts—the conceptual as well as the non-conceptual—does not exist.

---

[6] Here we find a major difference between Hegel's and Adorno's attempt. In sharp contrast to Adorno's focus on nonidentity, in Hegel's philosophy the absolute itself *is* the identity of identity and nonidentity. See G. W. F. Hegel, *Jenaer Schriften 1801–1807*, Werke 2, 7th edition (Frankfurt am Main: Suhrkamp, 2013), 96 ff.

Keeping that in mind, I want to propose some criteria that fit our under-standing of Critical Theories—without saying that all of them have to be ful-filled or that they are complete. According to Horkheimer's essay, 'Traditional and Critical Theory',[7] Critical Theories are non-positivist approaches. Strictly speaking, Critical Theories are normative, stressing that in fact normativity is a necessary part of every theory and this should be made explicit. Moreover, Critical Theories include, at least implicitly, the objective of the emancipated society. They ask how things emerged, how they came about. Some seek to provide a diagnosis of our time, as is the case, for example, with Axel Honneth's *Freedom's Right: The Social Foundations of Democratic Life*.[8] Some Critical Theories are interdisciplinary. But most importantly, they are self-reflective theories: reflecting their methods, their societal context, and the process of "doing" theory itself. Critical Theories are therefore meta-theories reflecting on their own conditions. We find this very pointedly for example in International Relations Theory, when Robert Cox writes: "Theory is always *for* someone and *for* some purpose."[9] Certainly, there are theories that do not exemplify these criteria, and maybe because of the elasticity of the term, using Wittgenstein's notion of family resemblances might help us out here in order to grasp the seemingly undefinable.

Adorno suggested making use of what he called "thought models" when looking at phenomena. This entailed that he uses a variety of concepts in a certain constellation in order to approach the object more closely without equating the object with the concept. This is the method he exercised in the third part of *Negative Dialectics* when he presents three models: *Freedom, World Spirit and Natural History* and *Meditations of Metaphysics*. In this approach, the object is still primary to the concepts or the subject making use of them. It is as if the thought models are trying to orbit the object, without losing either determinateness or accuracy: "The call for binding statements without a system is a call for thought models [...] A model covers the specific, and more than specific, without letting it evaporate in its more general super-content. Philosophical thinking is the same as thinking in models."[10] I think it is possible to regard different approaches to Critical Theory as such thought models. The plurality of models demonstrates once more that there is not one

---

[7] See Max Horkheimer, "Traditional and Critical Theory", in: Paul Connerton (ed.), *Critical Sociology: Selected Readings* (Harmondsworth: Penguin, 1976).

[8] See Axel Honneth, *Freedom's Right: The Social Foundations of Democratic Life* (New York: Columbia University Press, 2014).

[9] Robert W. Cox, "Social Forces, States and World Orders: Beyond International Relation's Theory", in *Millennium: Journal of International Studies* 1981, 2:10, 126–155, 128.

[10] Theodor W. Adorno, *Negative Dialectics*, 29.

proper way to look at things. All we can do is to make use of various models and their constellations to examine a given phenomenon. These are some of the criteria that might lead us to an understanding of the varieties of Critical Theory we encounter today.

The Good Life and Adorno's Form of Philosophy

The way of theorising I have adumbrated above might be a good framework for elaborating on the question of how a good life might look. Why is that so? The question seems to be hard to answer against the background of contemporary neo-liberal society, which goes along with what Rahel Jaeggi calls "ethical austerity" (*ethische Enthaltsamkeit*).[11] There is a widely accepted view that everyone has to decide for him- or herself what a good life is. In our society the question of how to lead life in a good way is sometimes even considered nothing but a matter of taste. There is no ground for talking about the good life in a "philosophical" way; there is no way to tackle the question as a general question to which one might find generally valid answers. So perhaps there is no direct way to an idea of the good life. But the rather negative, critical way of theorising that goes beyond a positive gesture of doing theory but nevertheless makes use of explicit normativity might be of some help.

Or is this question out of date now? Is it in fact a question that needs no longer bother us? I think there is no reason to claim that the question of the good life has no relevance today. Quite the contrary: against the background of what we call "negative freedom" where no inner nor outer obstacles hinder us to do what we want, it is crucially important to make normative judgements and to elaborate on the good; we have to determine ourselves since nobody else does. And we *are* aware of that, even though it is fashionable to deny it. Talking about morality, law or politics also means talking about the good life as such—albeit in a rather implicit way. One consideration we should bear in mind here is that the question of the good life was once the central question of philosophy. As Adorno puts it right at the beginning of his *Minima Moralia*:

> The melancholy science from which I make this offering to my friend relates to a region that from time immemorial was regarded as the true field of philosophy, but which, since the latter's conversion into method, has lapsed into

---

intellectual neglect, sententious whimsy and finally oblivion: the teaching of the good life.[12]

This passage illustrates one reason why I have chosen Adorno as the key reference in seeking to bring together Critical Theory and ethics. Even though Adorno makes strong efforts—most prominently in *Minima Moralia*—to present himself as a deeply negative thinker (he stresses that the "wrong life cannot be lived rightly"[13] and, in an anti-Hegelian attitude, that "the whole is the false"[14]), he focuses constantly on the idea of a well-lived life. He cannot find such an idea in the fascist society of the 1940s, where the individual was entirely liquidated and subjectivity as such was endangered. Right at the beginning of *Minima Moralia* he claims: "The subject still feels sure of its autonomy, but the nullity demonstrated to subjects by the concentration camp is already overtaking the form of subjectivity itself."[15] Against this background, it was simply impossible to think or even to write about the good life. But Adorno did so—silently, implicitly, in a negative manner which gets interrupted now and then, by using the open form of aphorisms and the method he calls *negative dialectics*, in comparison to the dialectical tradition that reached its peak in Hegel's philosophy. Moreover, Adorno, in contrast to thinkers such as Habermas or Honneth, focused more strongly on the individual, regarded as the starting point for every kind of ethics (without, of course, forgetting society as another constitutive element). In making this strong statement right at the beginning of *Minima Moralia*, Adorno seems to recommend combining his critique with a somewhat vague idea of ethics.

Bringing together Adorno and ethics is quite an unusual project. This is because in the established reading Adorno and ethics do *not* fit together—rather, they seem to be contradictory. According to widespread interpretations, all Adorno did in this regard was to develop some kind of moral philosophy. He is not perceived to have written about the good life, or the right life, to use his more normative concept.[16] This is, as mentioned before, because Adorno's

---

[12] Theodor W. Adorno, *Minima Moralia*, 15.

[13] Ibid, 39.

[14] Ibid, 50.

[15] Ibid, 16.

[16] I would like to make one short conceptual remark: Adorno does not make use of the term "the good life" *(das gute Leben)* at all. Instead, he uses the term "das richtige Leben" which would be "the right life" in a direct translation. But in the English version of *Dedication (Zueignung)* we find "the teaching of the good life" (Theodor W. Adorno, *Minima Moralia*, 15), which is a rather loose translation of "Lehre vom richtigen Leben". In making use of "the right life" *(das richtige Leben)* in the original version, instead of "the good life"

writings are perceived to be highly negative.[17] Adorno himself even seemed quite proud of his own gesture of deep negativity. In sharp contrast, any kind of ethics must talk about the good and consequently, ethics must be positive in a descriptive and also in a normative sense; it must talk about how things ought to be right.

One serious problem arises at this point. It seems to be much harder to outline what a concept of the good life is than to say what we might mean by using the term "Critical Theory". I do not want to talk about all the different kinds of ideas of the good life we find in the history of philosophy, such as in Aristotle, or Epictetus. When elaborating on the good life from a critical perspective, I think there are three crucial aspects that are all interwoven with one another, and which were already adapted by Adorno in the twentieth century.

First, I reject the distinction between morality and ethics brought about by Kant's equation of the good and the happy life. For Kant, the good or well-lived life is not much more than the happy life of individuals, so the ethical sphere becomes subjective, since it is considered to be completely arbitrary and a bare

(das gute Leben), I think Adorno wants to mark some kind of distance between his approach and the Aristotelian tradition. But looking at the English translation, it is striking that we constantly find "the good life" instead of "the right life". I will go along with the translation and use the two terms synonymously. I think it is legitimate to do this sort of equation since they basically refer to the same object: a life well-lived of individuals in the context of a well-constituted society.

[17] Adorno was emphatic about doing negative philosophy, about doing *negative* dialectics, distancing his philosophy from Hegel's highly positive approach (in Adorno's view) by stressing the falseness of the whole in a polemical manner, and not making any attempts to get over its immanent negativity. We find this rather common reading of Adorno in the writings of Jochen Hörisch; see Hörisch, *Es gibt (k)ein richtiges Leben im Falschen* (Frankfurt am Main: Suhrkamp, 2003), and Ulrich Raulff; Raulff, "Nachwort: Die Minima Moralia nach fünfzig Jahren: Ein philosophisches Volksbuch im Spiegel seiner frühen Kritik", in Andreas Bernard & Ulrich Raulff, *Theodor W. Adorno. 'Minima Moralia' neu gelesen,* (Frankfurt am Main: Suhrkamp, 2003), 123–131; and also Alexander Garcia-Düttmann, *So ist es: Ein philosophischer Kommentar zu Adornos "Minima Moralia"* (Frankfurt am Main: Suhrkamp, 2004). Nevertheless, when reading Martin Seel we do find a positive centre of Adorno's philosophy; see Seel, *Adornos Philosophie der Kontemplation* (Frankfurt am Main: Suhrkamp Verlag, 2004, 7ff. But Seel claims that Adorno's concept of contemplation is the positive glimmer of hope in his otherwise deeply dark and bleak writings. I claim that what Adorno calls "contemplation" is only one aspect of the good life or the right society. There are many more aspects that should be taken into account. Let us consider Rahel Jaeggi, who comes back to Adorno numerous times when talking about "forms of life", which arise in order to solve bundles of concrete problems that appear within society at a certain time and need to be overcome. But Jaeggi also insists on the fact that we cannot address ethics by using the writings of Adorno. Fabian Freyenhagen goes a bit further when talking about how to live "less wrongly"; see Freyenhagen, *Adorno's Practical Philosophy: Living Less Wrongly* (Cambridge, MA: Cambridge University Press, 2013).

matter of taste whether a person is happy or not.[18] That is why, consequently, the ethical sphere must be distinguished from the sphere of morality, which refers to intersubjective relations. Even though there are plenty of uses of the concepts "ethics" and "morality", I suggest sticking to Ronald Dworkin's distinction for illustrative purposes: what we name "ethics" deals with the question *how to lead a good life*. How can I myself have a good life? It focuses on the individual, on the singular existence of each person. Morality, on the other hand, deals with the question *how to treat other people right*.[19] How should I behave towards others? Do we have any obligations towards each other? What do we owe one another? Hence ethics refers, once again, to the individual sphere. In contrast, morality relates, as we have seen, to the intersubjective sphere. Against this understanding, I argue, in line with Adorno, that the concept of the good life is bound to both, the individual sphere and the collective sphere of intersubjectivity. We find this for example in Adorno's well-known lectures, *Problems of Moral Philosophy*.[20]

This distinction between ethics and morality is closely related to another well-established distinction that Adorno rejects: the distinction between the public and the private spheres. The private is defined as the sphere deprived of the public. Whatever I do, or whatever I omit, as a private citizen is not of any concern to the public, as long as I act in accordance with the laws. Only things belonging to the public—such as laws, the state, and other institutions like the political or societal system—are publicly negotiated. Adorno disagrees, and I follow him here: I do not think that it is possible to talk about the good life while separating the private sphere from the public one. The good life is not only about institutions, such as the legal system, governments, or distributive justice. The concept refers to considerably more than that. It refers to everyday practices, how we look upon ourselves, how we treat one another in domestic life, how we handle the objects around us, how we care for society as a whole.

Looking at the little sketches and episodes Adorno presents to us in *Minima Moralia* (which I would like to translate freely as "tiny pieces of morality"), the author does not focus on "large historical categories."[21] Unlike Hegel in his

---

[18] See Immanuel Kant, *Kritik der reinen Vernunft*, ed. Wilhelm Weischedel (Frankfurt am Main: Suhrkamp, 1974), A 806. See also Immanuel Kant: *Kritik der praktischen Vernunft*, edited by Wilhelm Weischedel (Frankfurt am Main: Suhrkamp, 1974), A 225.

[19] See Ronald Dworkin, *Justice for Hedgehogs* (Cambridge: Harvard University Press, 2013), 13.

[20] Theodor W. Adorno, *Problems of Moral Philosophy*, edited by Thomas Schröder, translated by Rodney Livingstone (Oxford: Polity Press, 2000).

[21] Theodor W. Adorno, *Minima Moralia*, 17.

Phenomenology of Spirit,[22] Adorno talks not about major historical events like the French Revolution. Instead, he writes about closing fridge doors, giving away ugly presents, the torture of marriage, or how bigoted bourgeois life can be. Instead of focusing on the general, he writes about riding a train or blossoming trees, saying: "There is nothing innocuous left. [...] Even the blossoming tree lies the moment its bloom is seen without the shadow of terror."[23] The very little things are where he starts. Life, as he finds it exemplified in all these episodes, is profoundly wrong.

Third, the good life always refers to the life of the individual in a well-constituted society. Both entities are necessarily bound together; there is some kind of ineluctable dialectical relation between them. The following passage illustrates this: "The change in the relations of production themselves depends largely on what takes place in the 'sphere of consumption', the mere reflection of production and the caricature of true life: in the consciousness and unconsciousness of individuals."[24] This passage gives us a hint that the good life can by no means be achieved by a single individual since individuality is thoroughly social. Moreover, it cannot be realised by only a subset of individuals within a society. Quite the contrary, the good life, as I understand the term, can *only* be actualised collectively, by society as a whole—the people and its institutions. That is why talking about the good life means talking about a specific form of "ethical life" *(Sittlichkeit).* Here I touch on Honneth's and—of course—Hegel's approaches.

To summarise: there can be no meaningful distinction between ethics and morality when talking about the good life. The public sphere is as constitutive of it as the private. Here again no sharp distinction can be made, since I am always a subject within a given society. Hence, the good life does not apply just to singular individuals but to society as a whole.

This leads to another central point: the general can only be actualised through the particular. From the beginning of *Minima Moralia* we find that "in an individualistic society the general not only realizes itself through the interplay of particulars, but society is essentially substance of the individual."[25] This for me is crucially important when looking at the form of *Minima Moralia,* which tries to cope with the general by concentrating on the particular that

---

[22] See G. W. F. Hegel, *Phänomenologie des Geistes,* Werke 3 (Frankfurt am Main: Suhrkamp, 1986), 431–441. G. W. F. Hegel: *Phenomenology of Spirit,* ed. and trans. Terry Pinkard (Cambridge: Cambridge University Press, 2018), 339–47.

[23] Theodor W. Adorno, *Minima Moralia,* 25.

[24] Ibid, 15.

[25] Ibid, 17.

exemplifies it. Let us have a look at the fragments of rightness within the overall wrongness. Adorno presents us with a broad variety of different aspects of life, and stresses the mutual interactions between different spheres of life. According to Adorno, they cannot be looked at separately. These aspects are what Adorno calls culture, art, and also the basic things of everyday life. We find plenty of descriptions and models of very detailed everyday situations; we find short aphorisms or essays on gift-giving, going to the movies, or on putting on slippers. *Minima Moralia* is basically about very concrete, ordinary, everyday activities that tend on first glance to appear as purely trivial.

The question arises: why does Adorno, who claims that his collection of aphorisms has to be regarded as part of philosophy, focus on issues like living in filthy flats? The answer is rather simple, because in doing so he wants to demonstrate that the general can only be actualised through the particular. Since content always corresponds to form, the aphorisms and short essays as short pieces of texts with sometimes a vague or even scrambled meaning correspond to the little sketches of life Adorno writes about. Assuming that the general—philosophy's main object—can only be realised through the particular, it might also be realised by the very form Adorno chose for his book. Therefore, this very loose and unorthodox, to say nothing of its unsystematic, form is—as Adorno proclaims—still part of philosophy.[26] When considering the content, the long list of examples of situations and incidents appears to be at first non-philosophical, as does its form. Adorno claims to write philosophy in *Minima Moralia*, but at the same time he claims that he does it in the most unusual way: no systematic intent, no rigorous argumentation, no strict coherence, but a strong focus on subjective experience. Adorno is even explicit in pointing this out:

> The specific approach of *Minima Moralia*, the attempt to present aspects of our shared philosophy from the standpoint of subjective experience, necessitates that the parts do not altogether satisfy the demands of the philosophy of which they are nevertheless a part. The disconnected and non-binding

---

[26] Referring directly to Hegel, Adorno claims: "Thus Hegel, whose method schooled that of *Minima Moralia*, argued the mere being-for-itself of subjectivity on all its levels. Dialectical theory, abhorring anything isolated, cannot admit aphorisms as such. In the most lenient instance they might, to use a term from the *Phenomenology of Mind*, be tolerated as 'conversation'. But the time for that has passed. Nevertheless, this book forgets neither the system's claim to totality, which would suffer nothing to remain outside it, nor that it remonstrates against this claim." (Theodor W. Adorno, *Minima Moralia*, 16).

character of the form, the renunciation of explicit theoretical cohesion, are meant as one expression of this.[27]

He seems to be telling the reader: look, doing philosophy is not possible anymore, neither is talking about the good life possible, but what I *can* do is to write about the damaged life in a damaged form. This is the specific form Adorno chooses in order to do justice to the well-known dialectic of content and form. There is no direct, clear and straight way to discuss the good life. Adorno found his own specific way of writing that acknowledged this fact.

A Brief Look at Adorno's Methodology

I shall now turn to Adorno's methodology. First, I want to outline what I mean when I talk about positivity and negativity (we also might use the terms "positive" and "negative"). Following Michael Theunissen, I want to highlight the double meaning of the two terms: the *descriptive* and the *normative* meaning.[28] The descriptive meaning is connected to *ponere/to posit*, while the second, normative dimension is illustrated by *affirmare/to affirm*. On the one hand we can identify negativity in terms of what *is* not (related to *ponere*, the descriptive meaning) while on the other we can refer to negativity as what pertains to what *should* not be (related to *affirmare*, the normative meaning). We find both dimensions in Adorno's writings. The negativity of what *should not be* is predominant; Adorno tells us repeatedly that things are deeply wrong with the way they are. However, we also find the descriptive form of negativity, most prominently in paragraph 100 *Sur l'eau*, where Adorno displays to us a form of practice where doing nothing but lying around and staring at the sky is an end in itself:

> *Rien faire comme une bête*, lying on water and looking peacefully at the sky, 'being, nothing else, without any further definition and fulfilment', might take the place of process, act, satisfaction, and so truly keep the promise of dialectical logic that it would culminate in its origin. None of the abstract concepts comes closer to fulfill utopia that that of eternal peace.[29]

Here, he describes an idea of a contemplative practice that *does not exist*. As this example points out, the descriptive and the prescriptive dimensions can be

[27] Ibid., 18.
[28] See Michael Theunissen, "Negativität bei Adorno", in Ludwig Friedeburg/Jürgen Habermas (eds.), *Adorno Konferenz 1983* (Frankfurt am Main: Suhrkamp, 1999), 41–65.
[29] Theodor W. Adorno, *Minima Moralia*, 157.

intimately related to one another. Even when Adorno tries to describe something in a dispassionate or fairly rational way, the normative comes into play. I contend that it is precisely this intertwining of the descriptive and the normative that makes his writings attractive to critical readers.

At this point we may ask whether Adorno remains negative, whether he just tells us what is wrong or what is not the case. Gerhard Schweppenhäuser calls this Adorno's "determinate negation of the given" *(bestimmte Negation des Bestehenden).*[30] If we could ask Adorno, he would probably say that critique must always be understood as negative; critique can neither be transferred into positive imperatives for action, nor lead to thinking about what might be good—as he puts it in his little text "Kritik".[31] Adorno claimed that there must be a strict distinction between theory and practice and that there is no path leading us from wrong to right. Critique always remains deeply negative. Every single negation—Adorno is talking about the "determinate negation" he takes from Hegel—leads to a new negation, not to positivity. Once again: each step out of negativity leads to a new negativity. The totality is negative, every part of it is negative and according to Adorno, in sharp contrast to Hegel, there is no way out of the negative.

Accordingly, for Adorno the aim of the critic is to tell us what is wrong. This is all he or she has to do. But I disagree with Adorno and his self-attribution as a critic. I think Adorno is not doing justice to his own writings when he points only towards their apparently negative character. He does no justice to their subversive potential, for, on this understanding, critique becomes toothless and loses its intensity. In contrast, I claim that by negating what is wrong it is possible to arrive at an idea of what might be right. And I want to push things even further and claim that, even though he would not admit it, Adorno himself makes this intellectual move in *Minima Moralia* and *Negative Dialectics* (as well as in other writings).

Only after we determine something to be wrong it is possible to envision something different that might be right—even though it will not be an exact reflection of its opposite, as Adorno mentions in § 153, *Finale*: "[C]onsummate negativity, once squarely faced, delineates the mirror image of its opposite. But it is also [...] impossible [...], because it presupposes a standpoint removed, even though by a hair's breadth, from the scope of existence."[32] And we can

---

[30] See Gerhard Schweppenhäuser, *Theodor W. Adorno zur Einführung*, 4th ed. (Hamburg: Junius, 2005), 136.

[31] Theodor W. Adorno, "Kritik", in: id., *Kulturkritik und Gesellschaft II. Eingriffe. Stichworte*, edited by Rolf Tiedemann, *Gesammelte Schriften*, vol. 10.2 (Frankfurt am Main: Suhrkamp, 2003), 785–793.

[32] Theodor W. Adorno, *Minima Moralia*, 247.

never escape from the scope of existence; we are always part of it. That is why the mirroring of negativity does not lead us straight to positivity. Not-A does not become A if we only turn it around. But by talking about what is deeply wrong, by talking about the distortions and the atrocious conditions, we always find little glimmers of hope, little fragments and traces of the right, of something different, something better. Horkheimer would say that we will not find any hints concerning "the radically other" *(das ganz Andere)*[33] by reading Adorno in this way. He would also say that our established concepts and categories cannot capture what is entirely different to all we know. They cannot capture it because it is far beyond our conceptual thinking. If we make use of conceptual thinking (which we inevitably do), we will only perpetuate what is already given. All we could ever envision would be "mere technique" and "reconstruction"[34] of what is.

I agree with Adorno's and Horkheimer's scepticism, but their ban on images, as well as their ban on talking about the better or emancipated society—in whatever vague manner—I consider to be wrong. Quite the contrary, an outline of the right is indeed possible without doing injustice to Adorno's attempt at rejecting bare positivity. By way of one example, Adorno talks about "identificatory thinking" *(identifizierendes Denken)*: "To think is to identify. Conceptual order is content to screen what thinking seeks to comprehend."[35] Identifactory or identifying thinking means to determine X as Y and so it follows that everything of X that is non-identical to Y is erased. Consequently, the non-identical, that is the non-conceptual, becomes negated in this act of identification; for us, it does not exist anymore. And for Adorno, this form of identification is actually an act of violation. We are violating the object when identifying it. And violation—violating things or people even in an epistemological way—is *wrong*.

So what could be right instead? Adorno would say, and I agree, that we need an ongoing awareness of non-identity and therefore *negative* dialectics because "[d]ialectics is the consistent sense of nonidentity."[36] We need an awareness that there is something non-identical inside the object which can never be subject to our concepts, something that might appear or present itself only in a non-conceptual way—in art for example. So here we might see that something

---

[33] See Max Horkheimer, "Die Sehnsucht nach dem ganz Anderen: Gespräch mit Helmut Gumnior 1970", in *Vorträge und Aufzeichnungen 1949–1973*, Gesammelte Schriften Vol. 7, edited by Gunzelin Schmid Noerr, (Frankfurt am Main: Fischer, 1985), 385–404.
[34] Theodor W. Adorno, *Minima Moralia*, 247.
[35] Theodor W. Adorno, *Negative Dialectics*, 5.
[36] Ibid.

we determine to be wrong already carries the nucleus or the index of the right. Reflecting on the problems of identifactory thinking leads us to the idea of non-identity and a more appropriate way of thinking. It even leads us to what Adorno calls the "cognitive utopia" which "would be to use concepts to unseal the nonconceptual with concepts, without making it their equal."[37]

We have seen that, if we interpreted the terms "position" *(Position)* and "negation" *(Negation)* as complementary, the negation of something implicitly points to a new position which might even guide us to an idea of an emancipated society: "If we imagine emancipated society as emancipation from precisely such totality, then vanishing-lines come into view that have little in common with increased production and its human reflections."[38] So here is the key for reading Adorno in a positive way. If we agree on that, we will find positive aspects of the good life when reading Adorno's deeply negative form of critique. I would like to stress once more that it is not possible to say that the mere opposite of the wrong must be the right. Just turning the negative aspects upside down does not make them positive elements of the right. Nonetheless, I am of the view that it *is* possible to figure out aspects of the right in Adorno—by using the interpretative power of the reader resonating with the texts. On this basis, I argue it is possible to fruitfully employ Adorno's negativity (and also its rare glimmers of hope) in thinking about the good life. Therefore, we need an active reader or recipient who goes beyond Adorno *with* Adorno.

It is here precisely that the concept of utopia comes into play. Utopia is, as we know, a dazzling term which began to lose its lustre during the twentieth century. However, Adorno can be understood as a utopian thinker—though clearly not as a pure or orthodox utopian thinker. The question then arises: what kind of utopian thinking can we find in Adorno's work? I suppose it would have to be a rather weak conception of utopia. If we transform the negativity of critique into something positive, we can develop something like a "soft" utopian concept from out of his writings. Utopia literally means "no place"; it refers to a society or a social order that has *not* been realised. But it *might* be realised one day; it *might* become reality. With Adorno we can try to imagine a good social order that at this point has no real existence. He sometimes calls this good social order the "emancipated society". With Adorno, we would not just start imagining how things might be better once we extricate ourselves entirely from the reality we are living in now. We would not illustrate something completely independent from what *is*. It is not by chance

---

[37] Ibid, 10.
[38] Theodor W. Adorno, *Minima Moralia*, 156.

that the last sentences of Adorno's introduction in *Negative Dialectics*, where he talks about the possibility of utopia and the nonbeing, are:

> Utopia is blocked off by possibility, never by immediate reality; this is why it seems abstract in the midst of extant things. The inextinguishable color comes from nonbeing. Thought is its servant, a piece of existence extending – however negatively – to that which is not. The utmost distance alone would be proximity; philosophy is the prism in which its color is caught.[39]

Horkheimer claims that each vision of the better is defective as long as it has its roots in reality. Here I totally disagree. It is not a lack, but a positive attribute of this kind of utopian thinking that is to be connected to the here and now, to what is actually the case. So our current reality becomes the basis for our ideas about a better future. Here we are engaged in some kind of immanent critique, when we compare what actually *is* with what our concepts normatively stand for. If we find contradictions or gaps between the normative concepts and reality, we have to provide alternatives—on both sides. We have to transform our reality and also modify our concepts in a never-ending process. In doing so, we acknowledge that reality itself is already normative in a Hegelian manner. By making use of this method we will certainly not reveal "the very different." My suggestion, rather, is reminiscent of Herbert Marcuse's understanding of utopia: *no where* becomes *now here*. We have to ask ourselves: what kind of possibilities and potentialities are hidden in the here and now? What is waiting to be discovered? What can we envision to be normatively right in the here and now that we find given to us?

Adorno (and also Horkheimer) would probably point out that by making use of this method we only end up reproducing the wrongness we are already in. We would thus perpetuate a giant tautology—as Adorno called Hegel's philosophy.[40] And I do not think they are completely wrong about that. Certainly, with the use of this movement we will not reveal "the very different". Yet I want to stress that we can find normatively right elements in the society in which we currently live. And we do not have to reject them; we do not have to leave them behind on our way towards the better. We do not have to remodel our practices entirely—which is not possible in any case. We should rather take a step back and decide: what do we want to keep? Which ones do we want to reject?

---

[39] Theodor W. Adorno, *Negative Dialectics*, 57.

[40] See Theodor W. Adorno, *Vorlesung über negative Dialektik*, ed. Rolf Tiedemann (Frankfurt am Main: Suhrkamp, 2007), 47.

An Illustration of the Good Life

We all know Adorno's famous sentence, "wrong life cannot be lived rightly."[41] I suggest that we modify the translation to: "There is no right life in the wrong."[42] But maybe there is a right life (of individuals) in the *right* (that means: in the right society at a specific moment). What would this right life in the right society look like? Obviously, this is a sorely difficult question. All I can do is illustrate some aspects we find vaguely sketched in Adorno's work. I would like to talk about four: subjectivity; the subject-object relation; the relationship a person has to other individuals, and the relationship a person has towards the totality of social practice.

We have seen that—even if Adorno is serious when making use of his anti-Hegelian statement "the whole is the false"[43]—we still find individuals who are resistant and who take a stand against the falseness of society.[44] Some subjectivity, in a good sense, remains. Adorno mentions it already in the dedication at the beginning of *Minima Moralia*: "Reduced and degraded essence tenaciously resists the magic that transforms it into a façade."[45] Thus there are individuals who experience with their hearts and their bodies that something is completely wrong. This highly positive connotation of subjectivity we find repeatedly in Adorno's writings. So what does he tell us about subjectivity and about individual subjects? As we have seen, Adorno claims that subjectivity is always located within society. And the individuals, the subjects, are at risk. Society dominates the individuals, even leading to their extinction. So, what would be right instead? Subjectivity would have to be in a completely different relation towards the whole of society—it would not be subjugated by society. Instead, each subject would be recognised in her particularity, by her unique qualities. And this would have a crucial influence on the individual's self-relation. Subjectivity would be recognised as something singular, unrepeatable, as having dignity.

What about the subject-object-relation? In *Minima Moralia* Adorno writes about the "disregarding of things" *(Nichtachtung für die Dinge)*: "But the thesis

---

[41] Theodor W. Adorno, *Minima Moralia*, 39.

[42] This translation appears to be closer to the German phrase: "Es gibt kein richtiges Leben im falschen." (Theodor W. Adorno, *Minima Moralia: Refexionen aus dem beschädigten Leben*, Gesammelte Schriften Vol. 4, (Frankfurt am Main: Suhrkamp, 2003), 43).

[43] Theodor W. Adorno, *Minima Moralia*, 50.

[44] About Hegel's understanding of self-consciousness and today's reality of it, Adorno writes: "Today self-consciousness no longer means anything but reflection on the ego as embarrassment, as realization of impotence: knowing that one is nothing." (Theodor W. Adorno, *Minima Moralia*, 50).

[45] Ibid., 15.

of this paradox leads to destruction, a loveless disregard for things which necessarily turns against people too."[46] In this case, finding out what might be right seems to be rather easy. It would be right if we were in a very sensitive or soft contact with things. Adorno writes about a kind of tenderness when getting in touch with objects *(Fühlung mit den Gegenständen)*. He also mentions a certain gentleness or delicateness when one is in touch with objects. Just like subjects, objects would also be respected as unique, valuable entities. They should be treated respectfully; we should care for them. We find in Adorno's writings both the "primacy of the object" and, in line with it, the idea of mimesis concerning the way we get in touch with the things we live with.[47] To be concrete: no fast eating, no cheap clothes, no abundance of things, no throwing away of things thoughtlessly. Be good to the things that serve you and surround you.

The same is true for the next relation concerning the moral sphere, the relation between and among different subjects. Adorno refers implicitly to the "end in itself" formula from Kant's categorical imperative when he criticises "a mode of human conduct adapted to production as an end in itself."[48] Here, he refers implicitly to a good social practice, where not production but people are ends in themselves. Each individual has to be treated in a careful and tender way, in contrast to mere instrumental rationality where the individual is nothing but a means to an end and so does not count at all. Quite the reverse; everyone has to be treated as end in him- or herself, always. In a praxis where the individual is given primacy (without negating the primacy of objects), tenderness would be the new guiding category for social life.

Additionally, when writing about the relation between and among different subjects, Adorno refers to Kant's *Perpetual Peace*[49]: "None of the abstract concepts comes closer to fulfilled utopia than that of eternal peace. Spectators on the sidelines of progress [...] have helped this intention to find expression, timidly, in the only way that its fragility permits."[50] How can we understand this paragraph? Sustainable peace among people, and even among different

---

[46] Ibid., 39.

[47] When talking about philosophy and mimesis, Adorno writes: "A thing that aims at what it is not a priori and is not authorized to control – such a thing, according to its own concept, is simultaneously part of a sphere beyond control, a sphere tabooed by conceptuality. To represent the mimesis it supplanted, the concept has no other way than to adopt something mimetic in its own conduct, without abandoning itself." (Theodor W. Adorno, *Negative Dialectics*, 14).

[48] Theodor W. Adorno, *Minima Moralia*, 156.

[49] See Immanuel Kant, *To Perpetual Peace: A Philosophical Sketch*, trans. Ted Humphry (Cambridge: Hacket Publishing, 2003).

[50] Theodor W. Adorno, *Minima Moralia*, 157.

nations and cultures, is possible. This means the absence of violence among people: no despotism, but the acknowledgement of personal dignity and the inviolability of the human person. It is utopia, but a kind of utopia that can one day be fulfilled. It is an ideal we can stick to, and we can try to achieve little by little, even if its full achievement will take considerable time.

And what about the totality of social practice? Adorno criticises "instrumental rationality" *(instrumentelle Zweckrationalität)* as the overall maxim of social practice. Instrumental rationality only focuses on means; it is blind concerning its ends. Adorno judges a form of society in which instrumental rationality dominates to be deeply wrong. But what would be the positive counterpart? Maybe it would be a society where we can find elements of contemplation. In such a society, I would take my time, look at situations, people, and things with respectful distance. And after having approached them I would treat them in a contemplative manner: "Perhaps the true society will grow tired of development and, out of freedom, leave possibilities unused, instead of storming under a confused compulsion to the conquest of strange stars."[51] Of course, I would also use means to reach my ends, but people and things would still have dignity and value—in accordance with the "end in itself" formula. I think in a good practice we would reflect on our goals and our ends constantly to avoid any kind of blindness towards our motivations or objectives. This practice would be much slower, more contemplative. The entirety of an individual's potential could legitimately remain unused. Being active would be one option; idleness would be another. The right society would be constituted by less hustling, no self-optimisation, but rather an ongoing reflection on the ends for the sake of which we are doing things. Society would not confront the individual in an antagonistic way. Instead, the interests of individuals and of society would converge. That does not mean that there would not be any differences or mismatches, but an agreement between societal and individual interests would itself be possible.

A New Reading of Adorno and Critical Theory

I come now to the last part and the question: what does all this mean for Critical Theory? I hope to have illustrated that we can do much with Critical Theory that has not been done yet. Adorno's writings are especially rich; we find a great variety of topics, the relevance of which remain contemporaneous with us, and call upon us to discuss them once again. I have tried to demonstrate that the negativity of critique and the positivity of a theory of the good

[51] Ibid.

life are compatible. Moreover, Critical Theory provides us with methods that can be inspiring for doing theoretical work and that seem to be appropriate for dealing with the problems we are facing now. Critique can help us not just to figure out what is wrong right now, but how things could be better in the future.

And this is the most important aspect to me: Critical Theory is and remains *normative* theory. Critical theorising is *normative* theorising. Living in contemporary neo-liberal society, we need a robust normative compass, which, as a self-reflective and strictly normative way of theorising, Critical Theory provides us with. And in order to live a good individual life in a well-constituted society, we need to talk about normativity in an explicit way. Besides that, we need a broad societal discourse of how we want to live together, and, generally speaking, of what is wrong and what is right. And then we have to demand the latter. In this way, critical theorising can lead to a critical attitude that brings the claim of normativity back in. And this is what we need today: to bring normativity back in without presupposing a well-defined telos of the right.

"Die Zeit auf ihren Begriff bringen"
A conversation with Antonia Hofstätter, Lydia Goehr, Helena Esther Grass, Martin Jay, Douglas Kellner, Stefan Müller-Doohm, and Sven-Olov Wallenstein

ANTONIA HOFSTÄTTER: In recent years, we have seen a growing tendency to define the present historical moment as exceptional. Symptomatic of this might be the advent of the concept of the Anthropocene, which seems to have coincided with a renewed faith in scientism and an emerging body of theories, such as new materialism or object-oriented ontology. Do you think that the contemporary moment constitutes some form of rupture, as some have claimed? And might this mean that critical theory is particularly relevant today? Or might it mean, on the contrary, that critical theory has become, in some ways, obsolete?

LYDIA GOEHR: I think, sadly, that these times are all too normal, that it is not a time of exception, but a time of normality. It began in 2001, when many of the most extreme consequences of what had been prepared through the '80s and '90s were coming to fruition. I don't see a state of exception, but a sad state of normality, but that's a very dialectical answer. And I think that critical theory can't proclaim itself obsolete, because it's the only theory that actually poses this question about the state of exception and normality. Critical theory can help us to understand the emerging or re-emerging positivism, which we face in the academy and the lack of support for the humanities, and help us to address its consequences. I think this is extremely urgent. Critical theory is able to ask people who put forward certain kinds of empirical questions to reflect on the very questions they pose. This is what Adorno did in the Radio Research Project: not to question the data but to question the questions. Critical theory has a particular role in the academy at the moment.

MARTIN JAY: The question you put about the rupture or the sense of radical newness that we are now experiencing is one with which historians always deal. We just celebrated the centenary of the great October Revolution. And one could argue that this was a turning point and that for seventy-three years there was something new in the world. But, of course, we now know that it was a turning point that didn't really turn. Russia today is closer to Tsarist Russia than to the Soviet Union. So, sometimes turning points were not as radical as we think. In the past few decades, we have experienced the fall of communism, the fall of apartheid, we have seen the 9/11 catastrophe, we experienced the Great Recession. There have been moments of rupture. And perhaps we can take populism and Trump, in particular, as an indicator of something radically new. But through all that, there has been continuity as well. And one of the points that critical theory always understood was that there is repetition—*das Immergleiche*—beneath the appearance of change. So it's premature to say whether this moment will be a moment of serious rupture in which we reach the tipping point on, say, climate change or refugees or anti-democratic populism. As for the relevance of critical theory, it seems to me that as a body of doctrine, as a stable set of texts, its time has passed. One has to see it as a ruin that we plunder for useful ways to deal with problems of today and tomorrow. We ought not to try to preserve the original moment. Critical theory was open-ended, it was historical, it was experimental, it knew that it was a creature of its own time and that moment has irreparably passed. So it gives us, let's say, potentials for use. But it doesn't give us a set of canonical texts, which we have simply to re-read and follow to the letter.

HELENA GRASS: I also think that we can't really say that critical theory, understood as a closed corpus of texts, remains particularly contemporary. Instead, the writings from the first generation—such as the texts of Horkheimer, Adorno, and Marcuse—have to be updated. We are no longer in the period between the 1930s and 1960s; fascism as we knew it in the first half of the 20th century is over. Obviously, the world has changed rather significantly. Though, at the same time, I think that critical thinking and critical theorising is something that we really need in this moment of history, and these 'classical' texts from the tradition of critical theory—such as Adorno's *Negative Dialectics* or Marcuse's *Reason and Revolution*—provide certain methods and topics that are still highly relevant if we want to grasp today's situation from a philosophical perspective. Perhaps, we should not only talk about critical theory—though I find this tradition very important—but about *critical thinking*, a thinking informed by critical theory, adapted and applied to present-day problems. I would agree that this moment does not present a complete rupture in history, and yet, there have been some noticeable changes: ten years ago, for instance, it was almost impossible to imagine the rise of populism or the renewed and very real threat of neo-fascist tendencies in many European countries. If you look at these phenomena from a critical perspective, you can step back and make judgements about such developments. And if we judge them as being normatively wrong, then we can begin to reflect on what alternatives would be better. I think a critical approach that proceeds from negativity to some kind of positivity can be effective and useful. It's not simply a matter of affirming what we find, but also of stepping back in order to examine and investigate the situation before us. Therefore, I think that critical theory will never be 'out of date' as such—as long as we understand it as a practice of critical thinking rather than a fixed theory. As with all things, critical theory and critical thinking has to change permanently to remain what it actually is: a critical enterprise, which tries to focus on and prioritise the objects it has in view, as Adorno stresses when he talks about the 'priority of the object'. If objects change, critical theory must change, too.

SVEN-OLOV WALLENSTEIN: It is undoubtedly true that the theories emerging around the Anthropocene and various versions of materialism and object-oriented ontology pose a challenge to the tradition of critical theory—not least in the perhaps somewhat ironic sense that some of them can be read as playing on Adorno's claim about the 'priority of the object'. What bothers me, from a philosophical point of view, is that the attempt of these theories to eschew 'correlationism' and to leap into the 'great outside' (to use the terms of perhaps its most serious proponent, Quentin Meillassoux) seems simply to evacuate the whole issue of epistemological checks, and to opt for a kind of speculative discourse that seeks support in what appears more like a philosopher's fantasy of science. I do think that the classical tradition of critical theory—especially Adorno's thoughts on nature—are still pertinent, since despite radically questioning the status of subjectivity, they nevertheless refuse simply to abandon it. In keeping with the Greek etymology of the term, philosophy should remain critical in the sense that it uncovers unexpected and challenging new distinctions—which in turn makes it possible to establish new connections—instead of abandoning itself to some type of "flat ontology" that obliterates the differences between consciousness and things, subjects and objects, intentional and non-intentional entities, etc., which sounds like a new version of the night in which all cows are black.

STEFAN MÜLLER-DOOHM: I'm highly sceptical about the concept of a state of exception, which, of course, goes back to Carl Schmitt. We need a sharp analytical conceptual language to address the structural transformations of modernity and its crisis-ridden developments, a language that is adequate to the phenomena in question. Incidentally, this was the common aim of the various forms of critical theory—from Adorno up to Habermas and Honneth: it was always crucial for them to give the present time its conceptual articulation. With regard to present societies, we face the dual task of investigating the causes of the progressive deformation of majoritarian democracy on the one hand, and of analysing the politically conspicuous forms of emerging nationalisms, nativisms, and populisms on the other. Furthermore, we need to inform people about the dangers of hegemonic global financial capitalism and to foster a greater awareness of rising social inequality in the world—the widening gap between extremely poor and extremely rich countries.

DOUGLAS KELLNER: In the 1960s you had a great upsurge of critical theory, because critical theory was connected with the student movement; it was connected with revolution on a global scale, as well as with social critique and revolt of different sorts. And this was only the time when critical theory was beginning to be translated and understood in its whole history. As for its actuality, in the 1980s you have Reagan, Thatcher, you have a right-wing reaction, and critical theory criticised this conservative revolution, which required radical responses. And then in the 1990s, you have the technological revolution and globalisation. Critical theory was in an excellent position to address both of these phenomena, because there had been a philosophy of technology in critical theory from the beginning. Critical theory formulated the changes from the family-market capitalism, which Marx addressed in the 19th century, to state monopoly capitalism. Thus it was logical that critical theory would address global capitalism, that is, a technological capitalism, in the 1990s, and this project has continued up to today.

ANTONIA HOFSTÄTTER: It seemed to me that there was, if not an open antagonism, then at least an elephant in the room throughout this conference. Namely, a certain tension between the earlier and later generations of critical theory. Some scholars—perhaps most notably Gérard Raulet in his paper on mimesis and reification—advanced the claim that something essential has been lost in the passage from Benjamin and Adorno to the present generation of critical theorists. Do you agree?

STEFAN MÜLLER-DOOHM: Critical theory is an open and plural project, which ought to be pursued as a learning process from one generation to the next. Each of its concepts, whether taken from its older writers—such as Adorno, Horkheimer, or Marcuse—or more recent proponents—such as Habermas and Honneth—as well as contemporary theorists, has its own historical origin and significance. This significance has to prove its mettle in explaining social antagonisms and crises. The different versions of critical theory share the task of understanding social realities from the perspective of changing historical situations by means of theorising. Critical theory, in all of its variations, aims to uncover the reasons for latent and manifest injustices, discrimination, and repression.

SVEN-OLOV WALLENSTEIN: Whether or not something is lost depends on what you're looking for, and what you assume should be or should have been there in the first place. Obviously, there have been substantial changes: say, the importance of Marx and the analysis of capital, crucial for many of the first generation, seem to have been replaced by theories of communication and consensus formation, while the importance of artworks not just for deciphering the contradictions of the present moment, but also for theory formation itself, seems to have diminished. Whether this is seen as a loss depends on your perspective. For me, the question of loss is less important than the question of what critical theory might become. The task will always be to understand the present in all its ramifications, and, in this context, the question of whether one is faithful to the past is of little use. The question is, rather, how to reinvent the past in order to move ahead. To me, art and aesthetic theory are central issues, which is why I consider the most recent developments, say, from Habermas onwards, to be less helpful. To establish a terrain for dialogue, a set of problems to be carried forward, seems to me a very interesting task.

LYDIA GOEHR: I have a very short answer: if something has been lost, then it applies only to those who have lost it. There are lots of critical theorists, young people in this country, in Germany and in America, who haven't lost something that early critical theory offered. In the last two days, much of the discussion has been about the 'big shots' of critical theory. Yet, if we were to give our attention to the 'little shots' of critical theory, we would see that there are lots of people doing critical theory in all kinds of ways. On the other hand, I do think that there has been a tendency to try to rationalise critical theory, to make it appeal to analytical philosophers, because of the domination of analytical philosophy in America. And people try to convert others by becoming like those others, and there are certainly problems in that regard. But as I said, there are lots of really good critical theorists working in what I deem to be very fruitful ways, with no loss.

MARTIN JAY: I think it's impossible to narrativise the first, second or third generations, either in terms of a super-decline or ascent. That is to say, there has been a continuity: there is a sense in which without Adorno, without

Marcuse, without Horkheimer, one couldn't really understand Habermas's project, and one couldn't understand Honneth's project without Habermas'. But there is also a sense that some of the, let's say, intuitive gestures of the early generation no longer seem as compelling to more recent thinkers. I think one can understand Habermas or Honneth's, let's call it, clarification of the premises of early critical theory—a pushing beyond certain statements about utopia, truth, beauty or goodness that was assumed in this kind of semi-metaphysical way that you find certainly in Benjamin, maybe Adorno, and sometimes in Horkheimer. They forced us to think more clearly about the normative sources of the critical impulses of the early generation. At the same time, some of the semantic energy of those early intuitions may be squandered by the overly clear, overly rational, sometimes rather dry formulations of the second and third generations. I think one of the great virtues of the tradition as a whole is that it does in fact have several generations, where people have been doing things differently. Critical theory has been given a new lease of life, and it is in dialogue with other traditions. I think this is useful in terms of creating an audience and so the audience sees critical theory not as a relic, but as an active interlocutor today.

DOUGLAS KELLNER: I think there has been a differentiation and pluralisation of critical theory from the beginning, starting with the immigration from Germany to America during World War II. And then, after the war, Adorno, Horkheimer, Pollock, and others returned to Germany, while Marcuse, Fromm and Löwenthal stayed in the United States. And in the 1970s and '80s, some scholars followed Habermas. I think it is true that there is some division between Habermasians and the original critical theory school. But there are many of us, who (exactly as others on this panel have indicated) see richness, variety, diversity, and important themes in all of these thinkers, whose work we can still use and apply today. So the relevance of critical theory seems still timely. Particularly, if you have this broad range of theories, there are bound to be certain ideas that are appropriate to analyse recent phenomena, such as authoritarian populism, Donald Trump, biotechnology, and other current issues.

HELENA GRASS: For me, it is difficult to talk about the first, the second, the third, and maybe even the fourth generation of critical theory, because each scholar in every generation is so different. Just take Adorno and his deep negativity, Marcuse and his account of utopia, or Horkheimer's strict materialism—they are distinct from one another. But they can equally be brought into dialogue with each other, as Adorno and Horkheimer demonstrated in practice. We find many different approaches in what we call 'critical theory' and we don't have to stick to any one of them in any orthodox way. On the contrary, we should consider ourselves to be free to take from each what might seem useful for our theorising. I think, for example, that Marcuse's concept of utopia fits together well with Adorno's negativity. We have a broad variety of themes and tools, which we can combine in any way we want—as long as it works. I think this kind of eclecticism can be a very productive way of doing critical theory. By picking what we want from each approach and by combining the methods and contents of each we can achieve good philosophy, sociology, political theory, etc. This enterprise is what we might call 'the future of critical theory'.

ANTONIA HOFSTÄTTER: Lastly, I'd like each of you to reflect on the last two days of this conference and to pick one moment or one issue that has contributed something new to your understanding of critical theory. Has there been anything that has challenged or reinforced your views of what it is that we do when we do critical theory?

HELENA GRASS: What I discovered during the last one and a half days is that I don't really have a clue what critical theory actually is. Since we have heard about epistemology, ontology, ethics, moral philosophy and also aesthetics, it's very difficult to define a single criterion or even a bunch of criteria to under-stand what critical theory actually *is*. Certainly, it has something to do with social emancipation, normativity, the relentless questioning of how things came to be; and it is an anti-positivist approach. I think it is crucial that there were scholars from many countries, from different generations and with different interests, and yet the conference still somehow cohered. So there must be some common ground, even if we can't pin it down. Maybe there is some kind of 'family resemblance', to use Wittgenstein's phrase. The conference demonstrated that critical theory is definitely still alive, that it remains quite a rich concept—and that it can be and *should* be developed even further.

MARTIN JAY: On the one hand, the generalisation of the concept 'critical theory' seems to imply that there is something common, something uniform, something we could create as a kind of brand that exists over time. On the other, there is this nominalist impulse, the impulse which says, 'now, wait a minute, Adorno wasn't saying the same thing as Marcuse, Fromm isn't arguing the same thing as Horkheimer'. So a conference like this is a site for the per-formance of that tension. Can we in fact find a unifying way to make the concept of critical theory meaningful, or are we engaged in a kind of open-ended search for something that could be relevant within a larger project? It seems to me that it is probably better to talk about *critical theorising* than critical theory, and that the activity of doing it is more important than the attempt to define it. We should think of critical theory as *in process* and this conference is a little piece of that process, which seems to be going on in many different places in the world.

DOUGLAS KELLNER: Well, the conference, with its variety and diversity of critical theorists, was a very rich one. Just to start with today, we had some very interesting papers that talked about both philosophical and aesthetic themes within critical theory. Over the last couple of days, we had all kinds of different papers on Habermas, on Adorno, on Marcuse, and we heard about Erich Fromm. To me this was very valuable in seeing the different perspectives. And it struck me that there was no conflict—with maybe a couple of exceptions— between the various schools of critical theory, just friendly dialogue. I also found a friendliness of dialogue between mostly Germans, Swedes and a couple of Americans. I thought it was a good sort of intercultural communication between the different groups.

SVEN-OLOV WALLENSTEIN: I think that the core issue, 'The Future of Critical Theory,' remained unanswered, perhaps rightly so. There was a wealth of historical analyses, interrogations of particular texts and thinkers, but a certain hesitation to map out a path towards the future—or perhaps, to use the plural form, *futures*, since the tradition appears evermore complex the more we look at it, which also means that the paths ahead must be multiple. What is clear is that the tasks that were once delineated at the beginning of this tradition have not disappeared. Rather, they must be grasped by vocabularies and concepts that can integrate the various changes in society, philosophy, the sciences, and the arts that have occurred in the interim between then and now.

STEFAN MÜLLER-DOOHM: The conference showed that open discussion and a readiness to engage in controversies have an illuminating and progressive function. During the course of the conference, it became clear that one cannot just stop at reconstructing critical theory from the perspective of a history of ideas. On the contrary, one has to draw on the whole spectrum of critical theory to address present problems. It seems to me to be particularly vital to build bridges between these critical analyses of the present so as to be better able to make interventions into the realm of the political public. Critical theory has to leave the ivory tower and be transformed into political practice—in the characteristic way in which, at different times, Adorno and Habermas pursued critical theory as public intellectuals. As an intellectual practice, critical theory has the task of advocating the enforcement of human rights. I agree with Habermas when he said that human rights form a realistic utopia that grounds the ideal goal of a just society in the institution of the constitutional state itself.

LYDIA GOEHR: I am not sure I have anything more to add. Parts of it have already been said about the richness and variety of approaches and so on. The only thing that I would say about the conference, as suggested by my last answer, is that I would have liked to have heard from younger people in the field. I think one of the tendencies of the aging process is that we come with well-formed views and we look for a way of affirming our views. We all have a standpoint, although critical theory is very much against 'standpoint-philosophy'. I feel myself bored by my own questions, which just re-affirm my own self-interests in particular subjects. So, if anything, it shows me that I wish I were not quite so old.

Contributors

ANDERS BARTONEK is Associate Professor of Philosophy at Söderörn University. His dissertation, *Philosophie im Konjunktiv: Nichtidentität als Ort der Möglichkeit des Utopischen in der negativen Dialektik Theodor W. Adornos* (2011), deals with Adorno's negative dialectics and the relation between non-identity and utopia. His other areas of research are German Idealism, theories of dialectics, labour, critique, Marxism, and Agamben's political philosophy. His latest book, *Kampen om kritiken,* was published in 2018.

ANNE BOISSIÈRE is Professor of Aesthetics and Philosophy of Art at the University of Lille. Recent publications include *Le mouvement à l'œuvre: Entre jeu et art* (2018), *La pensée musicale de Theodor W. Adorno: L'épique et le temps* (2011), *Adorno: La vérité de la musique moderne* (1999). She was also a guest editor for "Actualités d'Adorno", Rue Descartes/23, Collège international de philosophie (1999).

CAMILLA FLODIN is currently Research Fellow in Comparative Literature at Södertörn University, Stockholm. She has published extensively on Adorno's aesthetics and the art–nature relationship in, for example, *British Journal for the History of Philosophy* and *Adorno Studies.* She is a contributor to the edited volume *Understanding Adorno, Understanding Modernism* (2020) as well as to the *Oxford Handbook of Adorno* (forthcoming), and is a co-editor for *Beyond Autonomy in Eighteenth-Century British and German Aesthetics* (2020).

LYDIA GOEHR is Professor of Philosophy at Columbia University. She is the author of The Imaginary Museum of Musical Works: An Essay in the Philosophy of Music (1992), The Quest for Voice: Music, Politics, and the Limits of Philosophy (1998), and Elective Affinities: Musical Essays on the History of Aesthetic Theory (2008). Her forthcoming book is Red Sea – Red Square – Red Thread: A Philosophical Detective Story.

HELENA ESTHER GRASS studied philosophy and political science in Dresden, Frankfurt am Main, and Chicago. She has formerly been a research assistant in philosophy, as well as in political science, at Goethe University, Frankfurt am Main. Since 2019, she has been a research assistant at Carl von Ossietzky University Oldenburg working on German Idealism and Critical Theory. She is presently working on a project on "Critical Theory and the Good Life". Her latest publications focus on the relation between Schopenhauer's and

Nietzsche's view on determination and freedom, on the impact of the concept of culture industry in the social sciences, and the possibility of asking for a better life in the twenty-first century.

ANTONIA HOFSTÄTTER is Assistant Professor at the division of German at the Department for Slavic and Baltic Languages, Dutch, and German at Stockholm University. She completed her PhD in 2017 at the University of Brighton with a thesis entitled *The Fabric of Critique: "Lending Voice to Suffering" in the Work of T.W. Adorno*. Her research focuses on early critical theory, specifically the relationship between aesthetics and critique. Recent articles have appeared in *Adorno Studies* and *Zeitschrift für kritische Theorie*. Together with Daniel Steuer, she is the co-editor of *Adorno's Rhinoceros: Art, Nature, Critique* (forthcoming)

SVEN ANDERS JOHANSSON is Professor of Comparative Literature at Mid-Sweden University in Sundsvall. His latest book publication is *Det cyniska tillståndet* from 2018; his forthcoming book, *Litteraturens slut* is under publication. Currently he is involved in the research project *The Seed Box: An Environmental Humanities Collaboratory* based at Linköping University. Johansson also writes critcism in the Swedish daily newspaper *Aftonbladet*.

DOUGLAS KELLNER is George Kneller Chair in the Philosophy of Education at UCLA and is author of many books on social theory, politics, history, and culture. His most recent books include: *American Nightmare: Donald Trump, Media Spectacle, and Authoritarian Populism* (2016), *The American Horror Show: Election 2016 and the Ascendency of Donald J. Trump* (2017), and the second 25th Anniversary revised edition of *Media Culture: Cultural Studies, Identities, and Politics in the Contemporary Moment* (2020).

STEFAN MÜLLER-DOOHM studied in Frankfurt under Theodor W. Adorno and Max Horkheimer and is now Professor Emeritus of Sociology and Director of the Forschungsstelle Intellektuellensoziologie (Research Centre on the Sociology of Intellectuals) at the University of Oldenburg. Among his recent publications are: *Adorno: A Biography* (2005) and *Habermas: A Biography* (2016), and *Habermas global*, co-edited with Luca Corchia and William Outhwaite (2019).

SHIERRY WEBER NICHOLSEN, Ph.D., is a trained and practicing psychoanalyst at a private practice in Seattle, Washington. She studied briefly with Adorno in

Frankfurt in the 1960s and is the translator of his *Prisms* (with Samuel M. Weber), *Notes to Literature,* and *Hegel: Three Studies,* as well as the author of *Exact Imagination, Late Work: On Adorno's Aesthetics* (1997) and numerous essays on Adorno. Her current interests are in the usefulness of psychoanalysis and critical theory for understanding large-scale social issues; see, for example, her *The Love of Nature and the End of the World: The Unspoken Dimensions of Environmental Concern* (2003).

GÉRARD RAULET is Professor Emeritus of History of Ideas at the University Paris Sorbonne. He was Director of the Research Program "Philosophie politique contemporaine" at the Centre National de la Recherche Scientifique between 1999 and 2003. He is currently Research program director at the Foundation Maison des sciences de l'homme (Paris) and Invited Professor at the Albert-Ludwigs-Universität Freiburg im Breisgau. He has written numerous essays and books on Critical theory and contemporary political philosophy, such as *Critical Cosmology: On Nations and Globalization* (2005). *La philosophie allemande depuis 1945* (2006), *Republikanische Legitimität und politische Philosophie heute* (2012), *Wissen in Bewegung: Theoriebildung unter dem Fokus von Entgrenzung und Grenzziehung* (with Sarah Schmidt, 2014), *Geschichte der politischen Ideengeschichte* (with Marcus Llanquem 2018), *Das befristete Dasein der Gebildeten: Benjamin und die französische Intelligenz* (2019), and *Politik des Ornaments,* 2020.

CECILIA SJÖHOLM is Professor of Aesthetics at Södertörn University. Her research focuses on the relation between art and politics in contemporary culture. She has published extensively on art, psychoanalysis and critical theory. Her latest book. *Doing Aesthetics with Arendt; How to See Things* (2015) looks at the way in which Hannah Arendt's reflections on art and aesthetics invite us to rethink her political concepts.

ARPAD-ANDREAS SÖLTER, Dr. Phil., was the director of the Goethe-Institut in Sweden between 2015 and 2020 before relocating to become the Head of the Goethe-Institut in Ljubljana, Slovenia. He also served as President of EUNIC (European Union National Institutes for Culture). Some of his most recent contributions on cultural, social and political theory include "Mirrors of Evil: Cultural criticism, critique of modernity, and Anti-Semitism in Heidegger's Thought"in Daniel Pedersen (ed.): *Cosmopolitism, Heidegger, Wagner – Jewish Reflections* (2017), "Philosophie ohne archimedischen Punkt: Imperative kritisch-rationalen Denkens für die offene Gesellschaft", in Giuseppe Franco (ed.), *Begegnungen mit Hans Albert – Eine Hommage* (2018), *Moderne und Kulturkritik. Jürgen Habermas und das Erbe der Kritischen Theorie* (1996), *Der fremde Blick: Perspektiven interkultureller Kommunikation und Hermeneutik. Ergebnisse der DAAD-Tagung in London,* ed. with Ingo Breuer (1997).

ANKE THYEN is former Professor of Philosophy at the University of Education, Ludwigsburg. She is the author of *Negative Dialektik und Erfahrung: Zur Rationalität des Nichtidentischen bei Adorno* (1989). Among her recent publications are "Kollektive Intentionalität und Sprachspiele", in Jochen Krautz (ed.), *Beziehungsweisen und Bezogenheiten* (2017), "Kooperation als Lebensform: Eine anthropologische Erläuterung der Rede vom Vorrang der Moral", in Martin Hoffmann, Reinold Schmücker, and Héctor Wittwer (eds.): Vorrang der Moral? (2017), and *Moral und Anthropologie: Untersuchungen zur Lebensform "Moral"* (2017).

ROLF WIGGERSHAUS is a free-lance publicist and lecturer. He studied philosophy, sociology and German studies in Tübingen and Frankfurt am Main. Among his publications are *Wittgenstein und Adorno: Zwei Spielarten modernen Philosophierens* (2012), *Theodor W. Adorno* (1998, *Die Frankfurter Schule: Geschichte, theoretische Entwicklung, politische Bedeutung* (1986), and *Sprachanalyse und Soziologie: Die sozialwissenschaftliche Relevanz von Wittgensteins Sprachphilosophie* (ed. 1975). His main areas of research are sociology of art and the relation between society and nature.

SVEN-OLOV WALLENSTEIN is Professor of Philosophy at Södertörn University. He is the translator of works by, among others, Winckelmann, Lessing, Kant, Hegel, Husserl, Heidegger, Derrida, Deleuze, and Adorno, as well as the author of numerous books on contemporary philosophy and aesthetics. Among his recent publications are *Adorno: Negativ dialektik och estetisk teori* (2019), *Spacing Philosophy: Lyotard and the Idea of the Exhibition* (2019, with Daniel Birnbaum), *Upplysningens estetik: Nedslag i 1700-talet* (2019), and *Deleuze och litteraturen* (2018, ed. with Johan Sehlberg), and *Architecture, Critique, Ideology: Writings on Architecture and Theory* (2016).

JOSEFINE WIKSTRÖM is researcher and critic working on the intersection between cultural theory and post-Kantian philosophy. She is a Senior Lecturer in Dance Theory at Uniarts, Stockholm and has also taught aesthetics at Södertörn University, Stockholm, and at Goldsmiths College in London. She completed her PhD in Philosophy at the CRMEP, Kingston University in London 2017.

She has published in *Radical Philosophy* and *Performance Research Journal* among others and is the co-editor of *Objects of Feminism* (2017). The title of her forthcoming book is *Practices of Relations* (2020).

Södertörn Philosophical Studies

1. Hans Ruin & Nicholas Smith (red.), *Hermeneutik och tradition: Gadamer och den grekiska filosofin* (2003)

2. Hans Ruin, *Kommentar till Heideggers Varat och tiden* (2005)

3. Marcia Sá Cavalcante Schuback & Hans Ruin (eds.), *The Past's Presence: Essays on the Historicity of Philosophical Thought* (2006)

4. Jonna Bornemark (red.), *Det främmande i det egna: Filosofiska essäer om bildning och person* (2007)

5. Marcia Sá Cavalcante Schuback (red.), *Att tänka smärtan* (2009)

6. Jonna Bornemark, *Kunskapens gräns, gränsens vetande: En fenomenologisk undersökning av transcendens och kroppslighet* (2009)

7. Carl Cederberg & Hans Ruin (red.), *En annan humaniora, en annan tid/Another humanities, another time* (2009)

8. Jonna Bornemark & Hans Ruin (eds.), *Phenomenology and Religion: New Frontiers* (2010)

9. Hans Ruin & Andrus Ers (eds.), *Rethinking Time: Essays on History, Memory, and Representation* (2011)

10. Jonna Bornemark & Marcia Sá Cavalcante Schuback (eds.), *Phenomenology of Eros* (2012)

11. Leif Dahlberg & Hans Ruin (red.), *Teknik, fenomenologi och medialitet* (2011)

12. Jonna Bornemark & Hans Ruin (eds.), *Ambiguity of the Sacred* (2012)

13. Brian Manning Delaney & Sven-Olov Wallentein (eds.), *Translating Hegel* (2012)

14. Sven-Olov Wallenstein & Jakob Nilsson (eds.), *Foucault, Biopolitics, and Governmentality* (2013)

15. Jan Patočka, *Inledning till fenomenologisk filosofi* (2013)

16. Jonna Bornemark & Sven-Olov Wallenstein (eds.), *Madness, Religion, and the Limits of Reason* (2015)

17. Björn Sjöstrand, *Att tänka det tekniska: En studie i Derridas teknikfilosofi* (2015)

18. Jonna Bornemark & Nicholas Smith (eds.), *Phenomenology of Pregnancy* (2016)

19. Ramona Rat, *Un-common Sociality: Thinking Sociality with Levinas* (2016)

20. Hans Ruin & Jonna Bornemark (red.), *Ad Marciam* (2017)

21. Gustav Strandberg, *Politikens omskakning: Negativitet, samexistens och frihet i Jan Patočkas tänkande* (2017)

22. Anders Bartonek & Anders Burman (eds.), *Hegelian Marxism: The Uses of Hegel's Philosophy in Marxist Theory from Georg Lukács to Slavoj Žižek* (2018)

23. Lars Kleberg, Tora Lane, Marcia Sá Cavalcante Schuback (eds.), *Words, Bodies, Memory: A Festschrift in honor of Irina Sandomirskaja* (2019)

24. Marcia Sá Cavalcante Schuback, Helena Mattsson, Kristina Riegert & Hans Ruin (red.), *Material: Filosofi, Estetik, Arkitektur: Festskrift till Sven-Olov Wallenstein* (2020)

25. Johan Sehlberg, *Of Affliction: The Experience of Thought in Gilles Deleuze by way of Marcel Proust* (2020)

26. Hans Ruin, *Reduktion och reflektion – En inledning till Husserls fenomenologi* (2020)

27. Anders Burman, Marcia Sá Cavalcante Schuback & Synne Myrebøe (red.), *En plats för tänkande. Essäer om universitetet och filosofin* (2020)

28. Anders Bartonek & Sven-Olov Wallenstein (ed.) *Critical Theory – Past, Present, Future,* (2021)

www.ingramcontent.com/pod-product-compliance
Lightning Source LLC
LaVergne TN
LVHW042349190726
843493LV00005B/960